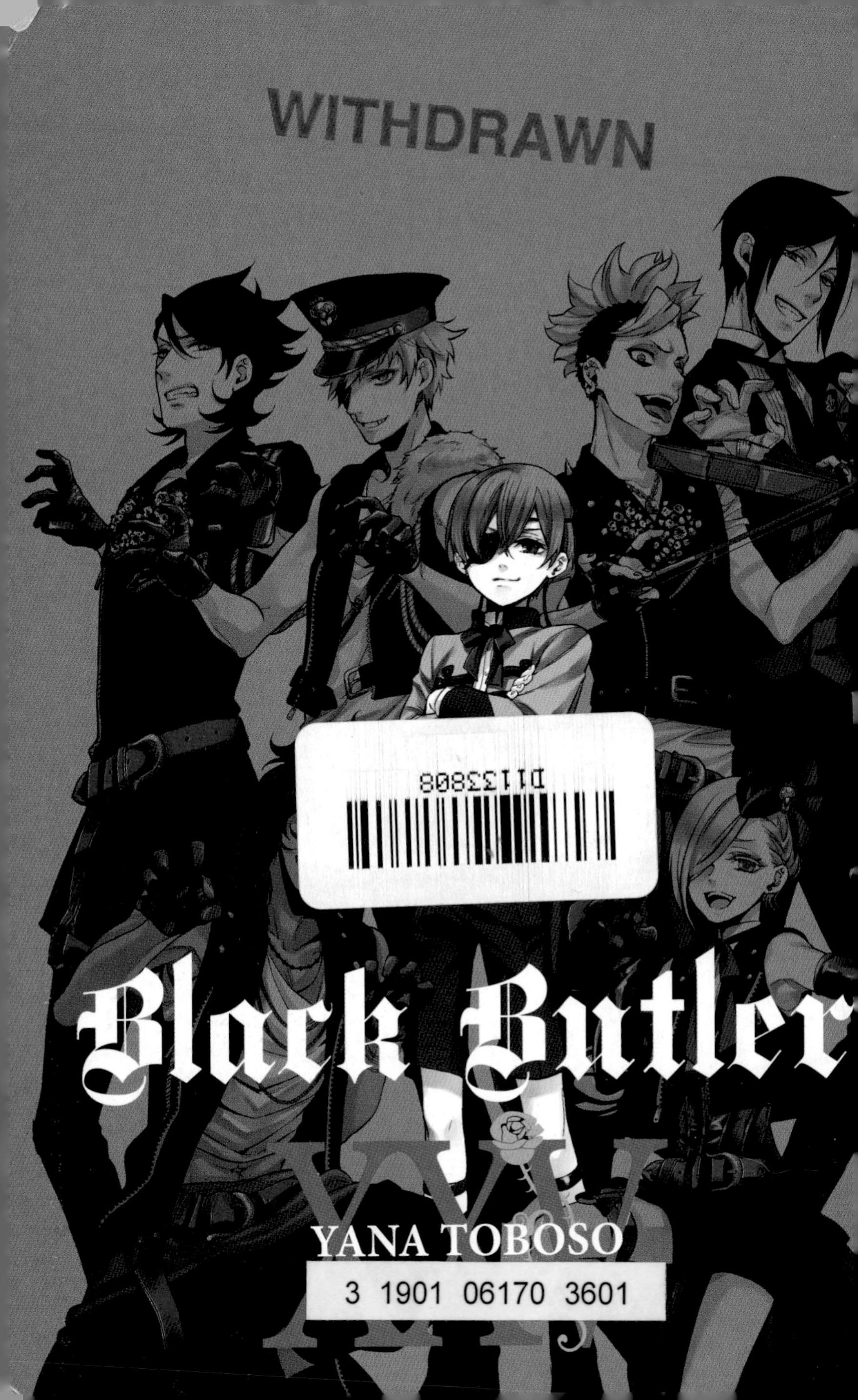

WITHDRAWN
D1133808
Black Butler
YANA TOBOSO
3 1901 06170 3601

Contents

CHAPTER 120

In the morning · · · · ◆ 3

The Butler, Listening Quietly

CHAPTER 121

At noon ◆ · ◆ · ◆ · ◆ · ◆ 23

The Butler, Unmoving

CHAPTER 122

In the afternoon · · · 57

The Butler, Lying in Wait

CHAPTER 123

In the evening ◆ · ◆ · ◆ 83

The Butler, Clarifying

CHAPTER 124

At night ◆ · ◆ · ◆ · ◆ 107

The Butler, Transporting

CHAPTER 125

At midnight ◆ · ◆ · ◆ 145

The Butler, Returning Home

PHANTOM FIVE
CONCERT

OCTOBER 1889
OCK

rea-6

PHANTOM

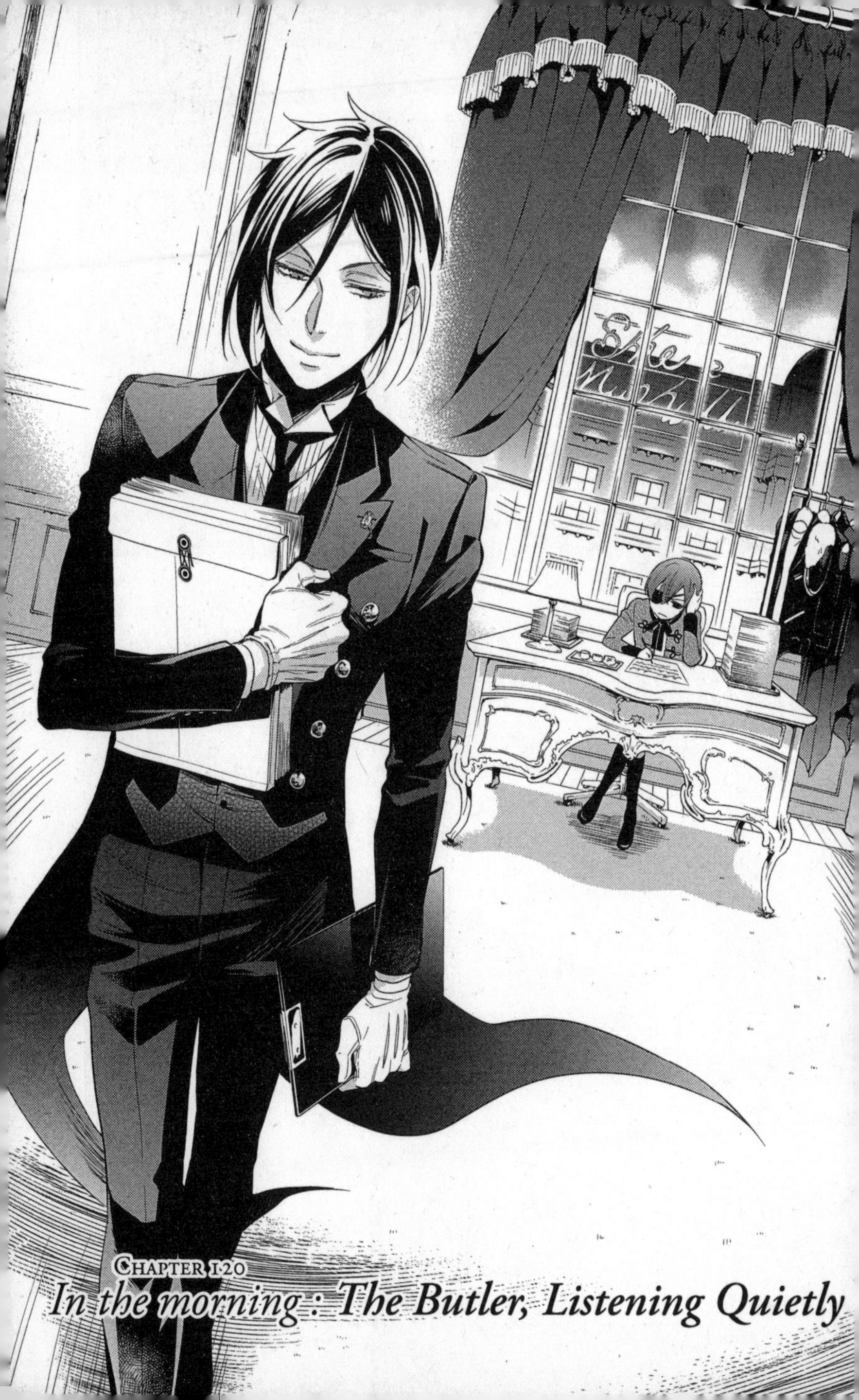

CHAPTER 120

In the morning : The Butler, Listening Quietly

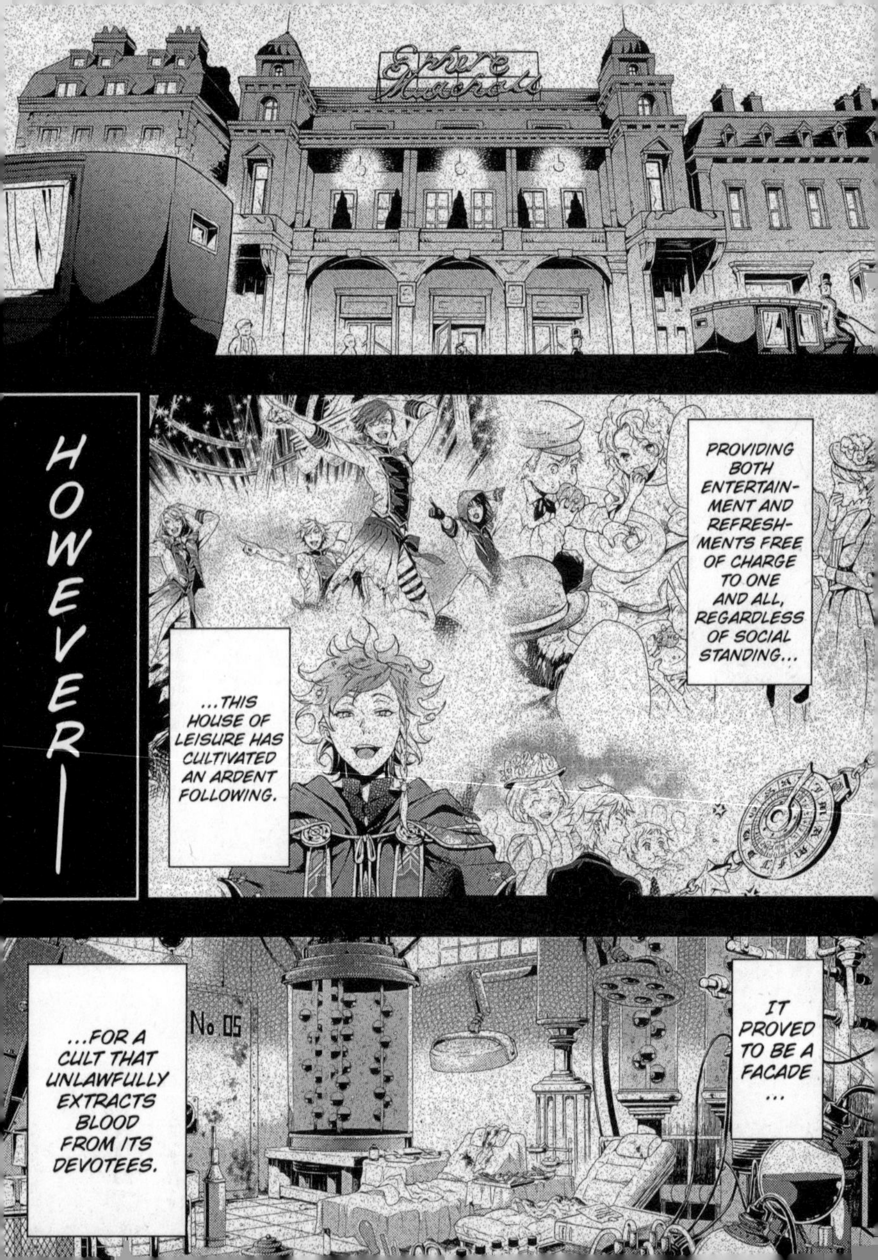
PROVIDING BOTH ENTERTAINMENT AND REFRESHMENTS FREE OF CHARGE TO ONE AND ALL, REGARDLESS OF SOCIAL STANDING...
...THIS HOUSE OF LEISURE HAS CULTIVATED AN ARDENT FOLLOWING.
HOWEVER—
IT PROVED TO BE A FACADE...
No. 05
...FOR A CULT THAT UNLAWFULLY EXTRACTS BLOOD FROM ITS DEVOTEES.

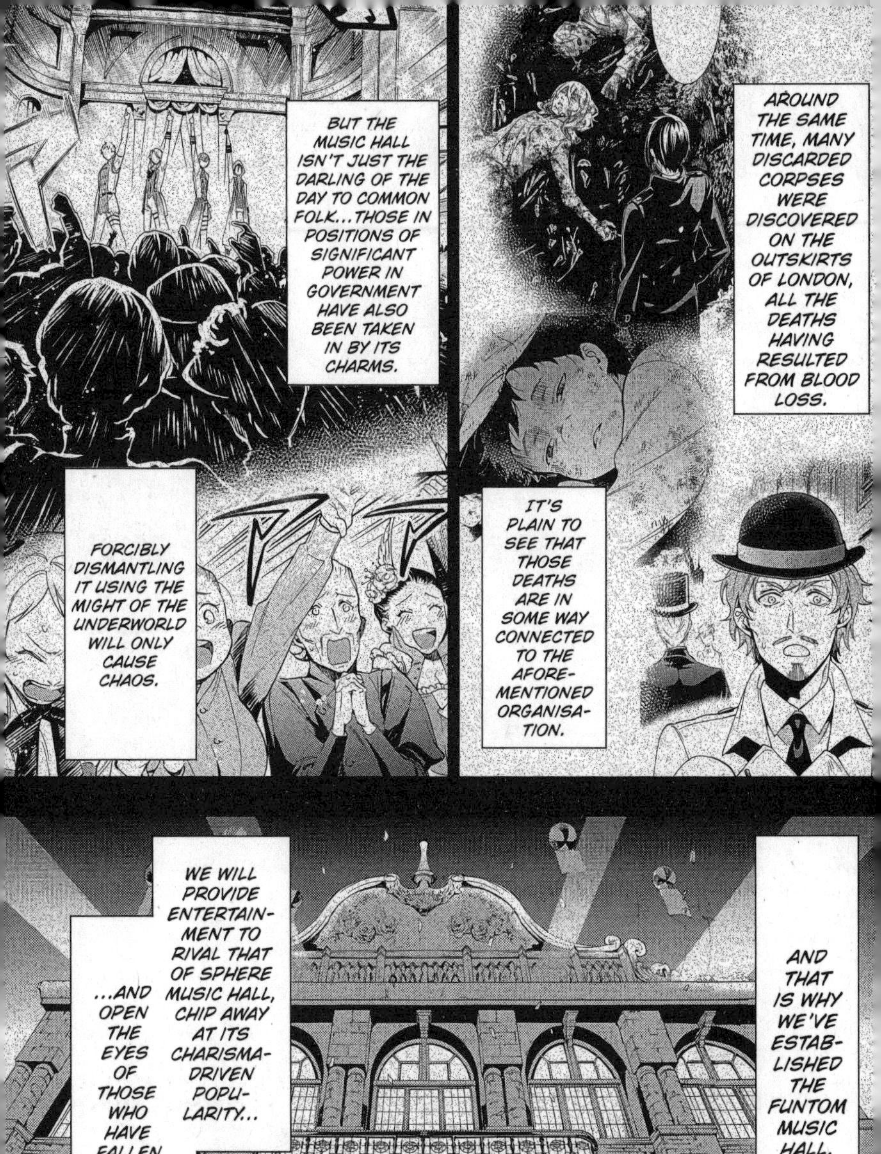
AROUND THE SAME TIME, MANY DISCARDED CORPSES WERE DISCOVERED ON THE OUTSKIRTS OF LONDON, ALL THE DEATHS HAVING RESULTED FROM BLOOD LOSS.
IT'S PLAIN TO SEE THAT THOSE DEATHS ARE IN SOME WAY CONNECTED TO THE AFORE-MENTIONED ORGANISA-TION.
BUT THE MUSIC HALL ISN'T JUST THE DARLING OF THE DAY TO COMMON FOLK...THOSE IN POSITIONS OF SIGNIFICANT POWER IN GOVERNMENT HAVE ALSO BEEN TAKEN IN BY ITS CHARMS.
FORCIBLY DISMANTLING IT USING THE MIGHT OF THE UNDERWORLD WILL ONLY CAUSE CHAOS.
AND THAT IS WHY WE'VE ESTAB-LISHED THE FUNTOM MUSIC HALL.
FUNTOM MUSIC HALL
WE WILL PROVIDE ENTERTAIN-MENT TO RIVAL THAT OF SPHERE MUSIC HALL, CHIP AWAY AT ITS CHARISMA-DRIVEN POPU-LARITY...
...AND OPEN THE EYES OF THOSE WHO HAVE FALLEN UNDER ITS SPELL.

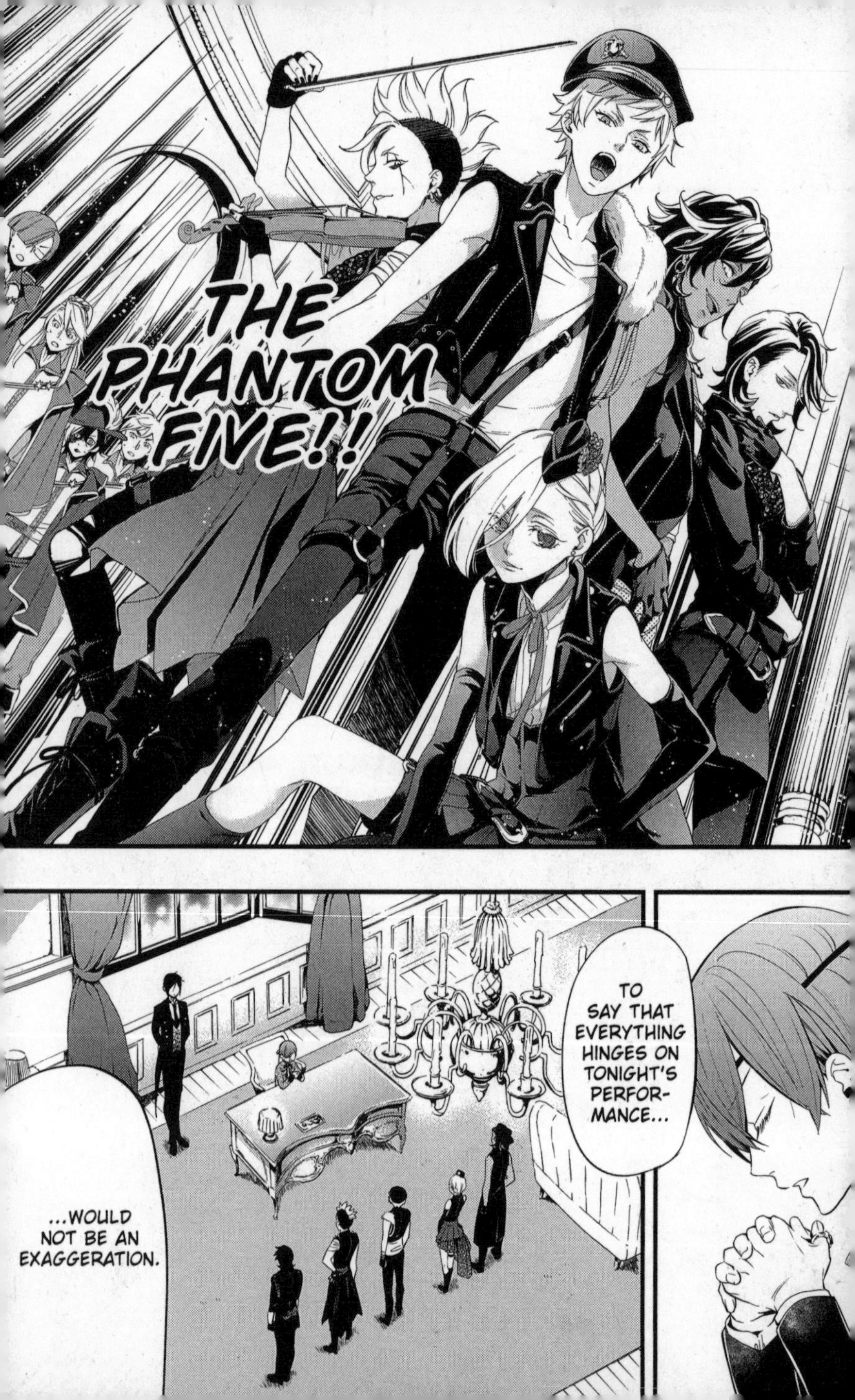
THE PHANTOM FIVE!!
TO SAY THAT EVERYTHING HINGES ON TONIGHT'S PERFORMANCE...
...WOULD NOT BE AN EXAGGERATION.

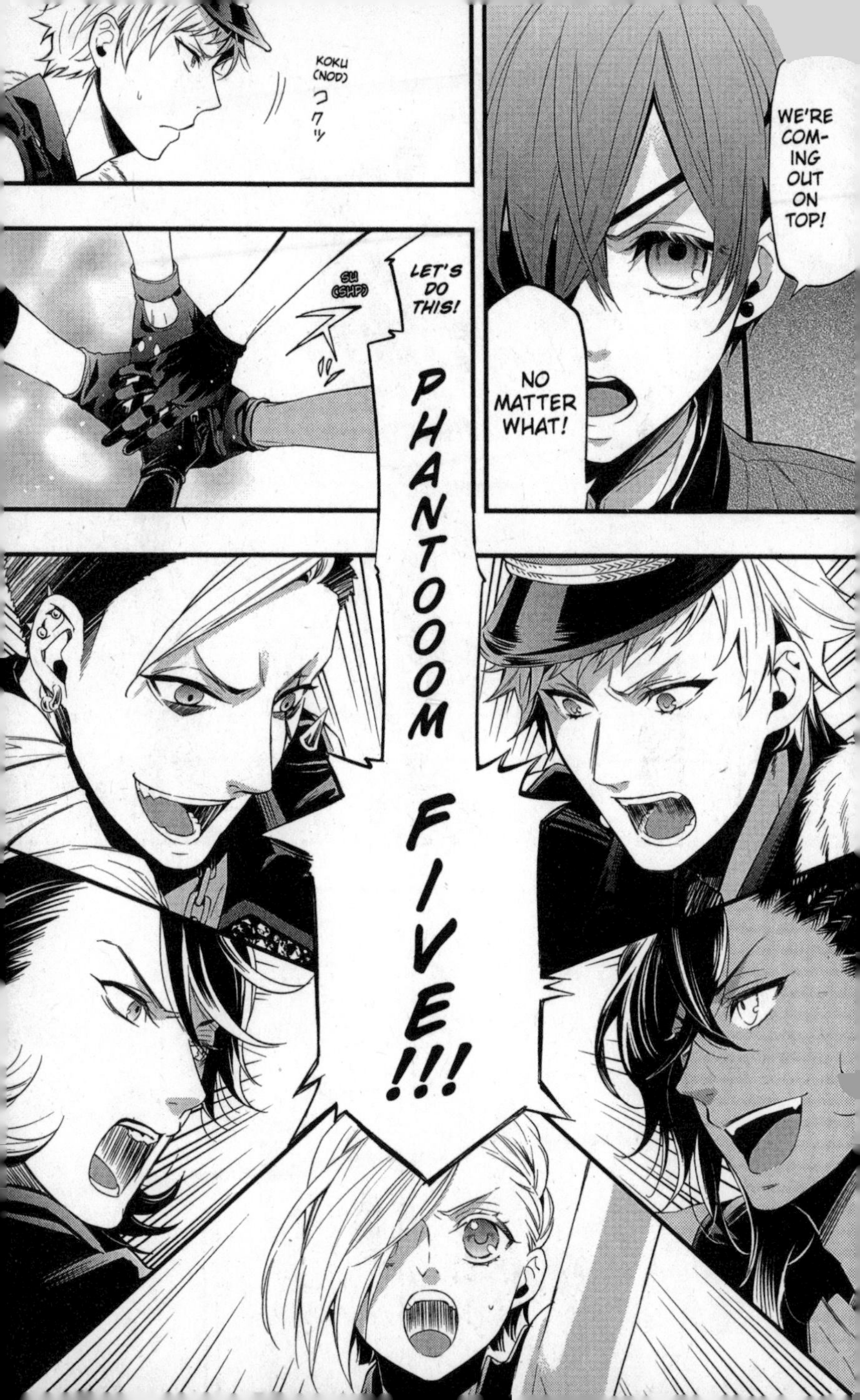
WE'RE COMING OUT ON TOP!
NO MATTER WHAT!
KOKU (NOD)
コクッ
LET'S DO THIS!
SU (SHP)
PHANTOOOOM FIVE!!!

FUNTOM MUSIC HALL!?

I CAN'T BELIEVE THEY'VE BUILT ONE OF THEIR OWN RIGHT IN FRONT OF OURS...

HEH...!

EASY, NOW... WE'RE ONLY TALKING ABOUT A PALE IMITATION THAT'S FAR TOO LITTLE, TOO LATE.

POPU-LARITY LIKE OURS CAN'T BE BUILT IN A DAY.

WANA

わな....?

WANA (TREMBLE)

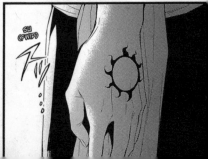

SU (FWIP)

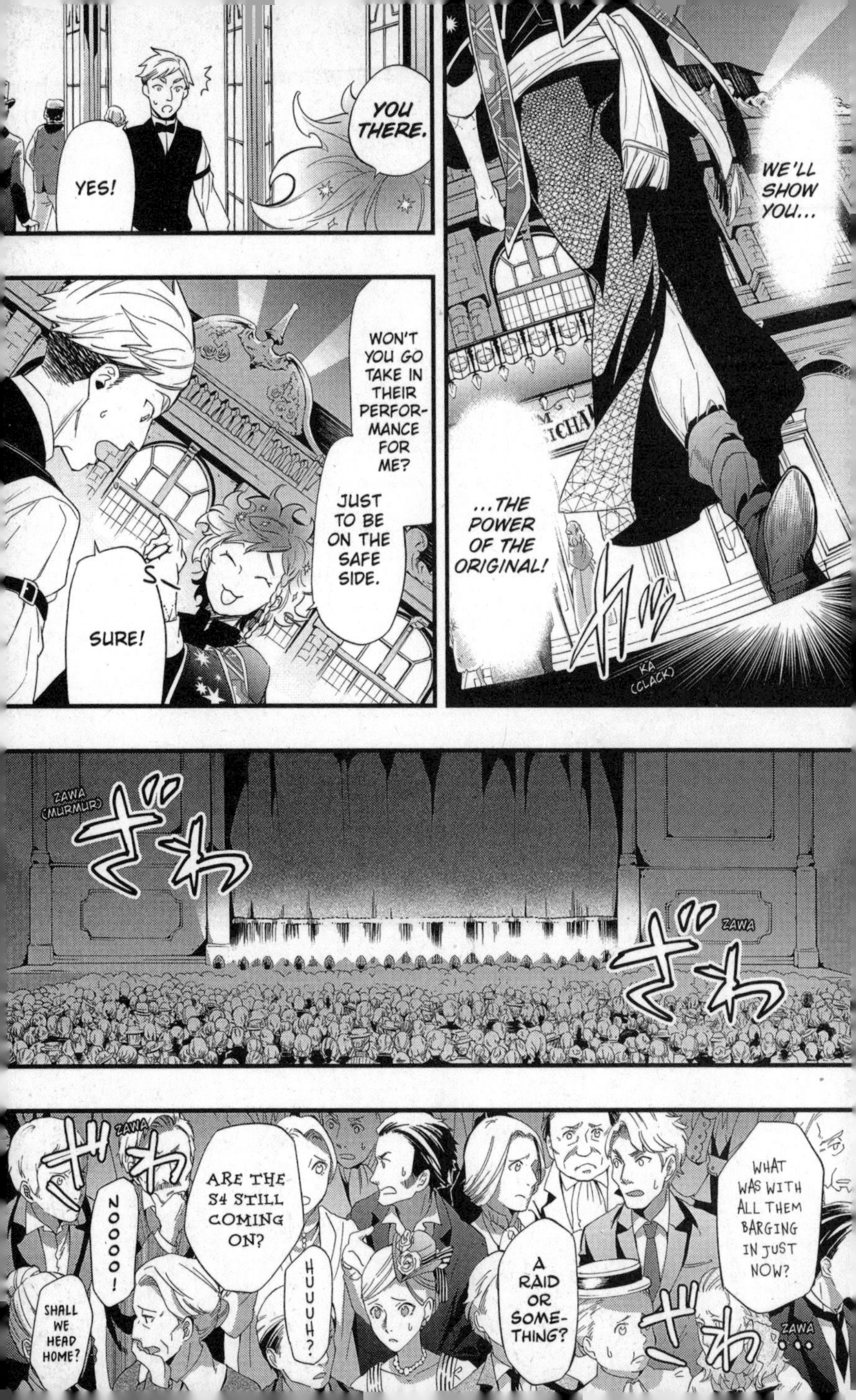
WE'LL SHOW YOU...
...THE POWER OF THE ORIGINAL!
KA (CLACK)
YOU THERE.
YES!
WON'T YOU GO TAKE IN THEIR PERFORMANCE FOR ME?
JUST TO BE ON THE SAFE SIDE.
SURE!
ZAWA (MURMUR)
ZAWA
WHAT WAS WITH ALL THEM BARGING IN JUST NOW?
ZAWA...
A RAID OR SOMETHING?
HUUUH?
ARE THE S4 STILL COMING ON?
NOOOOO!
ZAWA
SHALL WE HEAD HOME?

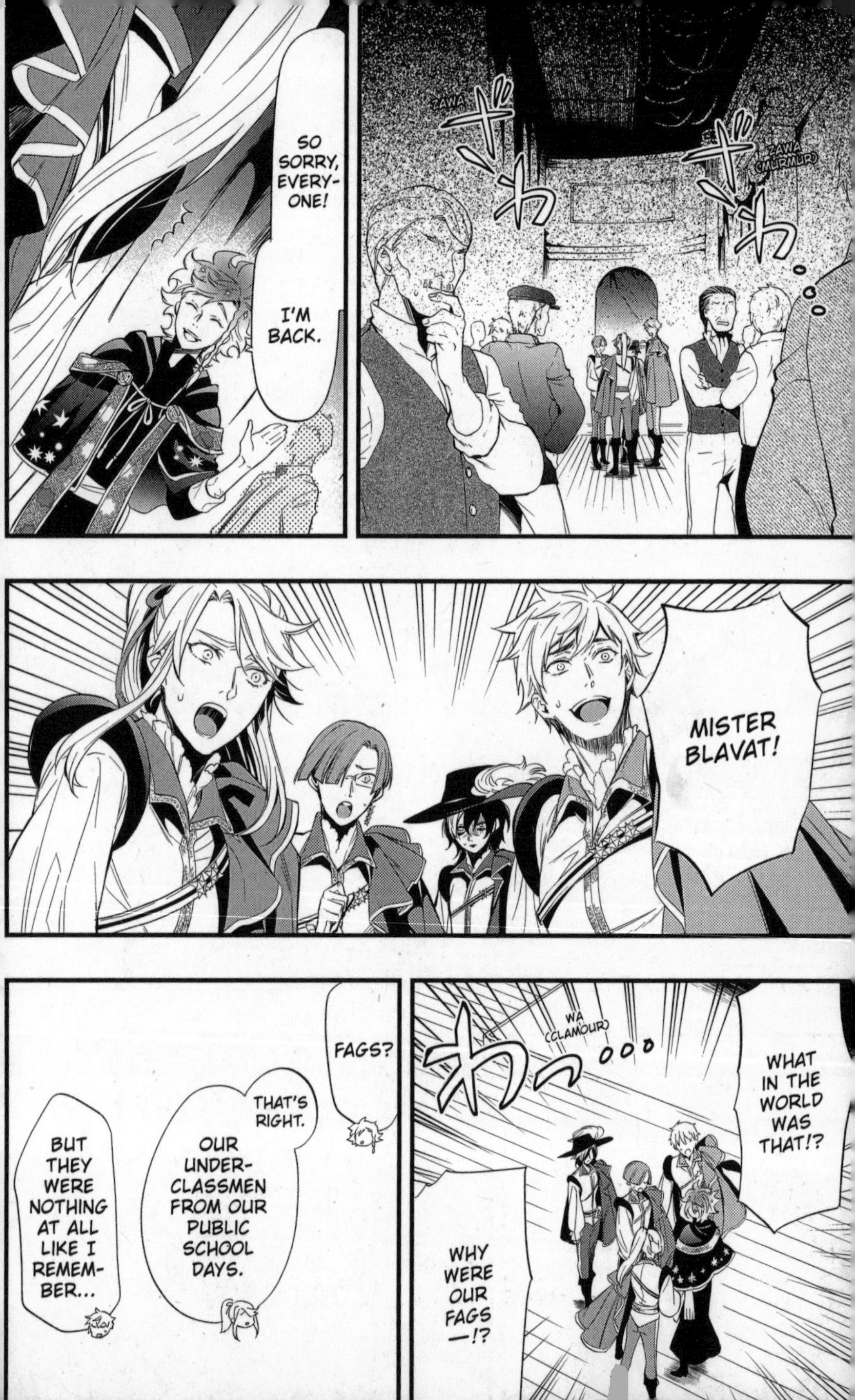
ZAWA (MURMUR)
ZAWA
SO SORRY, EVERY-ONE!
I'M BACK.
MISTER BLAVAT!
WA (CLAMOUR)
WHAT IN THE WORLD WAS THAT!?
WHY WERE OUR FAGS—!?
FAGS?
THAT'S RIGHT.
OUR UNDER-CLASSMEN FROM OUR PUBLIC SCHOOL DAYS.
BUT THEY WERE NOTHING AT ALL LIKE I REMEM-BER…

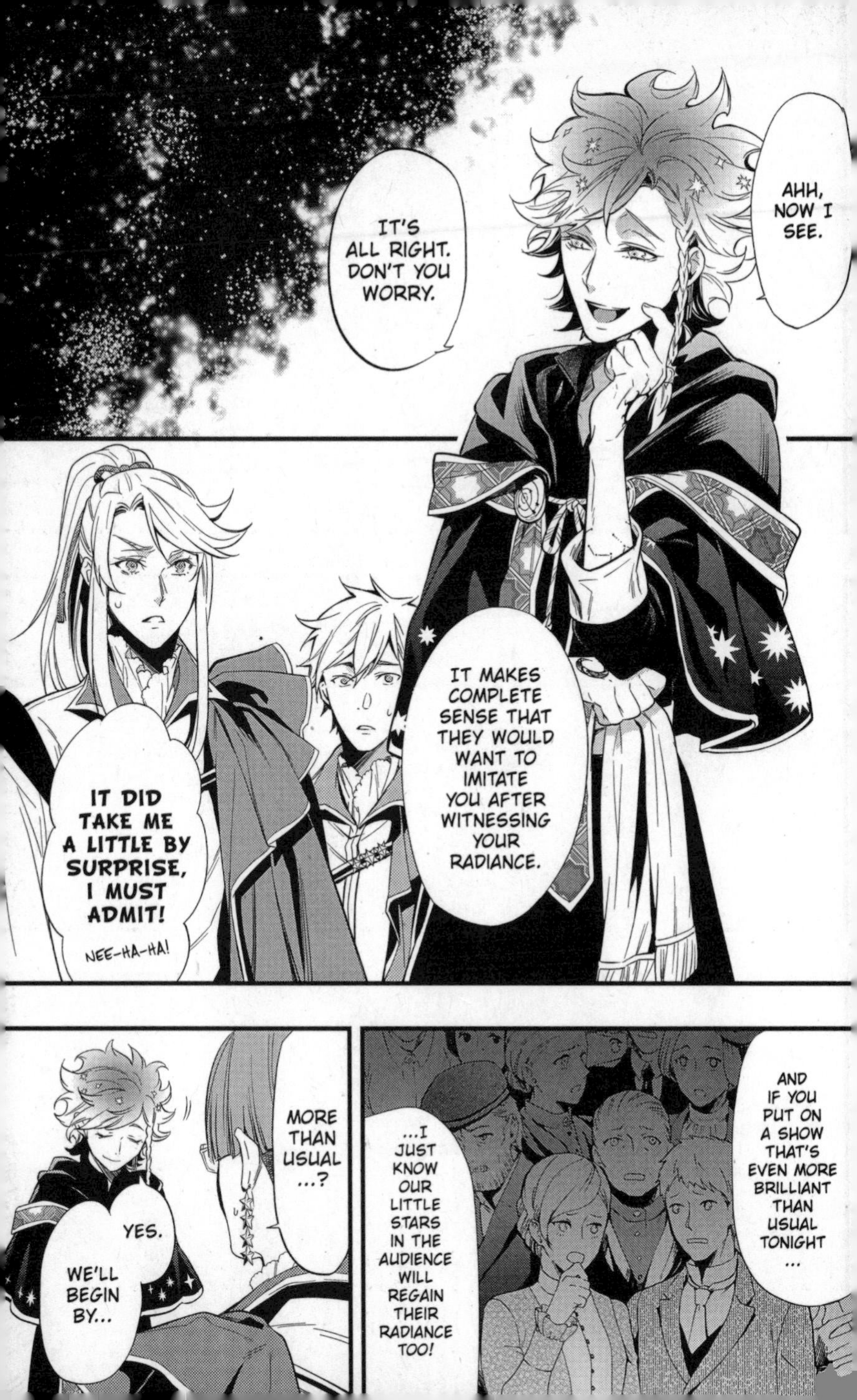
AHH, NOW I SEE.
IT'S ALL RIGHT. DON'T YOU WORRY.
IT MAKES COMPLETE SENSE THAT THEY WOULD WANT TO IMITATE YOU AFTER WITNESSING YOUR RADIANCE.
IT DID TAKE ME A LITTLE BY SURPRISE, I MUST ADMIT!
NEE-HA-HA!
AND IF YOU PUT ON A SHOW THAT'S EVEN MORE BRILLIANT THAN USUAL TONIGHT...
...I JUST KNOW OUR LITTLE STARS IN THE AUDIENCE WILL REGAIN THEIR RADIANCE TOO!
MORE THAN USUAL...?
YES.
WE'LL BEGIN BY...

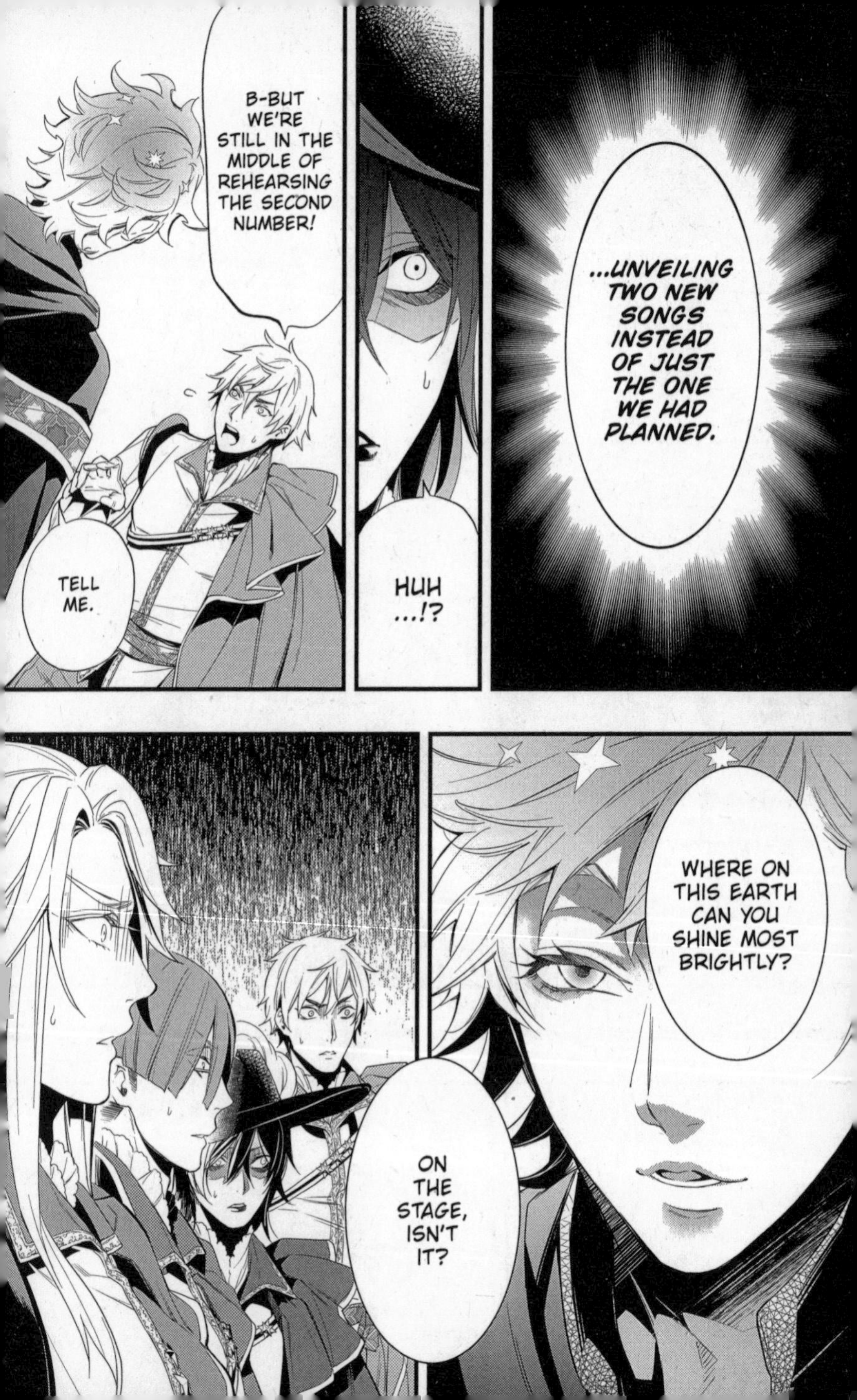
...UNVEILING TWO NEW SONGS INSTEAD OF JUST THE ONE WE HAD PLANNED.
HUH ...!?
B-BUT WE'RE STILL IN THE MIDDLE OF REHEARSING THE SECOND NUMBER!
TELL ME.
WHERE ON THIS EARTH CAN YOU SHINE MOST BRIGHTLY?
ON THE STAGE, ISN'T IT?

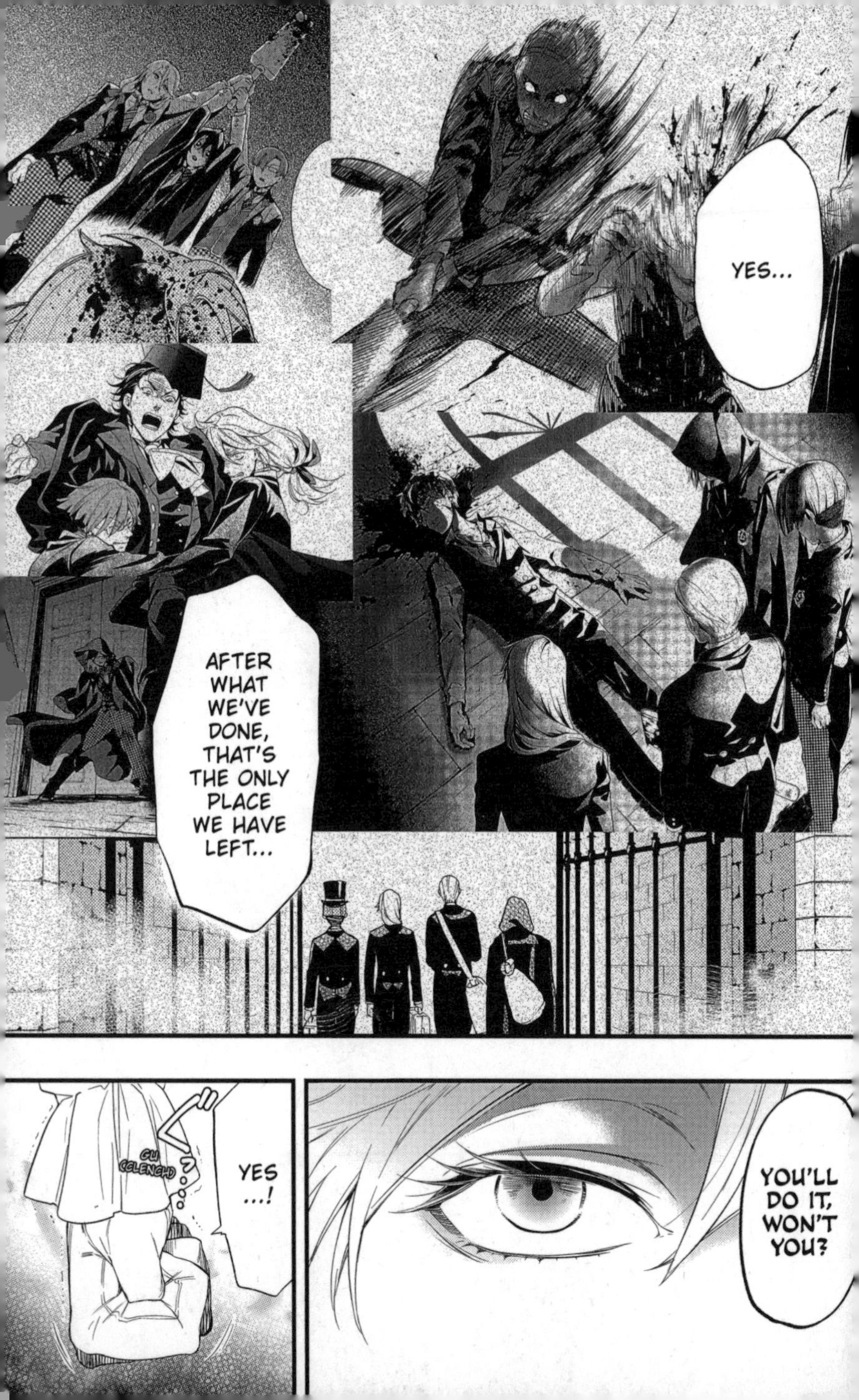
YES...
AFTER WHAT WE'VE DONE, THAT'S THE ONLY PLACE WE HAVE LEFT...
YOU'LL DO IT, WON'T YOU?
YES ...!
GU (CLENCH)

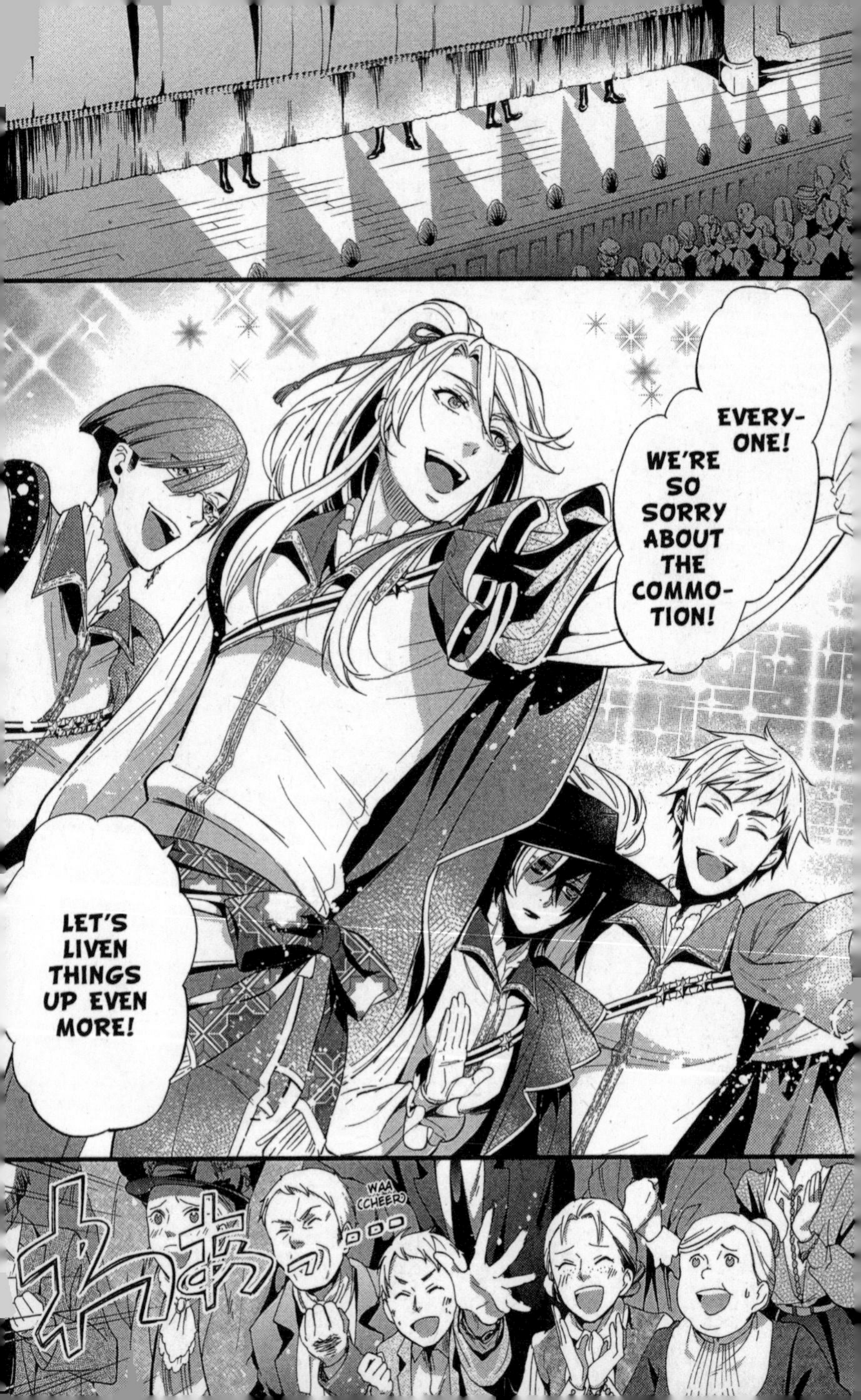
EVERY-ONE! WE'RE SO SORRY ABOUT THE COMMOTION!
LET'S LIVEN THINGS UP EVEN MORE!
WAA (CHEER)

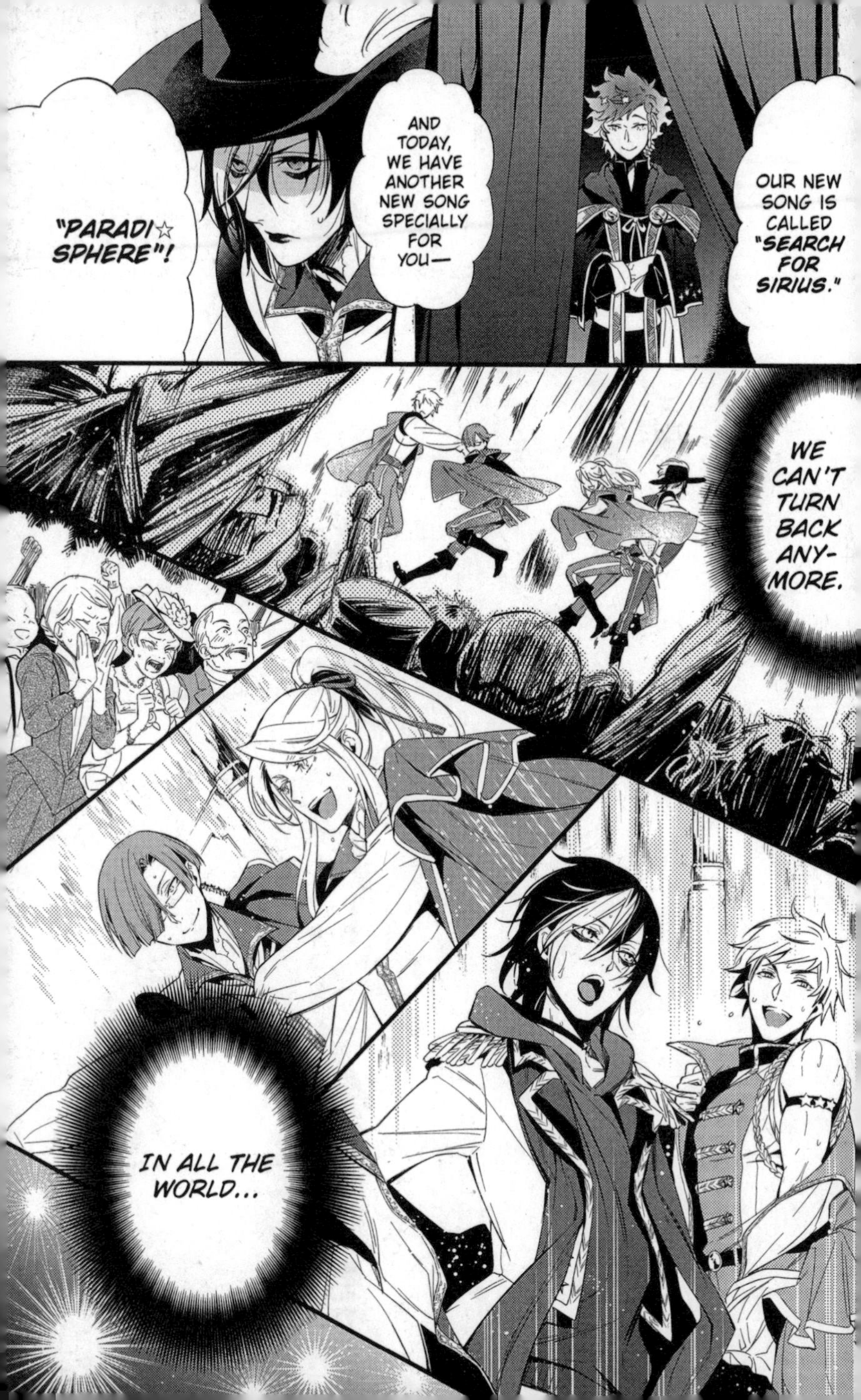
OUR NEW SONG IS CALLED "SEARCH FOR SIRIUS."
AND TODAY, WE HAVE ANOTHER NEW SONG SPECIALLY FOR YOU—
"PARADI☆SPHERE"!
WE CAN'T TURN BACK ANY-MORE.
IN ALL THE WORLD...

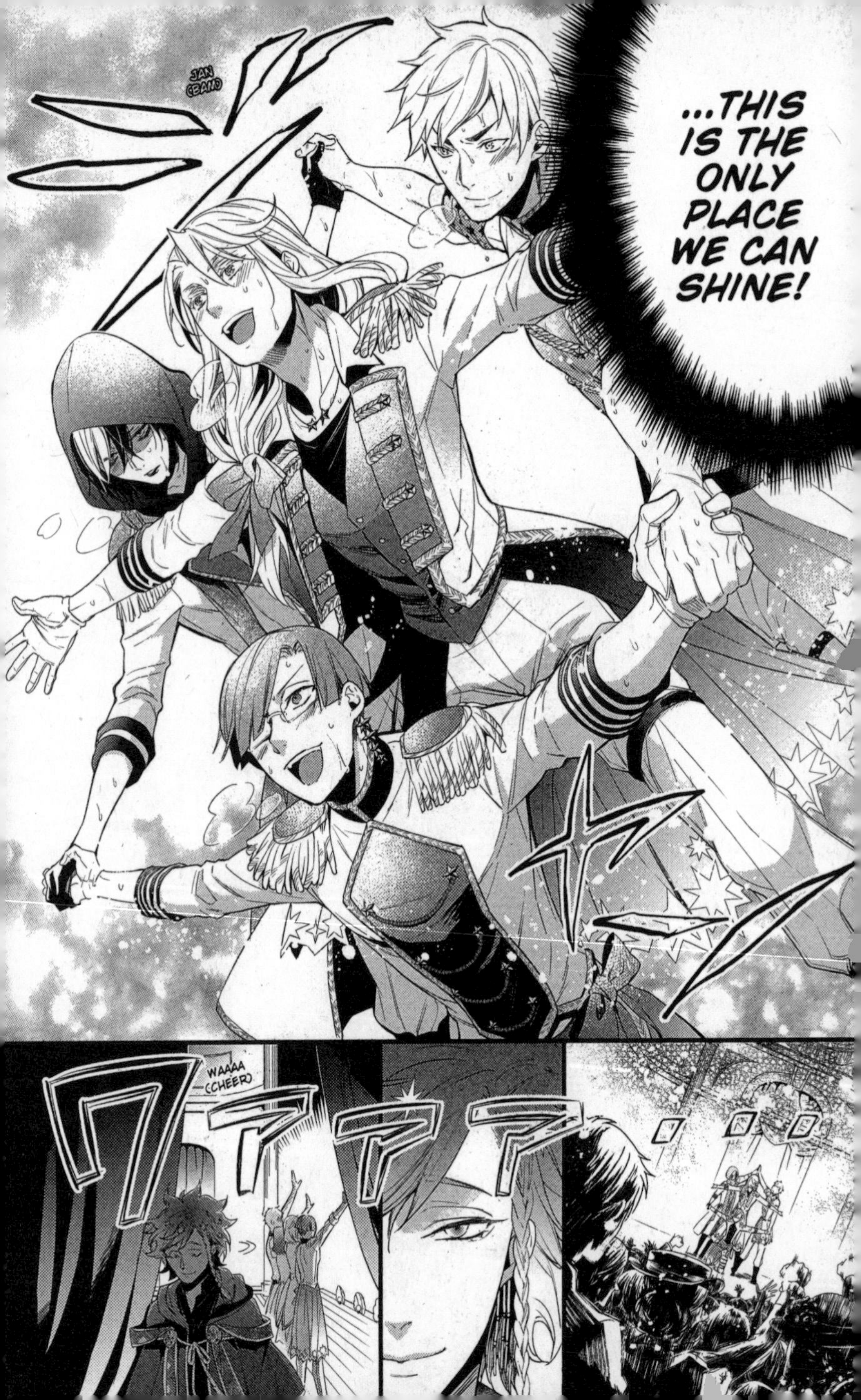
...THIS IS THE ONLY PLACE WE CAN SHINE!
JAN (BAM)
WAAAA (CHEER)

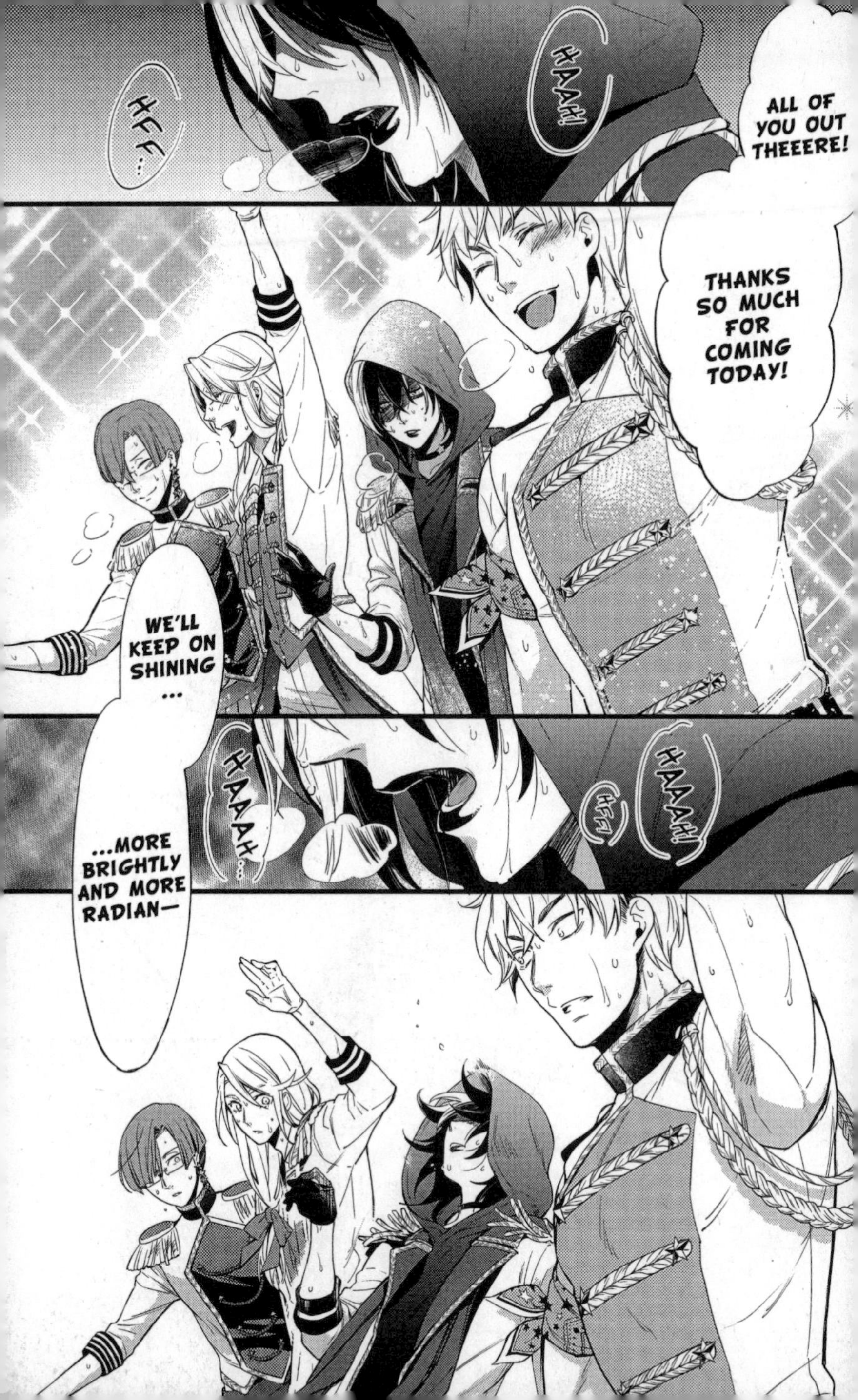
ALL OF YOU OUT THEEERE!
HAAH!
HFF...
THANKS SO MUCH FOR COMING TODAY!
WE'LL KEEP ON SHINING...
HAAAH!
HFF
HAAAH...
...MORE BRIGHTLY AND MORE RADIAN—

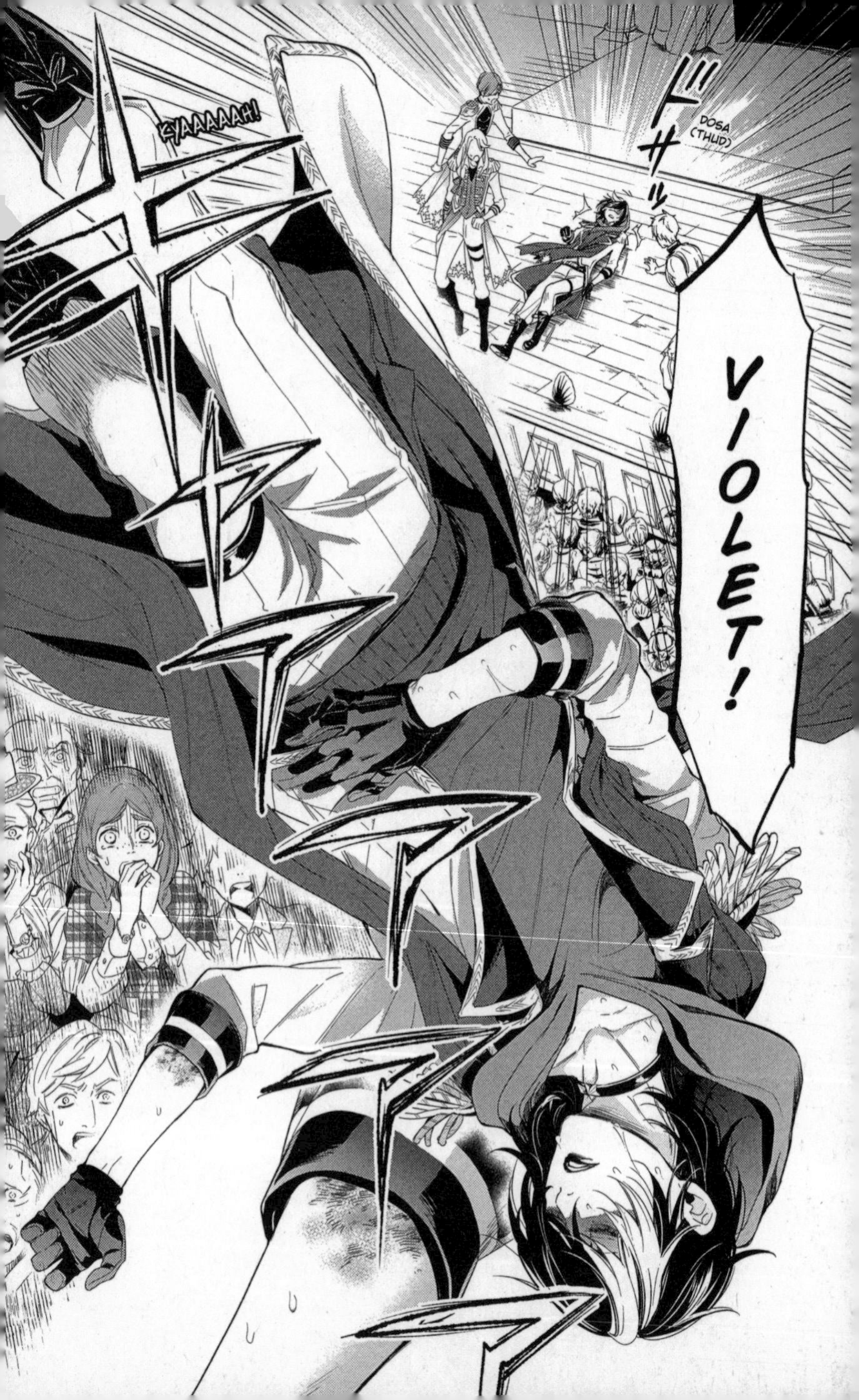
VIOLET!
DOSA (THUD)
KYAAAAAH!

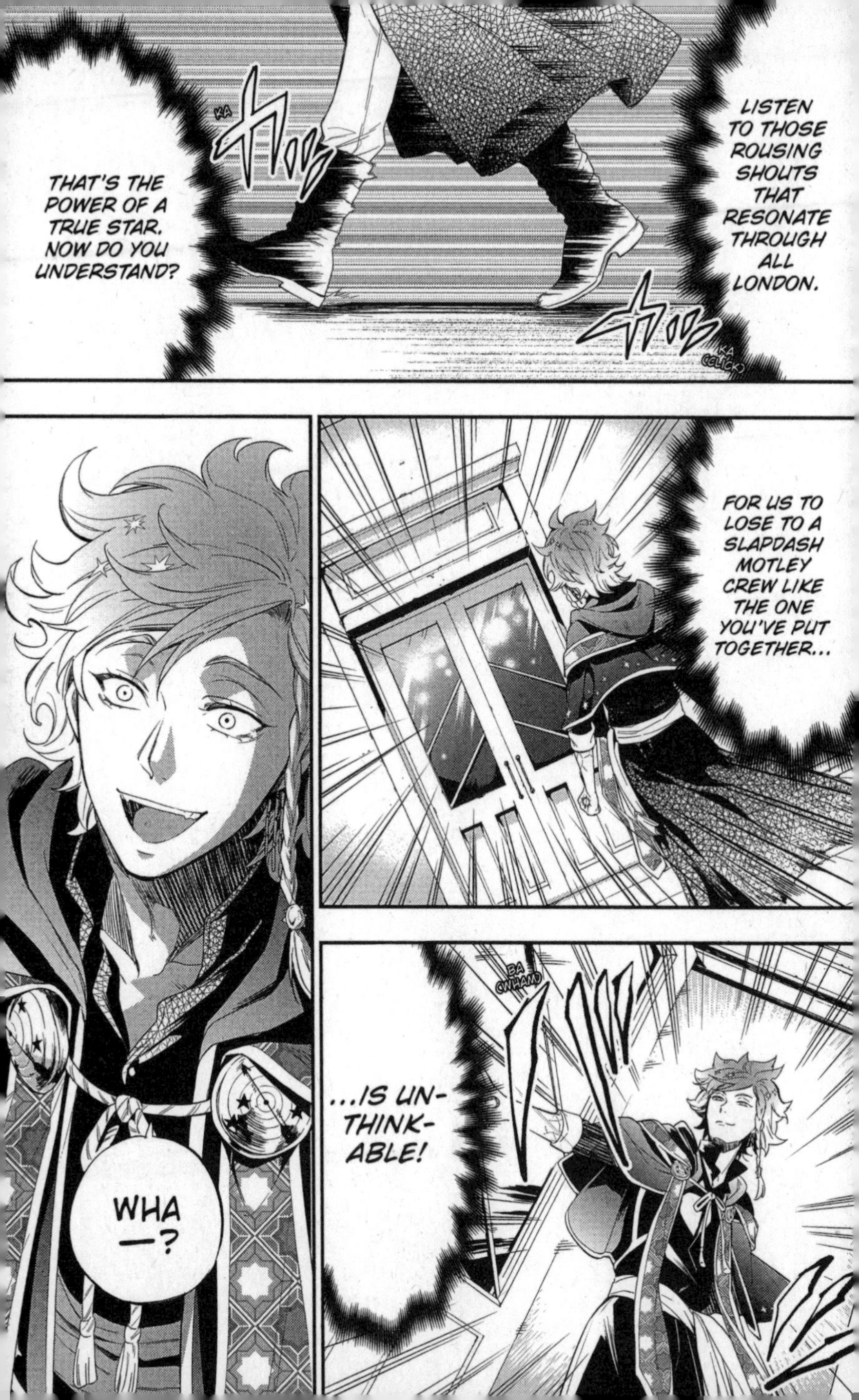
LISTEN TO THOSE ROUSING SHOUTS THAT RESONATE THROUGH ALL LONDON.
KA
THAT'S THE POWER OF A TRUE STAR. NOW DO YOU UNDERSTAND?
KA (CLICK)
FOR US TO LOSE TO A SLAPDASH MOTLEY CREW LIKE THE ONE YOU'VE PUT TOGETHER...
BA (WHAM)
...IS UN-THINK-ABLE!
WHA—?

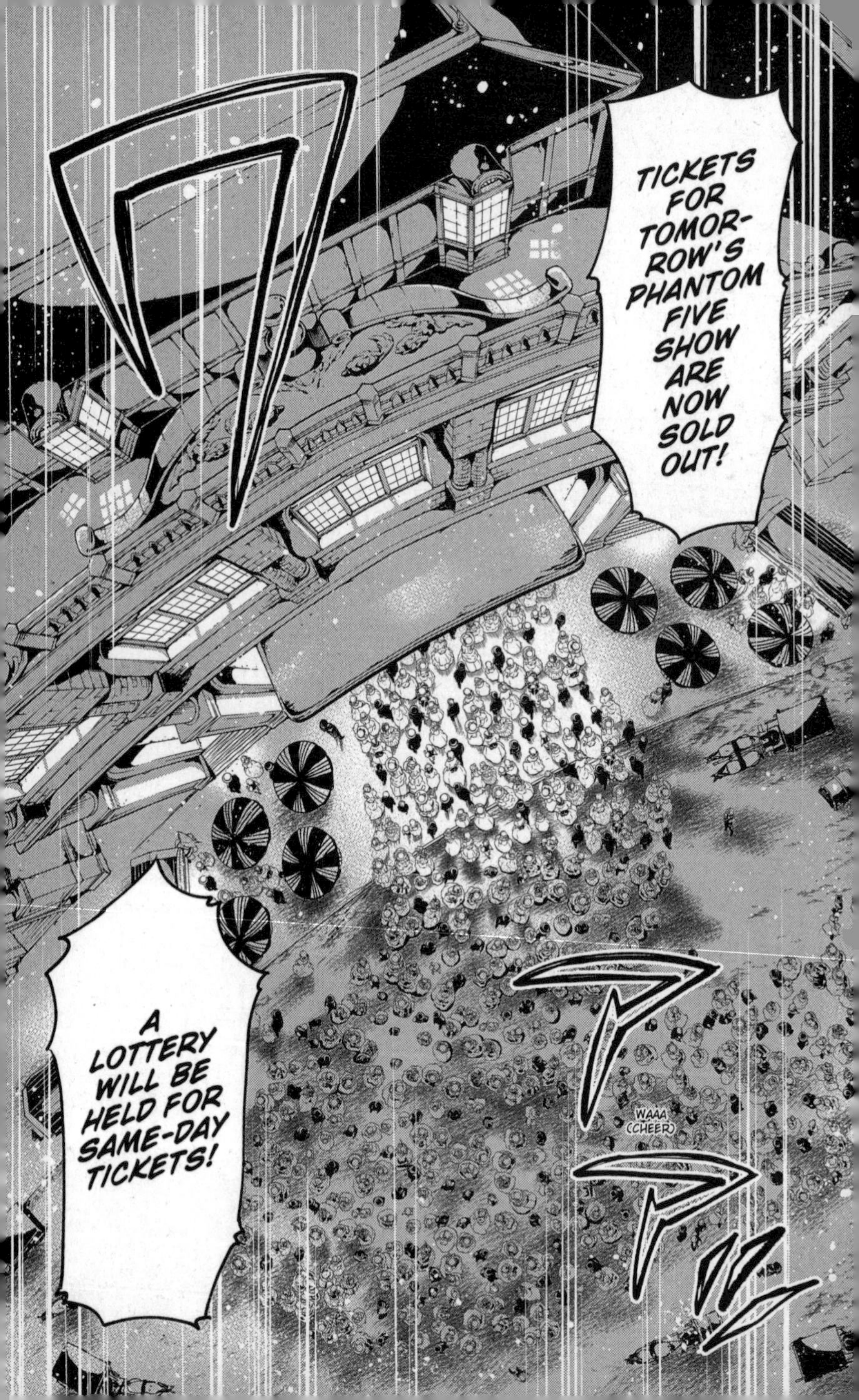
TICKETS FOR TOMORROW'S PHANTOM FIVE SHOW ARE NOW SOLD OUT!
A LOTTERY WILL BE HELD FOR SAME-DAY TICKETS!
WAAA (CHEER)

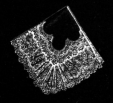

Black Butler

Chapter 121
At noon : The Butler, Unmoving

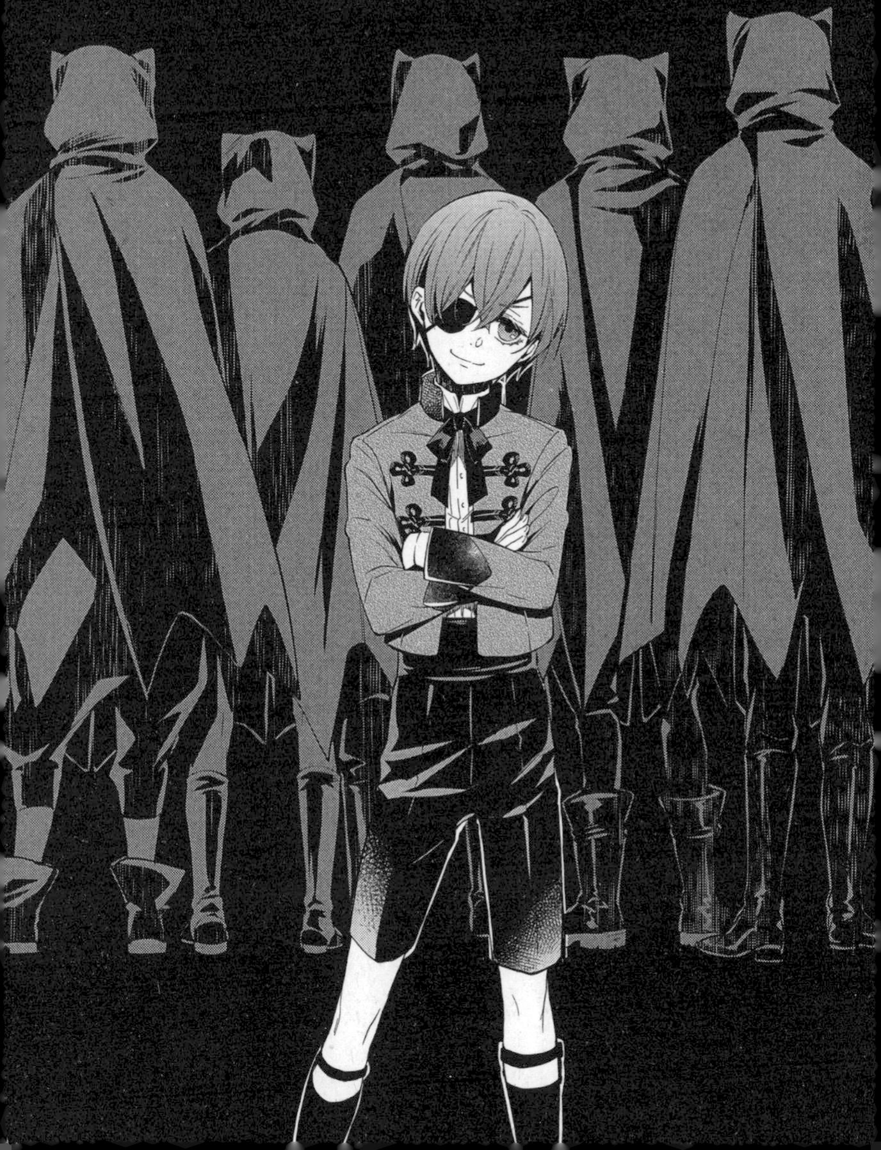

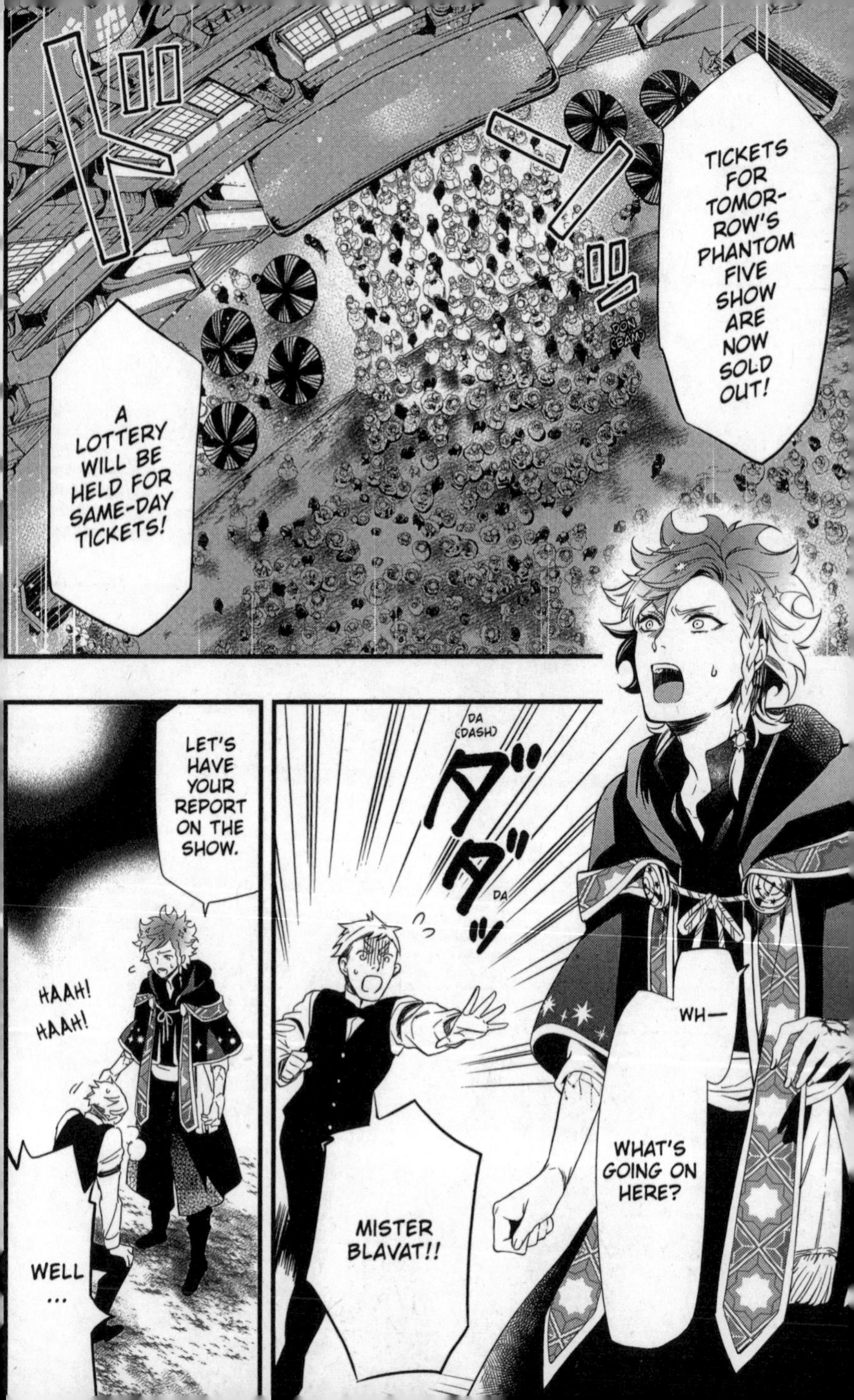
TICKETS FOR TOMORROW'S PHANTOM FIVE SHOW ARE NOW SOLD OUT!
DON (BAM)
A LOTTERY WILL BE HELD FOR SAME-DAY TICKETS!
DA (DASH)
DA
MISTER BLAVAT!!
WH—
WHAT'S GOING ON HERE?
LET'S HAVE YOUR REPORT ON THE SHOW.
HAAH! HAAH!
WELL...

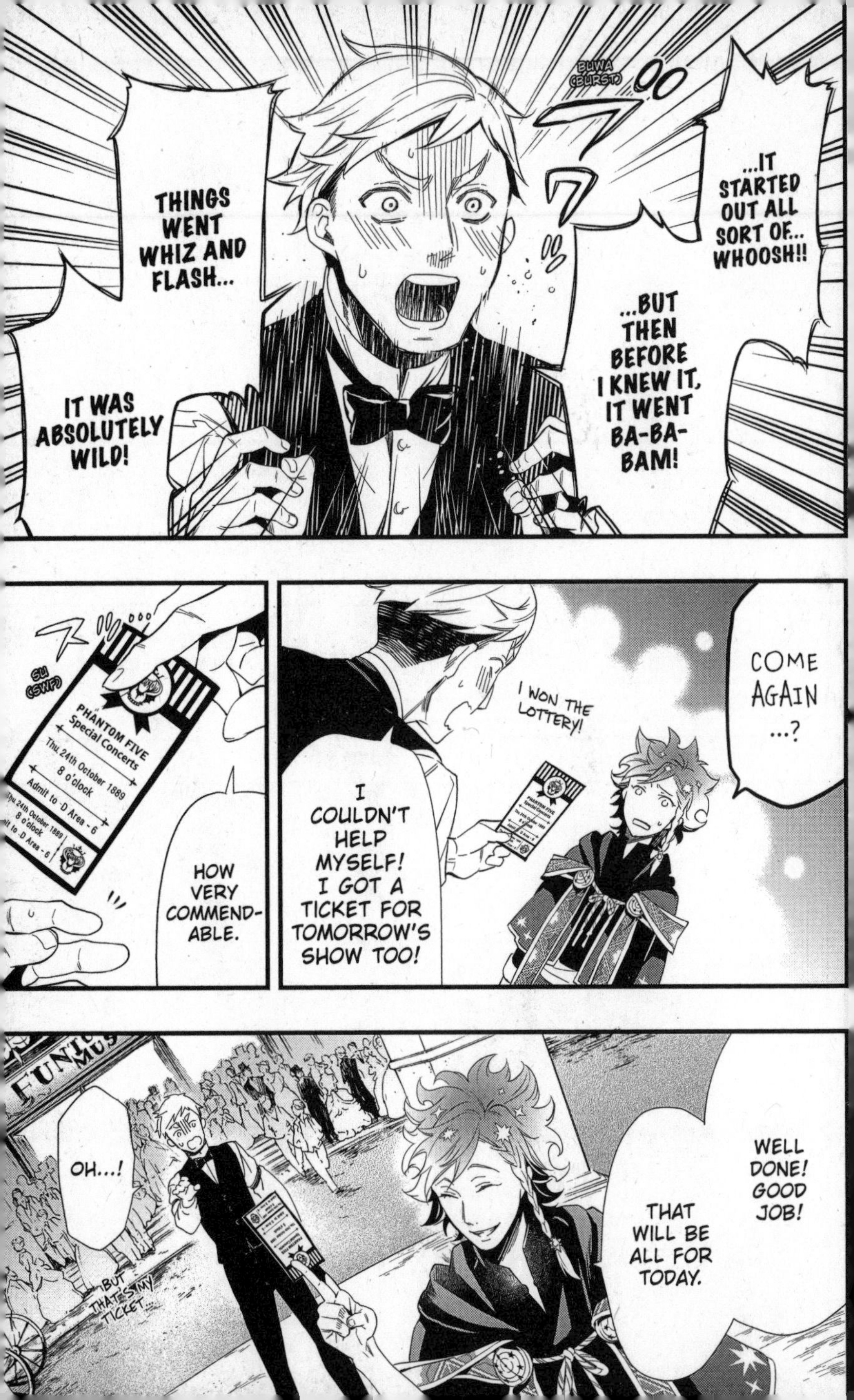
...IT STARTED OUT ALL SORT OF... WHOOSH!!
BUWA (BURST)
...BUT THEN BEFORE I KNEW IT, IT WENT BA-BA-BAM!
THINGS WENT WHIZ AND FLASH...
IT WAS ABSOLUTELY WILD!
COME AGAIN ...?
I WON THE LOTTERY!
I COULDN'T HELP MYSELF! I GOT A TICKET FOR TOMORROW'S SHOW TOO!
SU (SWIP)
PHANTOM FIVE Special Concerts
Thu. 24th October 1889
8 o'clock
Admit to -D Area - 6
HOW VERY COMMEND-ABLE.
WELL DONE! GOOD JOB!
THAT WILL BE ALL FOR TODAY.
OH...!
BUT THAT'S MY TICKET...

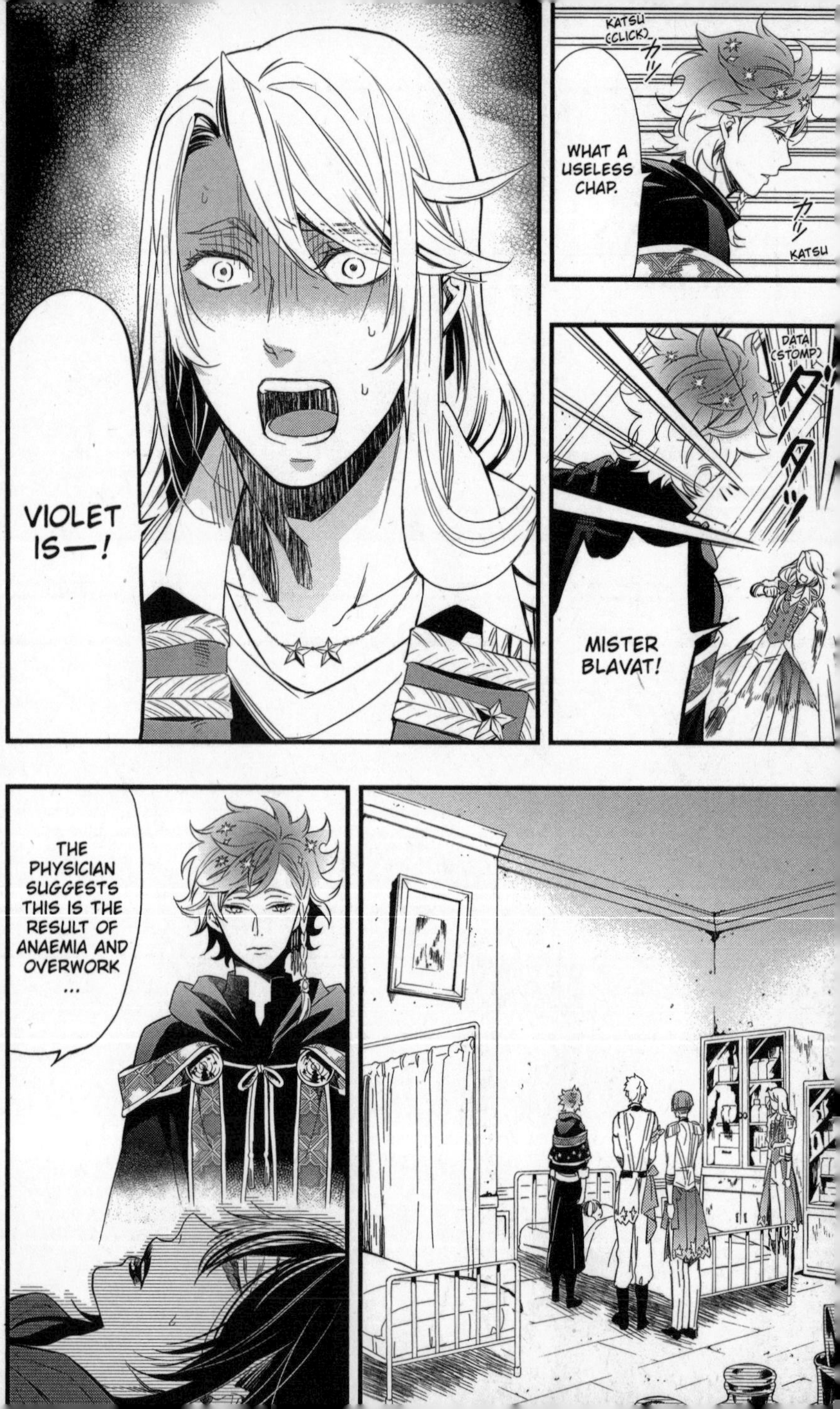
KATSU (CLICK)
WHAT A USELESS CHAP.
KATSU
DATA (STOMP)
MISTER BLAVAT!
VIOLET IS—!
THE PHYSICIAN SUGGESTS THIS IS THE RESULT OF ANAEMIA AND OVERWORK ...

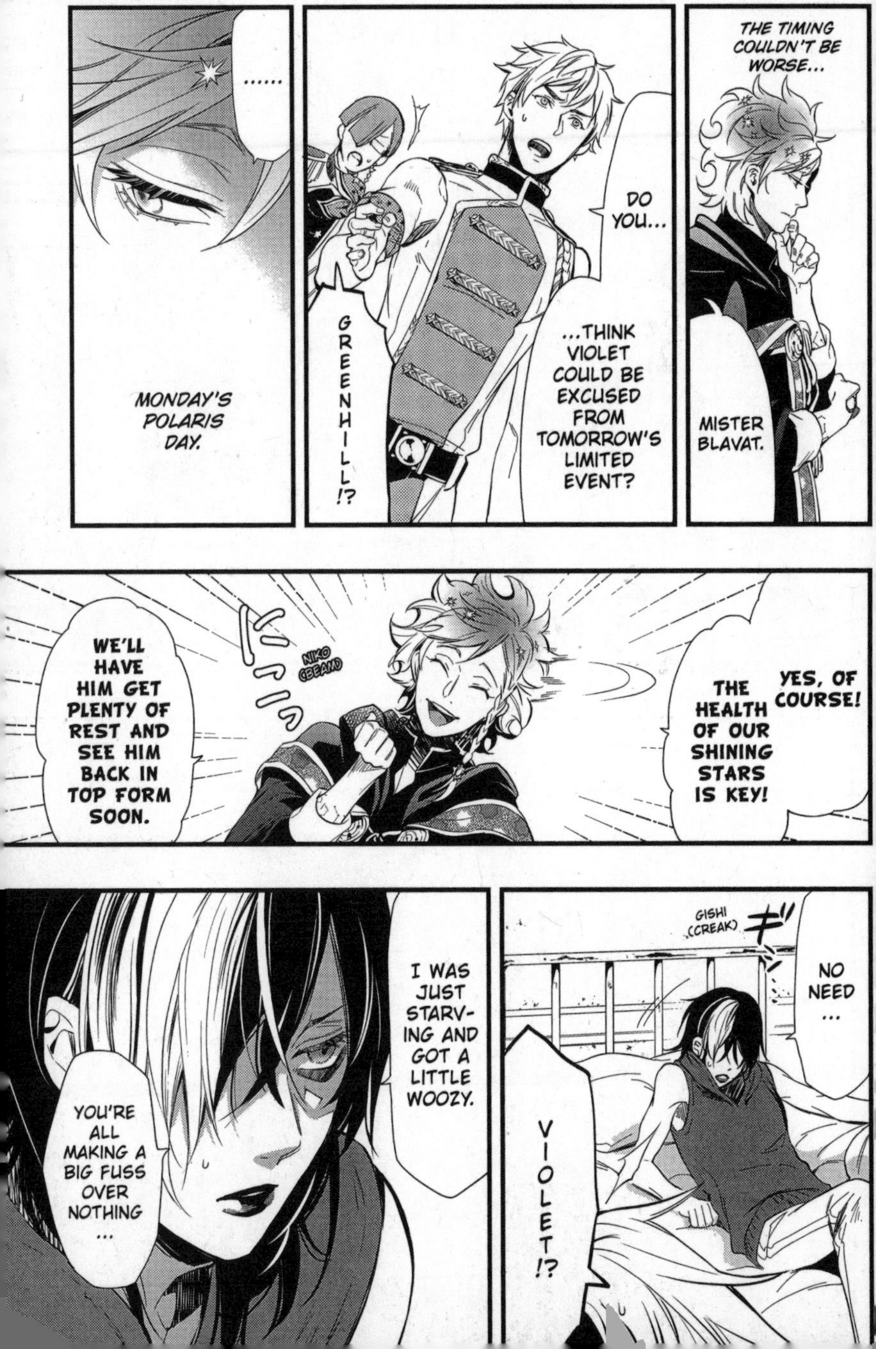
THE TIMING COULDN'T BE WORSE...
MISTER BLAVAT.
DO YOU...
...THINK VIOLET COULD BE EXCUSED FROM TOMORROW'S LIMITED EVENT?
GREENHILL!?
......
MONDAY'S POLARIS DAY.
YES, OF COURSE!
THE HEALTH OF OUR SHINING STARS IS KEY!
NIKO (BEAM)
WE'LL HAVE HIM GET PLENTY OF REST AND SEE HIM BACK IN TOP FORM SOON.
NO NEED...
GISHI (CREAK)
VIOLET!?
I WAS JUST STARVING AND GOT A LITTLE WOOZY.
YOU'RE ALL MAKING A BIG FUSS OVER NOTHING...

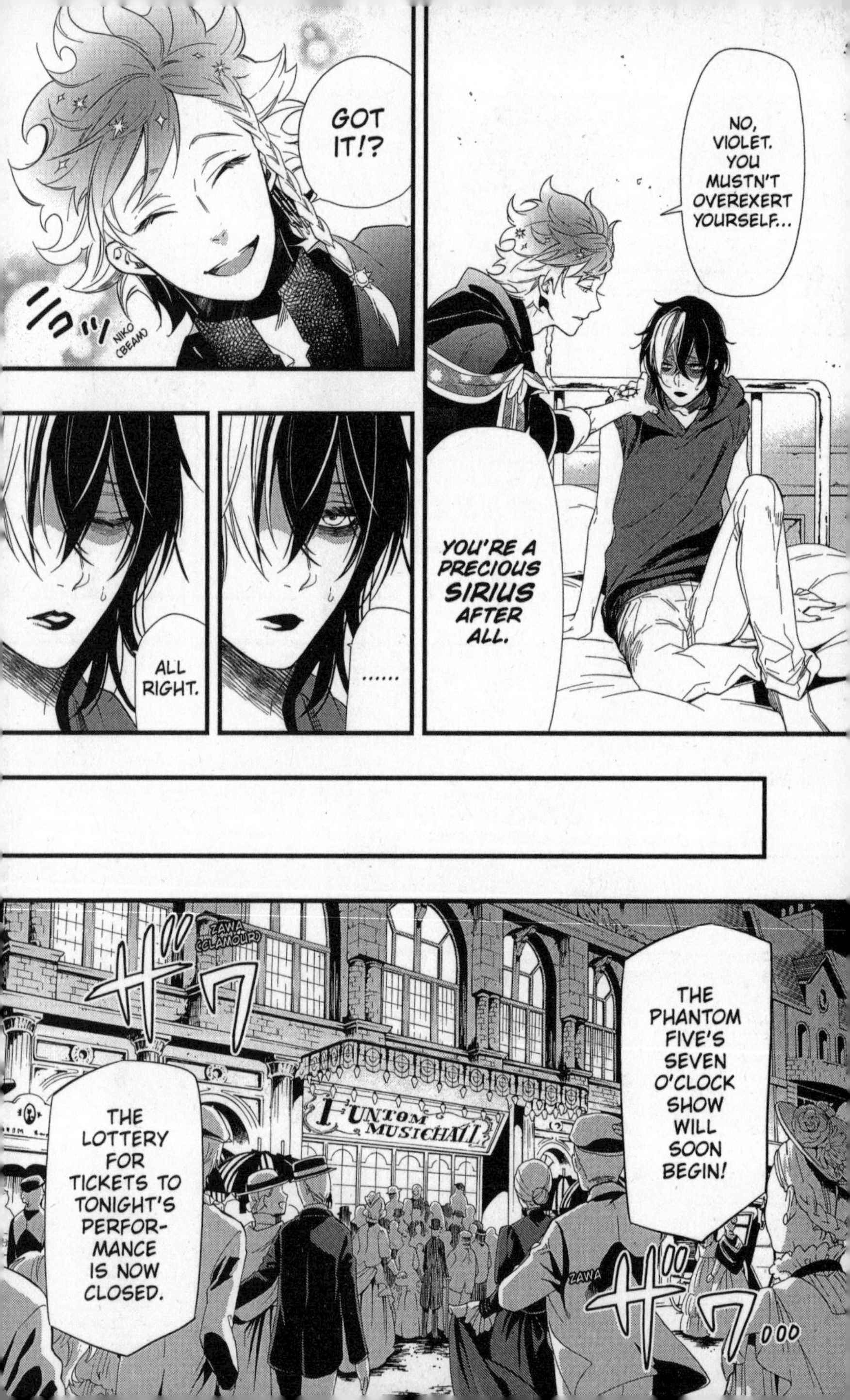
NO, VIOLET. YOU MUSTN'T OVEREXERT YOURSELF...
YOU'RE A PRECIOUS SIRIUS AFTER ALL.
GOT IT!?
ニコッ
NIKO (BEAM)
......
ALL RIGHT.
THE PHANTOM FIVE'S SEVEN O'CLOCK SHOW WILL SOON BEGIN!
ザワ
ZAWA (CLAMOUR)
THE LOTTERY FOR TICKETS TO TONIGHT'S PERFORMANCE IS NOW CLOSED.
ザワ
ZAWA

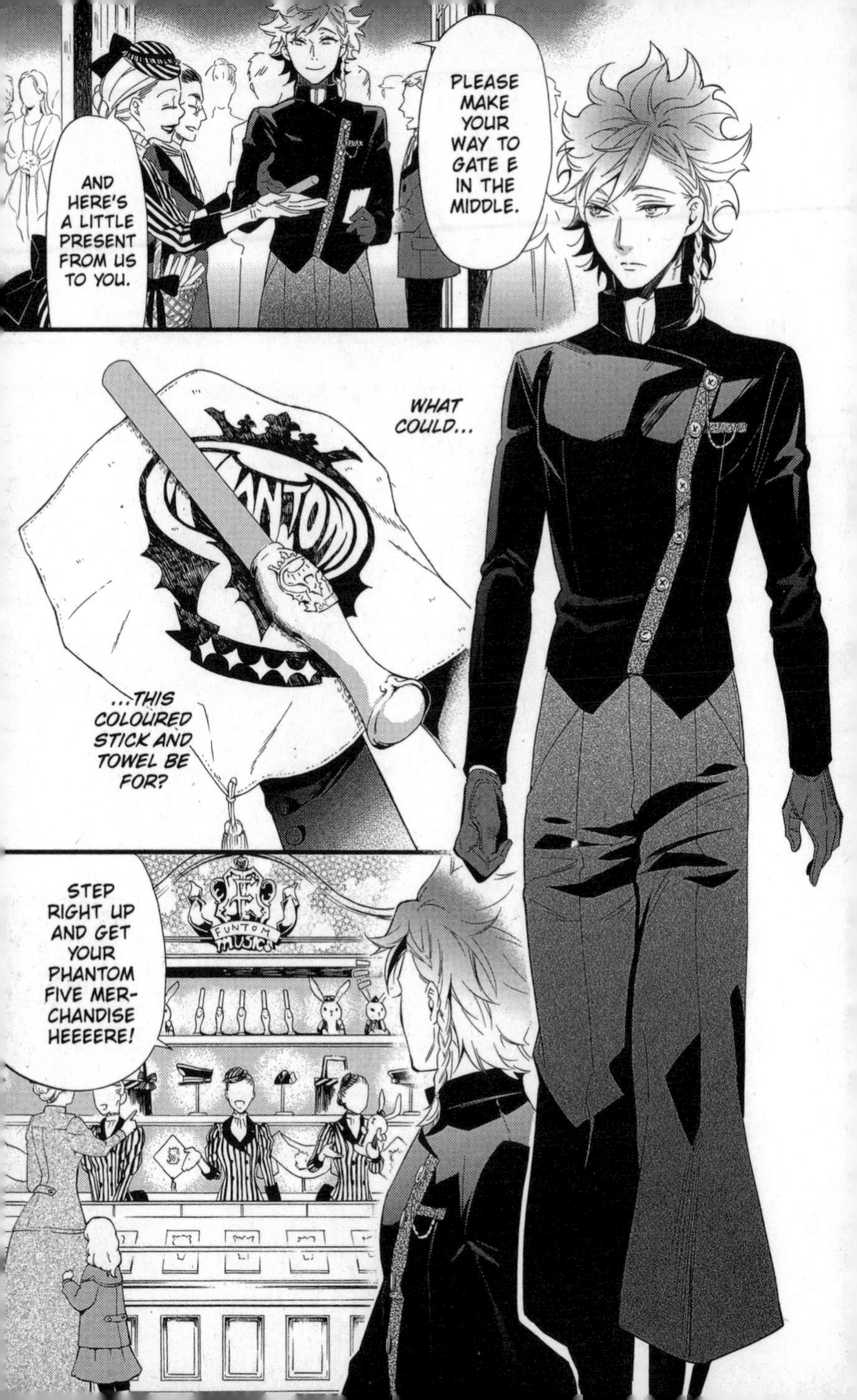
PLEASE MAKE YOUR WAY TO GATE E IN THE MIDDLE.
AND HERE'S A LITTLE PRESENT FROM US TO YOU.
WHAT COULD...
...THIS COLOURED STICK AND TOWEL BE FOR?
FUNTOM MUSIC
STEP RIGHT UP AND GET YOUR PHANTOM FIVE MER-CHANDISE HEEEERE!

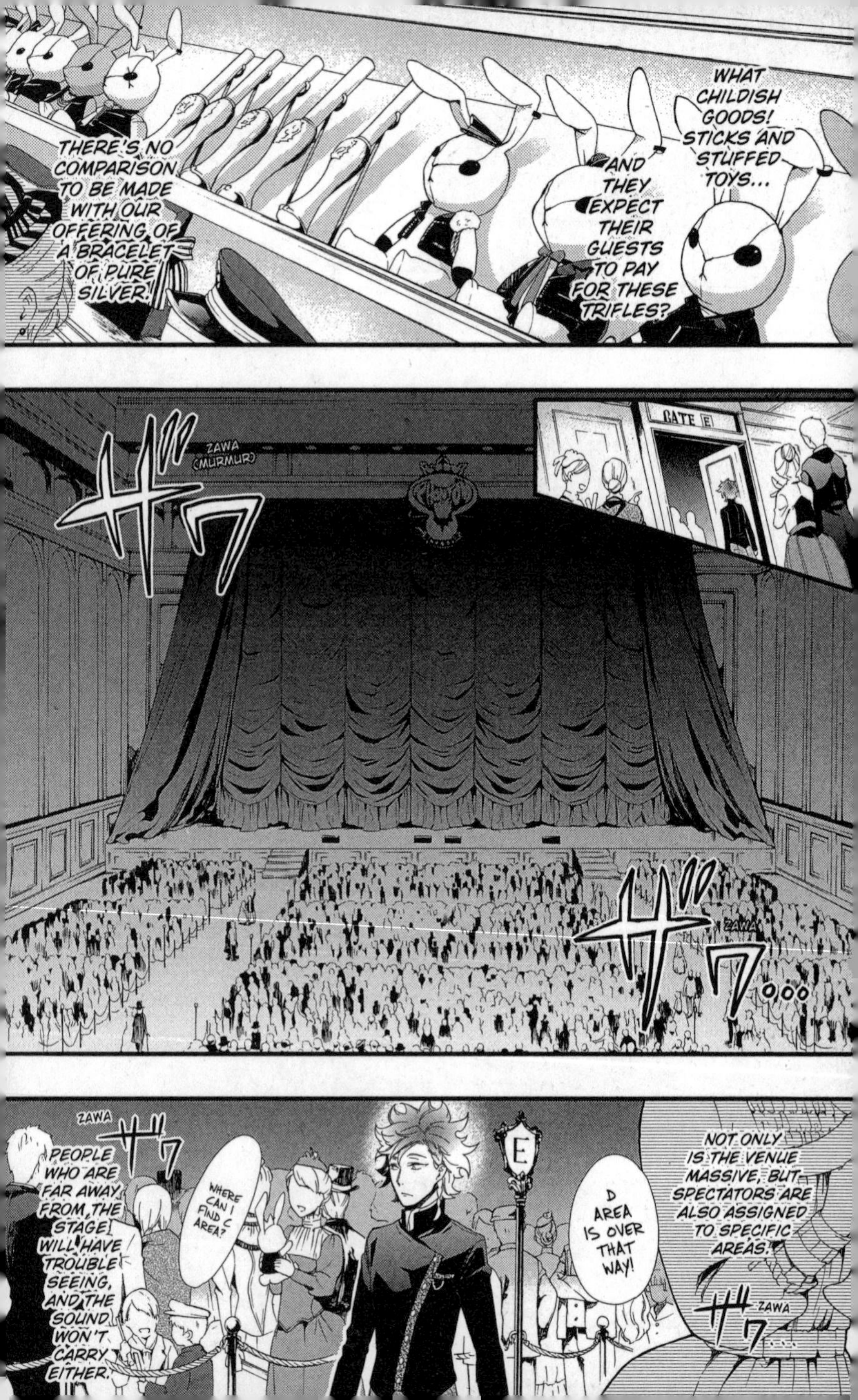
WHAT CHILDISH GOODS! STICKS AND STUFFED TOYS...
AND THEY EXPECT THEIR GUESTS TO PAY FOR THESE TRIFLES?
THERE'S NO COMPARISON TO BE MADE WITH OUR OFFERING OF A BRACELET OF PURE SILVER!
GATE E
ZAWA (MURMUR)
ZAWA
NOT ONLY IS THE VENUE MASSIVE, BUT SPECTATORS ARE ALSO ASSIGNED TO SPECIFIC AREAS.
ZAWA
D AREA IS OVER THAT WAY!
E
WHERE CAN I FIND C AREA?
ZAWA
PEOPLE WHO ARE FAR AWAY FROM THE STAGE WILL HAVE TROUBLE SEEING, AND THE SOUND WON'T CARRY EITHER.

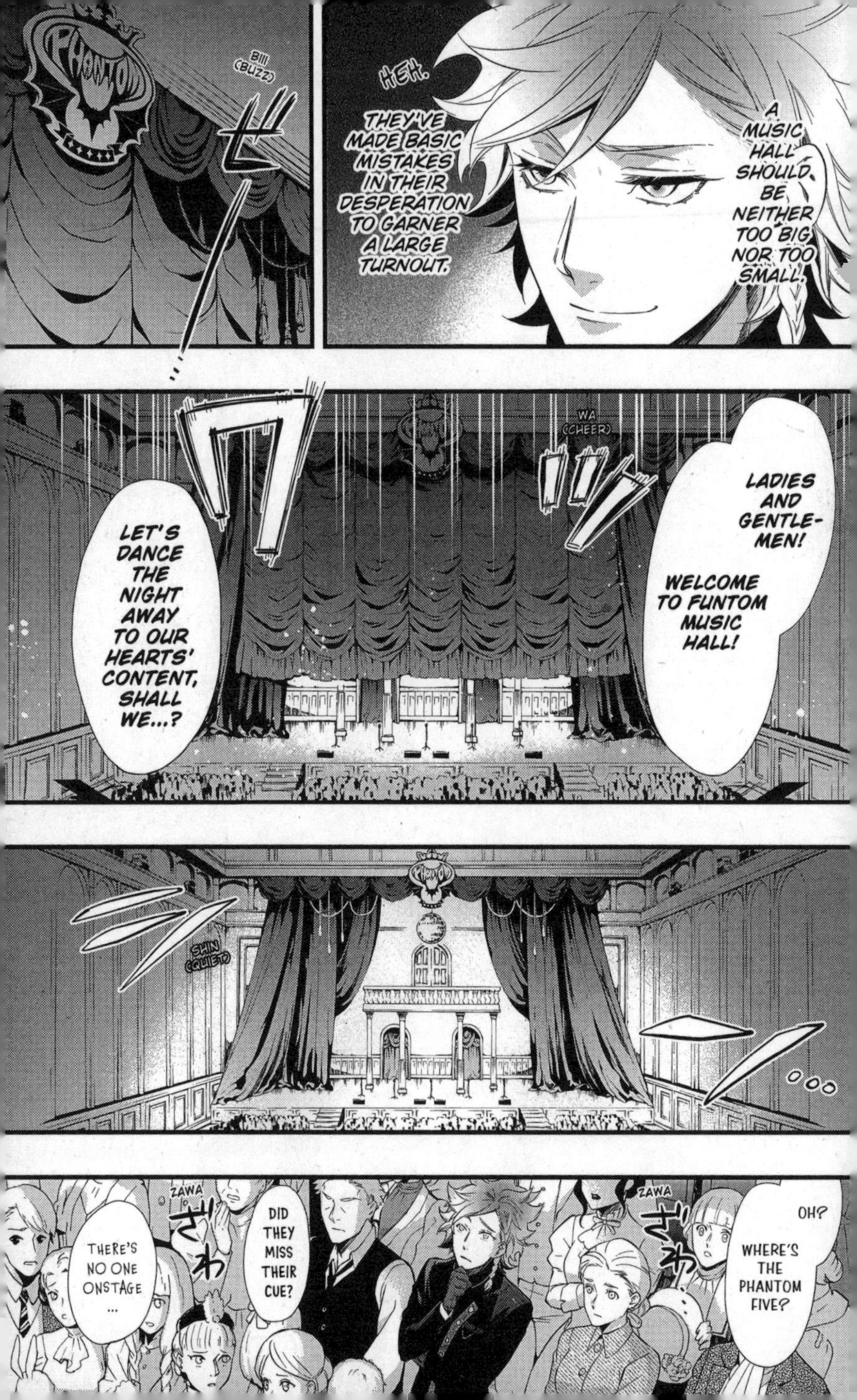
HEH.
A MUSIC HALL SHOULD BE NEITHER TOO BIG NOR TOO SMALL.
THEY'VE MADE BASIC MISTAKES IN THEIR DESPERATION TO GARNER A LARGE TURNOUT.
BIII (BUZZ)
WA (CHEER)
LADIES AND GENTLE-MEN!
WELCOME TO FUNTOM MUSIC HALL!
LET'S DANCE THE NIGHT AWAY TO OUR HEARTS' CONTENT, SHALL WE...?
SHIN (QUIET)
ZAWA
OH?
WHERE'S THE PHANTOM FIVE?
ZAWA
DID THEY MISS THEIR CUE?
THERE'S NO ONE ONSTAGE ...

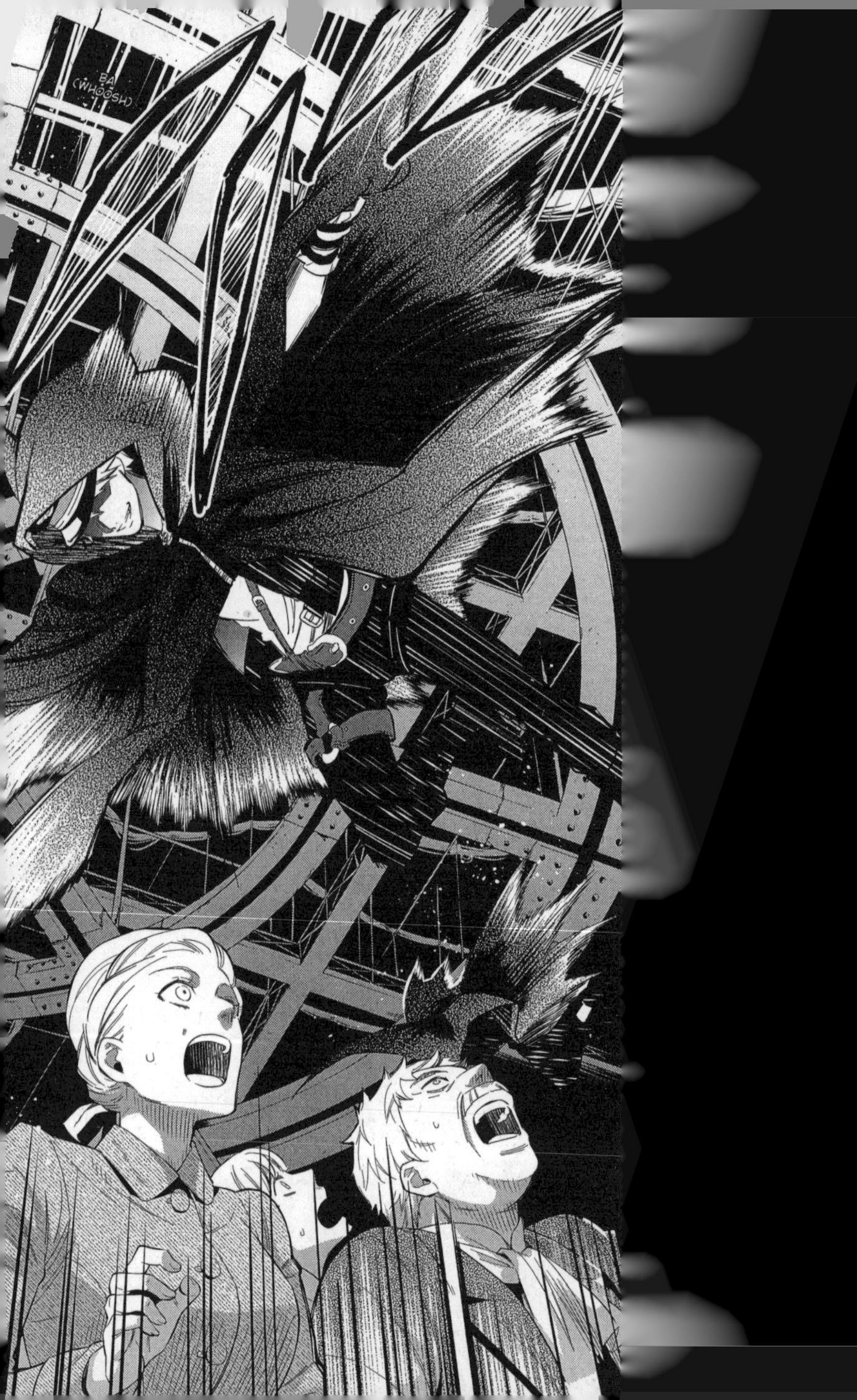
BA
(WHOOSH)

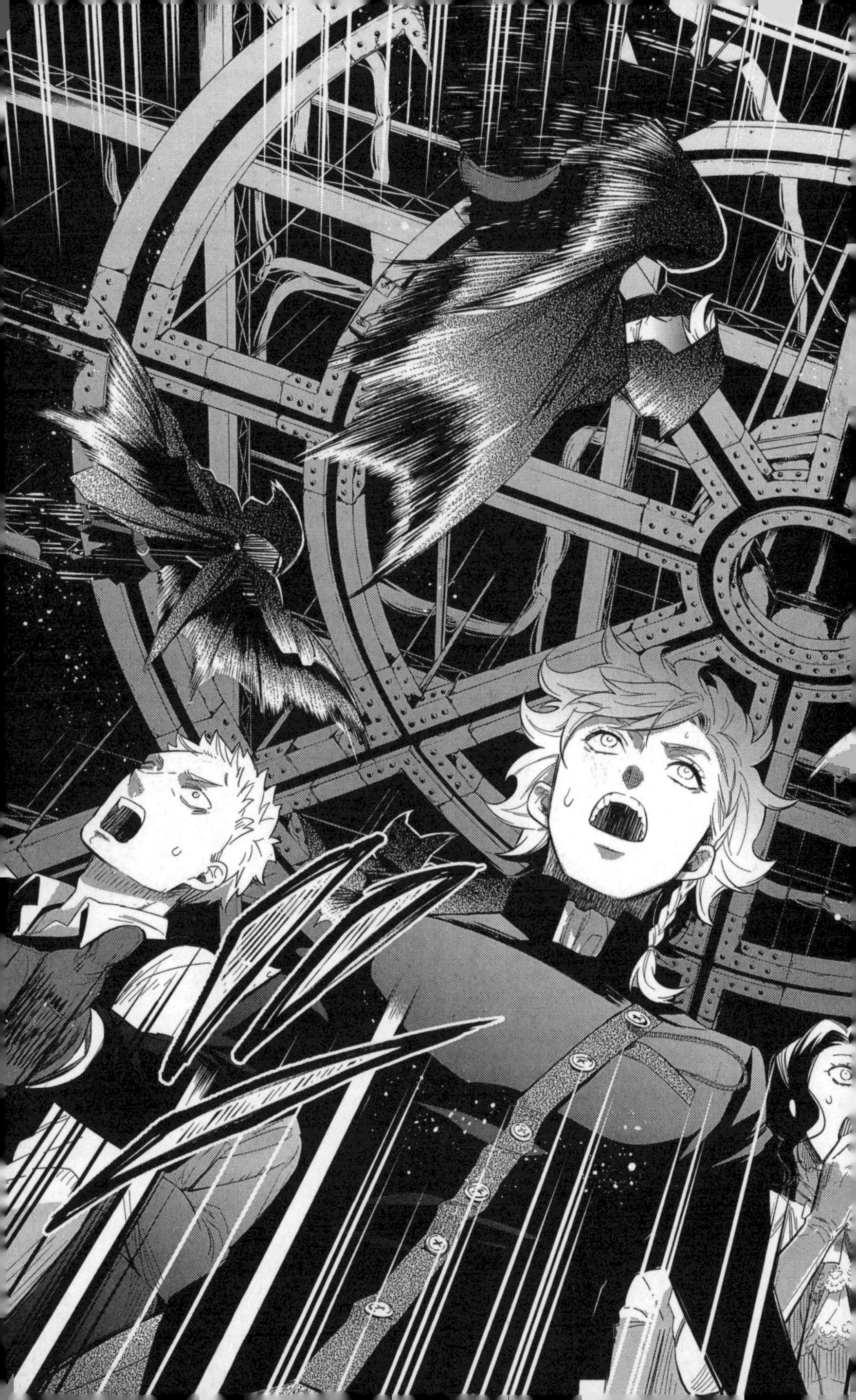

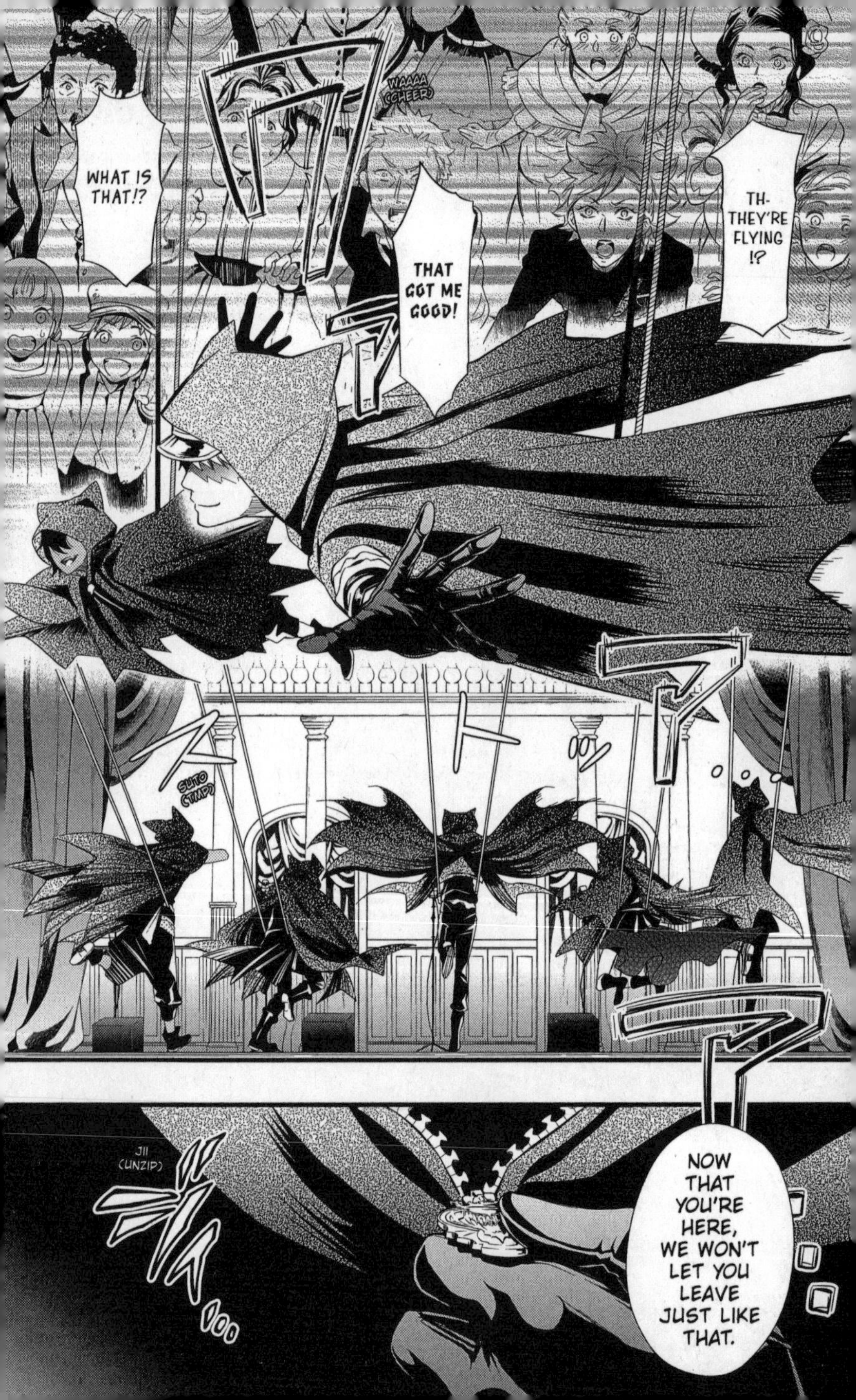
TH-THEY'RE FLYING!?
WAAAA (CHEER)
THAT GOT ME GOOD!
WHAT IS THAT!?
SUTO (TMP)
NOW THAT YOU'RE HERE, WE WON'T LET YOU LEAVE JUST LIKE THAT.
JII (UNZIP)

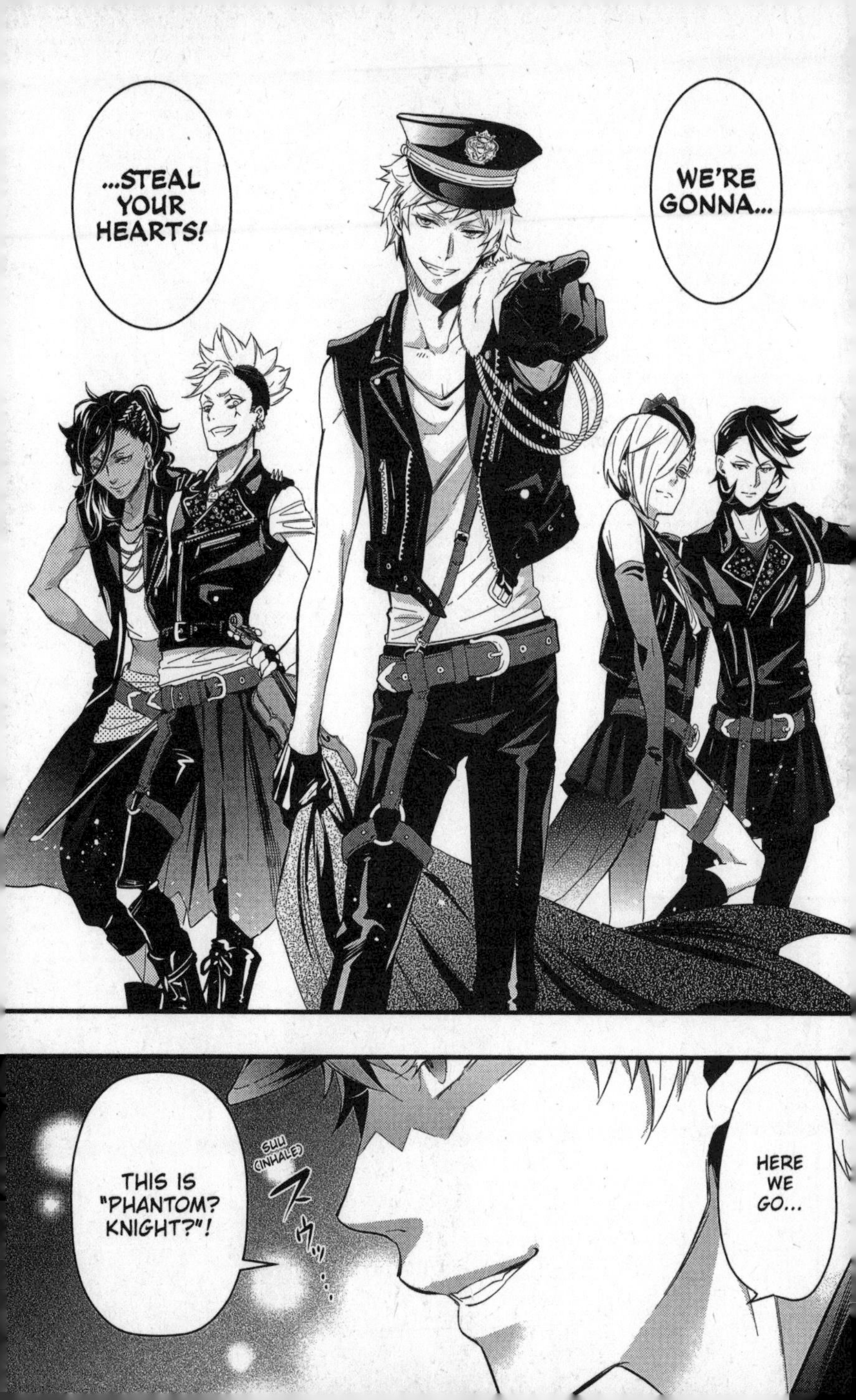
WE'RE GONNA...
...STEAL YOUR HEARTS!
HERE WE GO...
SUU (INHALE)
THIS IS "PHANTOM? KNIGHT?"!

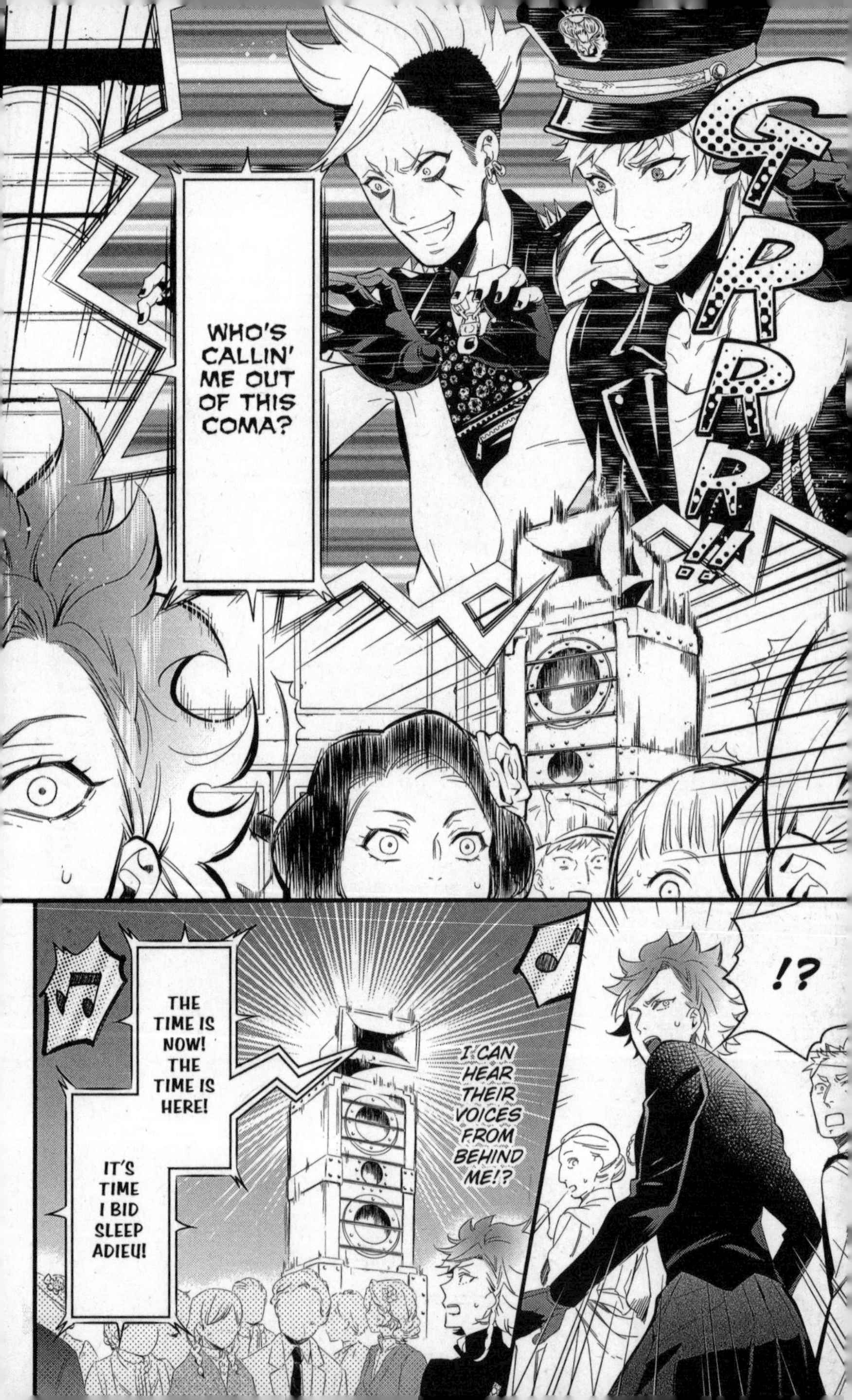
GRRR!!
WHO'S CALLIN' ME OUT OF THIS COMA?
!?
I CAN HEAR THEIR VOICES FROM BEHIND ME!?
THE TIME IS NOW! THE TIME IS HERE!
IT'S TIME I BID SLEEP ADIEU!

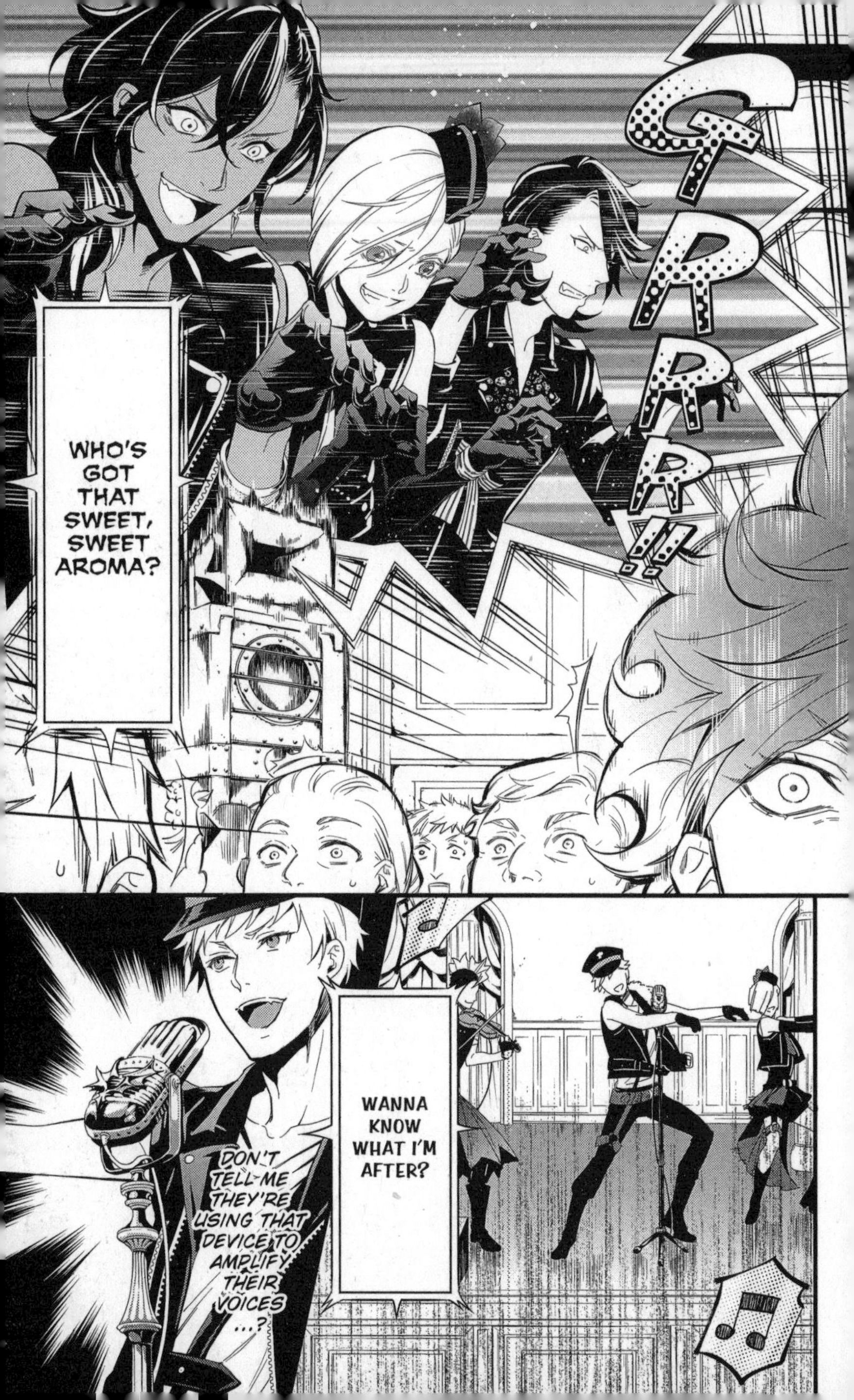
GRRR!!
WHO'S GOT THAT SWEET, SWEET AROMA?
WANNA KNOW WHAT I'M AFTER?
DON'T TELL ME THEY'RE USING THAT DEVICE TO AMPLIFY THEIR VOICES...?

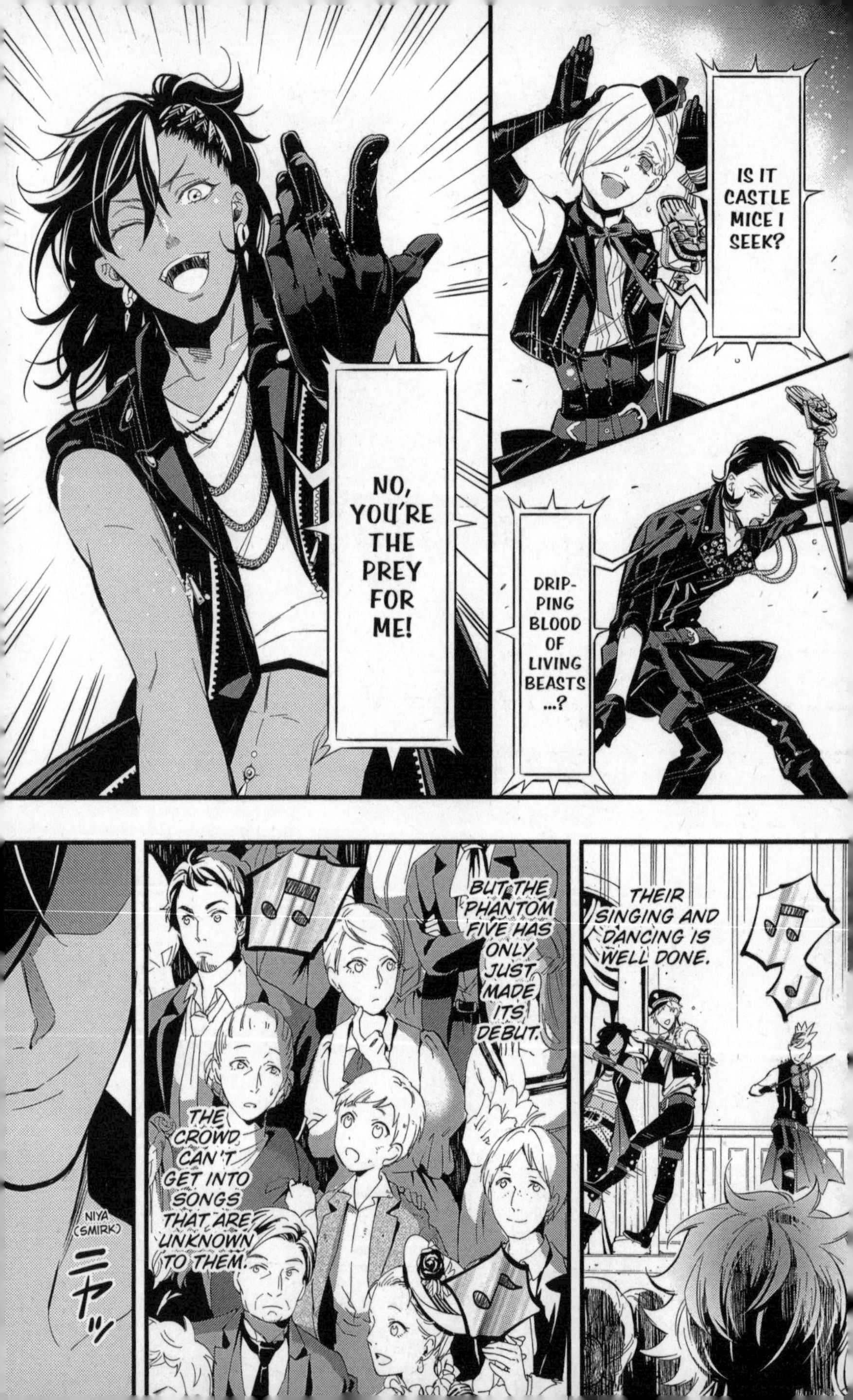
IS IT CASTLE MICE I SEEK?
DRIP-PING BLOOD OF LIVING BEASTS ...?
NO, YOU'RE THE PREY FOR ME!
THEIR SINGING AND DANCING IS WELL DONE.
BUT THE PHANTOM FIVE HAS ONLY JUST MADE ITS DEBUT.
THE CROWD CAN'T GET INTO SONGS THAT ARE UNKNOWN TO THEM.
NIYA (SMIRK)
ニヤッ

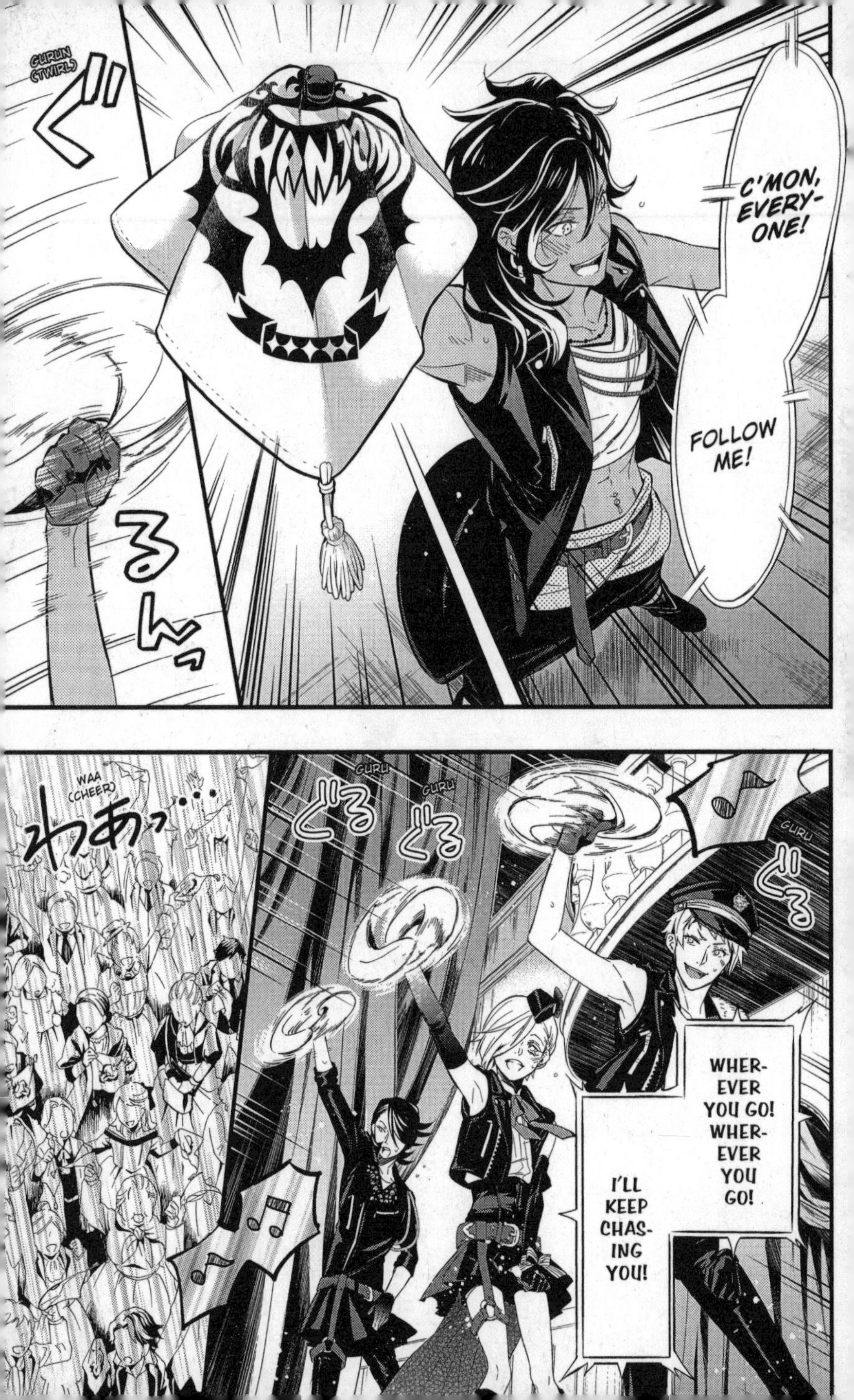

C'MON, EVERYONE!
FOLLOW ME!
GURUN (TWIRL)
くるんっ
GURU
ぐる
WHEREVER YOU GO! WHEREVER YOU GO!
I'LL KEEP CHASING YOU!
GURU GURU
ぐるぐる
WAA (CHEER)
わあっ

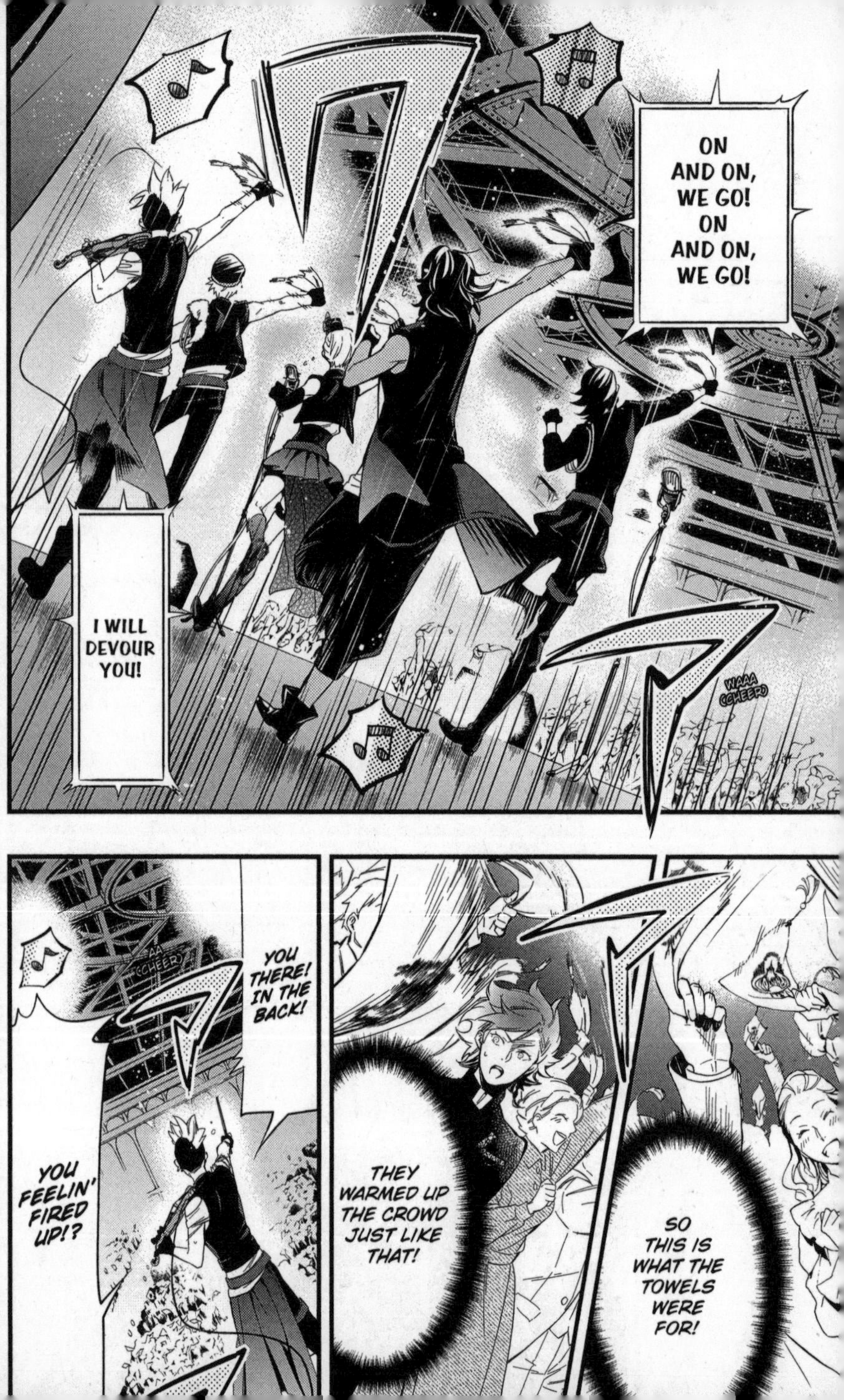
ON AND ON, WE GO! ON AND ON, WE GO!
I WILL DEVOUR YOU!
WAAA (CHEER)
THEY WARMED UP THE CROWD JUST LIKE THAT!
SO THIS IS WHAT THE TOWELS WERE FOR!
AA (CHEER)
YOU THERE! IN THE BACK!
YOU FEELIN' FIRED UP!?

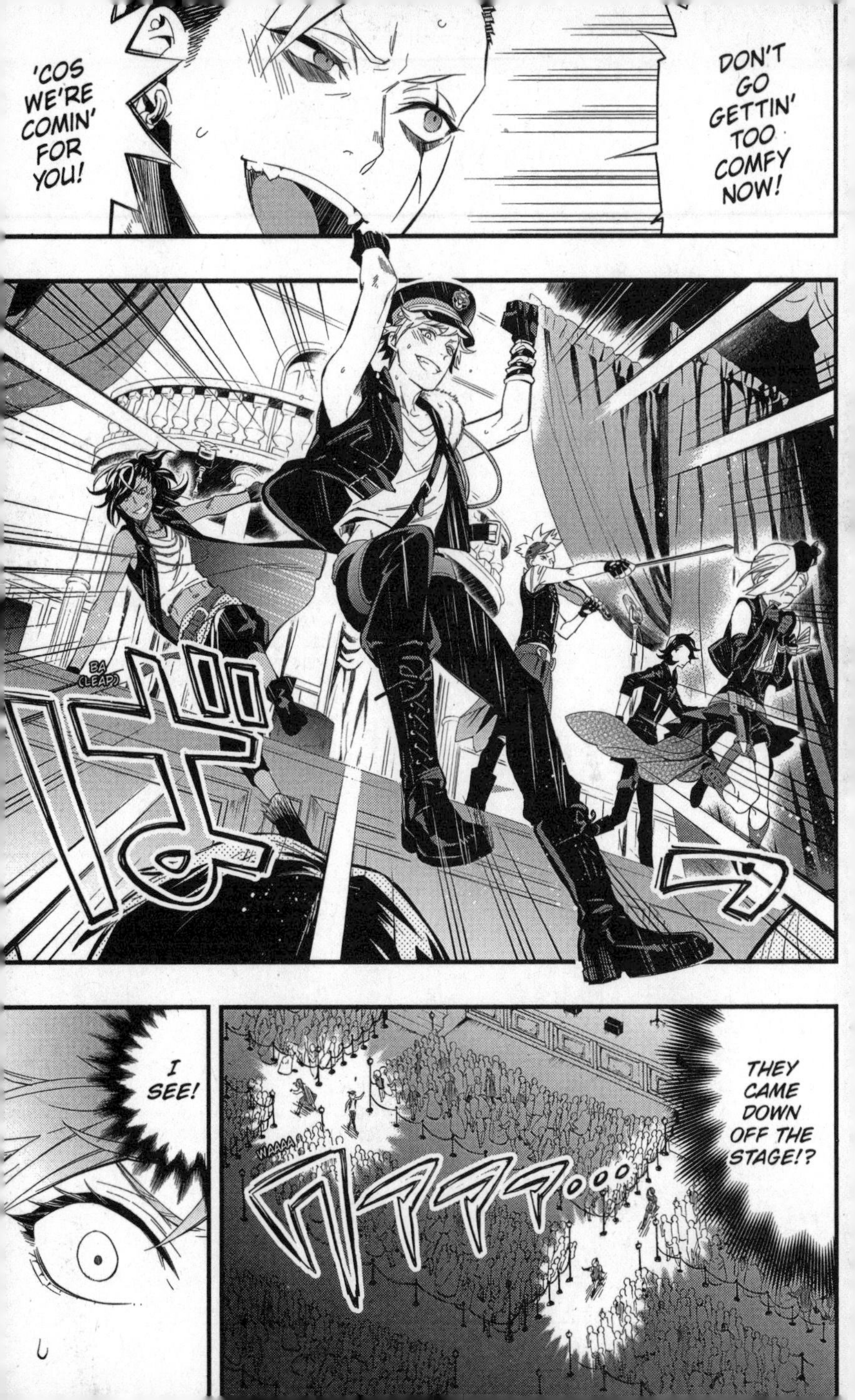
DON'T GO GETTIN' TOO COMFY NOW!
'COS WE'RE COMIN' FOR YOU!
BA (LEAP)
THEY CAME DOWN OFF THE STAGE!?
WAAAA
I SEE!

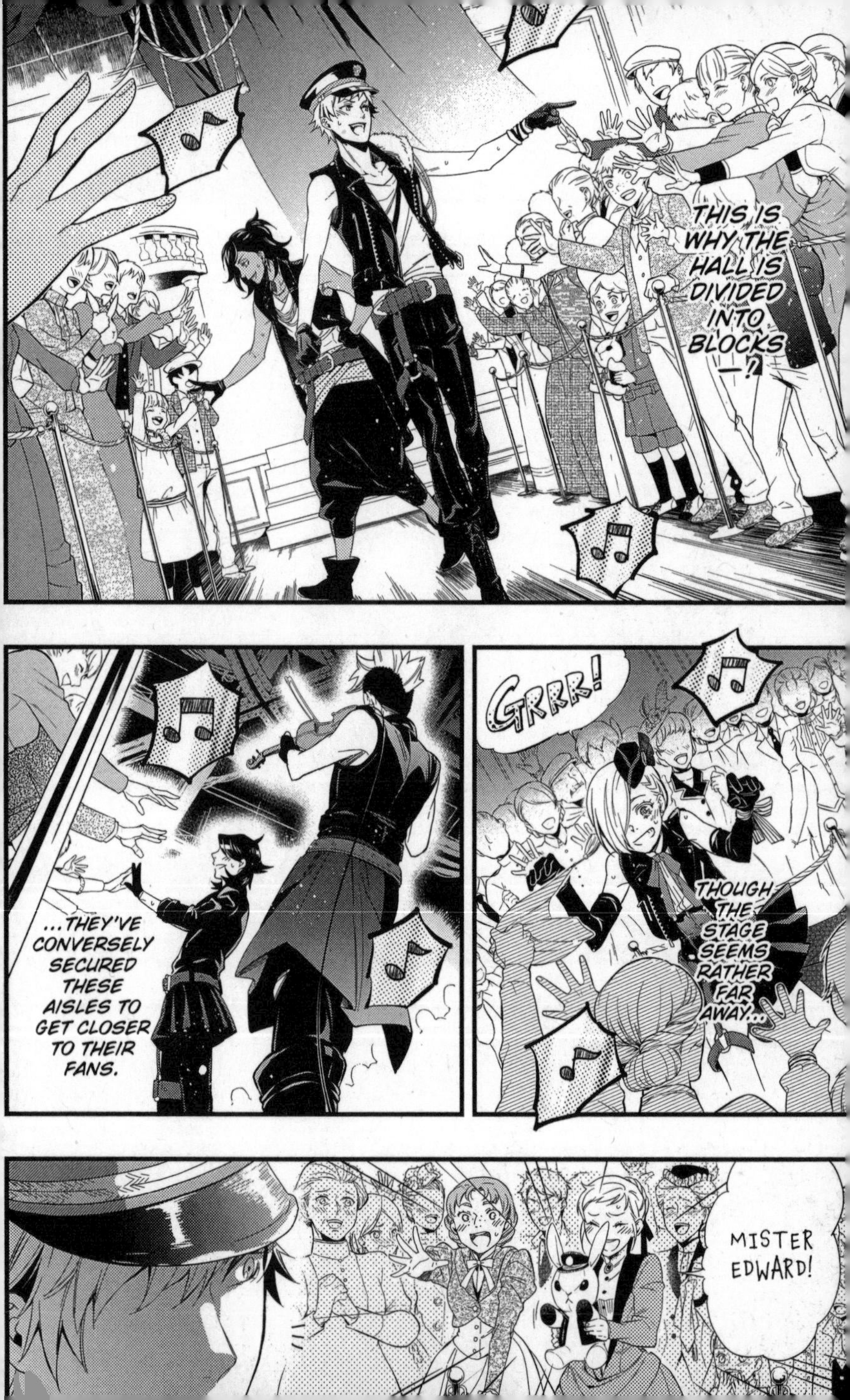
THIS IS WHY THE HALL IS DIVIDED INTO BLOCKS—!?
GRRR!
THOUGH THE STAGE SEEMS RATHER FAR AWAY...
...THEY'VE CONVERSELY SECURED THESE AISLES TO GET CLOSER TO THEIR FANS.
MISTER EDWARD!

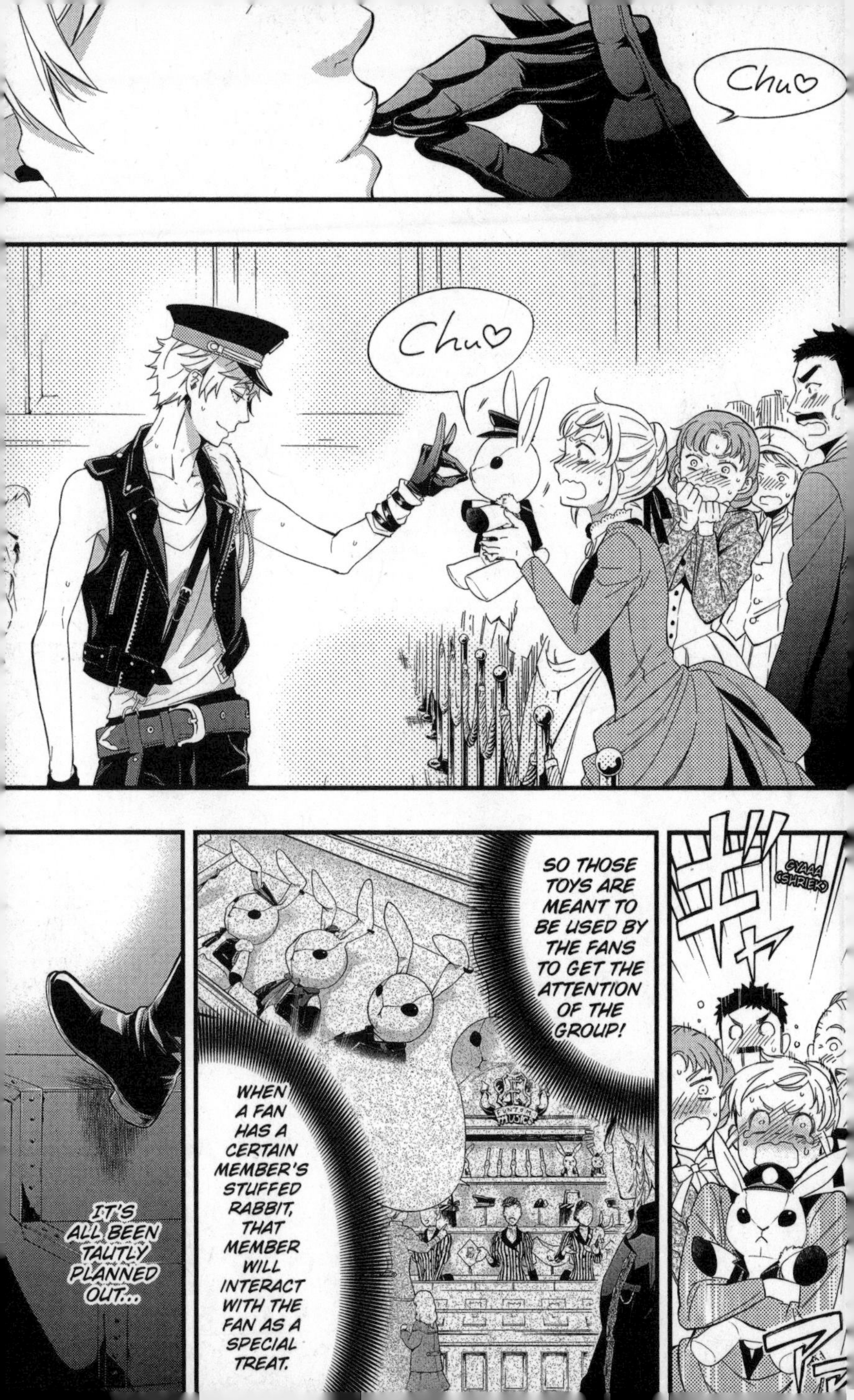
Chu♡
Chu♡
GYAAA (SHRIEK)
SO THOSE TOYS ARE MEANT TO BE USED BY THE FANS TO GET THE ATTENTION OF THE GROUP!
WHEN A FAN HAS A CERTAIN MEMBER'S STUFFED RABBIT, THAT MEMBER WILL INTERACT WITH THE FAN AS A SPECIAL TREAT.
IT'S ALL BEEN TAUTLY PLANNED OUT...

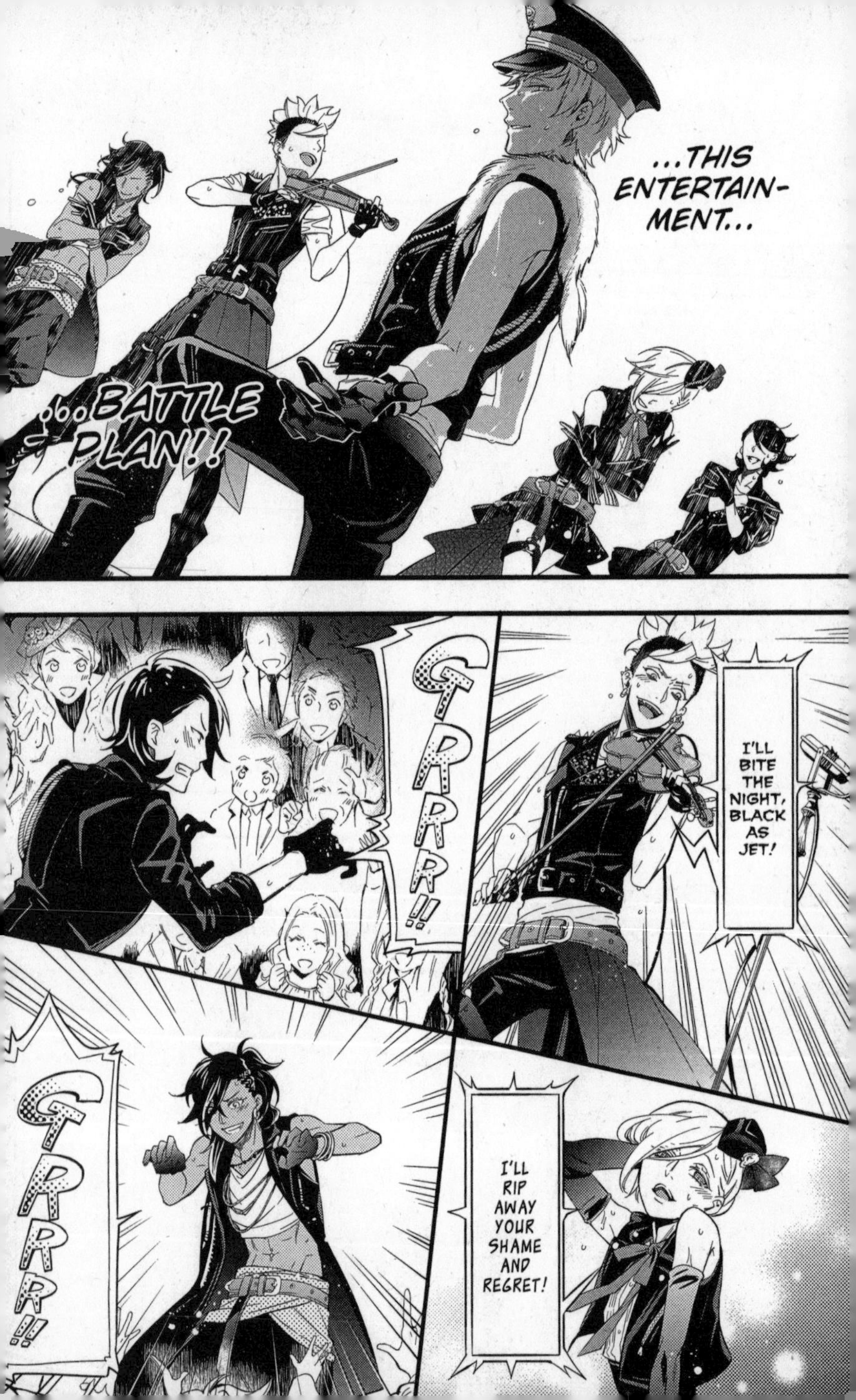
...THIS ENTERTAINMENT...
...BATTLE PLAN!!
I'LL BITE THE NIGHT, BLACK AS JET!
GRRRR!!
I'LL RIP AWAY YOUR SHAME AND REGRET!
GRRRR!!

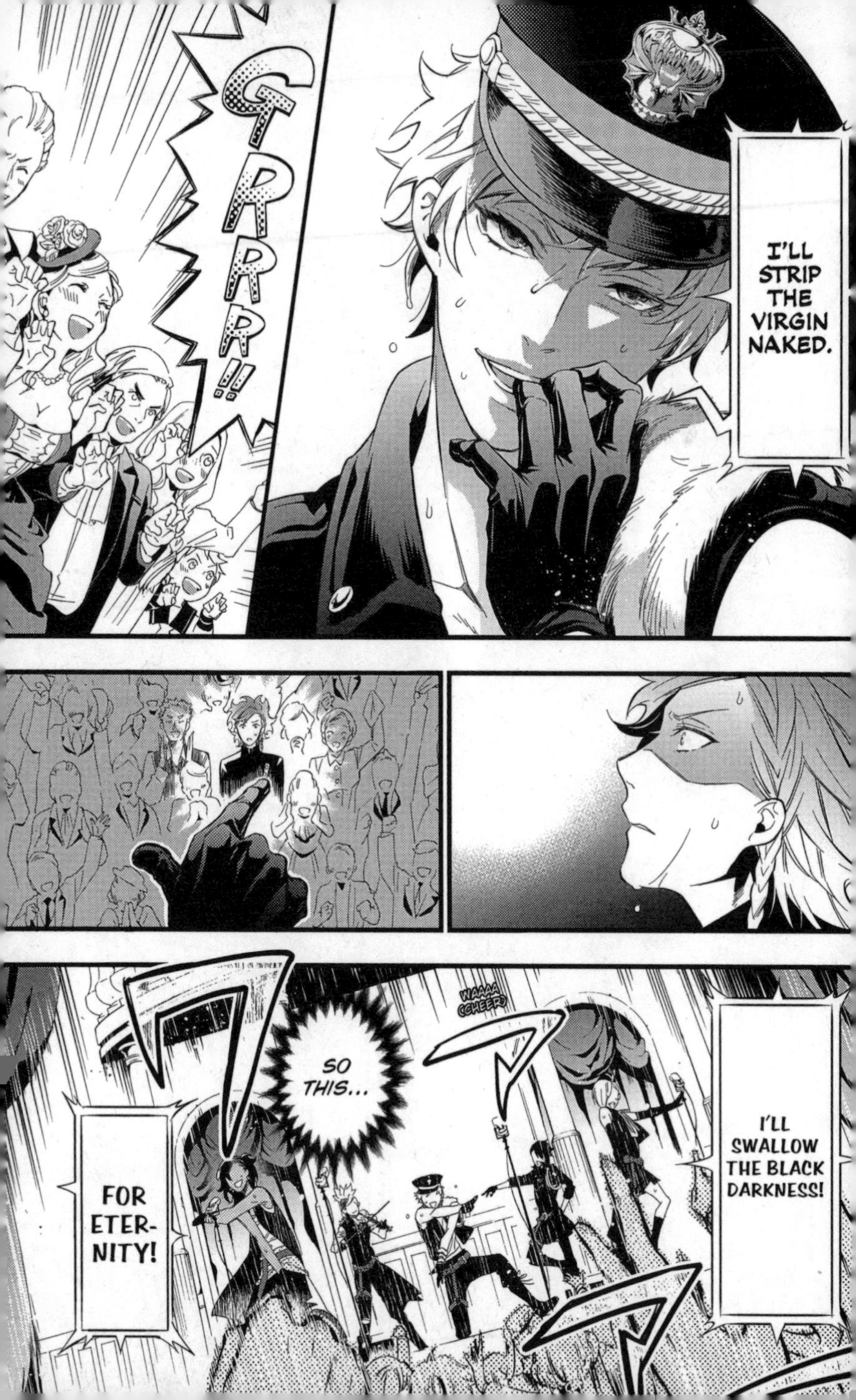
I'LL STRIP THE VIRGIN NAKED.
GRRRR!!
I'LL SWALLOW THE BLACK DARKNESS!
WAAAA (CHEER)
SO THIS...
FOR ETER-NITY!

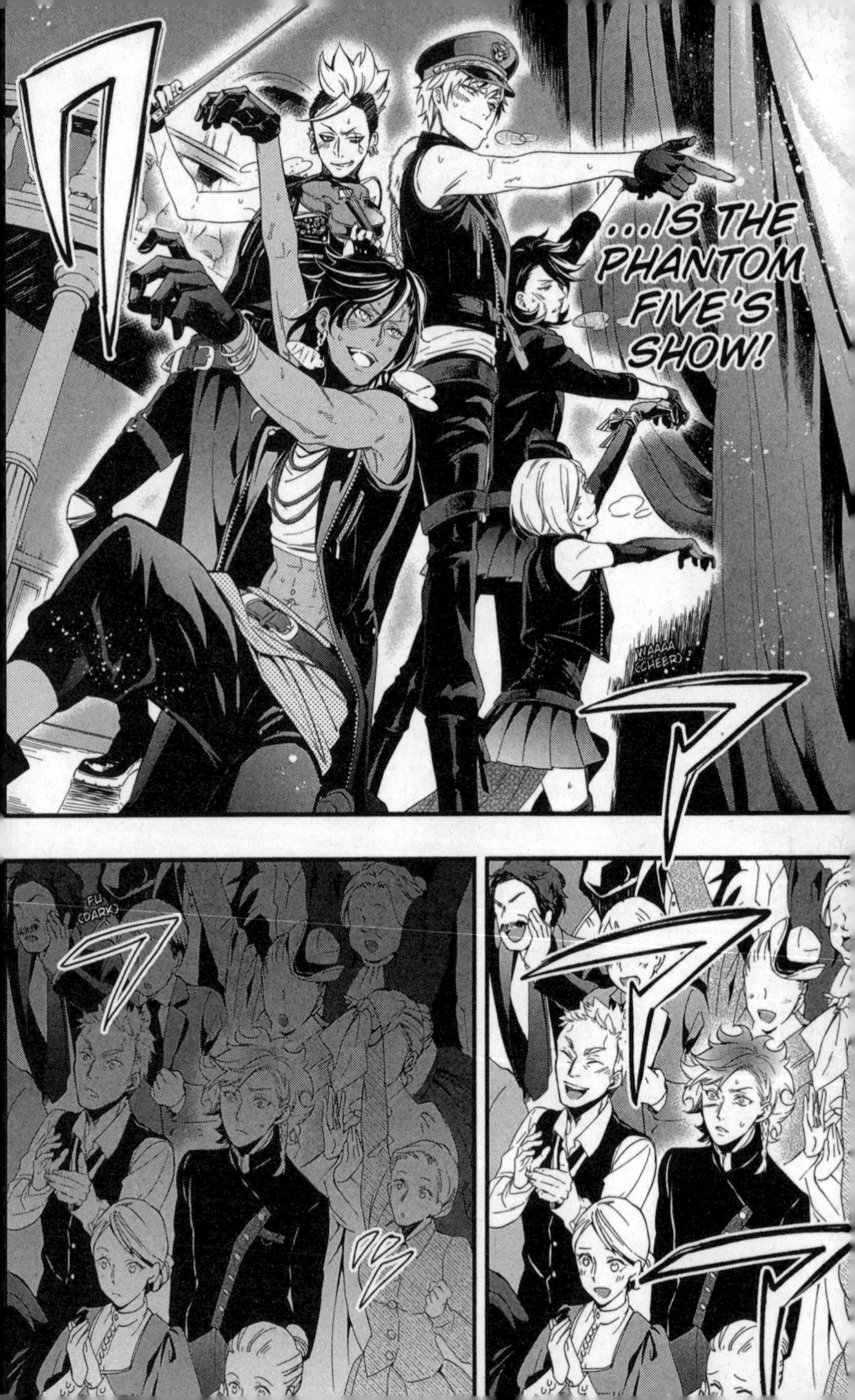
...IS THE PHANTOM FIVE'S SHOW!
WAAAA (CHEER)
FU (DARK)

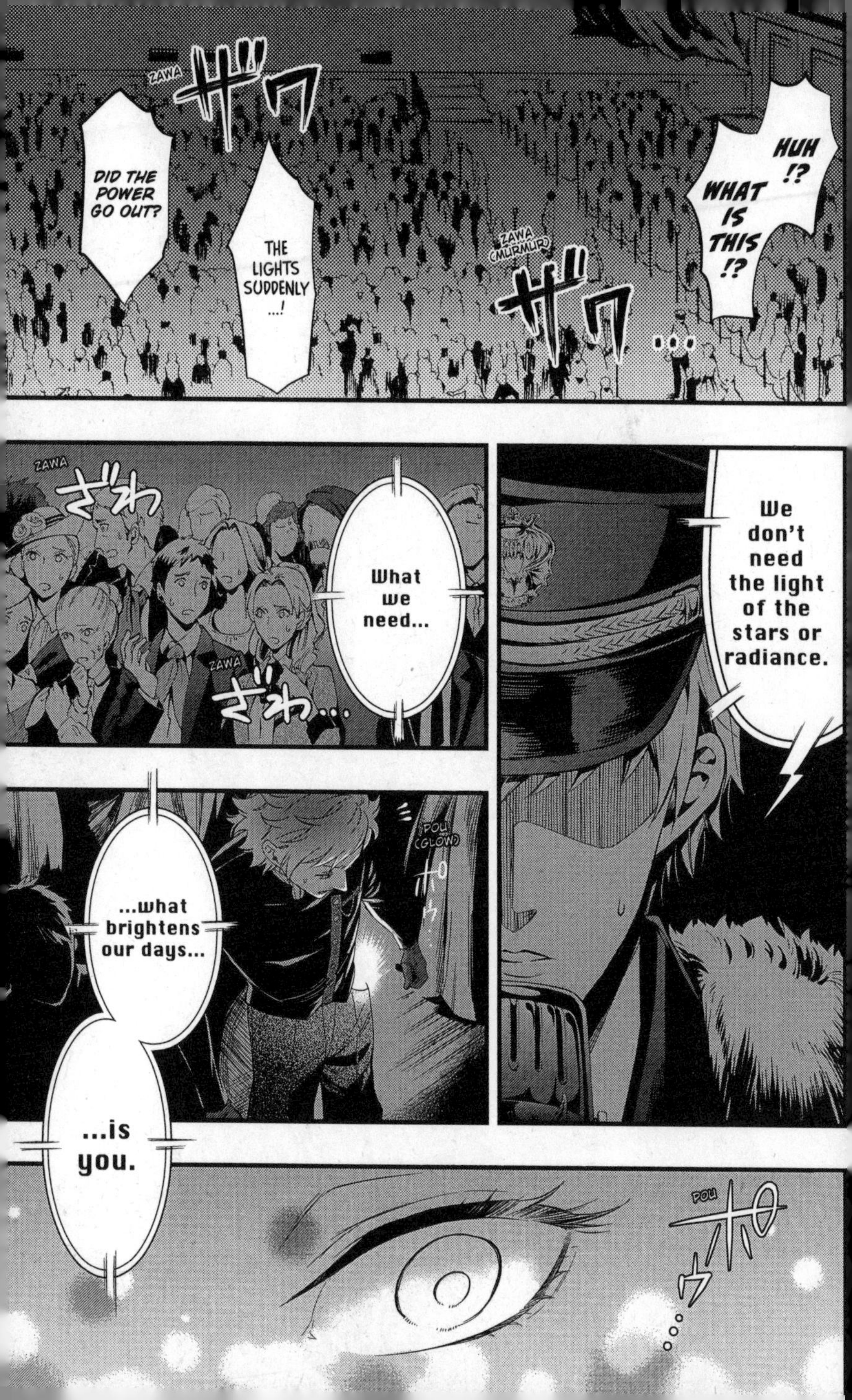
HUH!? WHAT IS THIS!?
ZAWA (MURMUR)
THE LIGHTS SUDDENLY...!
DID THE POWER GO OUT?
ZAWA
We don't need the light of the stars or radiance.
ZAWA
What we need...
ZAWA
POU (GLOW)
...what brightens our days...
...is you.
POU

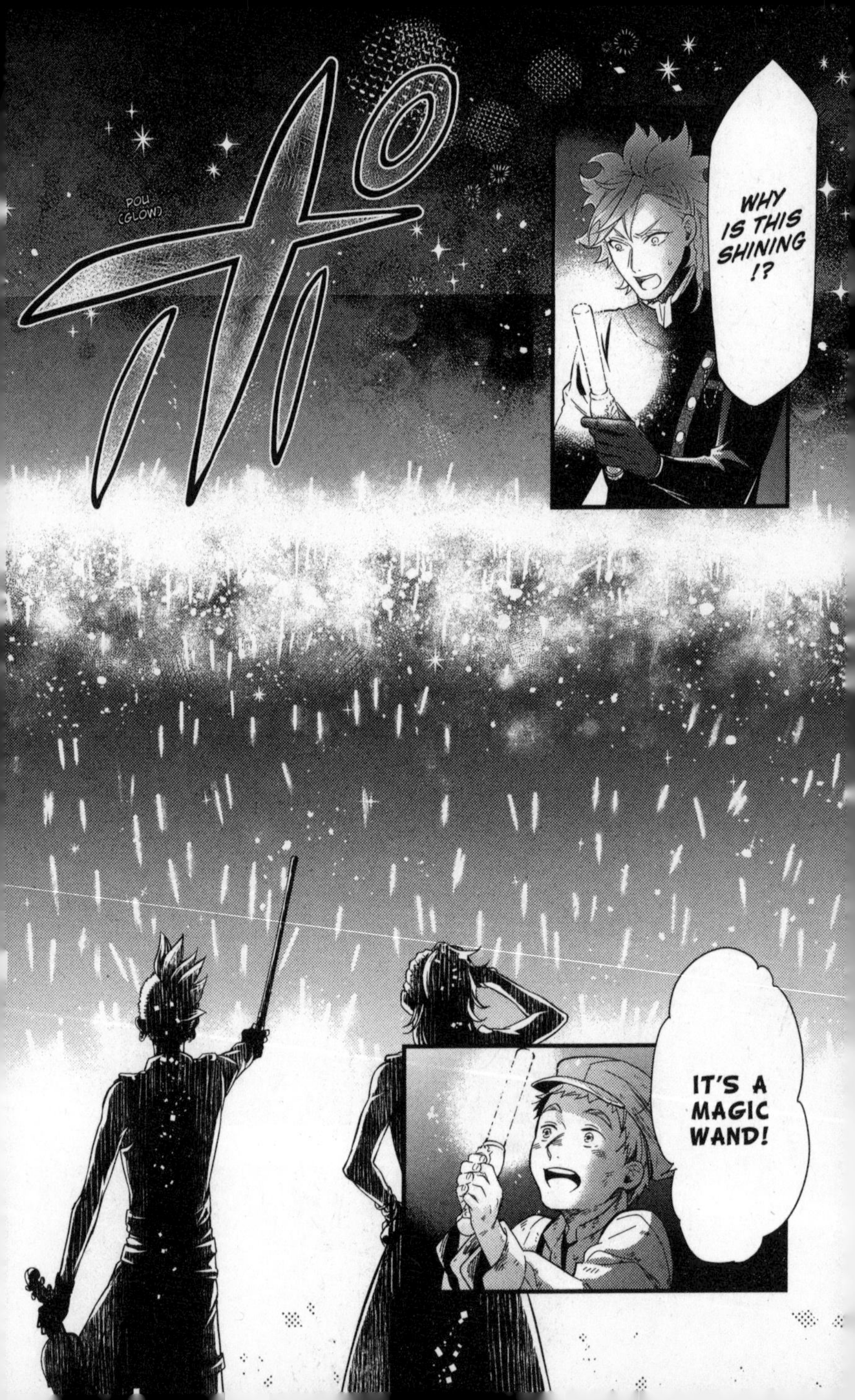
POU (GLOW)
WHY IS THIS SHINING !?
IT'S A MAGIC WAND!

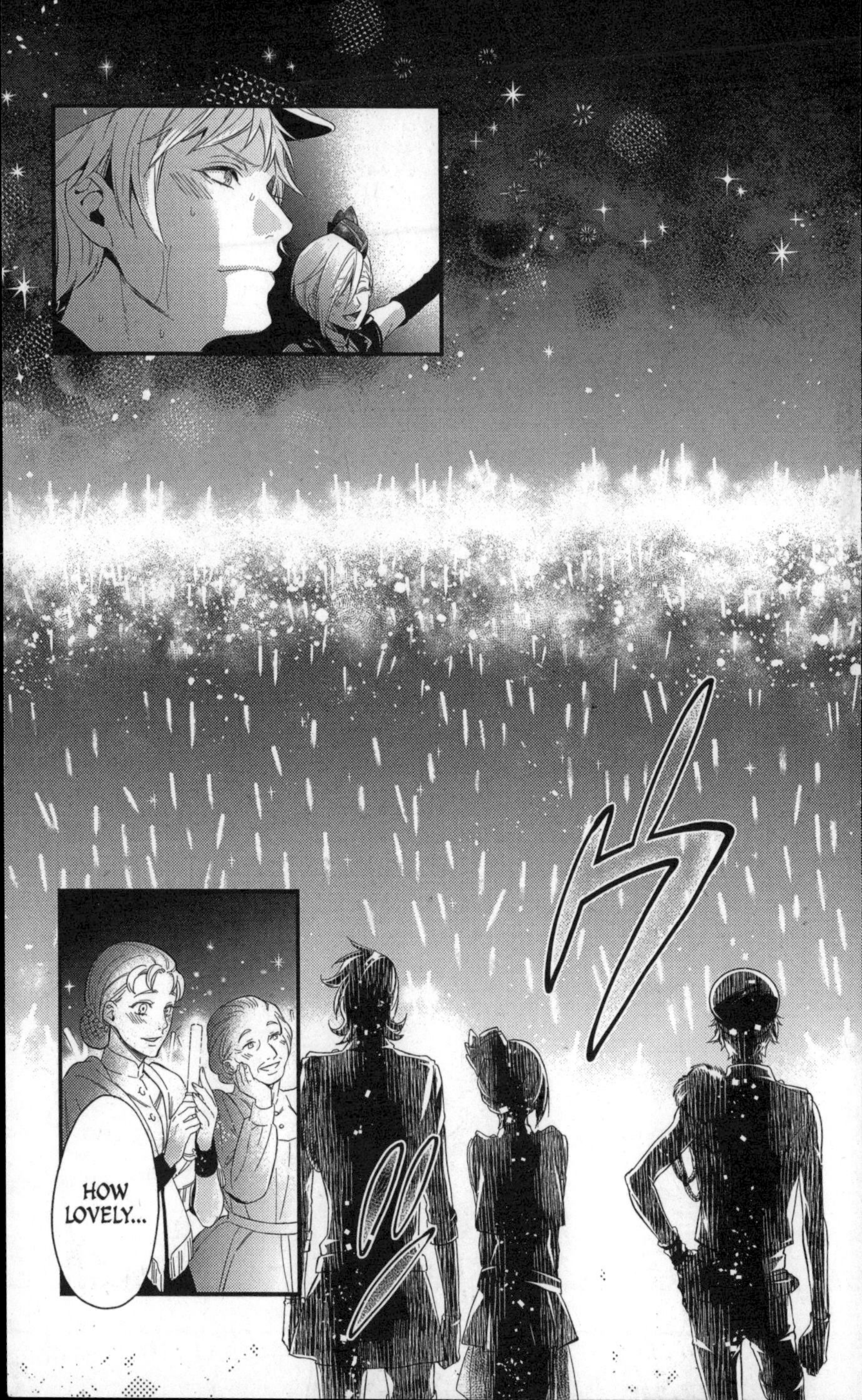
HOW LOVELY...

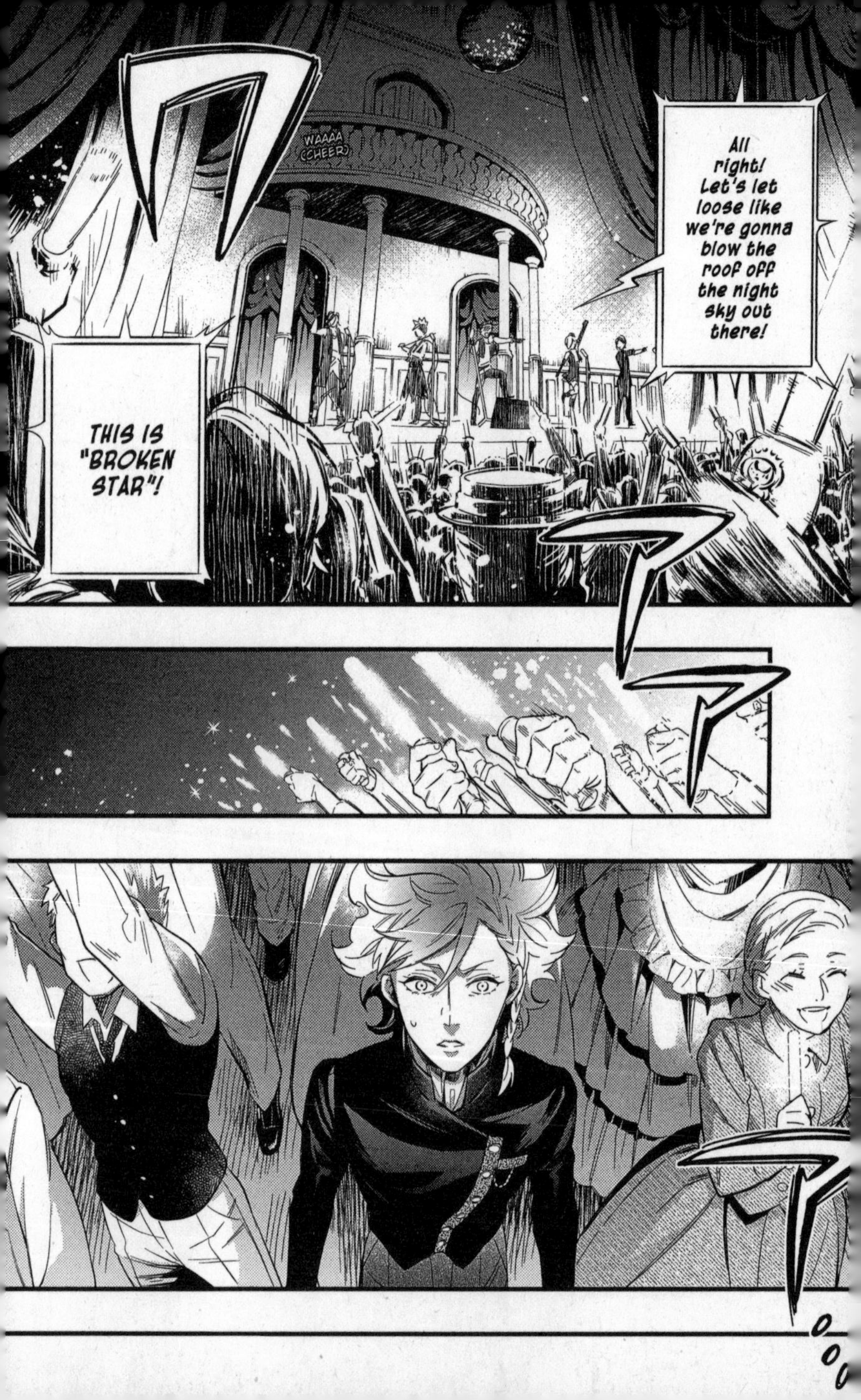
All right! Let's let loose like we're gonna blow the roof off the night sky out there!
THIS IS "BROKEN STAR"!
WAAAA (CHEER)

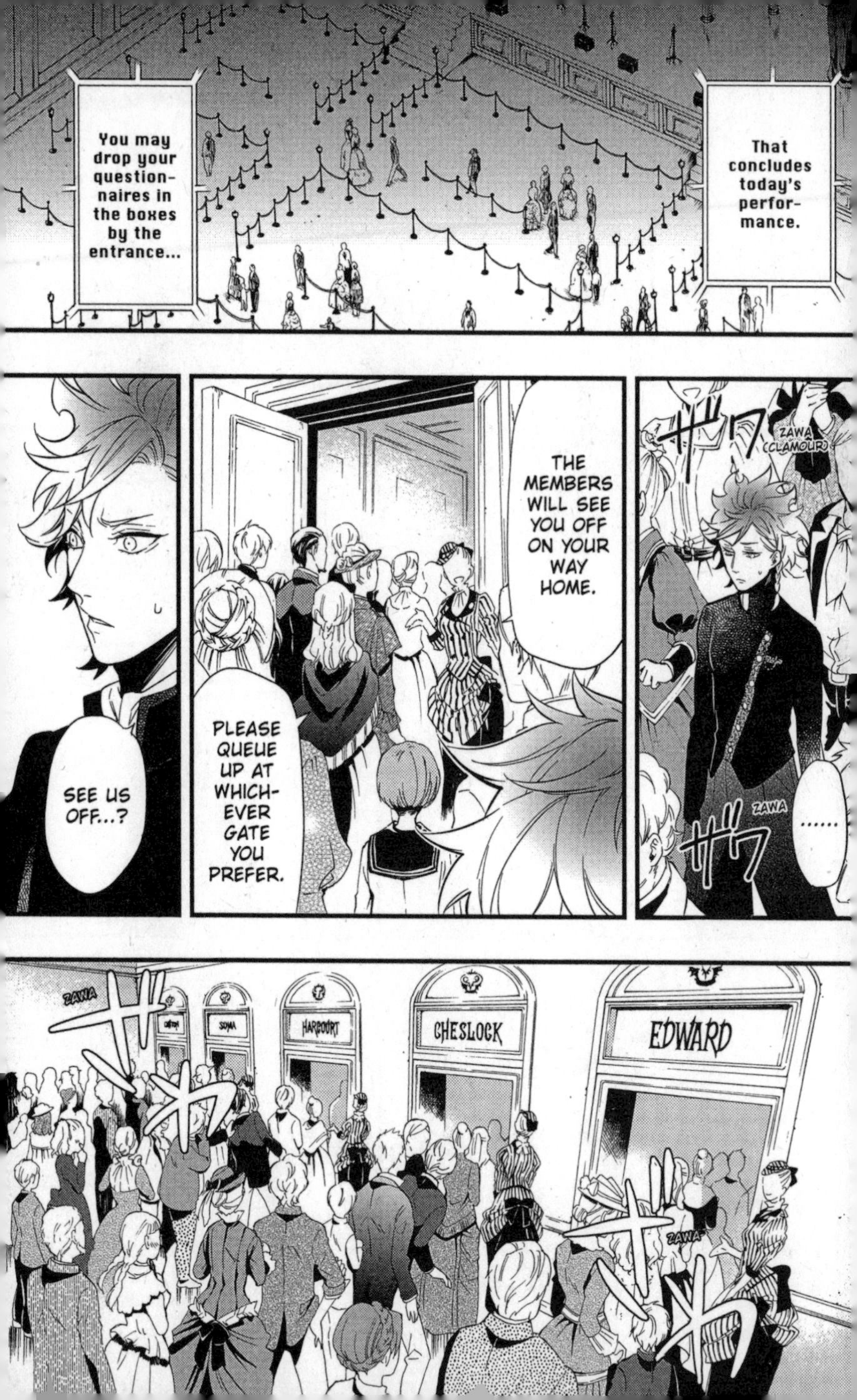
That concludes today's performance.
You may drop your questionnaires in the boxes by the entrance...
ZAWA (CLAMOUR)
ZAWA
......
THE MEMBERS WILL SEE YOU OFF ON YOUR WAY HOME.
PLEASE QUEUE UP AT WHICHEVER GATE YOU PREFER.
SEE US OFF...?
EDWARD
ZAWA
CHESLOCK
HARCOURT
SOMA
ZAWA

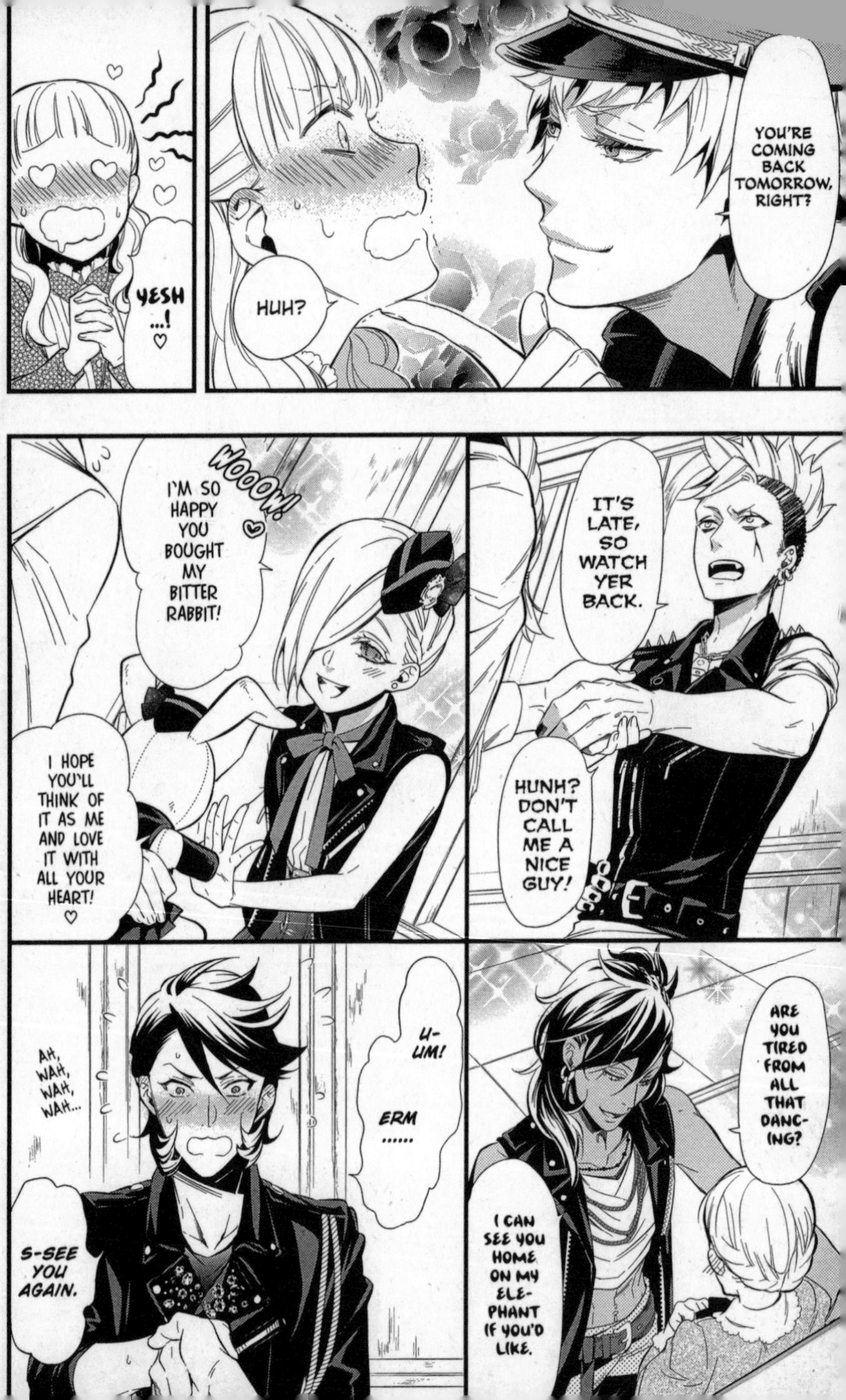

YOU'RE COMING BACK TOMORROW, RIGHT?
HUH?
YESH ...! ♡
IT'S LATE, SO WATCH YER BACK.
HUNH? DON'T CALL ME A NICE GUY!
WOOOW!
I'M SO HAPPY YOU BOUGHT MY BITTER RABBIT! ♡
I HOPE YOU'LL THINK OF IT AS ME AND LOVE IT WITH ALL YOUR HEART! ♡
ARE YOU TIRED FROM ALL THAT DANC-ING?
I CAN SEE YOU HOME ON MY ELE-PHANT IF YOU'D LIKE.
U-UM!
ERM ......
AH, WAH, WAH, WAH...
S-SEE YOU AGAIN.

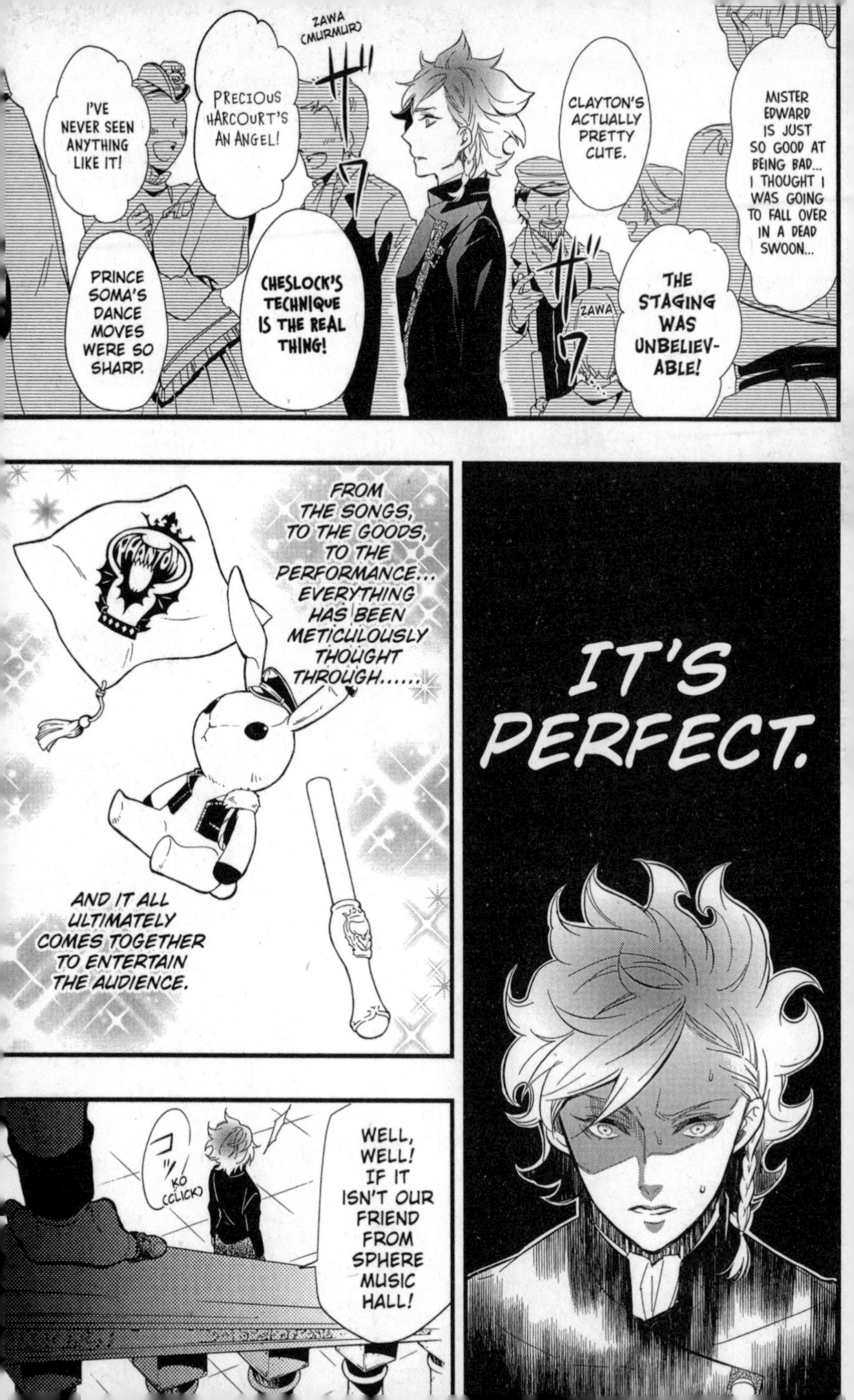
MISTER EDWARD IS JUST SO GOOD AT BEING BAD... I THOUGHT I WAS GOING TO FALL OVER IN A DEAD SWOON...
CLAYTON'S ACTUALLY PRETTY CUTE.
ZAWA (MURMUR)
PRECIOUS HARCOURT'S AN ANGEL!
I'VE NEVER SEEN ANYTHING LIKE IT!
ZAWA
THE STAGING WAS UNBELIEV-ABLE!
CHESLOCK'S TECHNIQUE IS THE REAL THING!
PRINCE SOMA'S DANCE MOVES WERE SO SHARP.
IT'S PERFECT.
FROM THE SONGS, TO THE GOODS, TO THE PERFORMANCE... EVERYTHING HAS BEEN METICULOUSLY THOUGHT THROUGH......
AND IT ALL ULTIMATELY COMES TOGETHER TO ENTERTAIN THE AUDIENCE.
WELL, WELL! IF IT ISN'T OUR FRIEND FROM SPHERE MUSIC HALL!
KO (CLICK)

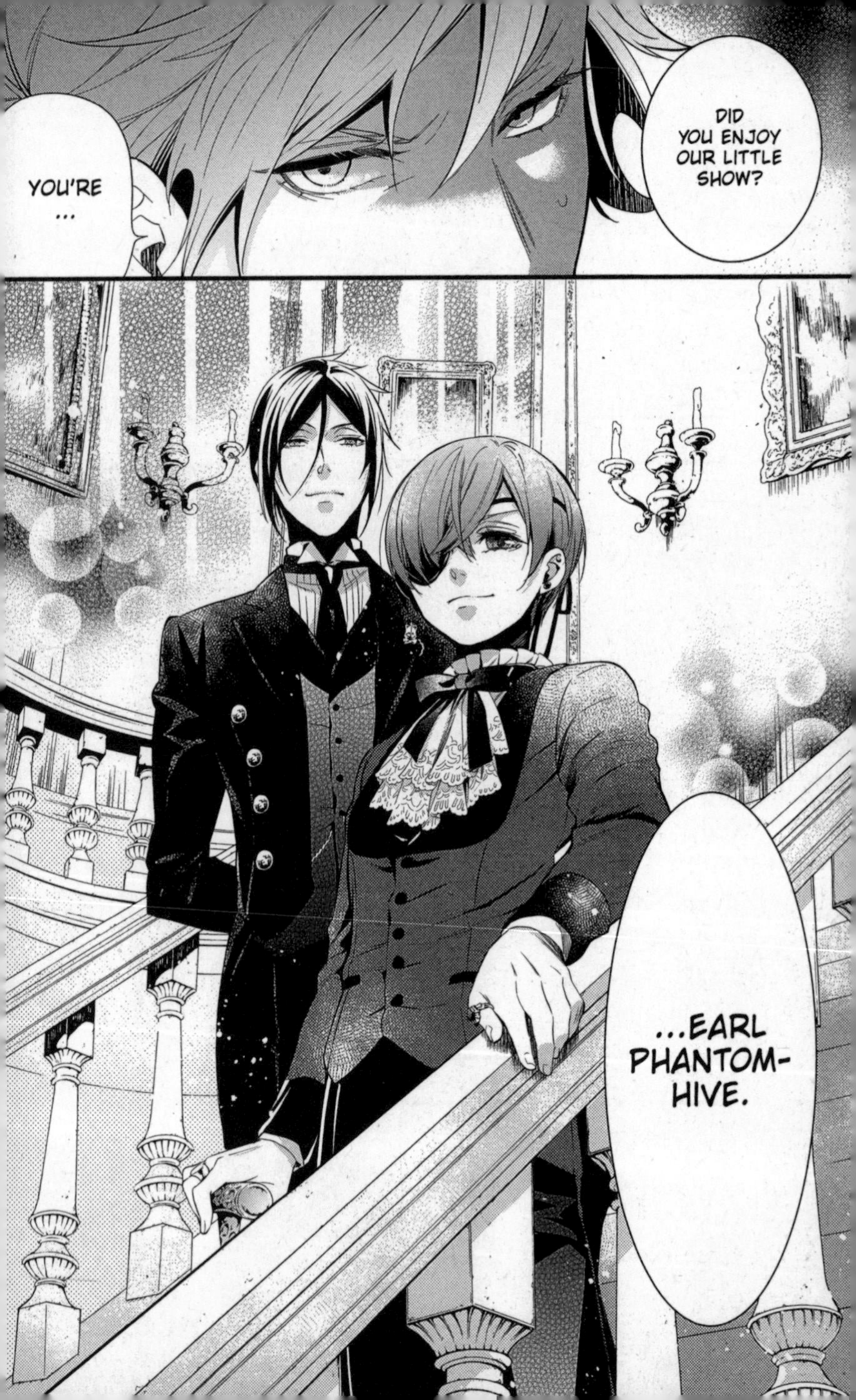
DID YOU ENJOY OUR LITTLE SHOW?
YOU'RE ...
...EARL PHANTOM-HIVE.

Black Butler

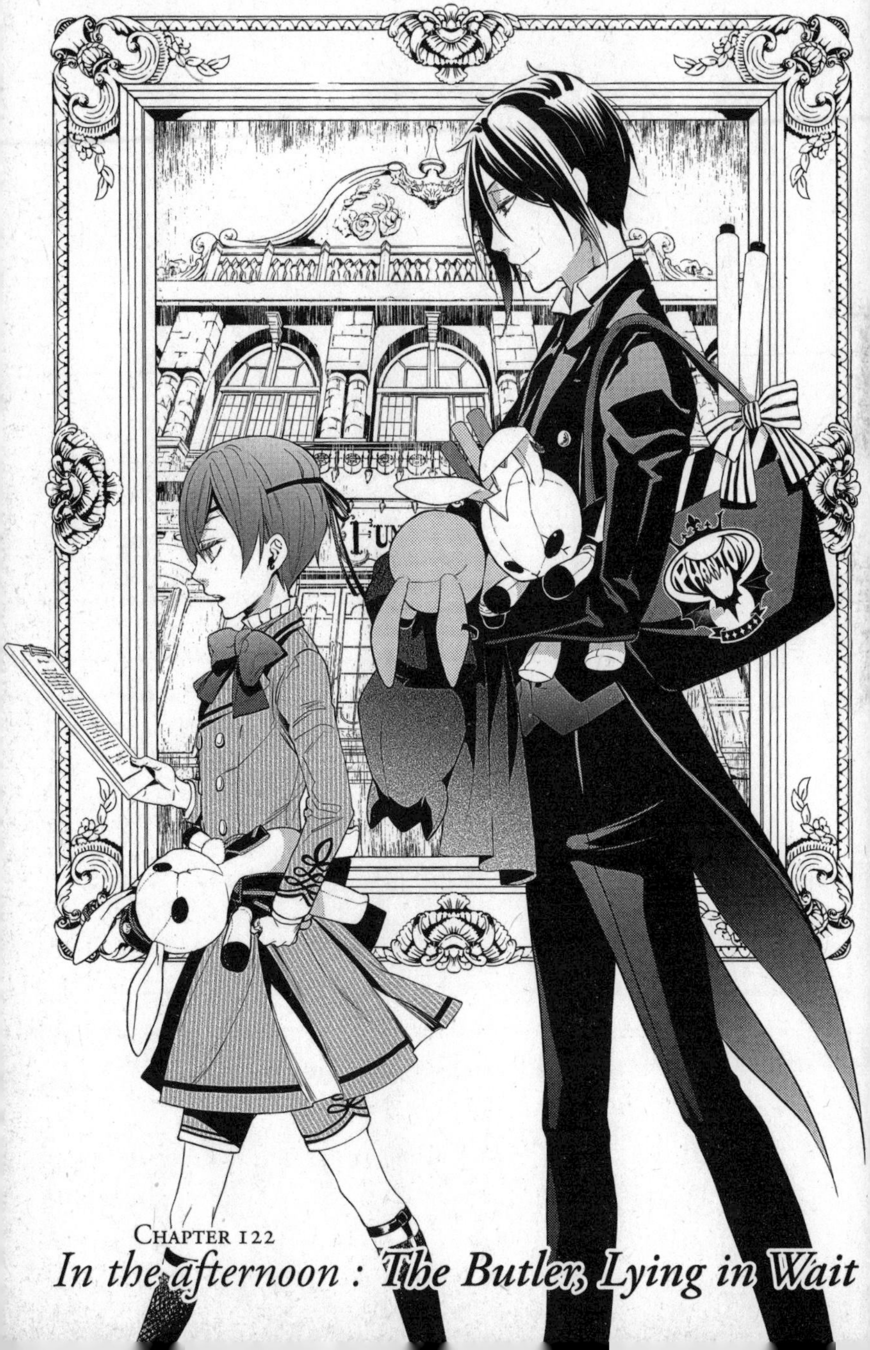

Chapter 122

In the afternoon : The Butler, Lying in Wait

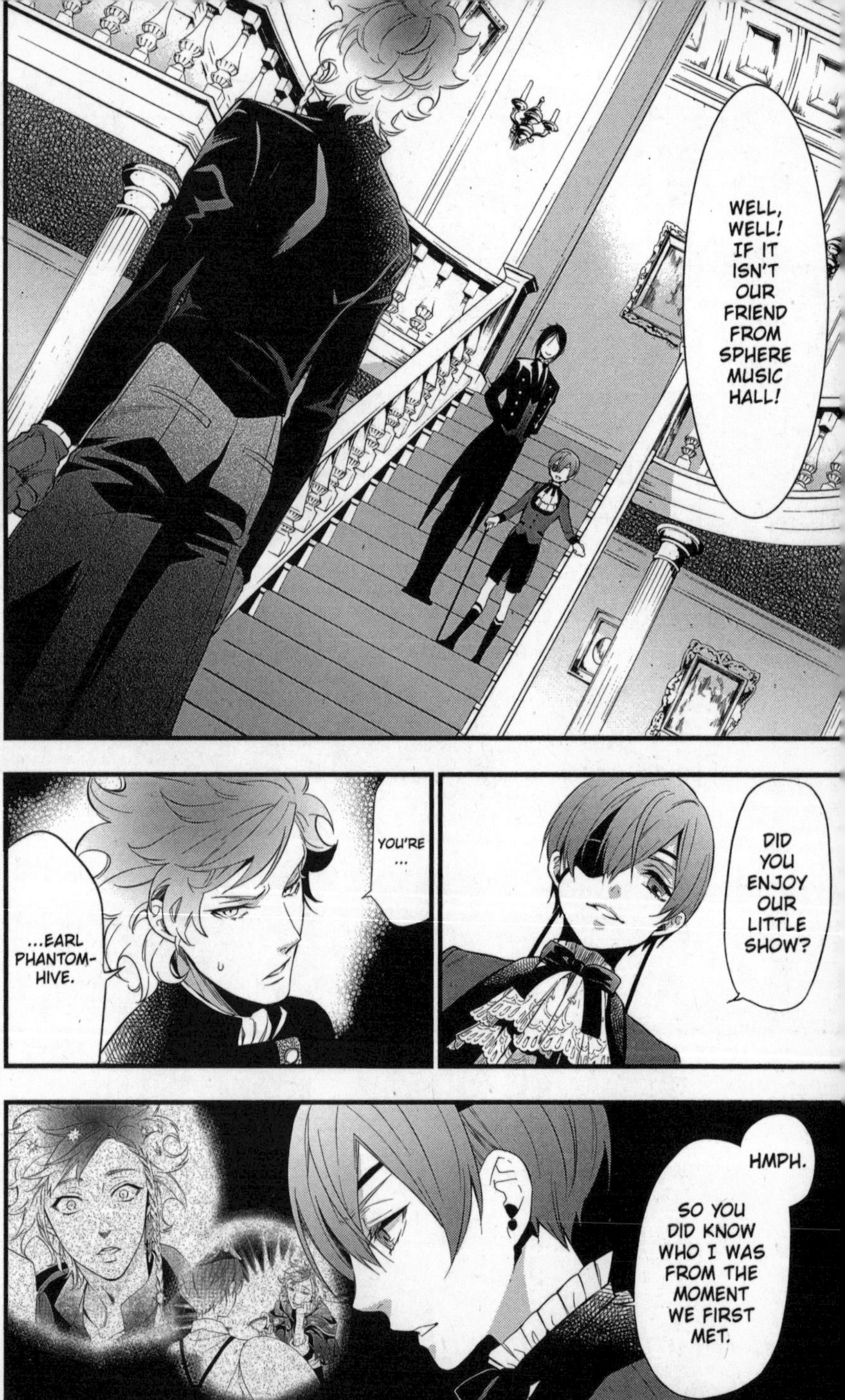
WELL, WELL! IF IT ISN'T OUR FRIEND FROM SPHERE MUSIC HALL!
DID YOU ENJOY OUR LITTLE SHOW?
YOU'RE ...
...EARL PHANTOM-HIVE.
HMPH.
SO YOU DID KNOW WHO I WAS FROM THE MOMENT WE FIRST MET.

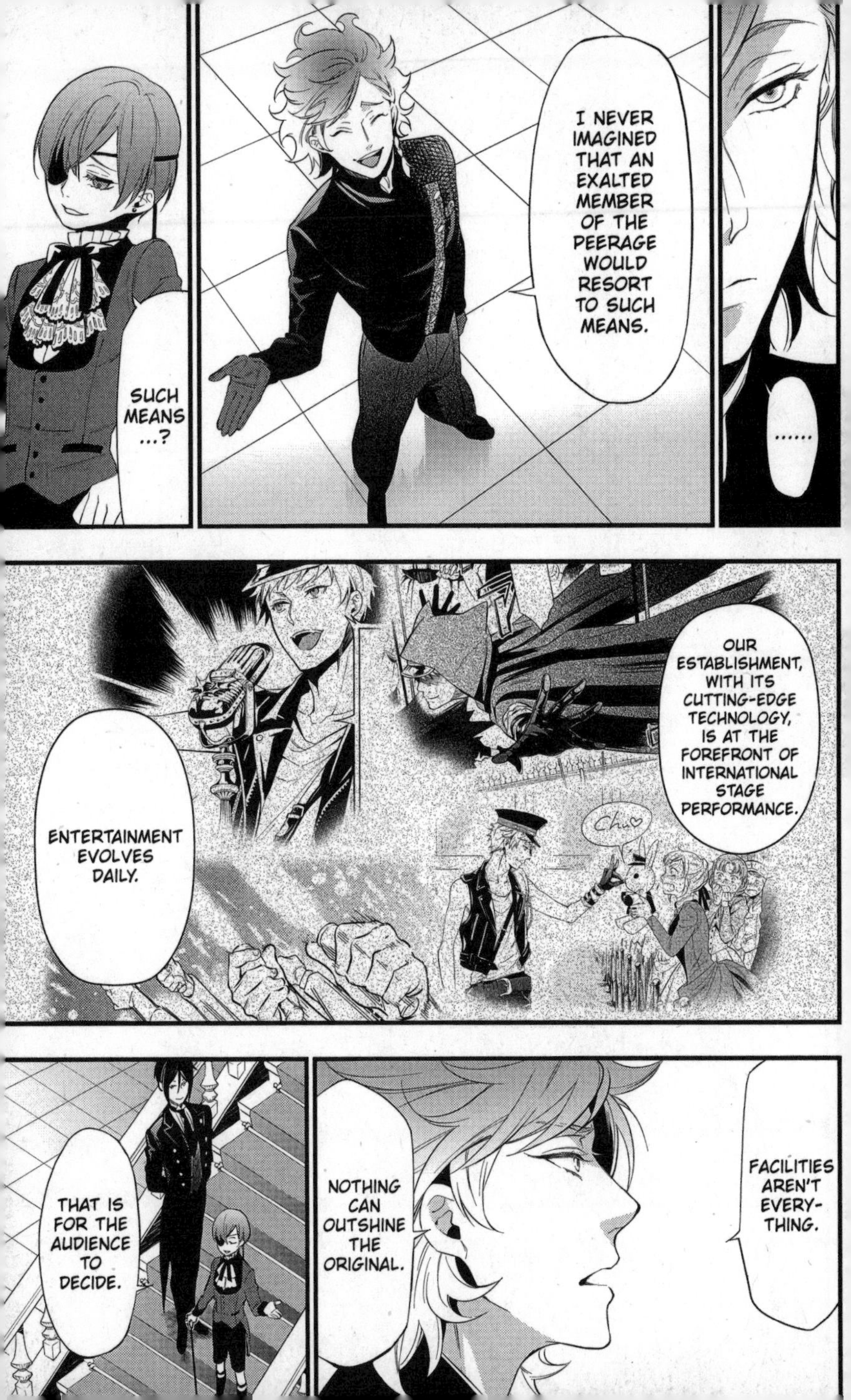
......
I NEVER IMAGINED THAT AN EXALTED MEMBER OF THE PEERAGE WOULD RESORT TO SUCH MEANS.
SUCH MEANS ...?
OUR ESTABLISHMENT, WITH ITS CUTTING-EDGE TECHNOLOGY, IS AT THE FOREFRONT OF INTERNATIONAL STAGE PERFORMANCE.
Chu♡
ENTERTAINMENT EVOLVES DAILY.
FACILITIES AREN'T EVERY-THING.
NOTHING CAN OUTSHINE THE ORIGINAL.
THAT IS FOR THE AUDIENCE TO DECIDE.

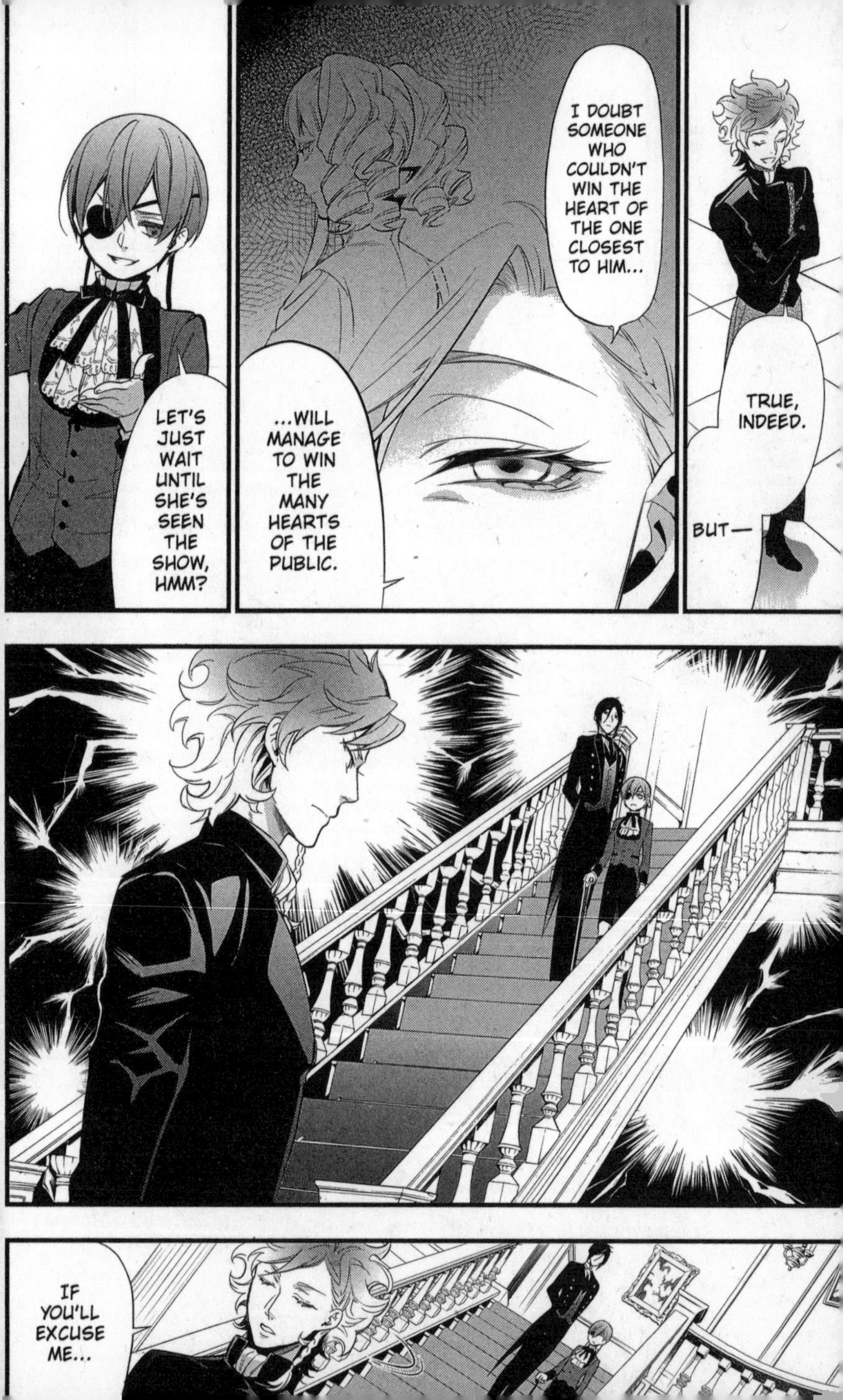
TRUE, INDEED.
BUT—
I DOUBT SOMEONE WHO COULDN'T WIN THE HEART OF THE ONE CLOSEST TO HIM...
...WILL MANAGE TO WIN THE MANY HEARTS OF THE PUBLIC.
LET'S JUST WAIT UNTIL SHE'S SEEN THE SHOW, HMM?
IF YOU'LL EXCUSE ME...

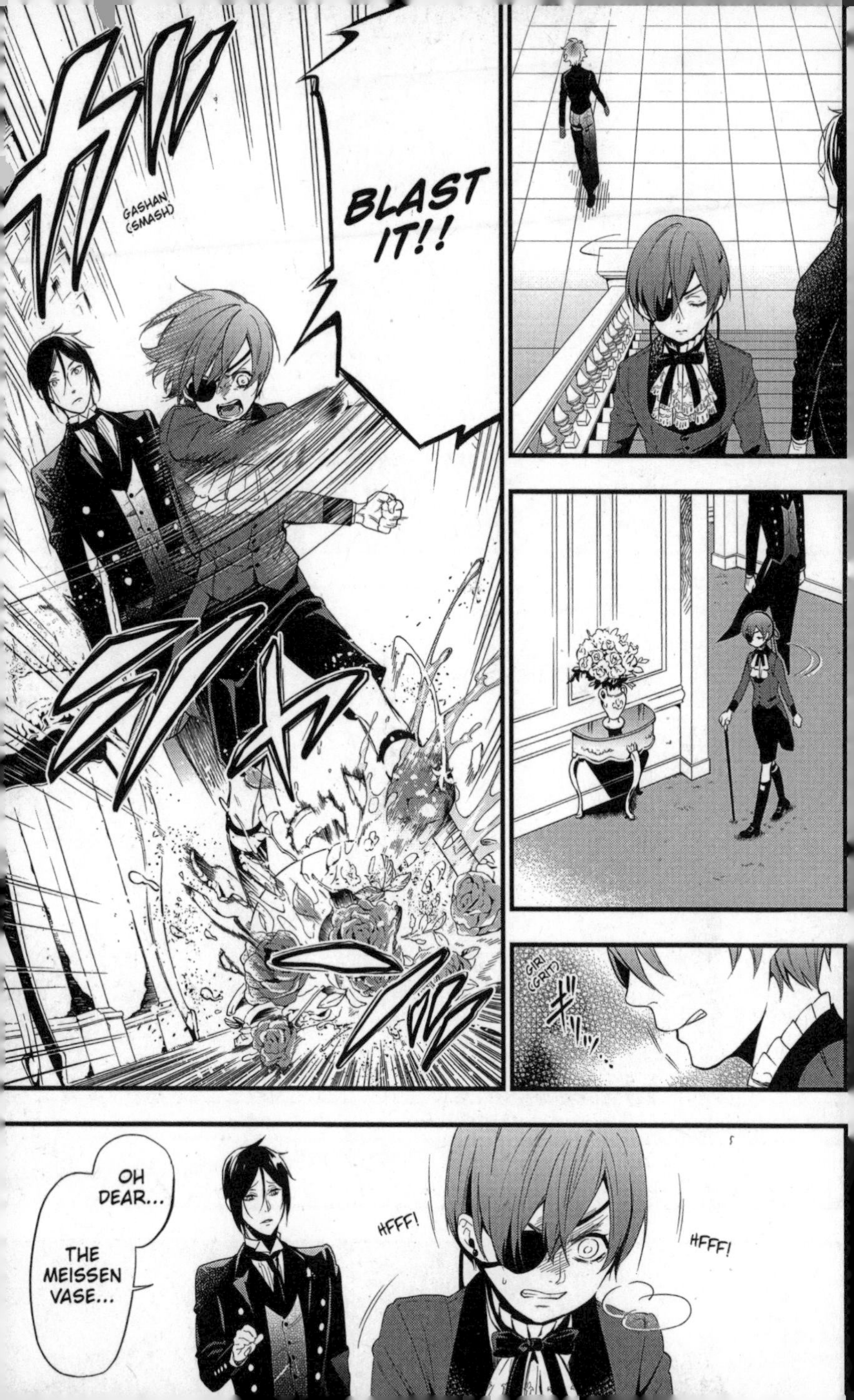
GIRI (GRIT)
BLAST IT!!
GASHAN (SMASH)
HFFF!
HFFF!
OH DEAR...
THE MEISSEN VASE...

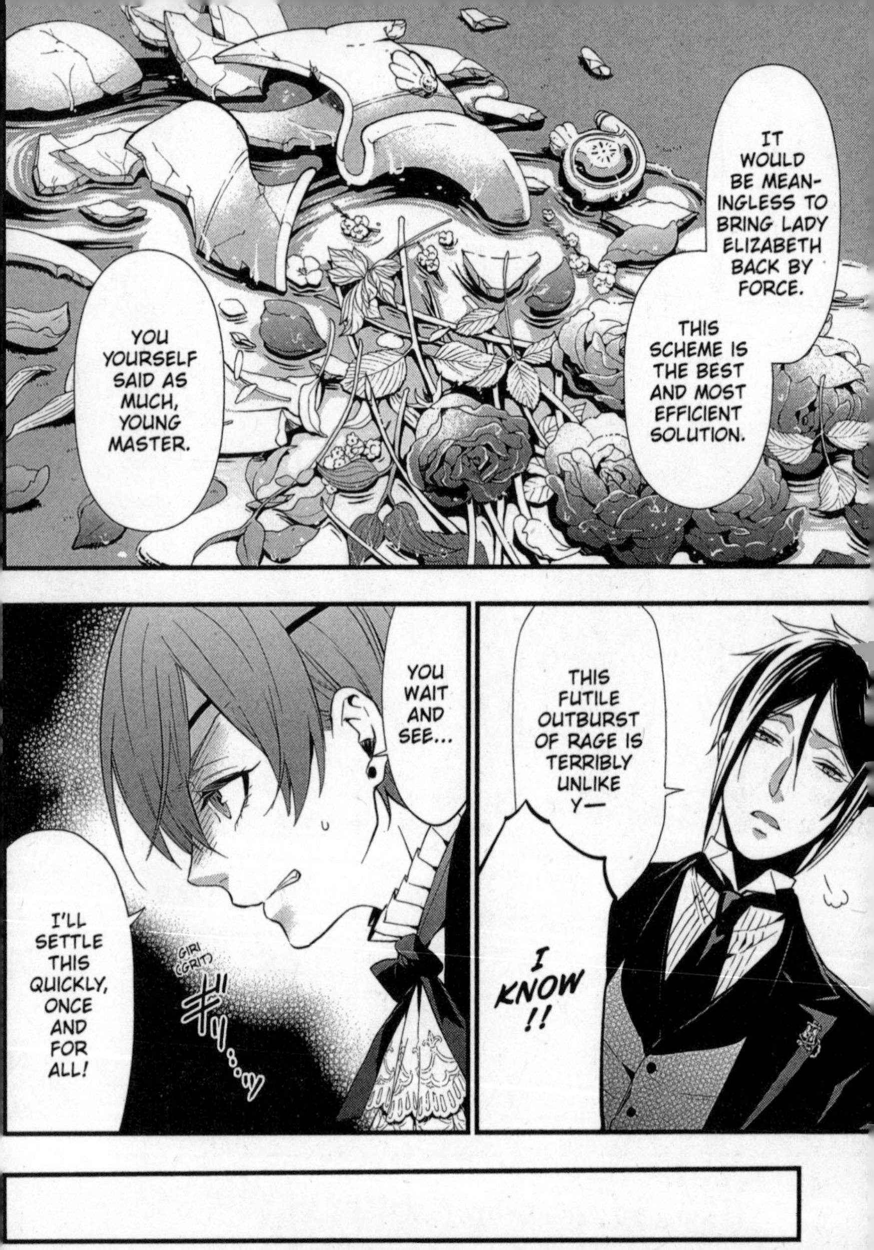
IT WOULD BE MEAN-INGLESS TO BRING LADY ELIZABETH BACK BY FORCE.
THIS SCHEME IS THE BEST AND MOST EFFICIENT SOLUTION.
YOU YOURSELF SAID AS MUCH, YOUNG MASTER.
THIS FUTILE OUTBURST OF RAGE IS TERRIBLY UNLIKE Y—
I KNOW!!
YOU WAIT AND SEE...
GIRI (GRIT)
I'LL SETTLE THIS QUICKLY, ONCE AND FOR ALL!

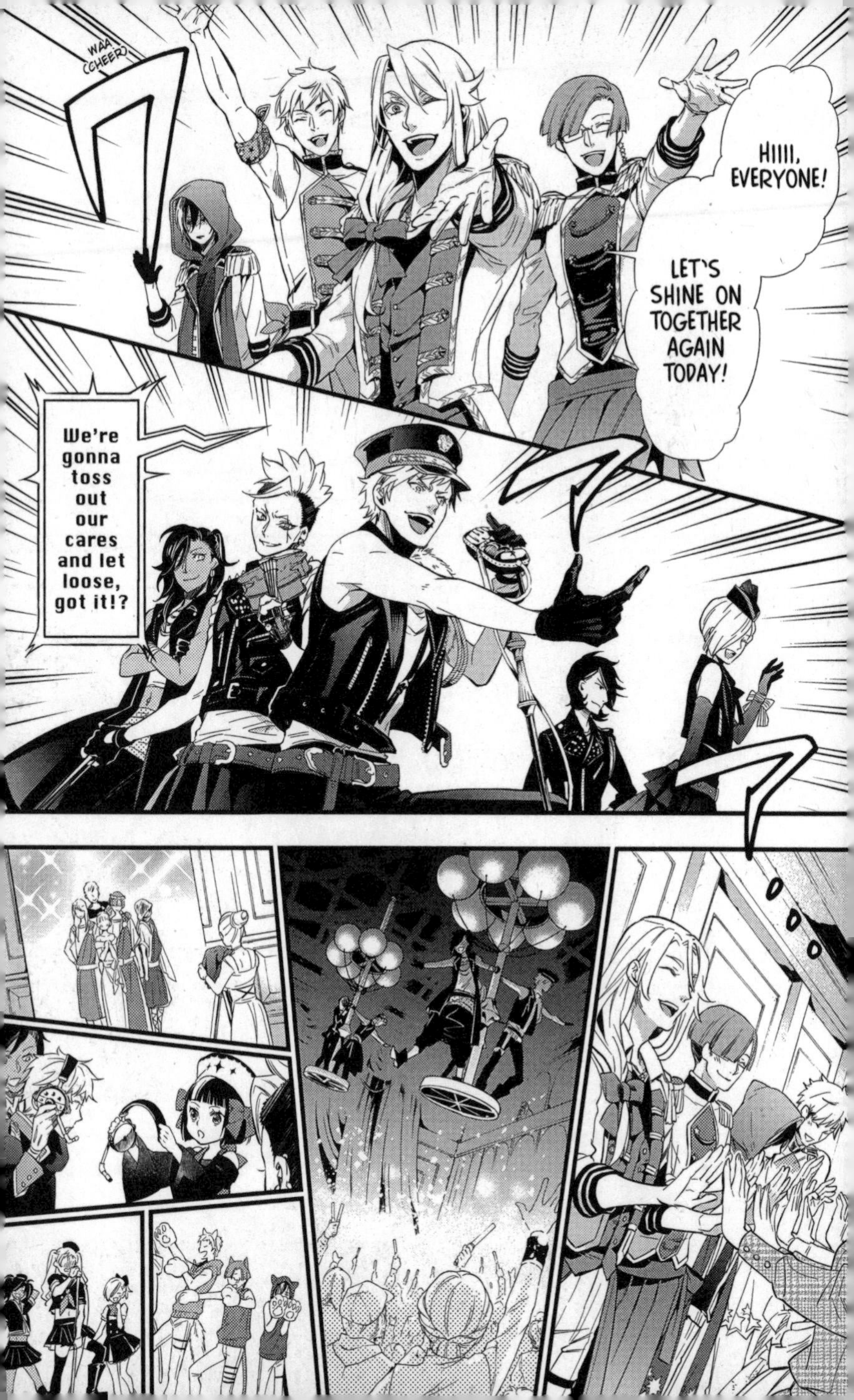
HIIII, EVERYONE!
LET'S SHINE ON TOGETHER AGAIN TODAY!
WAA (CHEER)
We're gonna toss out our cares and let loose, got it!?

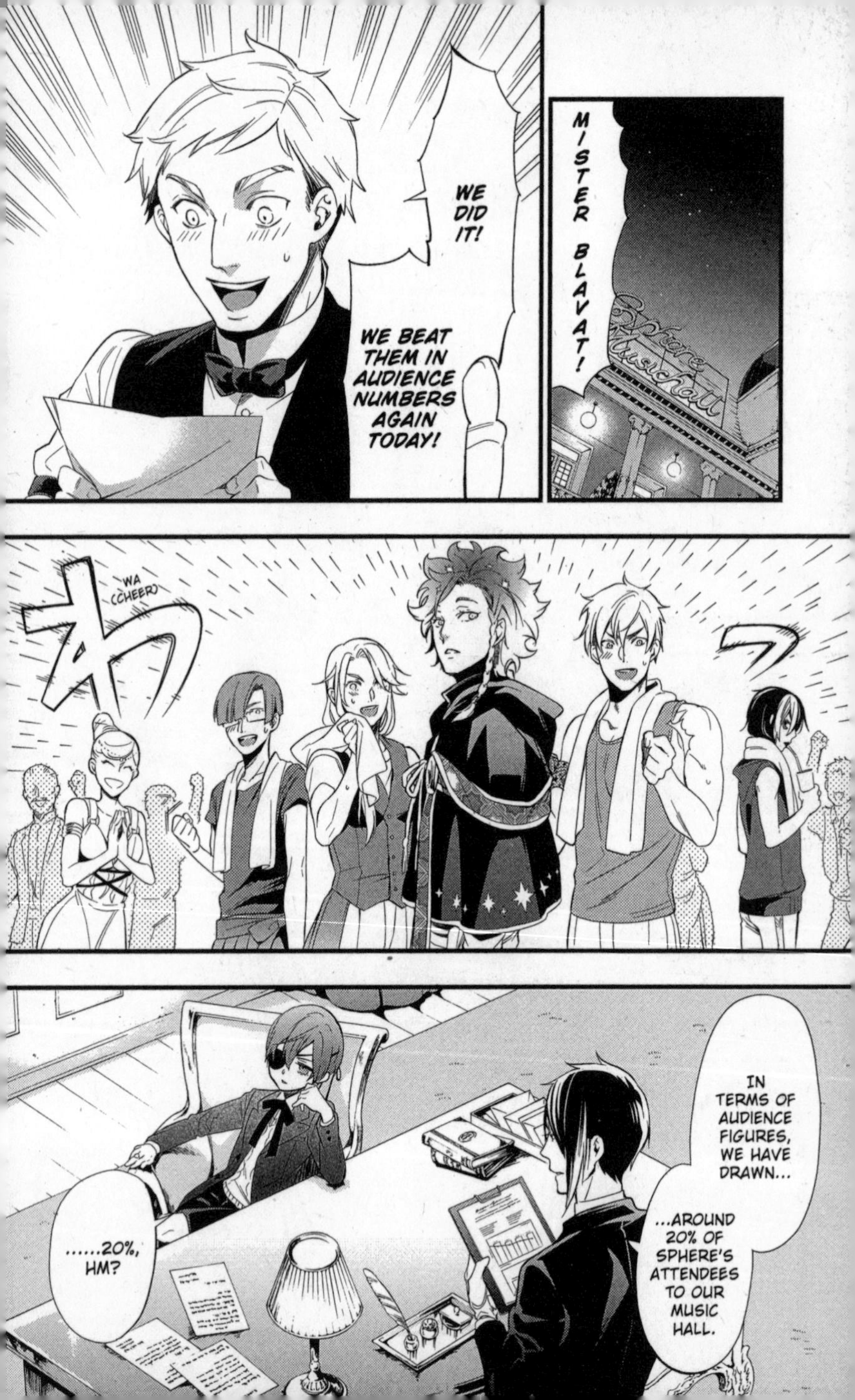
MISTER BLAVAT!
WE DID IT!
WE BEAT THEM IN AUDIENCE NUMBERS AGAIN TODAY!
WA (CHEER)
IN TERMS OF AUDIENCE FIGURES, WE HAVE DRAWN...
...AROUND 20% OF SPHERE'S ATTENDEES TO OUR MUSIC HALL.
......20%, HM?

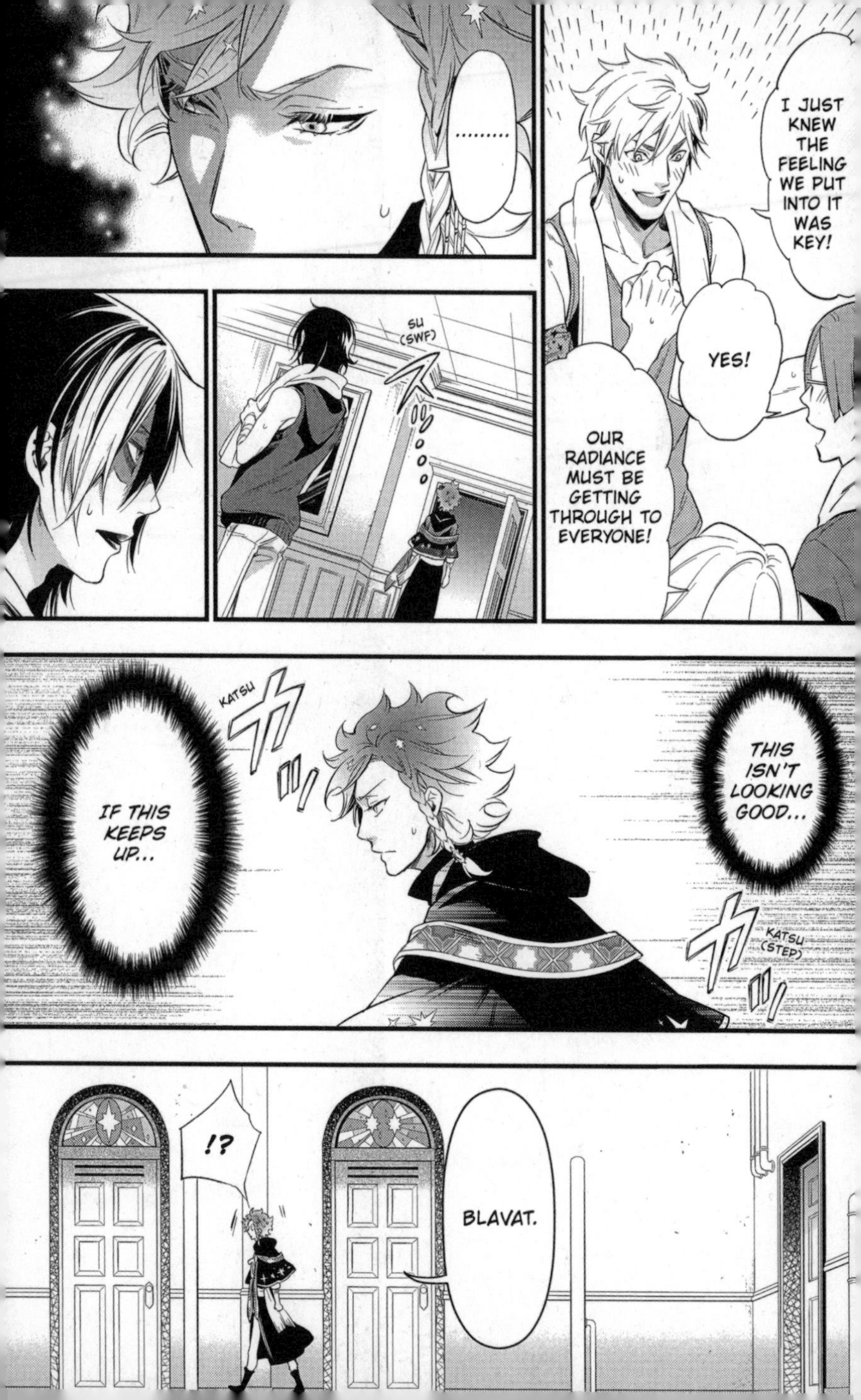
I JUST KNEW THE FEELING WE PUT INTO IT WAS KEY!
YES!
OUR RADIANCE MUST BE GETTING THROUGH TO EVERYONE!
....
SU (SWF)
THIS ISN'T LOOKING GOOD...
KATSU (STEP)
KATSU
IF THIS KEEPS UP...
BLAVAT.
!?

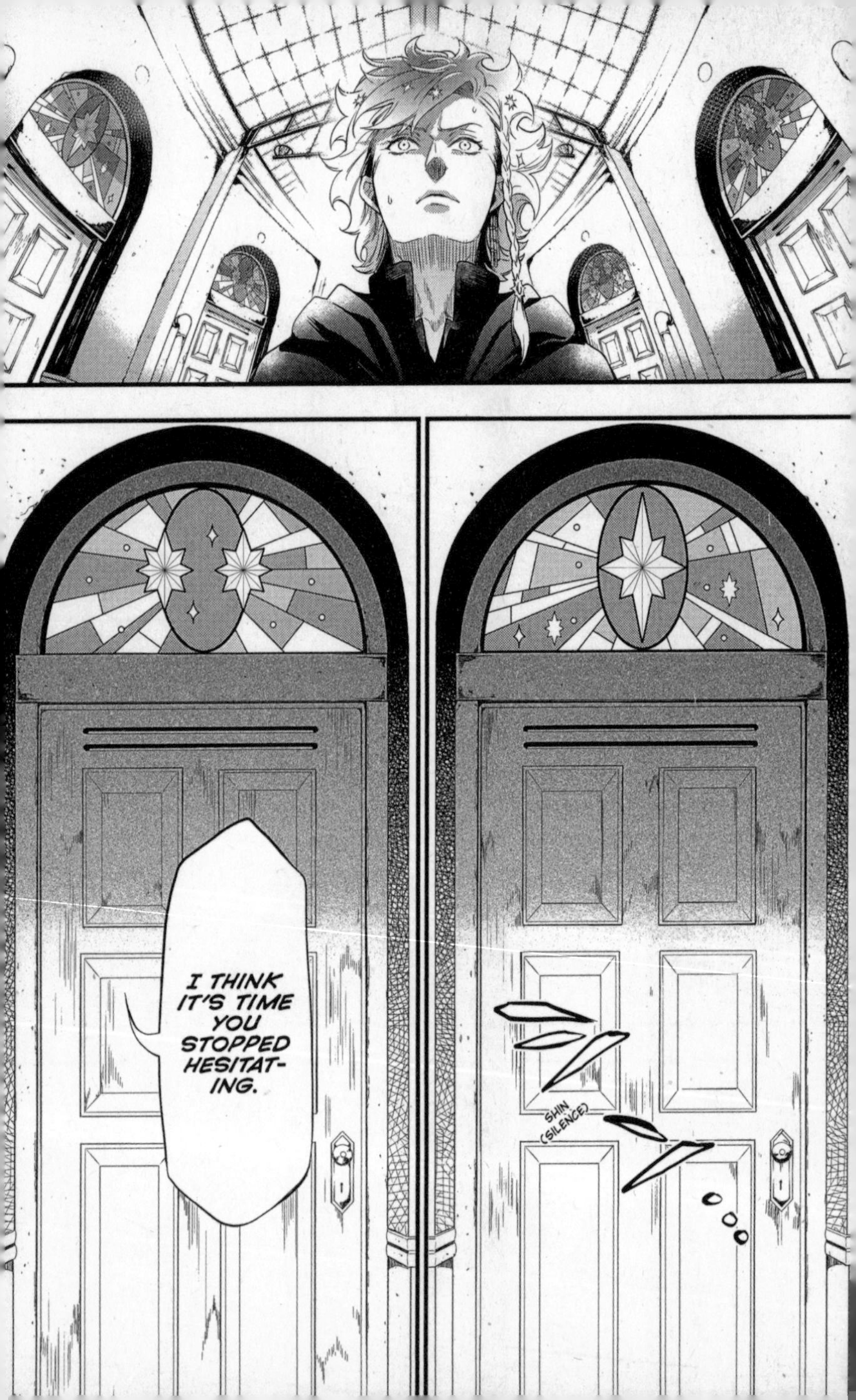
SHIN (SILENCE)
I THINK IT'S TIME YOU STOPPED HESITAT-ING.

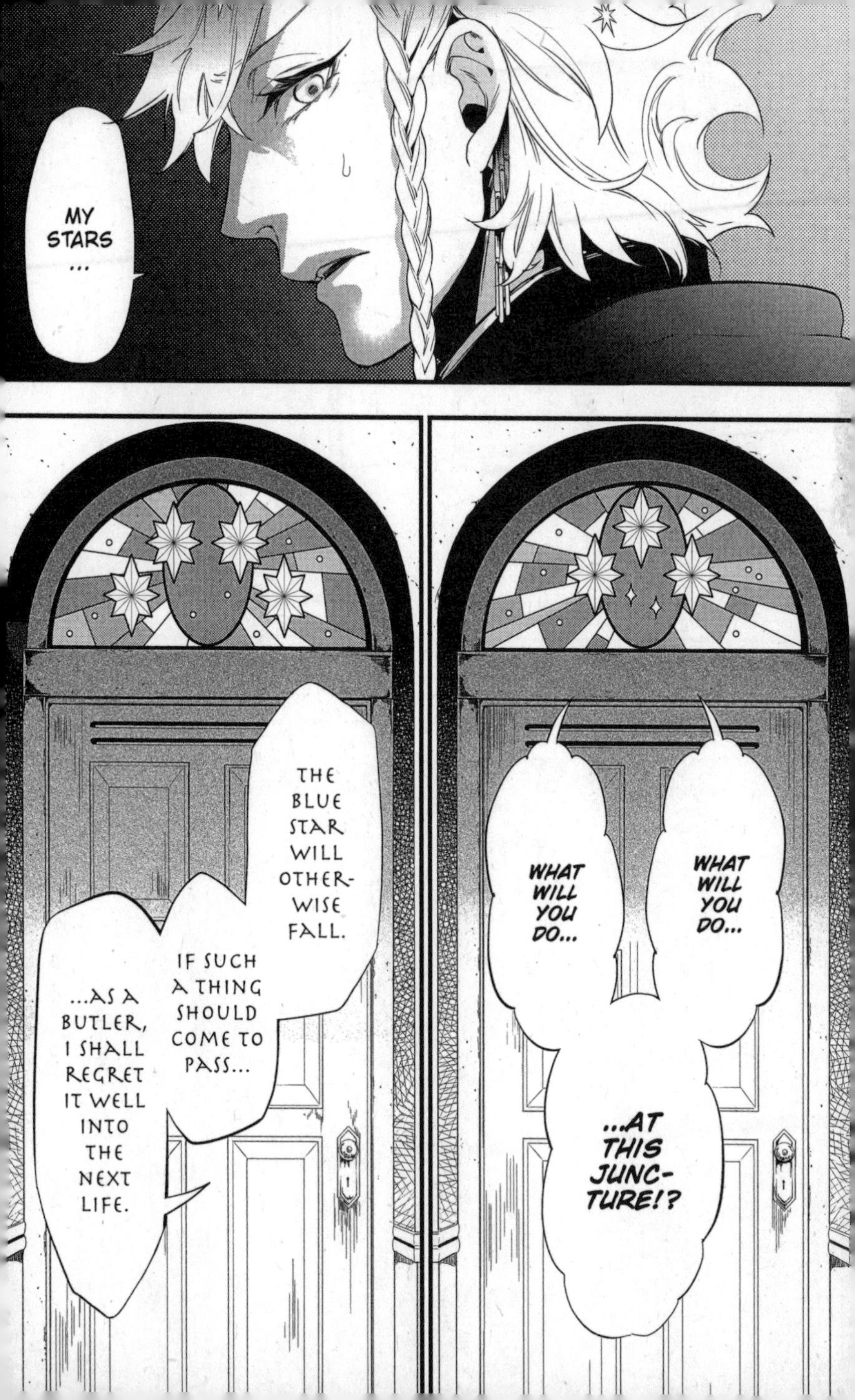
MY STARS ...
WHAT WILL YOU DO...
WHAT WILL YOU DO...
...AT THIS JUNC-TURE!?
THE BLUE STAR WILL OTHER-WISE FALL.
IF SUCH A THING SHOULD COME TO PASS...
...AS A BUTLER, I SHALL REGRET IT WELL INTO THE NEXT LIFE.

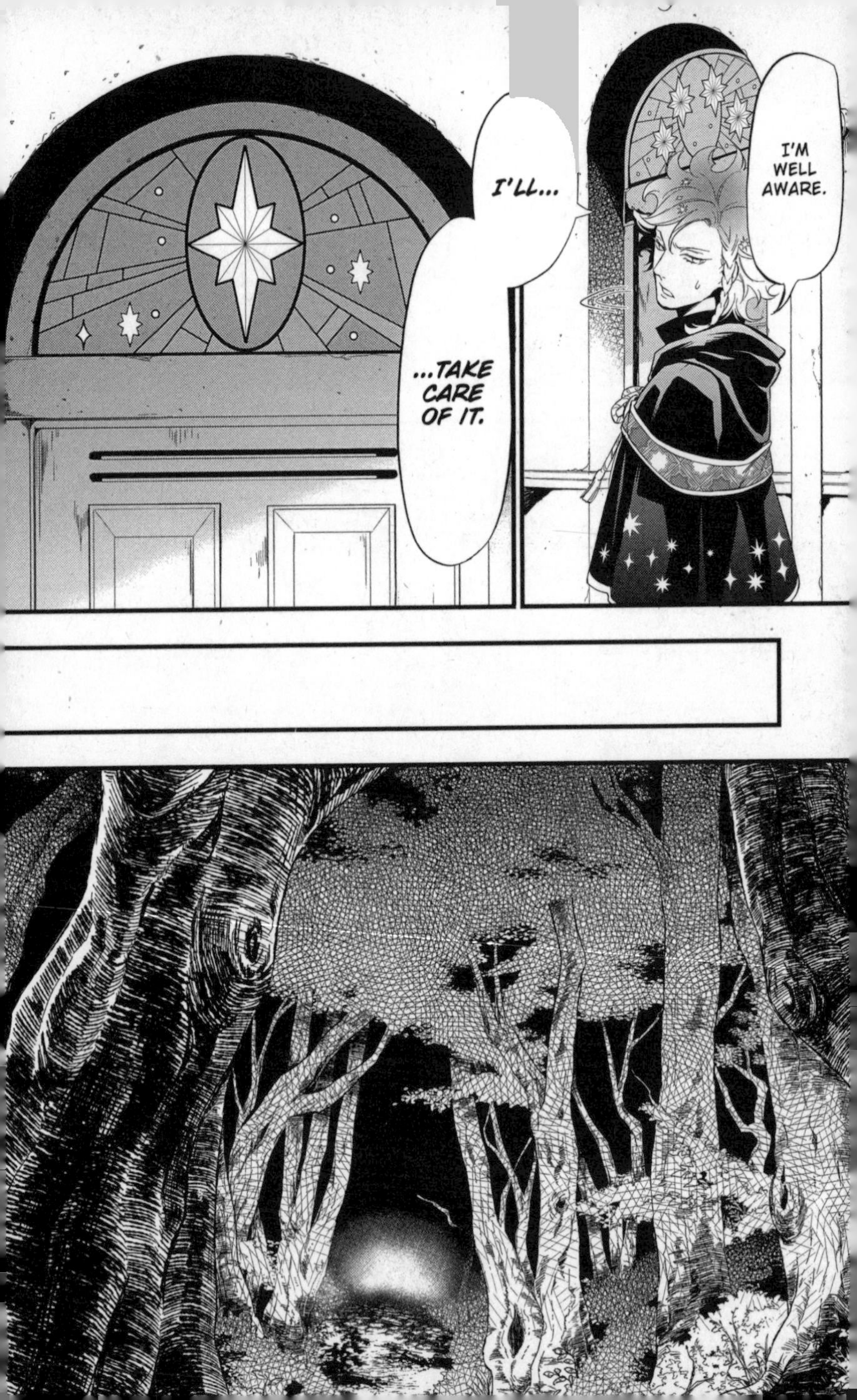
I'M WELL AWARE.
I'LL...
...TAKE CARE OF IT.

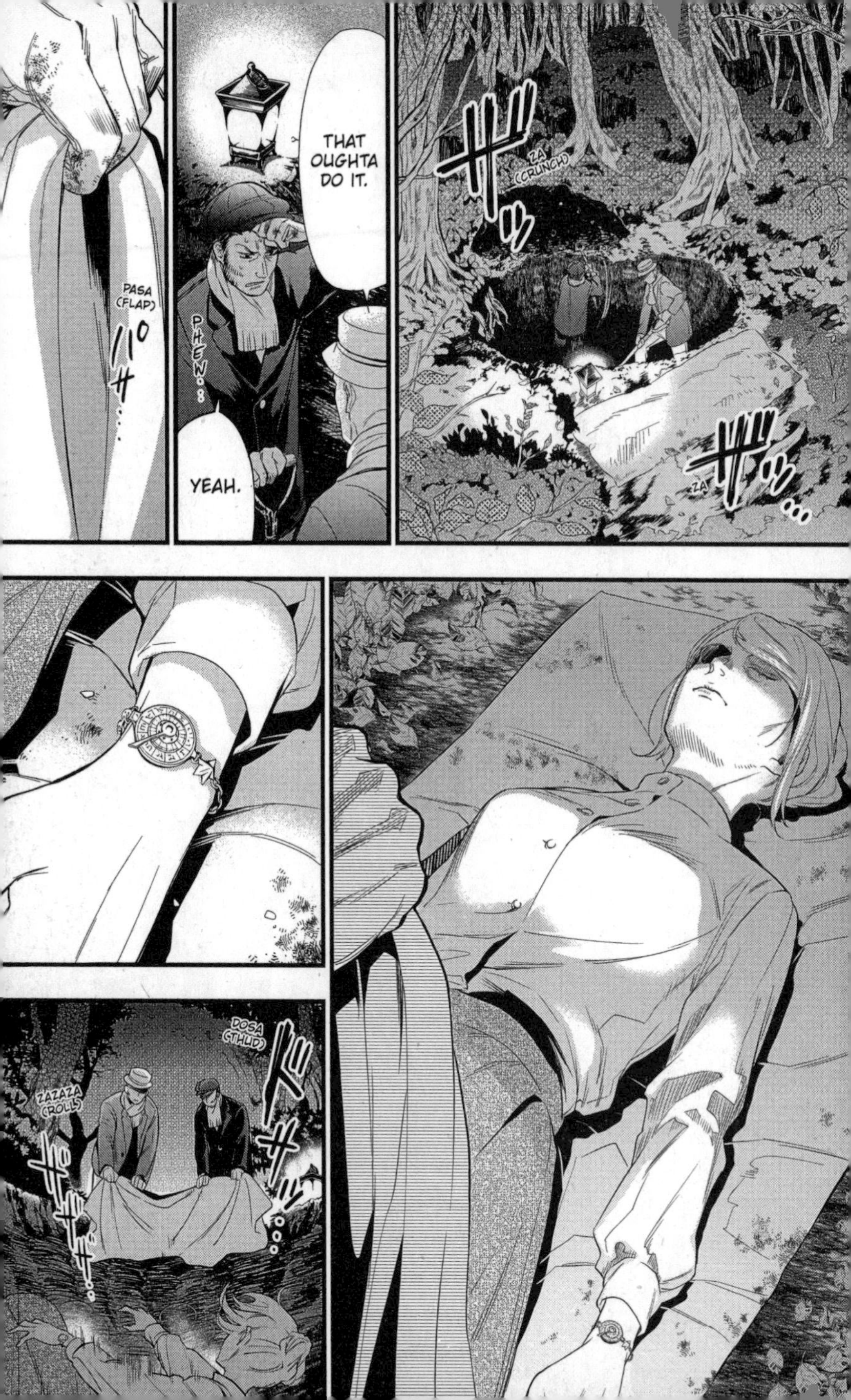
ZA (CRUNCH)
ZA...
THAT OUGHTA DO IT.
PHEW...
YEAH.
PASA (FLAP)
DOSA (THUD)
ZAZAZA (ROLL)

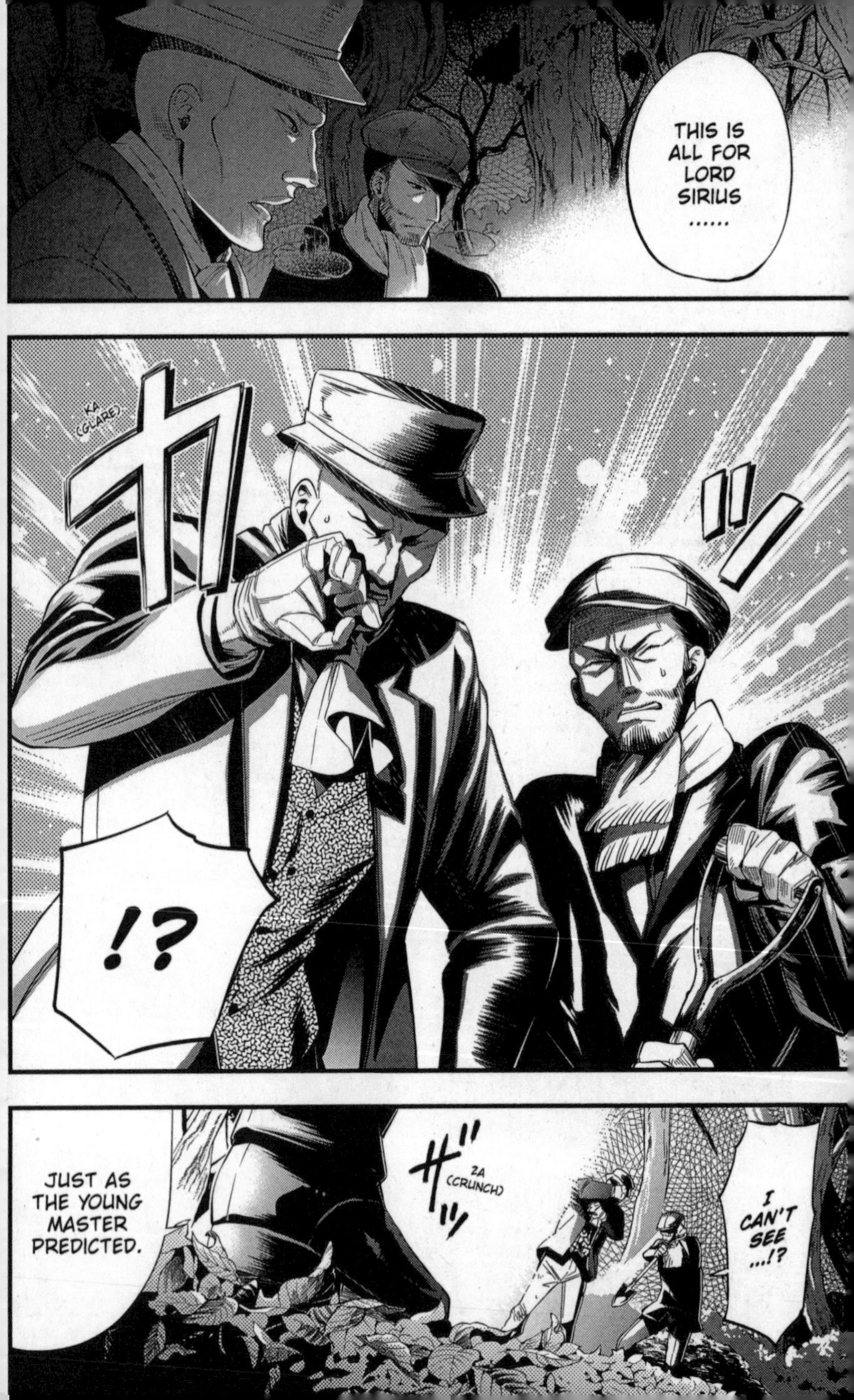
THIS IS ALL FOR LORD SIRIUS ......
KA (GLARE)
!?
I CAN'T SEE ...!?
ZA (CRUNCH)
JUST AS THE YOUNG MASTER PREDICTED.

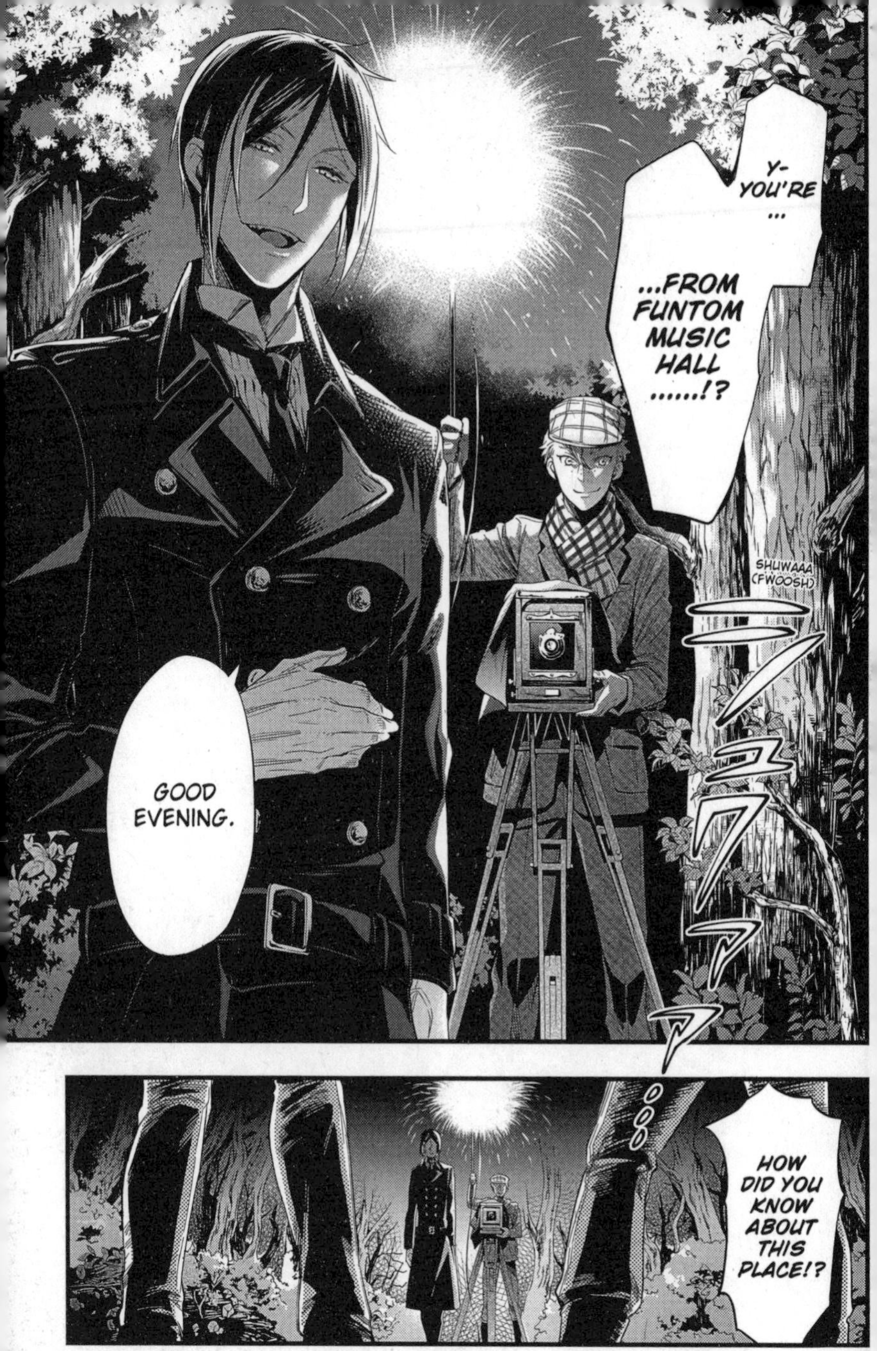
Y-YOU'RE ...
...FROM FUNTOM MUSIC HALL ......!?
SHUWAAA (FWOOSH)
GOOD EVENING.
HOW DID YOU KNOW ABOUT THIS PLACE!?

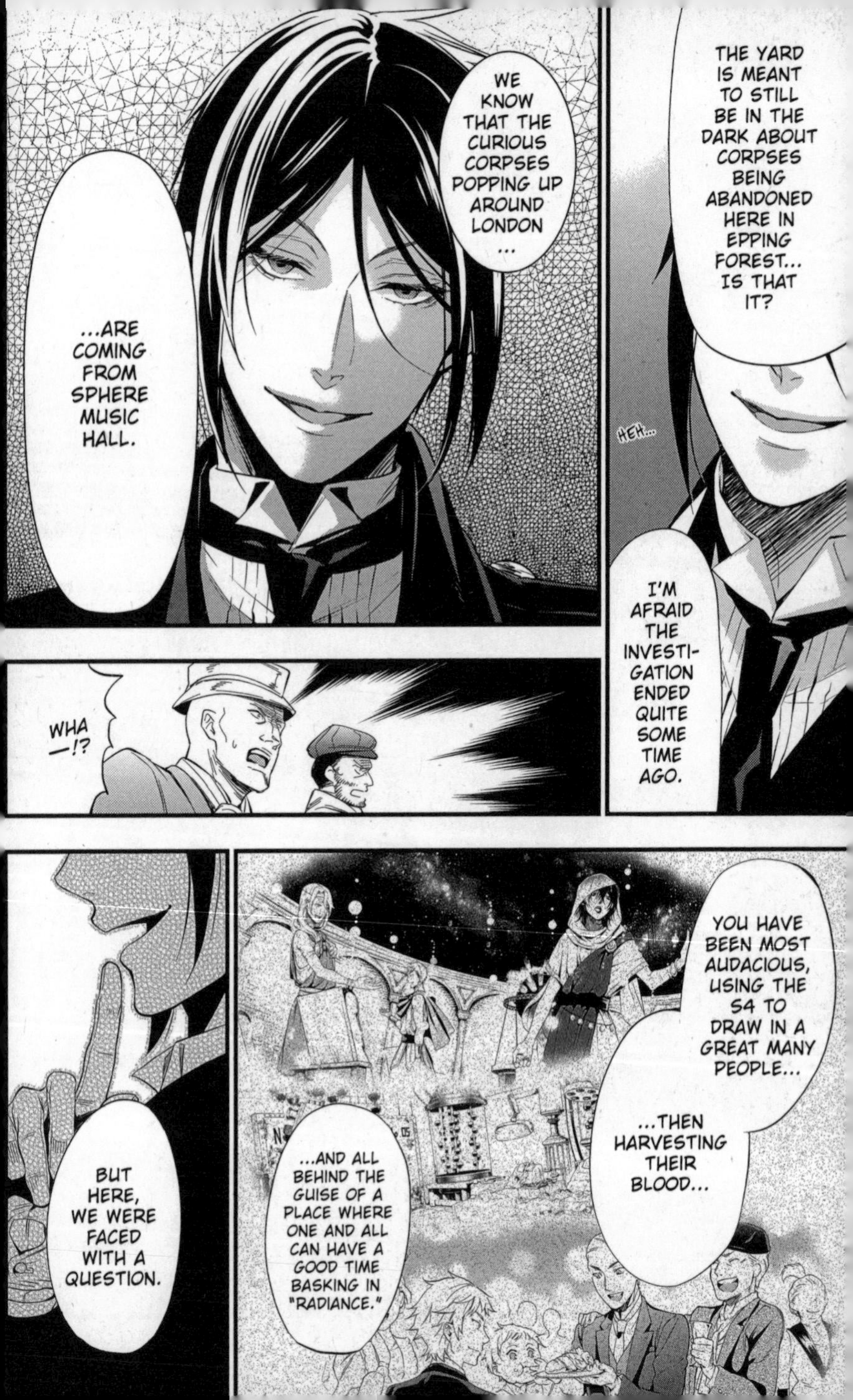
THE YARD IS MEANT TO STILL BE IN THE DARK ABOUT CORPSES BEING ABANDONED HERE IN EPPING FOREST... IS THAT IT?
HEH...
I'M AFRAID THE INVESTIGATION ENDED QUITE SOME TIME AGO.
WE KNOW THAT THE CURIOUS CORPSES POPPING UP AROUND LONDON...
...ARE COMING FROM SPHERE MUSIC HALL.
WHA—!?
YOU HAVE BEEN MOST AUDACIOUS, USING THE S4 TO DRAW IN A GREAT MANY PEOPLE...
...THEN HARVESTING THEIR BLOOD...
...AND ALL BEHIND THE GUISE OF A PLACE WHERE ONE AND ALL CAN HAVE A GOOD TIME BASKING IN "RADIANCE."
BUT HERE, WE WERE FACED WITH A QUESTION.

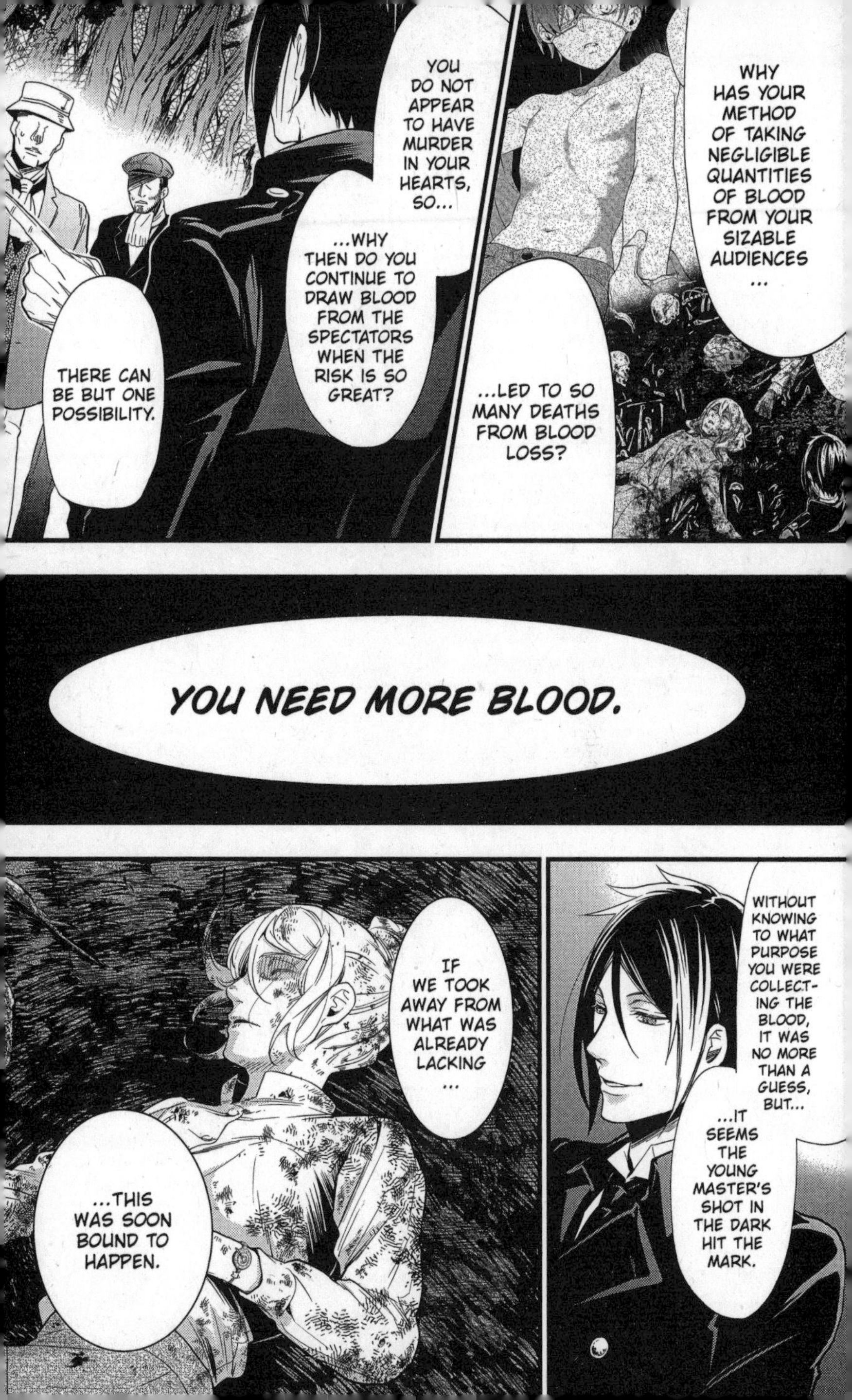
WHY HAS YOUR METHOD OF TAKING NEGLIGIBLE QUANTITIES OF BLOOD FROM YOUR SIZABLE AUDIENCES ...
...LED TO SO MANY DEATHS FROM BLOOD LOSS?
YOU DO NOT APPEAR TO HAVE MURDER IN YOUR HEARTS, SO...
...WHY THEN DO YOU CONTINUE TO DRAW BLOOD FROM THE SPECTATORS WHEN THE RISK IS SO GREAT?
THERE CAN BE BUT ONE POSSIBILITY.
YOU NEED MORE BLOOD.
WITHOUT KNOWING TO WHAT PURPOSE YOU WERE COLLECT-ING THE BLOOD, IT WAS NO MORE THAN A GUESS, BUT...
...IT SEEMS THE YOUNG MASTER'S SHOT IN THE DARK HIT THE MARK.
IF WE TOOK AWAY FROM WHAT WAS ALREADY LACKING ...
...THIS WAS SOON BOUND TO HAPPEN.

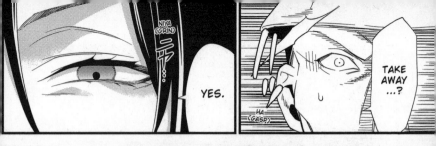

NIYA (GRIND)

YES.

TAKE AWAY...?

HA (GASP)

THE TRUE INTENT OF FUNTOM MUSIC HALL...

...WAS TO STEAL SPHERE'S AUDIENCE AND PUT A DENT IN YOUR BLOOD TOTALS...

...IN ORDER TO INDUCE MORE DEATHS FROM BLOOD LOSS!

ALL WE HAD TO DO THEN WAS WAIT FOR YOU HERE AT YOUR FAVOURITE CORPSE BURIAL SITE.

JUST AS I WOULD EXPECT FROM THE YOUNG MASTER.

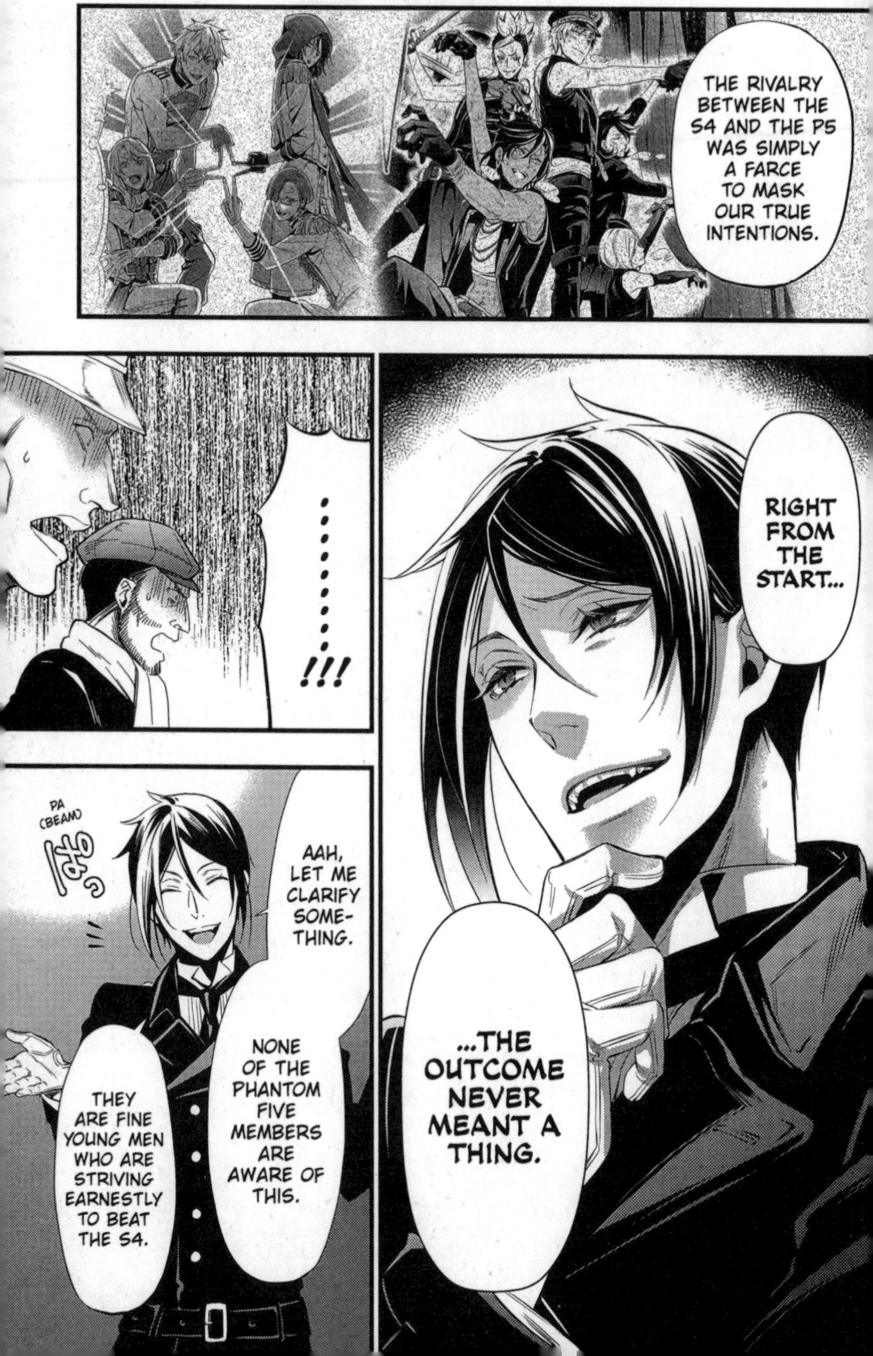
THE RIVALRY BETWEEN THE S4 AND THE P5 WAS SIMPLY A FARCE TO MASK OUR TRUE INTENTIONS.
RIGHT FROM THE START...
...THE OUTCOME NEVER MEANT A THING.
.........!!!
AAH, LET ME CLARIFY SOME-THING.
PA (BEAM)
NONE OF THE PHANTOM FIVE MEMBERS ARE AWARE OF THIS.
THEY ARE FINE YOUNG MEN WHO ARE STRIVING EARNESTLY TO BEAT THE S4.

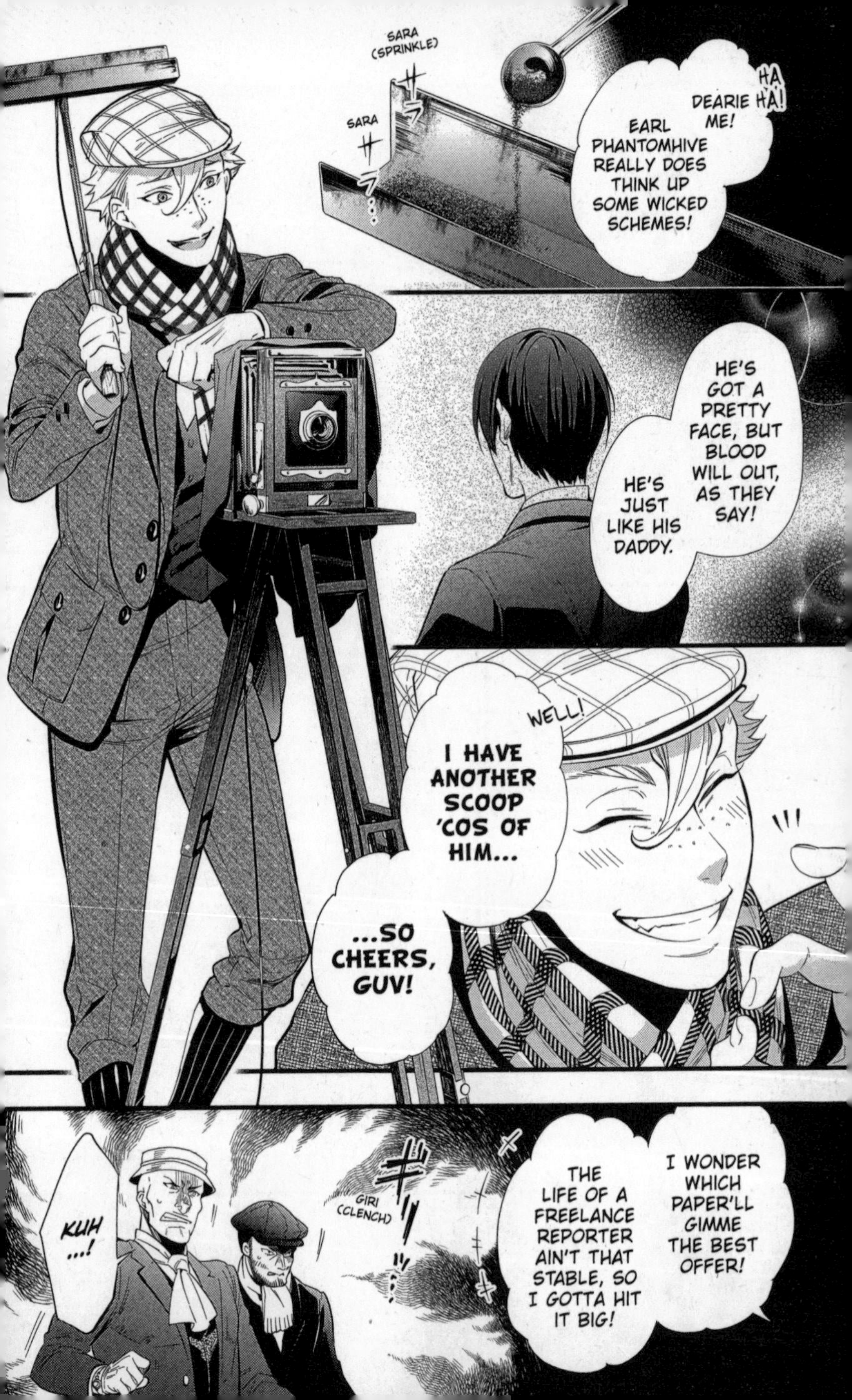
HA HA!
DEARIE ME!
EARL PHANTOMHIVE REALLY DOES THINK UP SOME WICKED SCHEMES!
SARA (SPRINKLE)
SARA
HE'S GOT A PRETTY FACE, BUT BLOOD WILL OUT, AS THEY SAY!
HE'S JUST LIKE HIS DADDY.
WELL!
I HAVE ANOTHER SCOOP 'COS OF HIM...
...SO CHEERS, GUV!
I WONDER WHICH PAPER'LL GIMME THE BEST OFFER!
THE LIFE OF A FREELANCE REPORTER AIN'T THAT STABLE, SO I GOTTA HIT IT BIG!
GIRI (CLENCH)
KUH ...!

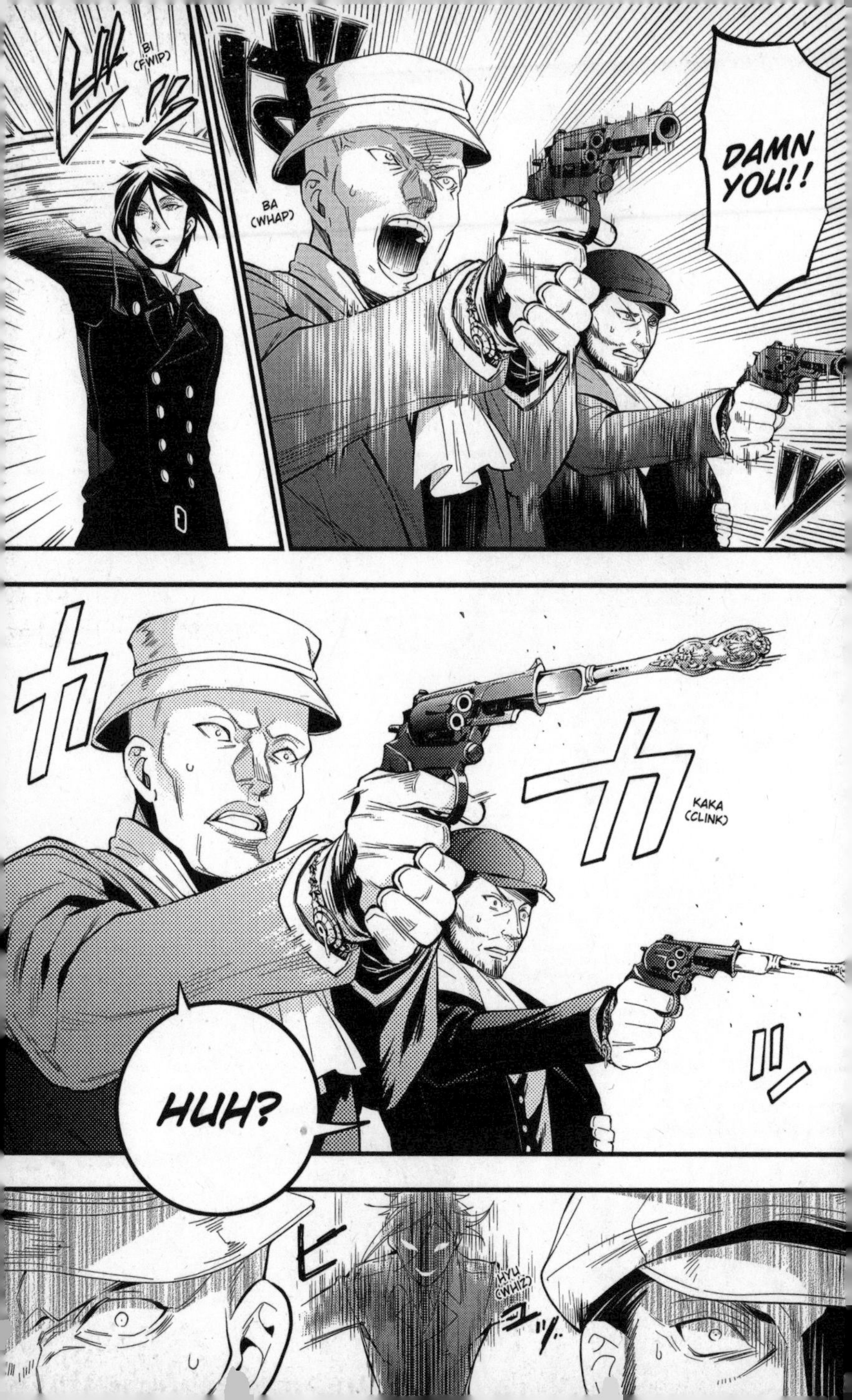
DAMN YOU!!
BA (WHAP)
BI (FWIP)
KAKA (CLINK)
HUH?
HYU (WHIZ)

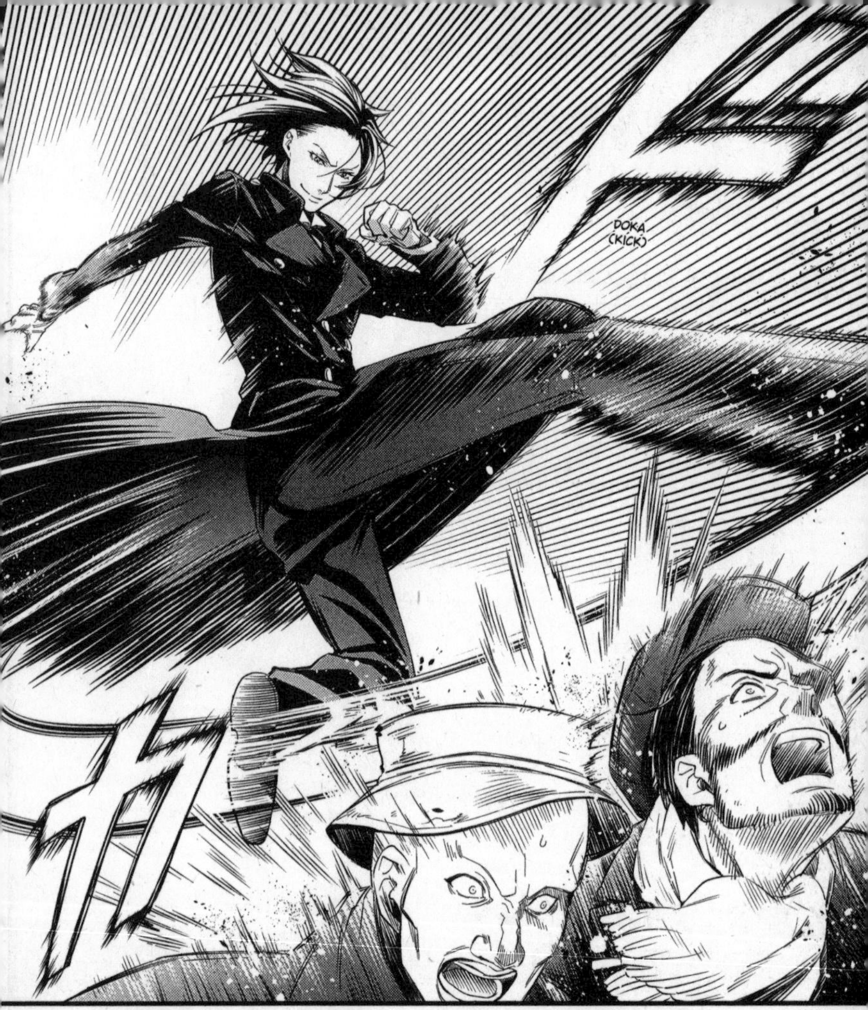
DOKA (KICK)
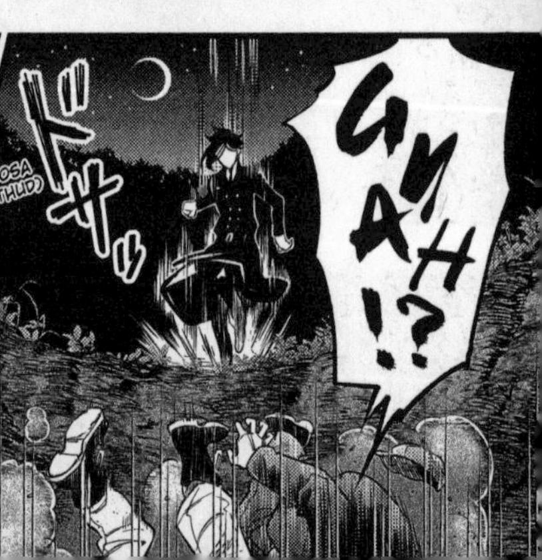
GWAH!?
DOSA (THUD)
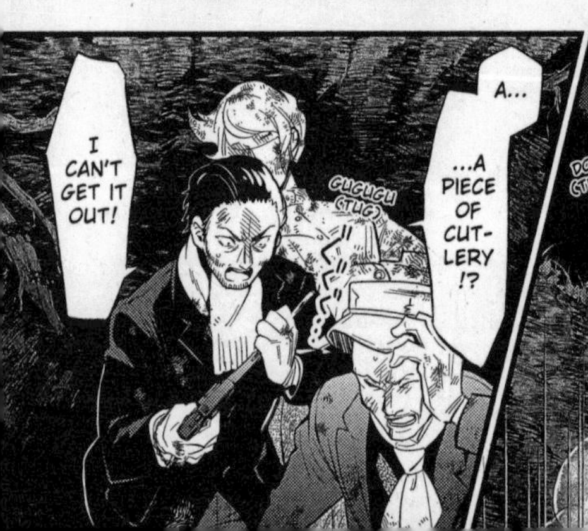
A...
...A PIECE OF CUT-LERY!?
GUGUGU (TUG)
I CAN'T GET IT OUT!

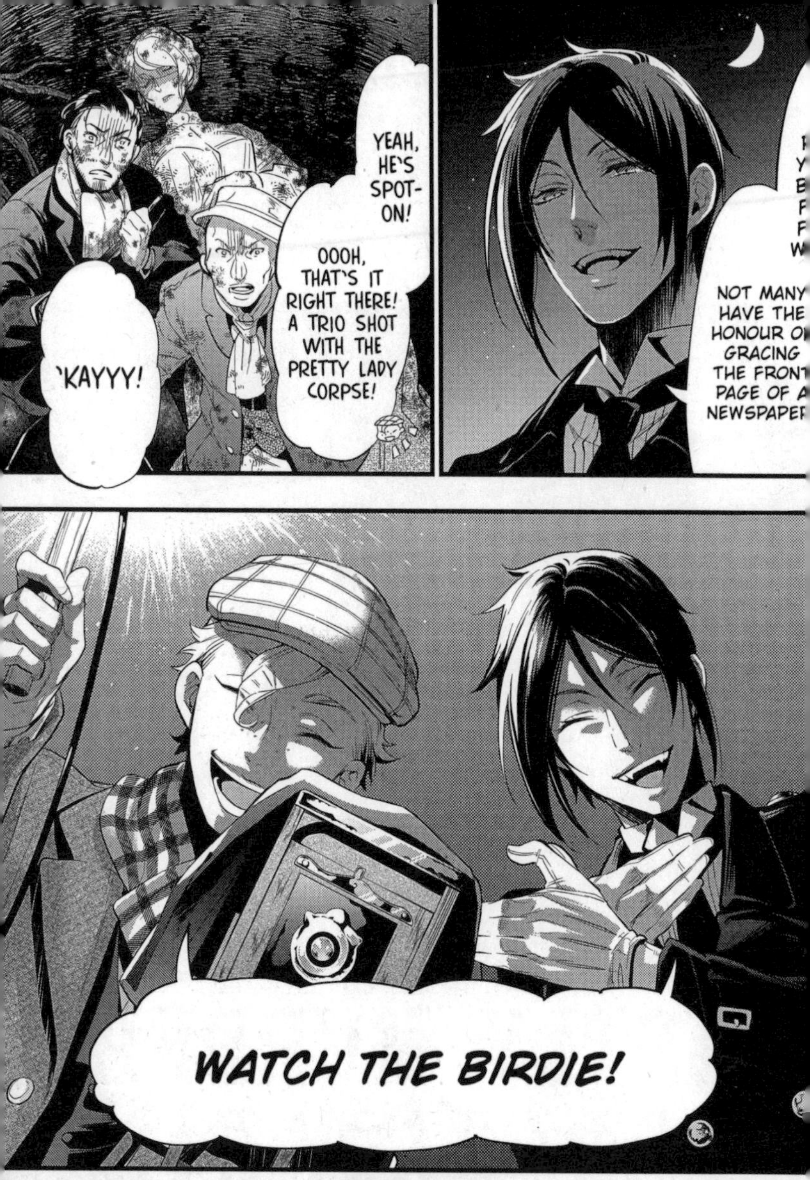
NOT MANY HAVE THE HONOUR O GRACING THE FRONT PAGE OF A NEWSPAPE
YEAH, HE'S SPOT-ON!
OOOH, THAT'S IT RIGHT THERE! A TRIO SHOT WITH THE PRETTY LADY CORPSE!
'KAYYY!
WATCH THE BIRDIE!

THE · PENNY · ILLUSTRATED · PAPER

AND · ILLUSTRATED TIMES

GHASTLY MURDER!

PERPETRATED BY

SPHERE MUSIC HALL

SPHERE MUSIC HALL MURDERS A SPECTATOR!

Black Butler

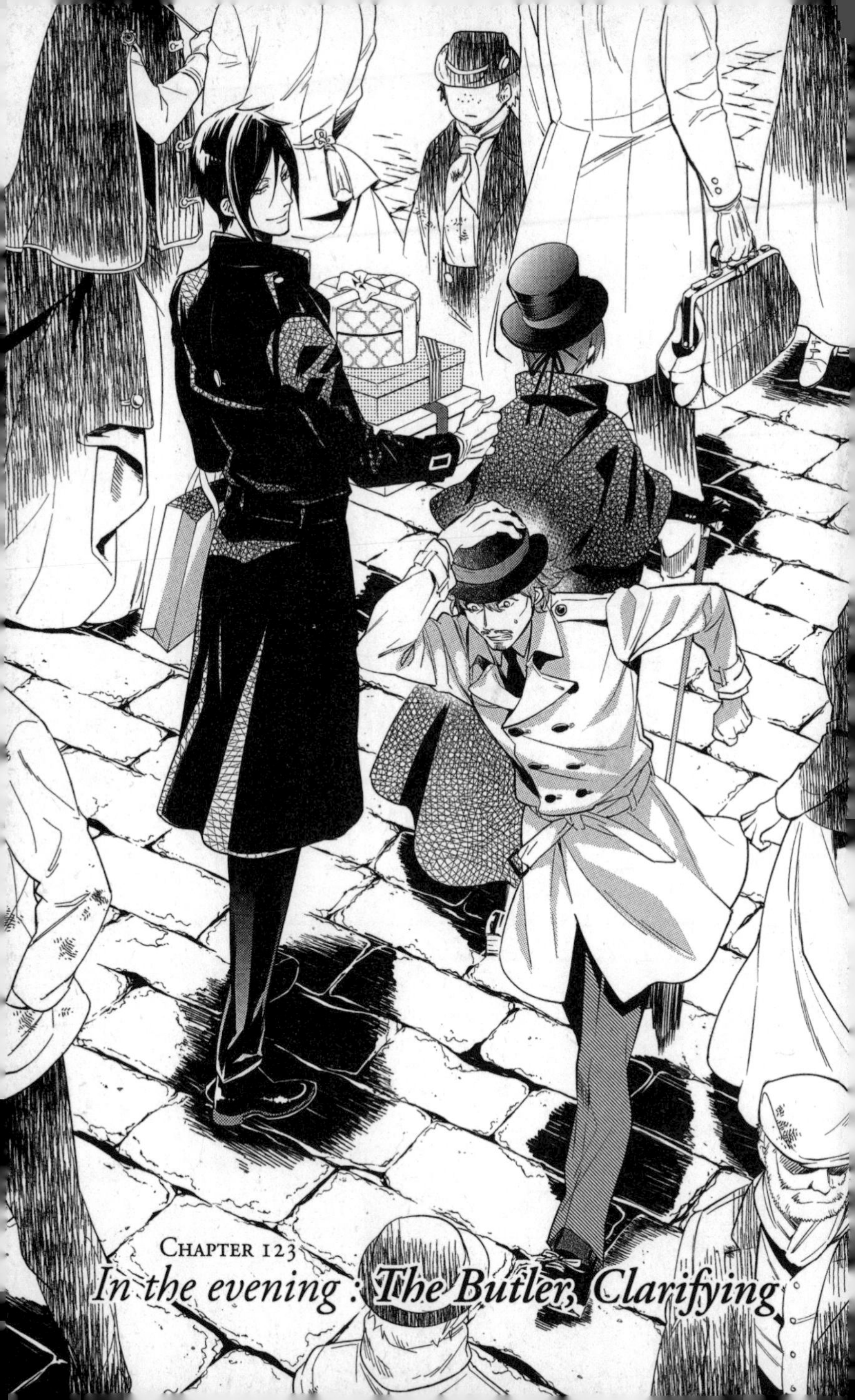

Chapter 123
In the evening : The Butler, Clarifying

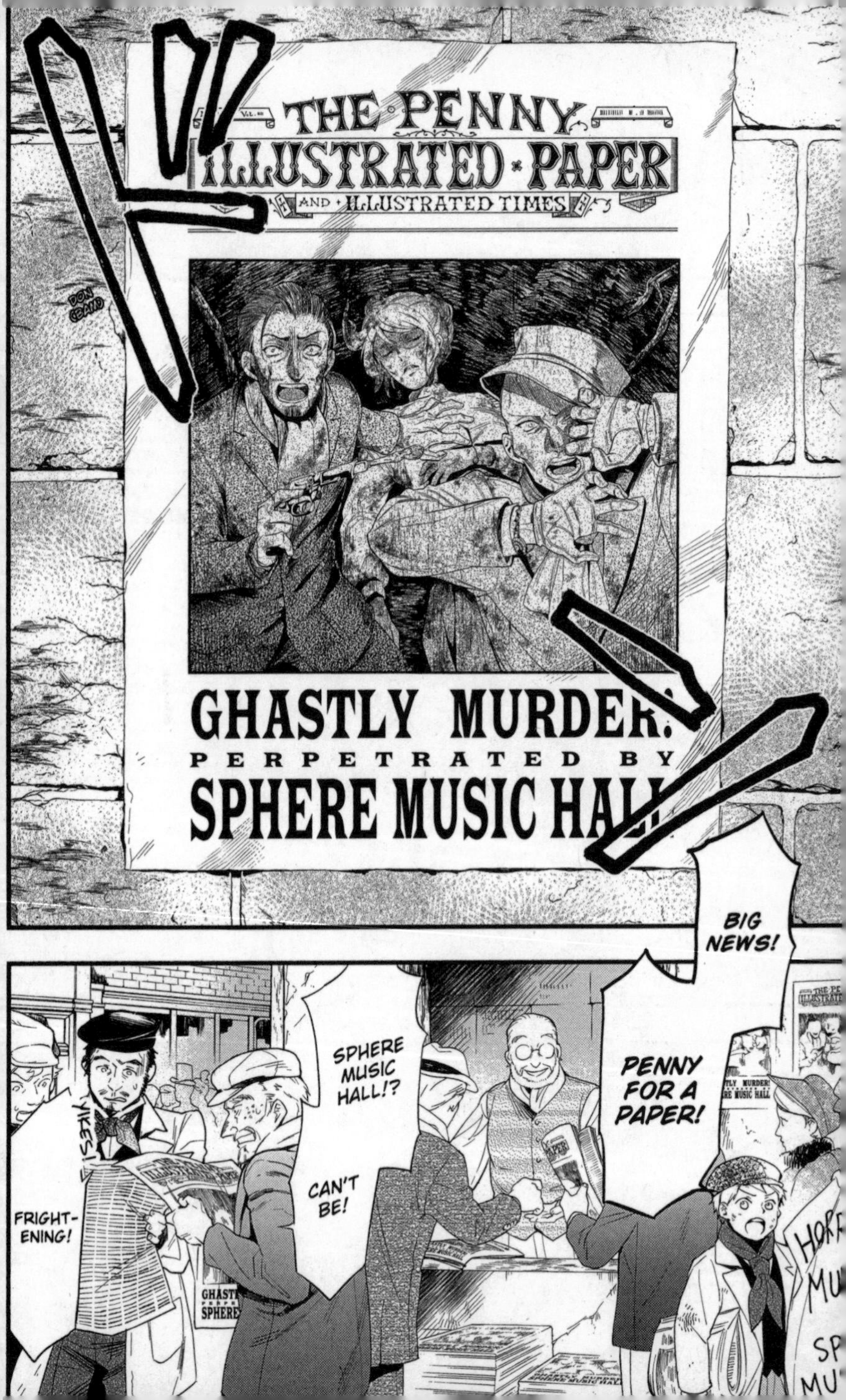
THE PENNY ILLUSTRATED PAPER
AND ILLUSTRATED TIMES
DON (BAM)
GHASTLY MURDER!
PERPETRATED BY
SPHERE MUSIC HALL!
BIG NEWS!
PENNY FOR A PAPER!
SPHERE MUSIC HALL!?
CAN'T BE!
YIKES!
FRIGHT-ENING!

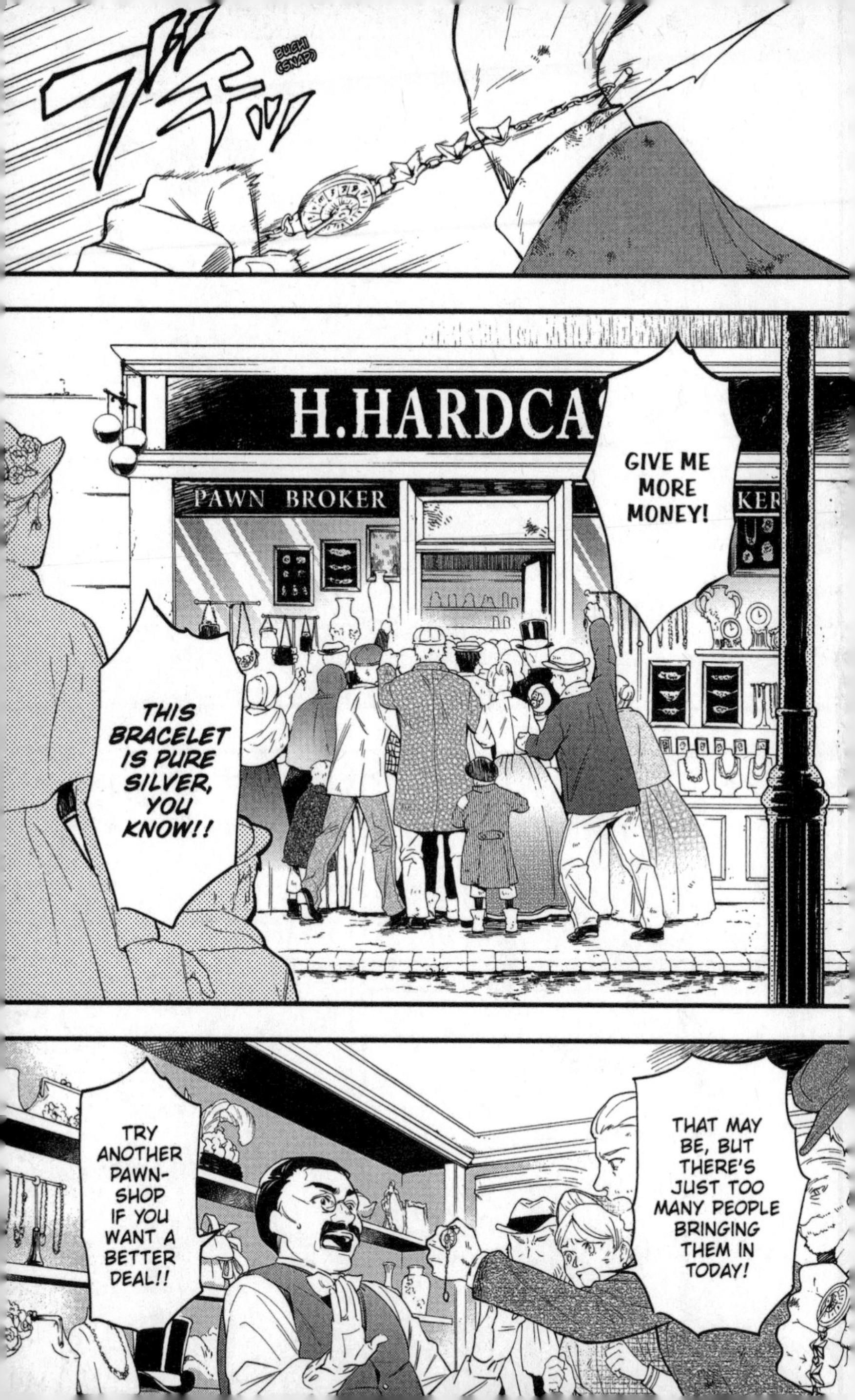
ブチッ
BUCHI (SNAP)
H.HARDCA
PAWN BROKER
KER
GIVE ME MORE MONEY!
THIS BRACELET IS PURE SILVER, YOU KNOW!!
THAT MAY BE, BUT THERE'S JUST TOO MANY PEOPLE BRINGING THEM IN TODAY!
TRY ANOTHER PAWN-SHOP IF YOU WANT A BETTER DEAL!!

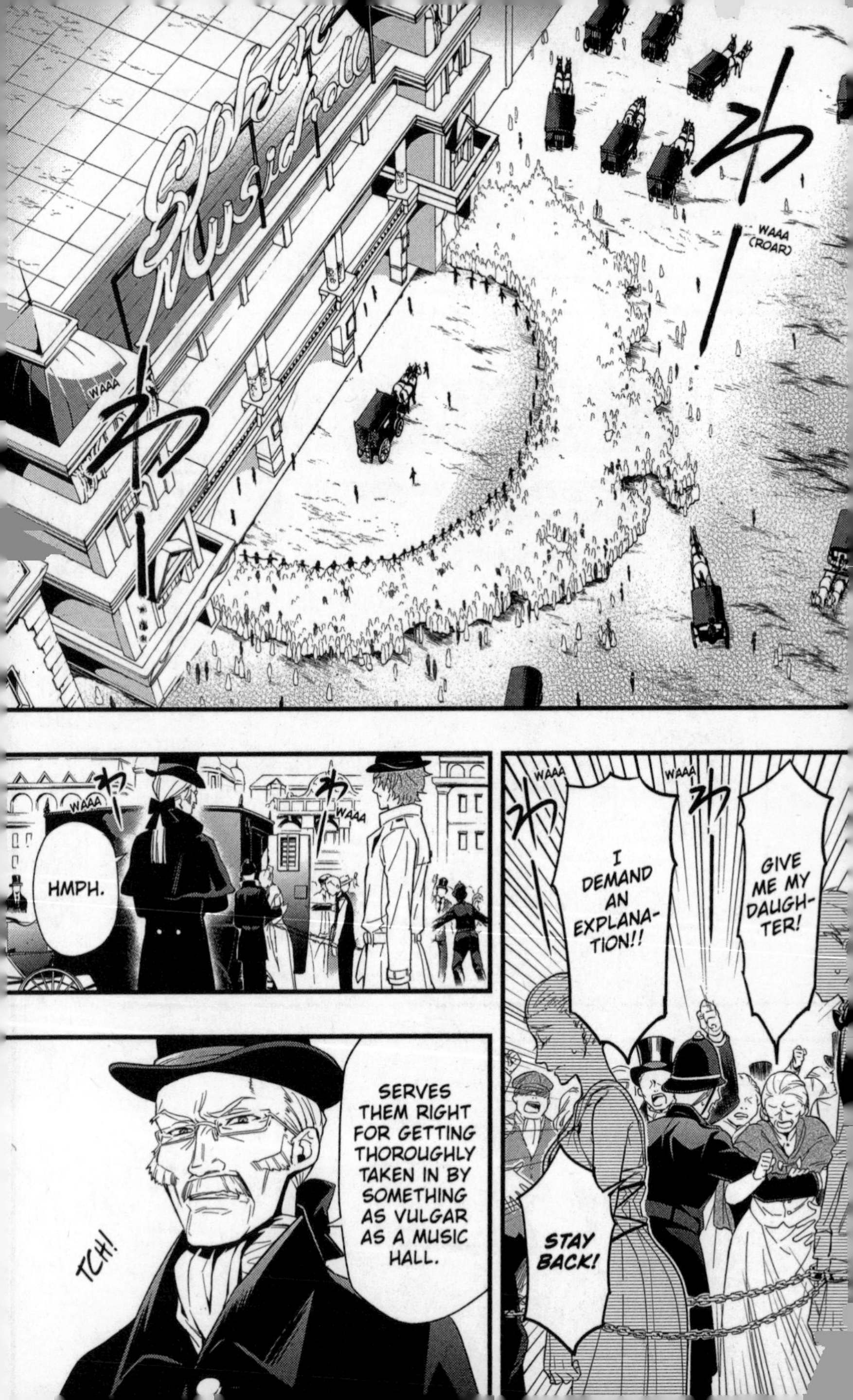
WAAA (ROAR)
WAAA
GIVE ME MY DAUGHTER!
WAAA
WAAA
I DEMAND AN EXPLANATION!!
STAY BACK!
WAAA
WAAA
HMPH.
SERVES THEM RIGHT FOR GETTING THOROUGHLY TAKEN IN BY SOMETHING AS VULGAR AS A MUSIC HALL.
TCH!

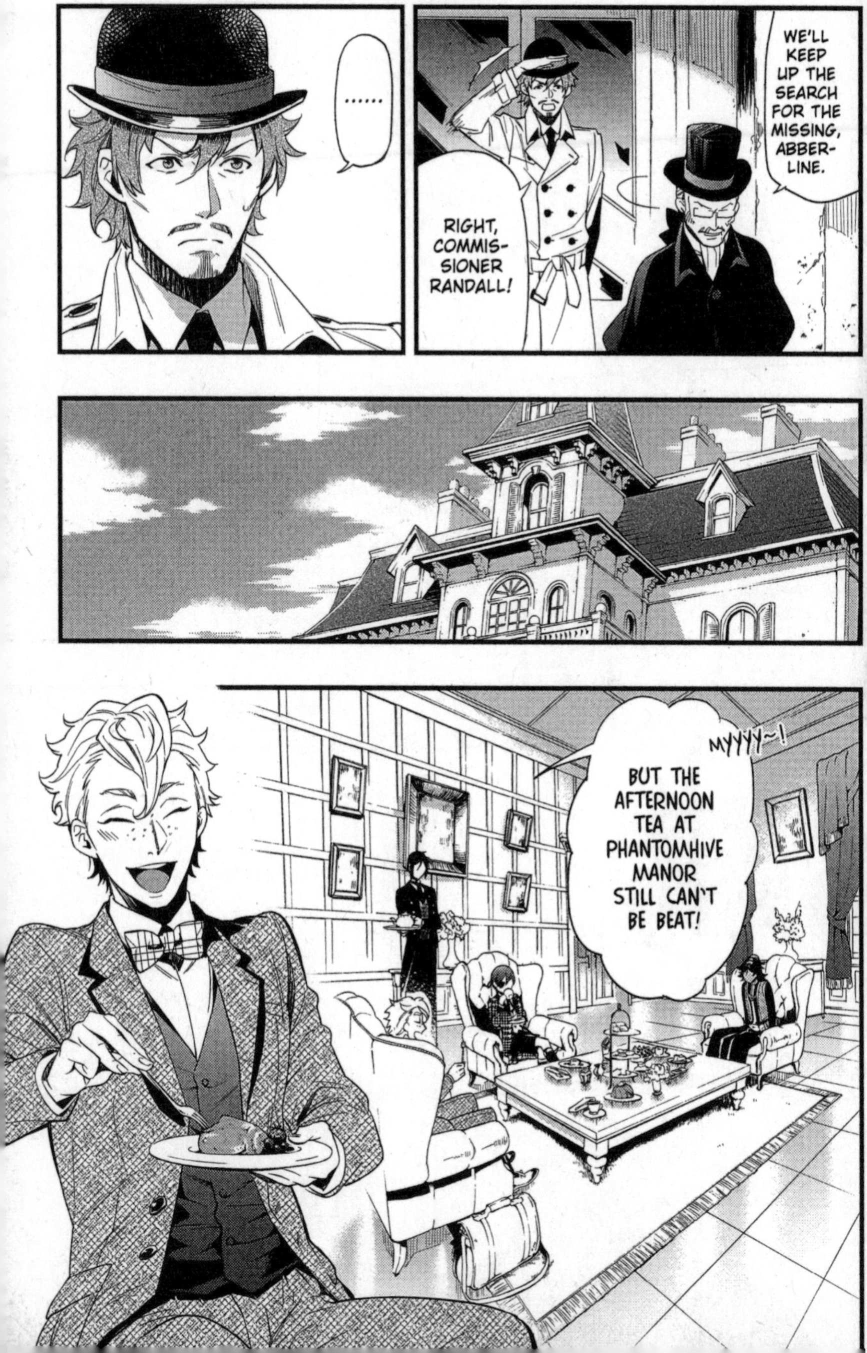
WE'LL KEEP UP THE SEARCH FOR THE MISSING, ABBER-LINE.
RIGHT, COMMIS-SIONER RANDALL!
......
MYYYY~!
BUT THE AFTERNOON TEA AT PHANTOMHIVE MANOR STILL CAN'T BE BEAT!

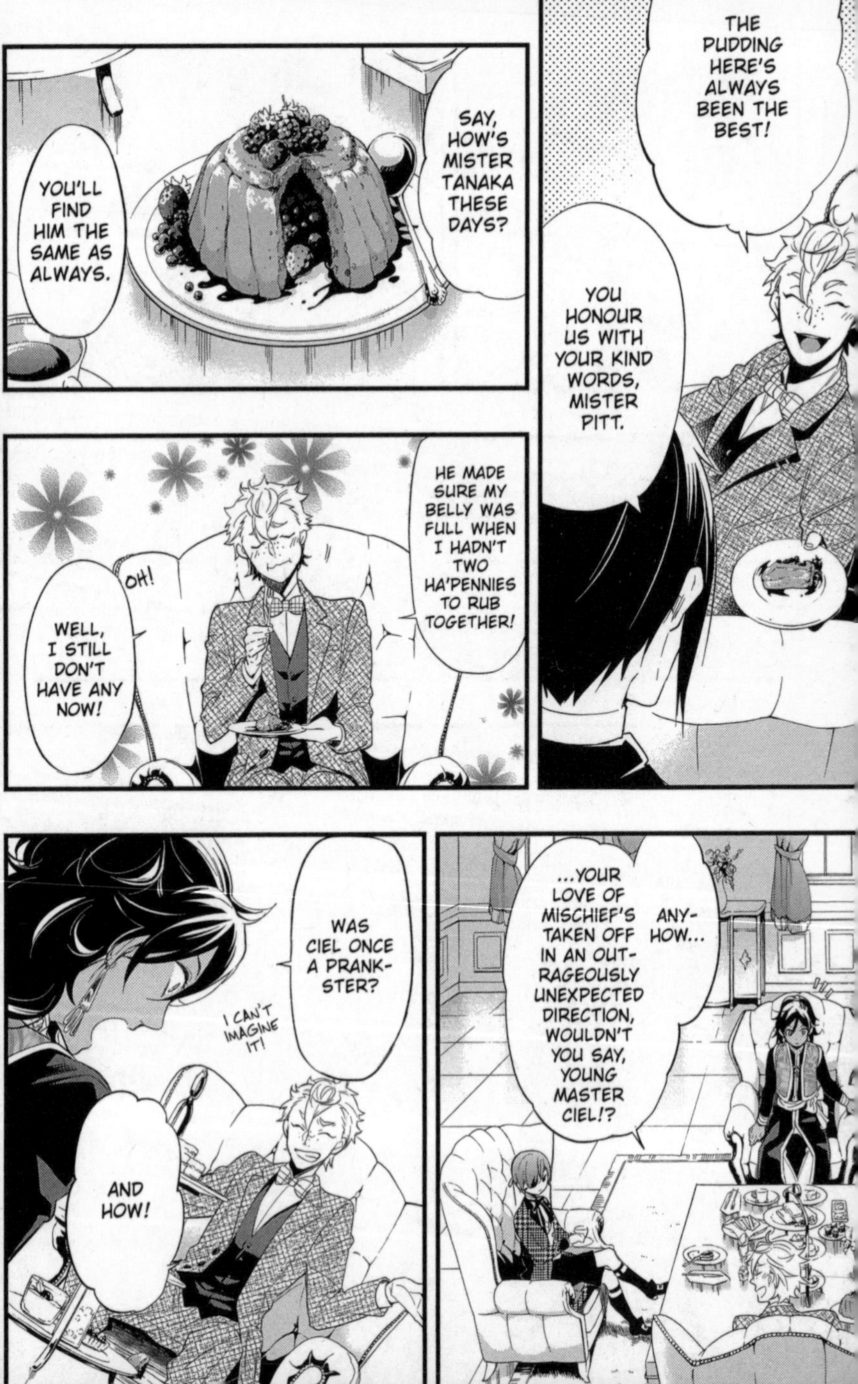
THE PUDDING HERE'S ALWAYS BEEN THE BEST!
YOU HONOUR US WITH YOUR KIND WORDS, MISTER PITT.
SAY, HOW'S MISTER TANAKA THESE DAYS?
YOU'LL FIND HIM THE SAME AS ALWAYS.
HE MADE SURE MY BELLY WAS FULL WHEN I HADN'T TWO HA'PENNIES TO RUB TOGETHER!
OH!
WELL, I STILL DON'T HAVE ANY NOW!
ANY-HOW...
...YOUR LOVE OF MISCHIEF'S TAKEN OFF IN AN OUT-RAGEOUSLY UNEXPECTED DIRECTION, WOULDN'T YOU SAY, YOUNG MASTER CIEL!?
WAS CIEL ONCE A PRANK-STER?
I CAN'T IMAGINE IT!
AND HOW!

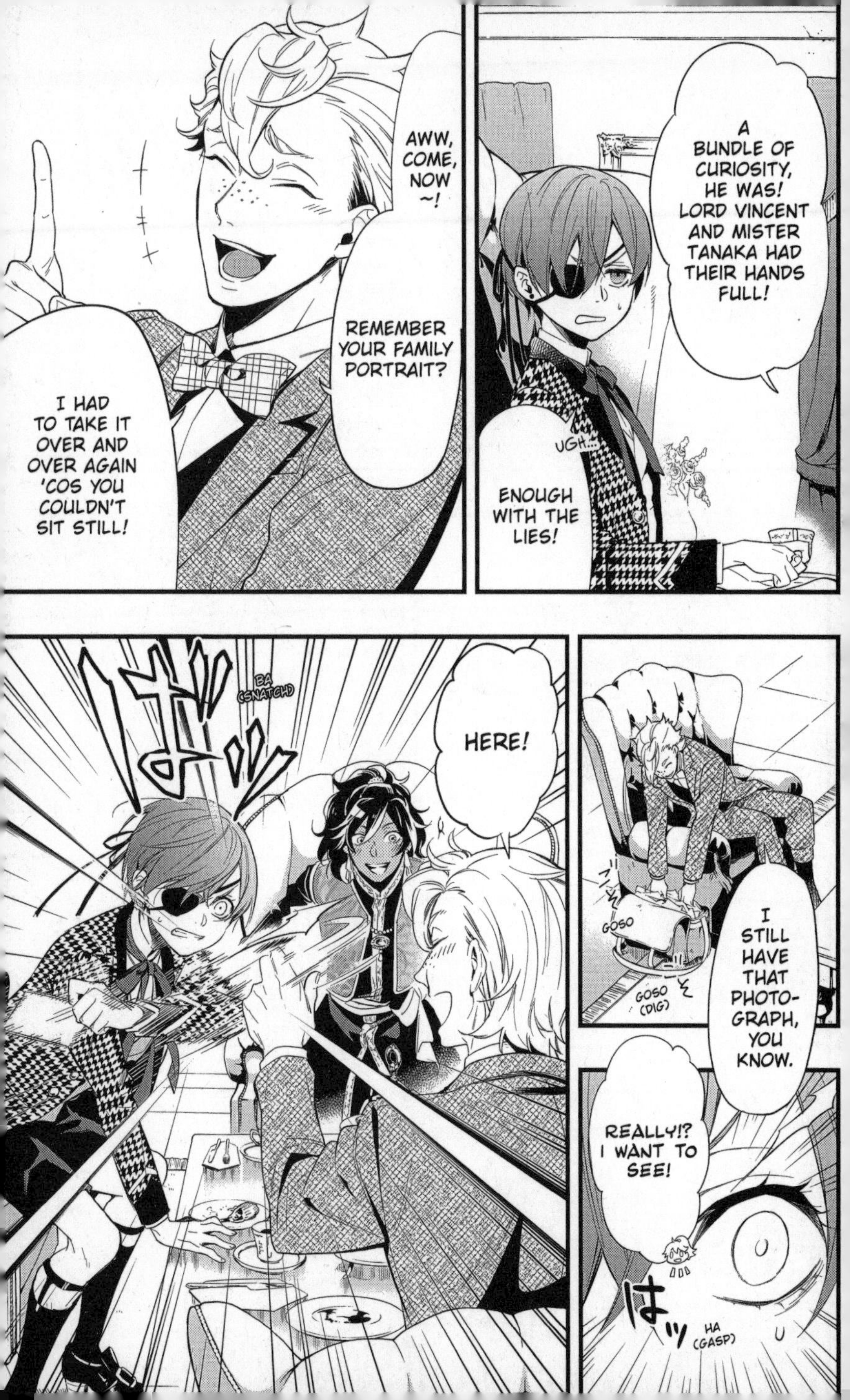
A BUNDLE OF CURIOSITY, HE WAS! LORD VINCENT AND MISTER TANAKA HAD THEIR HANDS FULL!
UGH...
ENOUGH WITH THE LIES!
AWW, COME, NOW ~!
REMEMBER YOUR FAMILY PORTRAIT?
I HAD TO TAKE IT OVER AND OVER AGAIN 'COS YOU COULDN'T SIT STILL!
GOSO
GOSO (DIG)
I STILL HAVE THAT PHOTOGRAPH, YOU KNOW.
REALLY!? I WANT TO SEE!
HA (GASP)
HERE!
BA (SNATCH)

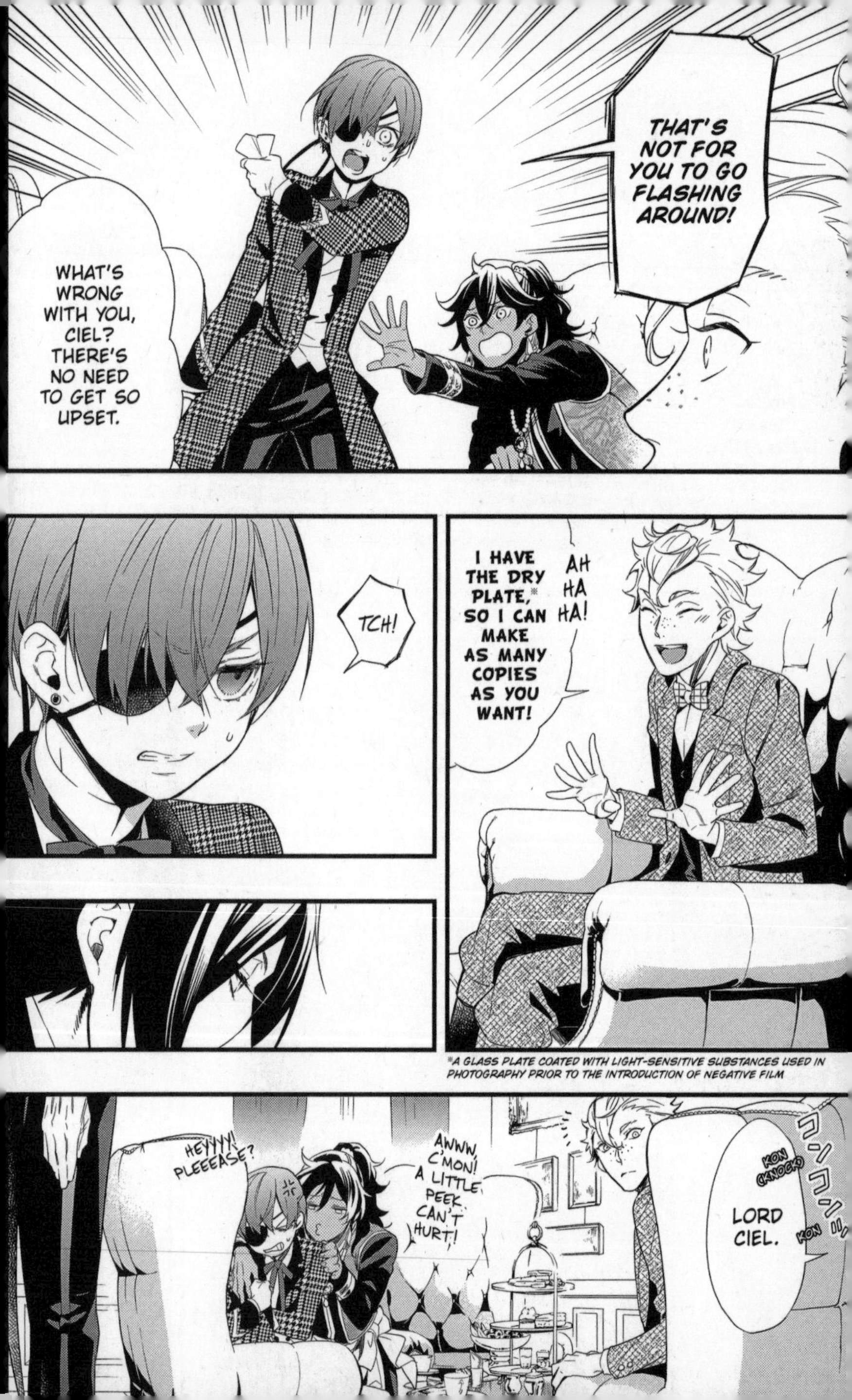
THAT'S NOT FOR YOU TO GO FLASHING AROUND!
WHAT'S WRONG WITH YOU, CIEL? THERE'S NO NEED TO GET SO UPSET.
AH HA HA!
I HAVE THE DRY PLATE,* SO I CAN MAKE AS MANY COPIES AS YOU WANT!
TCH!
KON KON (KNOCK)
LORD CIEL.
AWWW, C'MON! A LITTLE PEEK CAN'T HURT!
HEYYY! PLEEEASE?

*A GLASS PLATE COATED WITH LIGHT-SENSITIVE SUBSTANCES USED IN PHOTOGRAPHY PRIOR TO THE INTRODUCTION OF NEGATIVE FILM

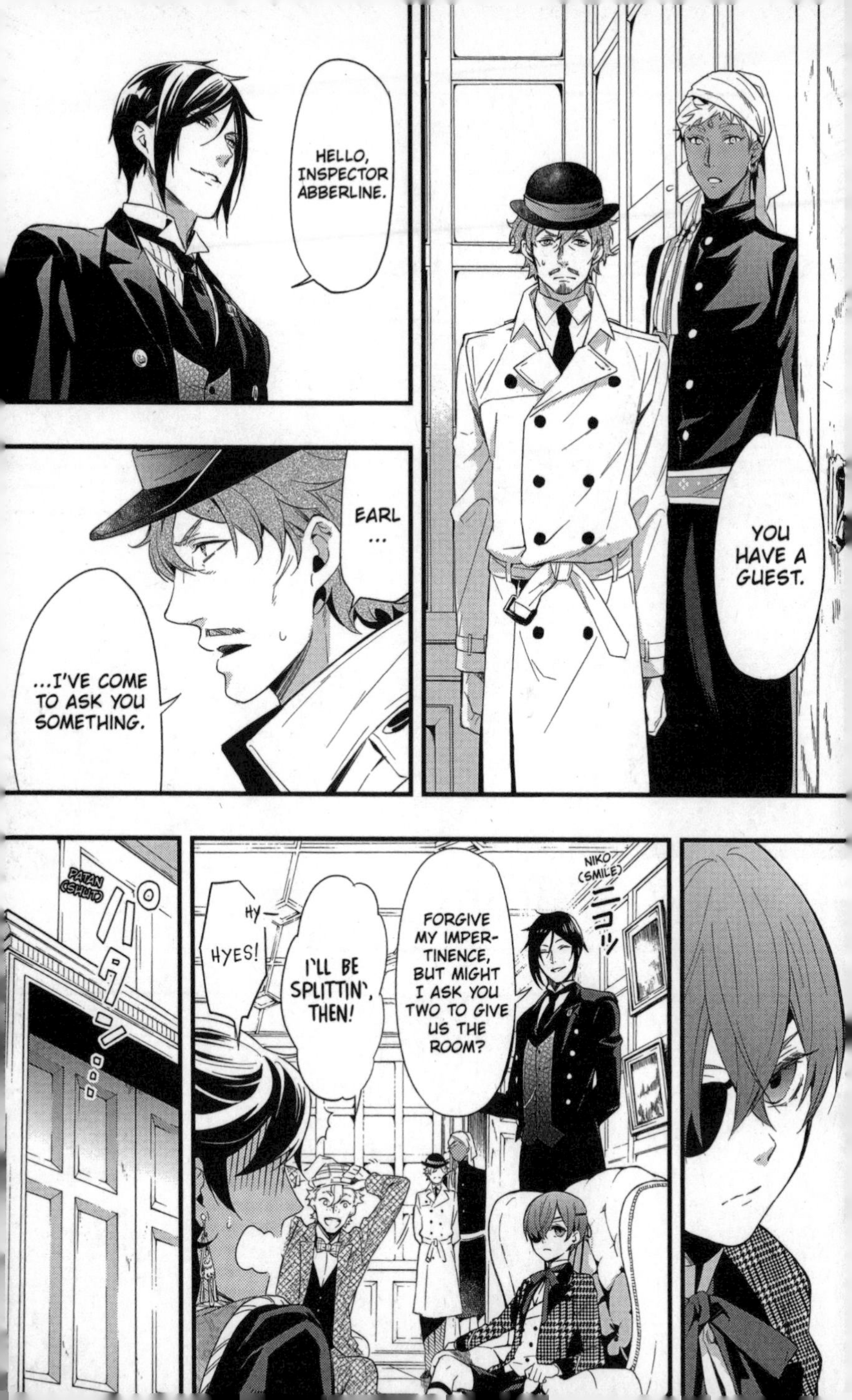
YOU HAVE A GUEST.
HELLO, INSPECTOR ABBERLINE.
EARL ...
...I'VE COME TO ASK YOU SOMETHING.
NIKO (SMILE)
ニコッ
FORGIVE MY IMPER-TINENCE, BUT MIGHT I ASK YOU TWO TO GIVE US THE ROOM?
I'LL BE SPLITTIN', THEN!
HY— HYES!
PATAN (SHUT)
パタン

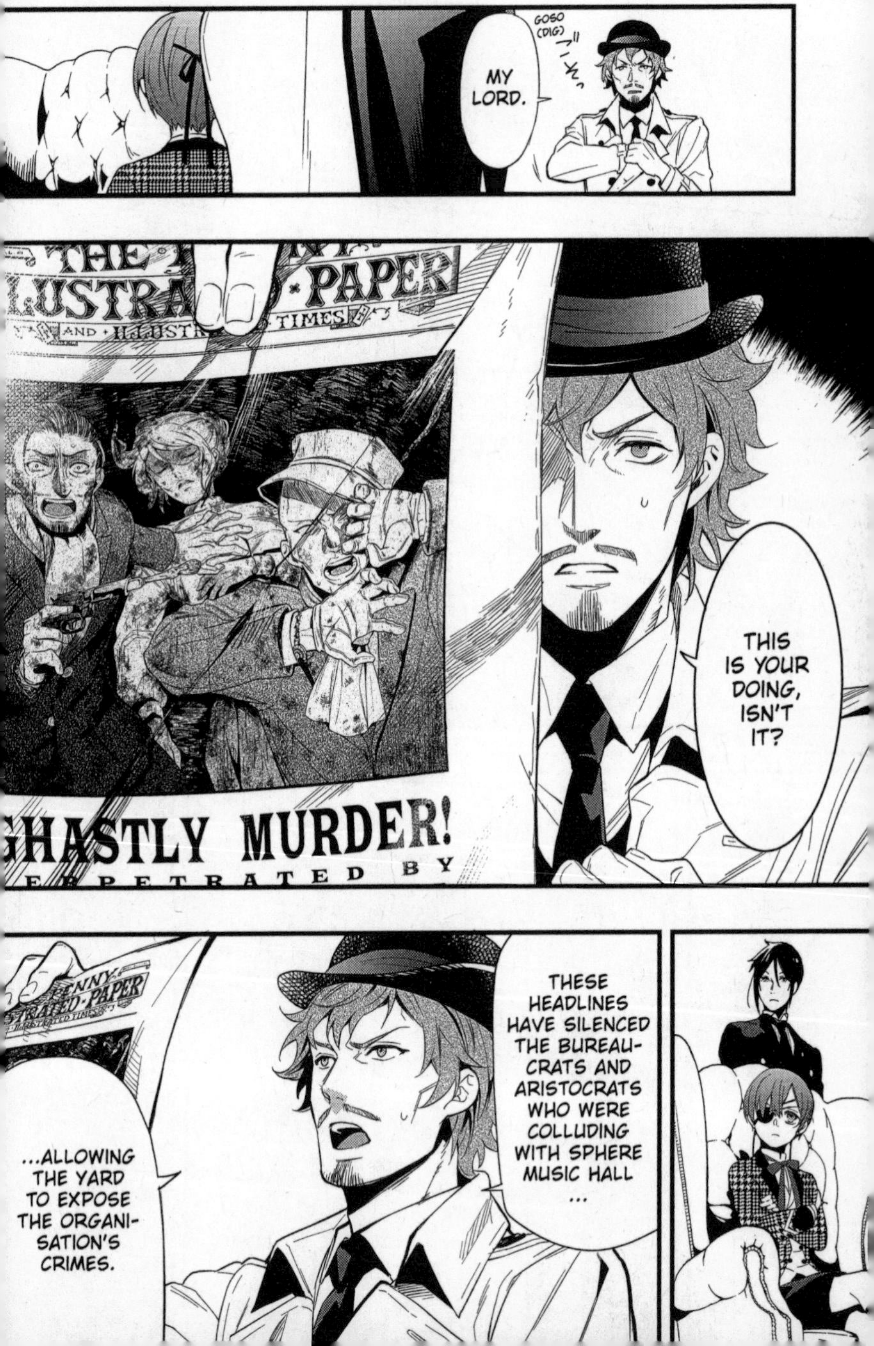
GOSO (DIG)
MY LORD.
THIS IS YOUR DOING, ISN'T IT?
GHASTLY MURDER!
THESE HEADLINES HAVE SILENCED THE BUREAU-CRATS AND ARISTOCRATS WHO WERE COLLUDING WITH SPHERE MUSIC HALL ...
...ALLOWING THE YARD TO EXPOSE THE ORGANI-SATION'S CRIMES.

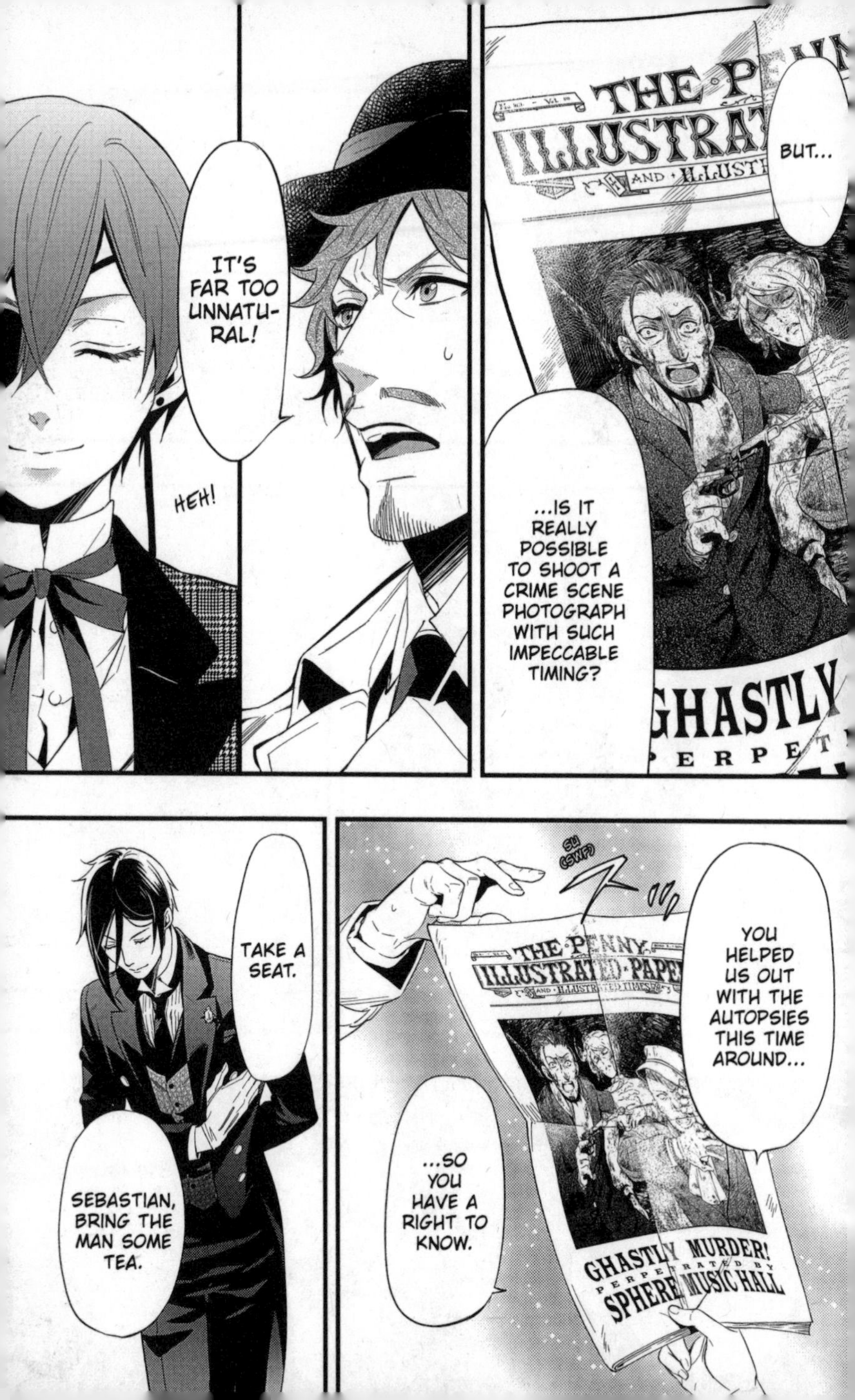
BUT...
...IS IT REALLY POSSIBLE TO SHOOT A CRIME SCENE PHOTOGRAPH WITH SUCH IMPECCABLE TIMING?
GHASTLY
IT'S FAR TOO UNNATU-RAL!
HEH!
SU (SWF)
YOU HELPED US OUT WITH THE AUTOPSIES THIS TIME AROUND...
...SO YOU HAVE A RIGHT TO KNOW.
THE PENNY ILLUSTRATED PAPER
AND ILLUSTRATED TIMES
GHASTLY MURDER!
PERPETRATED BY
SPHERE MUSIC HALL
TAKE A SEAT.
SEBASTIAN, BRING THE MAN SOME TEA.

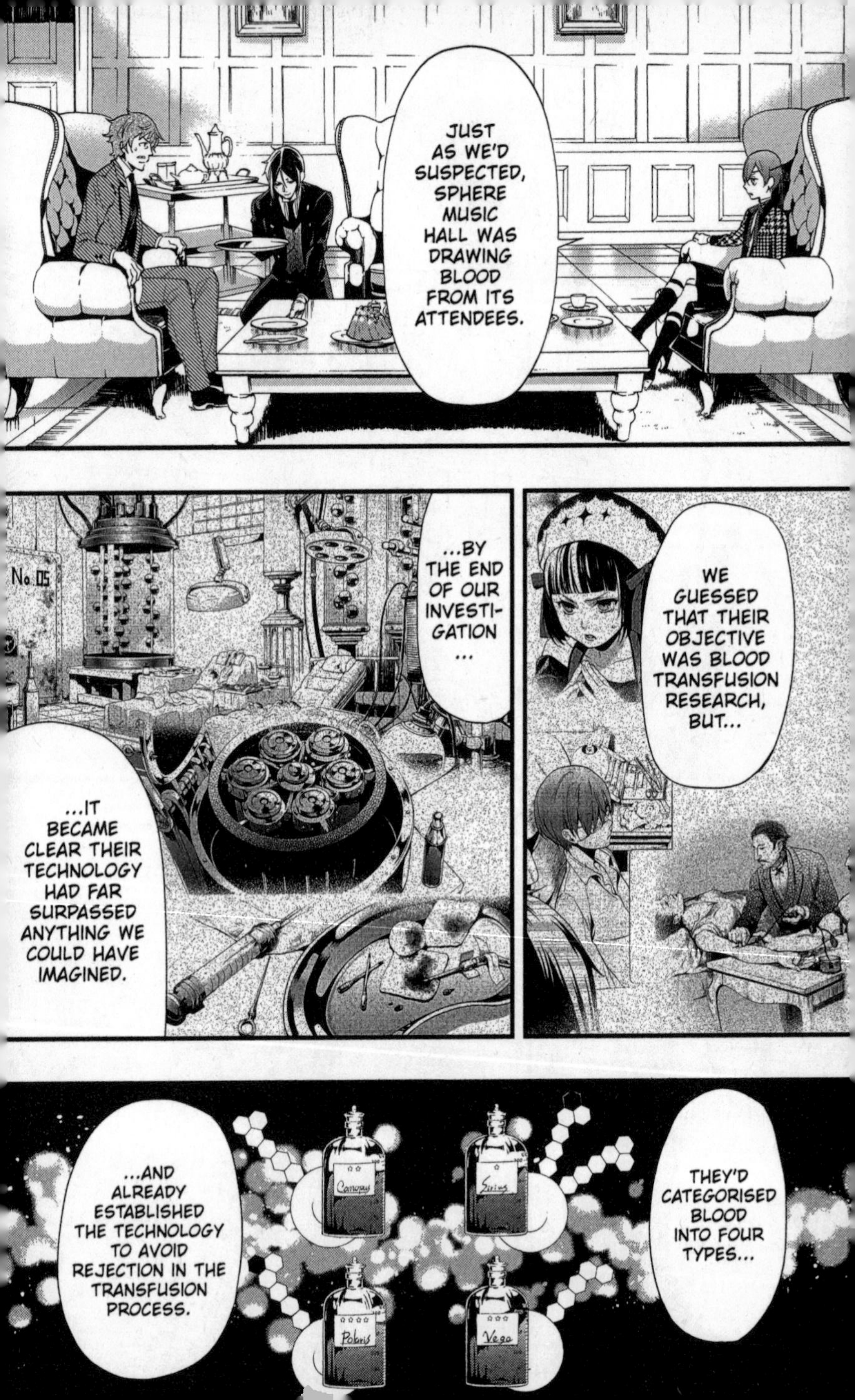
JUST AS WE'D SUSPECTED, SPHERE MUSIC HALL WAS DRAWING BLOOD FROM ITS ATTENDEES.
WE GUESSED THAT THEIR OBJECTIVE WAS BLOOD TRANSFUSION RESEARCH, BUT...
No. 05
...BY THE END OF OUR INVESTIGATION...
...IT BECAME CLEAR THEIR TECHNOLOGY HAD FAR SURPASSED ANYTHING WE COULD HAVE IMAGINED.
THEY'D CATEGORISED BLOOD INTO FOUR TYPES...
Sirius
Canopus
Vega
Polaris
...AND ALREADY ESTABLISHED THE TECHNOLOGY TO AVOID REJECTION IN THE TRANSFUSION PROCESS.

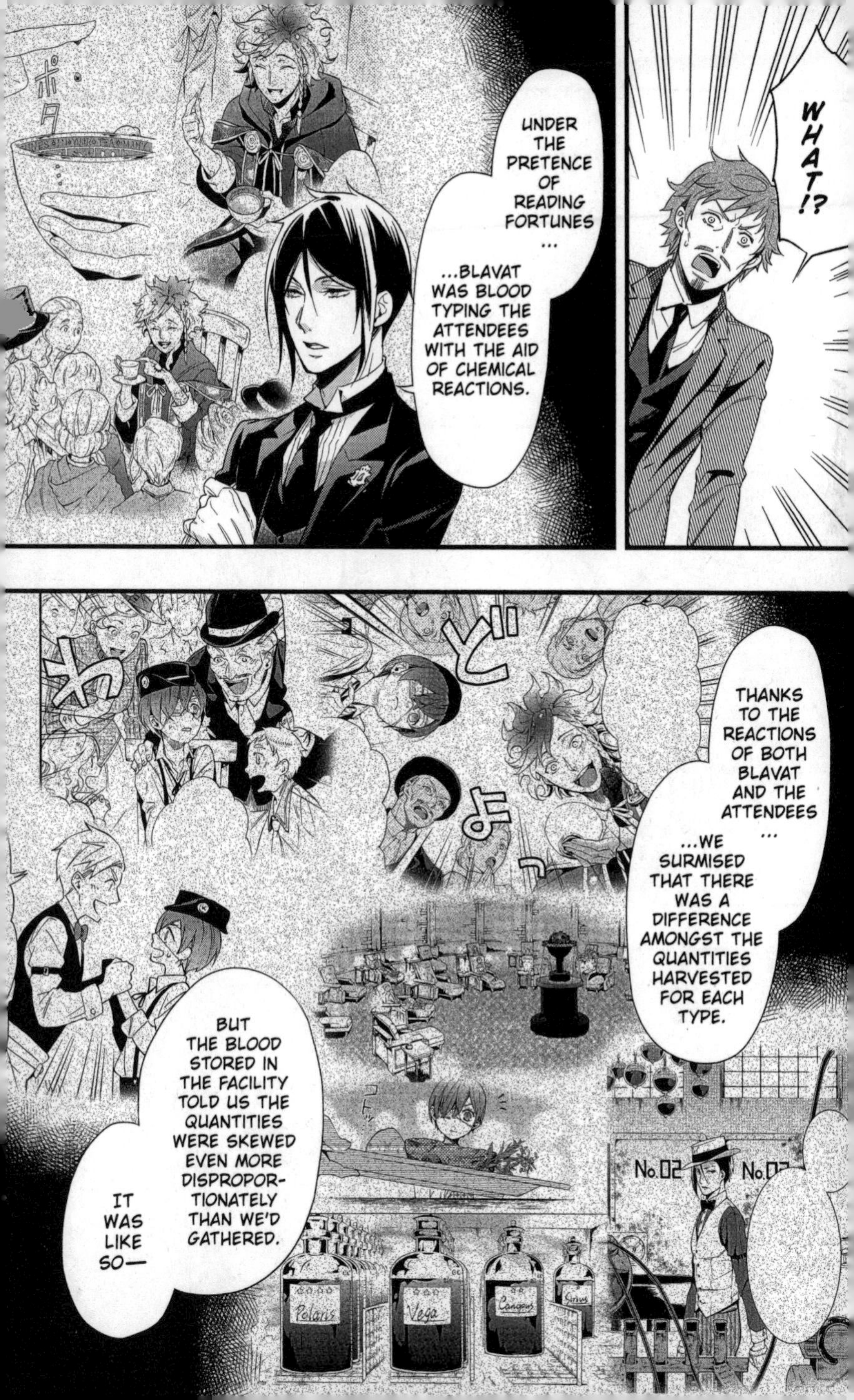
WHAT!?
UNDER THE PRETENCE OF READING FORTUNES ...
...BLAVAT WAS BLOOD TYPING THE ATTENDEES WITH THE AID OF CHEMICAL REACTIONS.
ポタ
THANKS TO THE REACTIONS OF BOTH BLAVAT AND THE ATTENDEES ...
...WE SURMISED THAT THERE WAS A DIFFERENCE AMONGST THE QUANTITIES HARVESTED FOR EACH TYPE.
No.02
BUT THE BLOOD STORED IN THE FACILITY TOLD US THE QUANTITIES WERE SKEWED EVEN MORE DISPROPOR-TIONATELY THAN WE'D GATHERED.
IT WAS LIKE SO—
Polaris
Vega
Canopus
Sirius

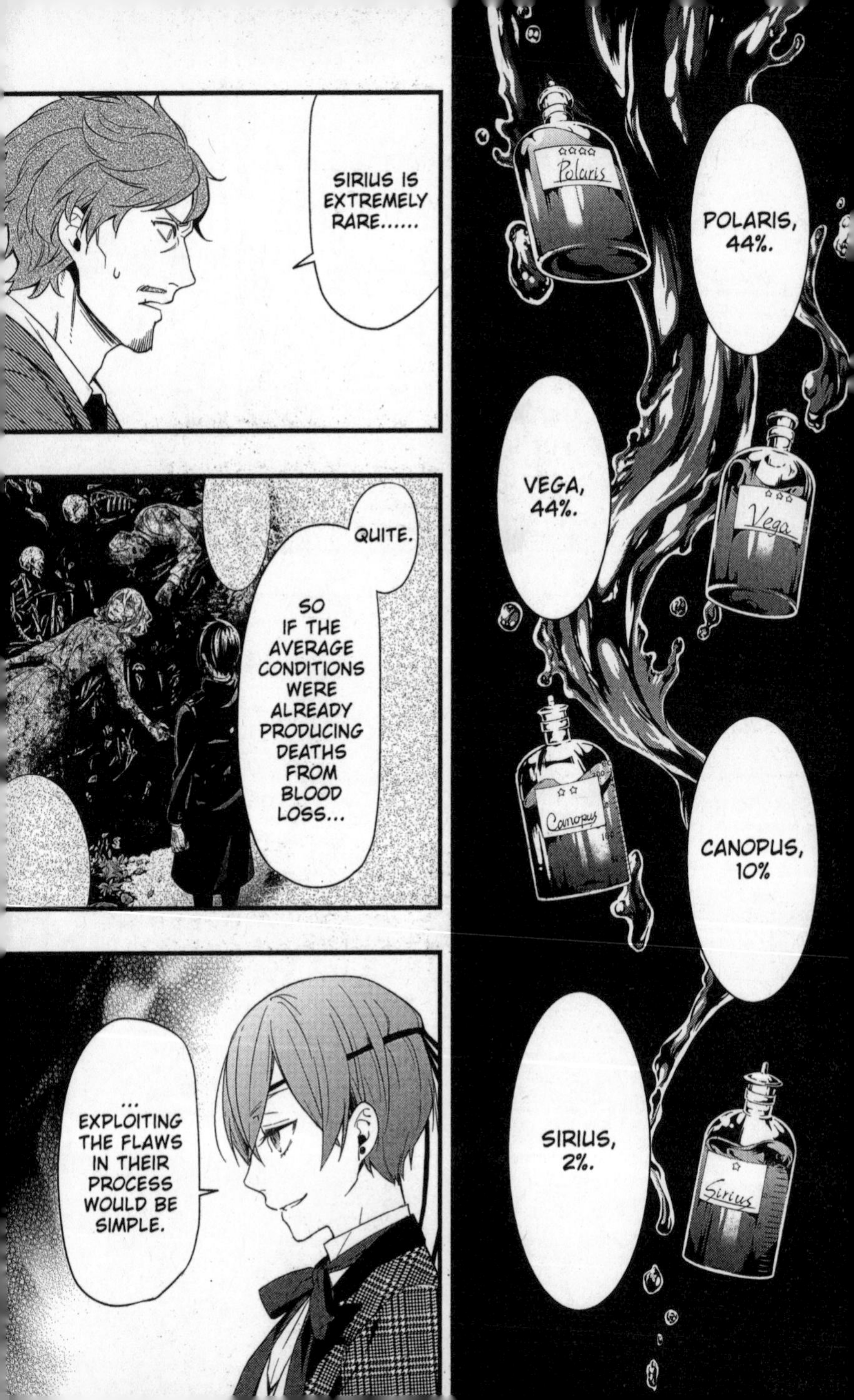
Polaris
POLARIS, 44%.
VEGA, 44%.
Vega
Canopus
CANOPUS, 10%
SIRIUS, 2%.
Sirius
SIRIUS IS EXTREMELY RARE......
QUITE.
SO IF THE AVERAGE CONDITIONS WERE ALREADY PRODUCING DEATHS FROM BLOOD LOSS...
...EXPLOITING THE FLAWS IN THEIR PROCESS WOULD BE SIMPLE.

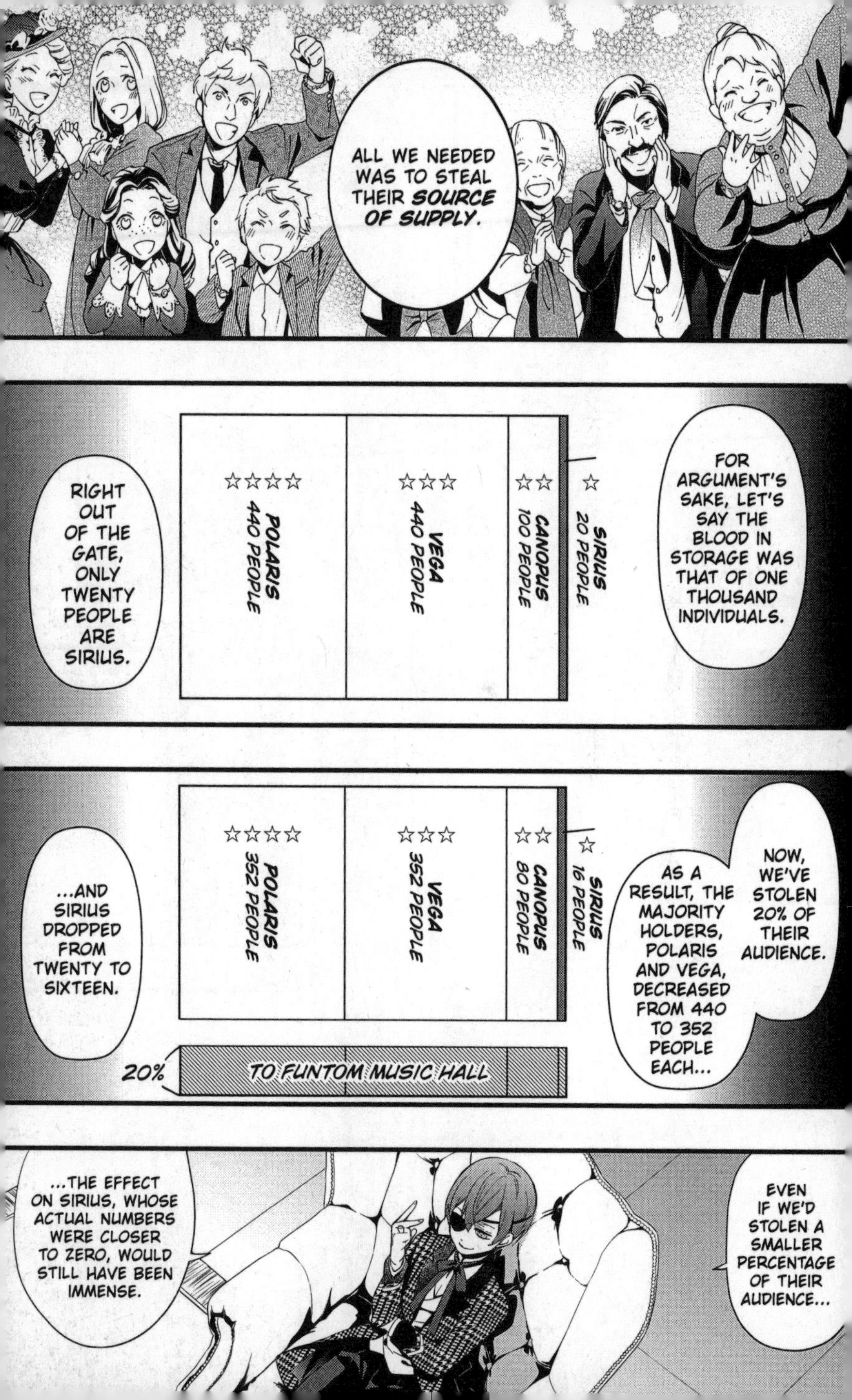
ALL WE NEEDED WAS TO STEAL THEIR *SOURCE OF SUPPLY.*
FOR ARGUMENT'S SAKE, LET'S SAY THE BLOOD IN STORAGE WAS THAT OF ONE THOUSAND INDIVIDUALS.
☆ SIRIUS 20 PEOPLE
☆☆ CANOPUS 100 PEOPLE
☆☆☆ VEGA 440 PEOPLE
☆☆☆☆ POLARIS 440 PEOPLE
RIGHT OUT OF THE GATE, ONLY TWENTY PEOPLE ARE SIRIUS.
NOW, WE'VE STOLEN 20% OF THEIR AUDIENCE.
AS A RESULT, THE MAJORITY HOLDERS, POLARIS AND VEGA, DECREASED FROM 440 TO 352 PEOPLE EACH...
☆ SIRIUS 16 PEOPLE
☆☆ CANOPUS 80 PEOPLE
☆☆☆ VEGA 352 PEOPLE
☆☆☆☆ POLARIS 352 PEOPLE
20%
TO FUNTOM MUSIC HALL
...AND SIRIUS DROPPED FROM TWENTY TO SIXTEEN.
EVEN IF WE'D STOLEN A SMALLER PERCENTAGE OF THEIR AUDIENCE...
...THE EFFECT ON SIRIUS, WHOSE ACTUAL NUMBERS WERE CLOSER TO ZERO, WOULD STILL HAVE BEEN IMMENSE.

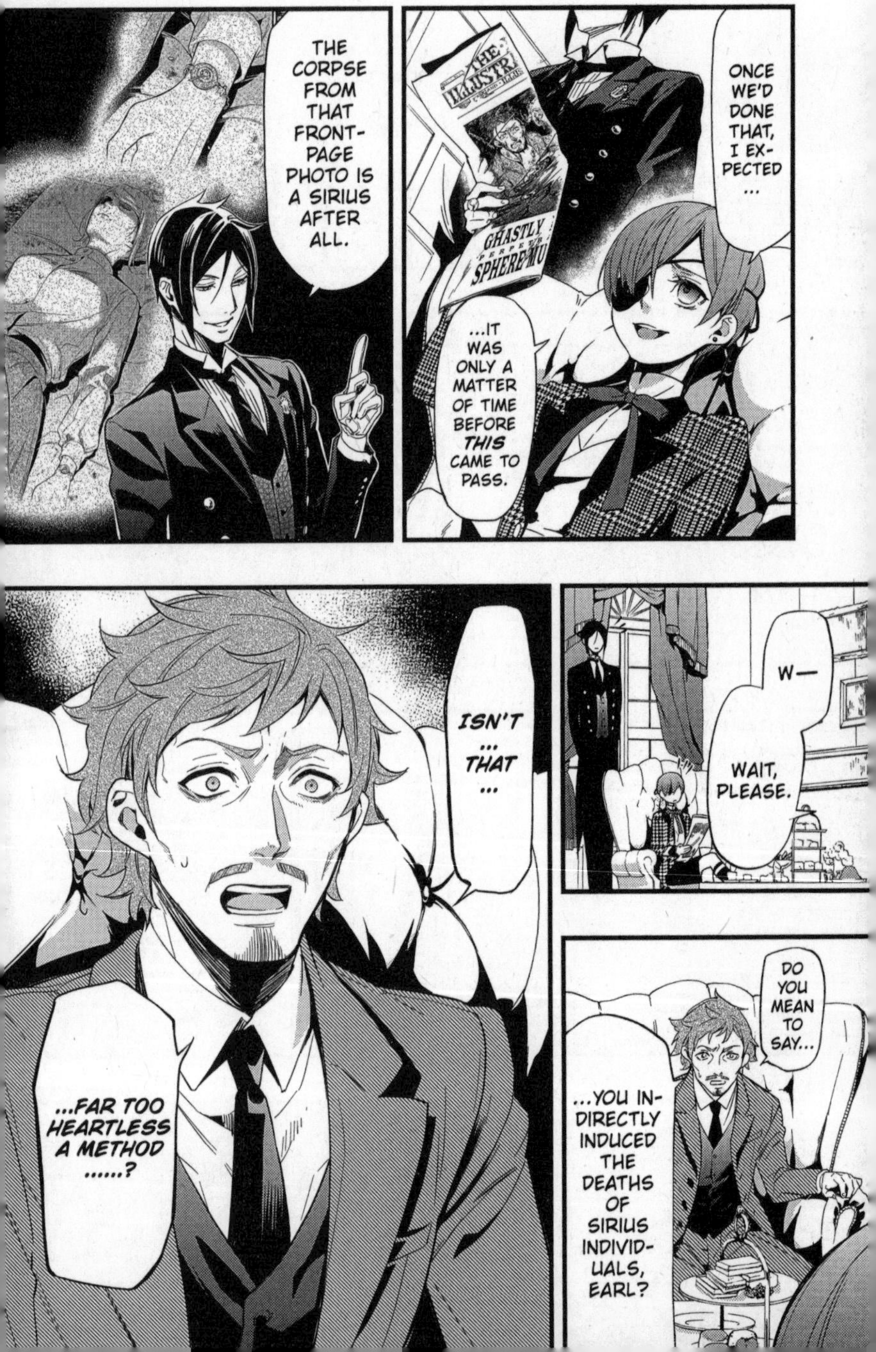

ONCE WE'D DONE THAT, I EX-PECTED ...
...IT WAS ONLY A MATTER OF TIME BEFORE *THIS* CAME TO PASS.
THE CORPSE FROM THAT FRONT-PAGE PHOTO IS A SIRIUS AFTER ALL.
W—
WAIT, PLEASE.
DO YOU MEAN TO SAY...
...YOU IN-DIRECTLY INDUCED THE DEATHS OF SIRIUS INDIVID-UALS, EARL?
ISN'T ... THAT ...
...FAR TOO HEARTLESS A METHOD ......?

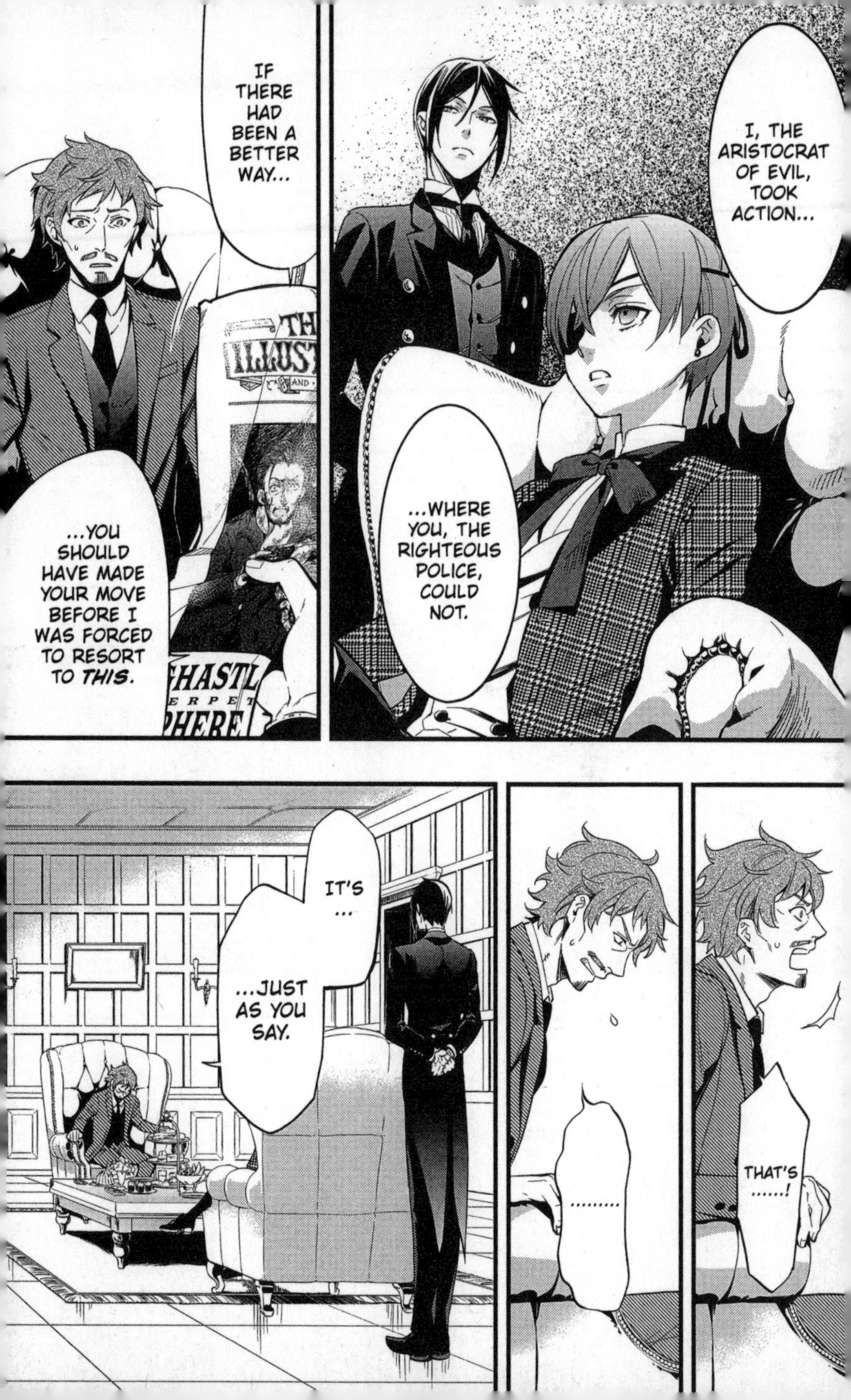
I, THE ARISTOCRAT OF EVIL, TOOK ACTION...
...WHERE YOU, THE RIGHTEOUS POLICE, COULD NOT.
IF THERE HAD BEEN A BETTER WAY...
...YOU SHOULD HAVE MADE YOUR MOVE BEFORE I WAS FORCED TO RESORT TO *THIS*.
THAT'S ......!
....
IT'S ...
...JUST AS YOU SAY.

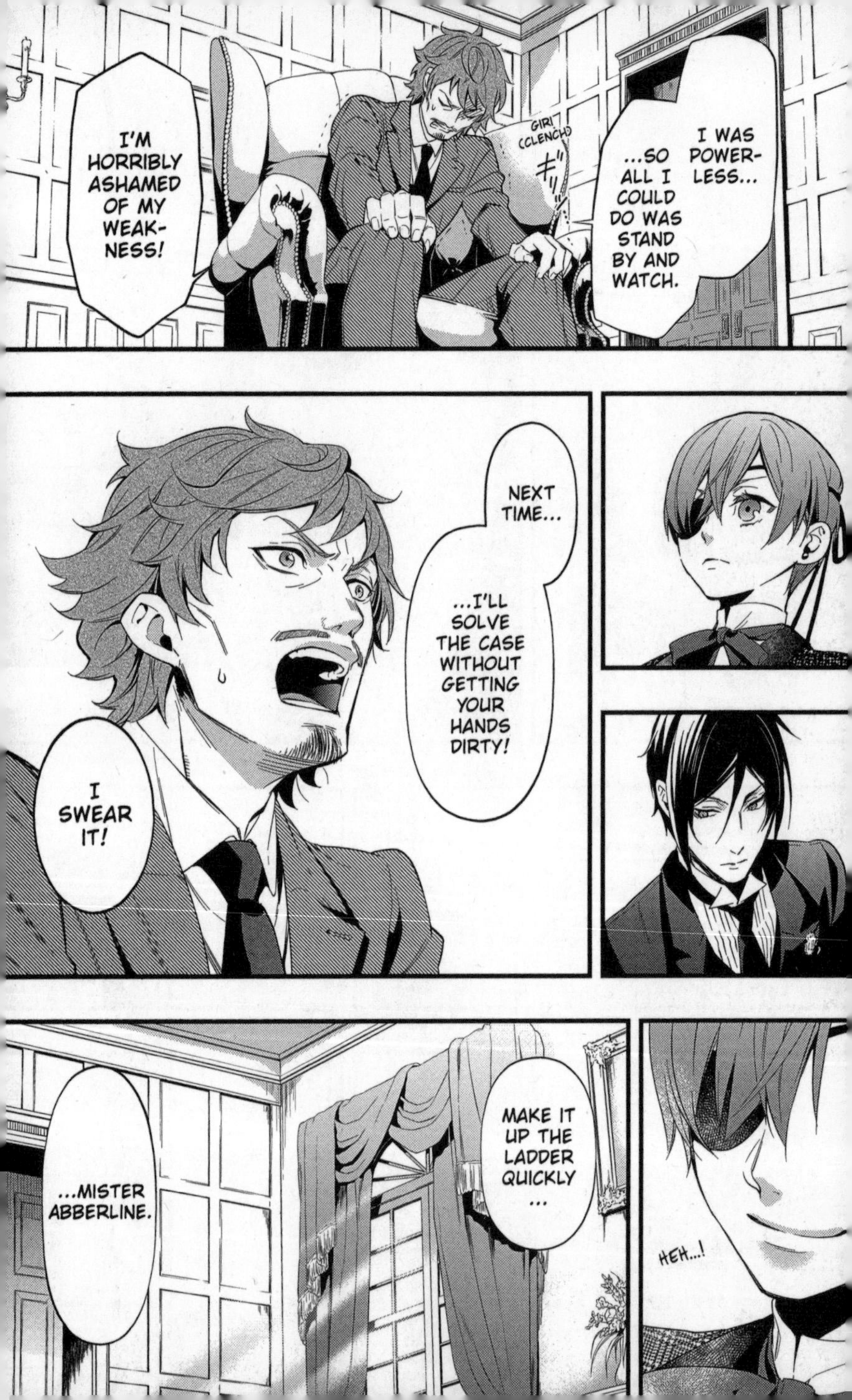
I WAS POWER-LESS...
...SO ALL I COULD DO WAS STAND BY AND WATCH.
GIRI (CLENCH)
I'M HORRIBLY ASHAMED OF MY WEAK-NESS!
NEXT TIME...
...I'LL SOLVE THE CASE WITHOUT GETTING YOUR HANDS DIRTY!
I SWEAR IT!
HEH...!
MAKE IT UP THE LADDER QUICKLY ...
...MISTER ABBERLINE.

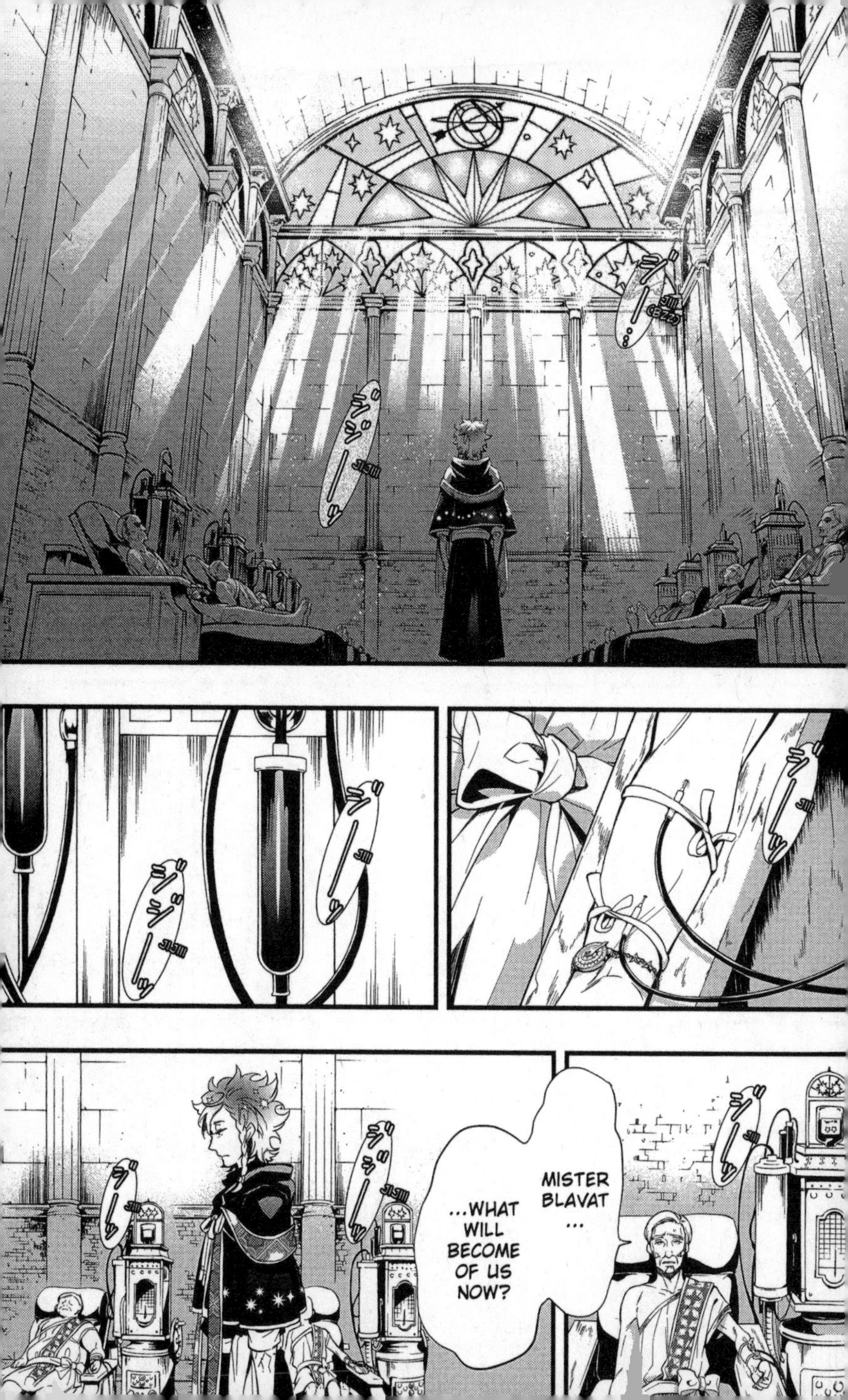
(BZZZ)
MISTER BLAVAT ...
...WHAT WILL BECOME OF US NOW?

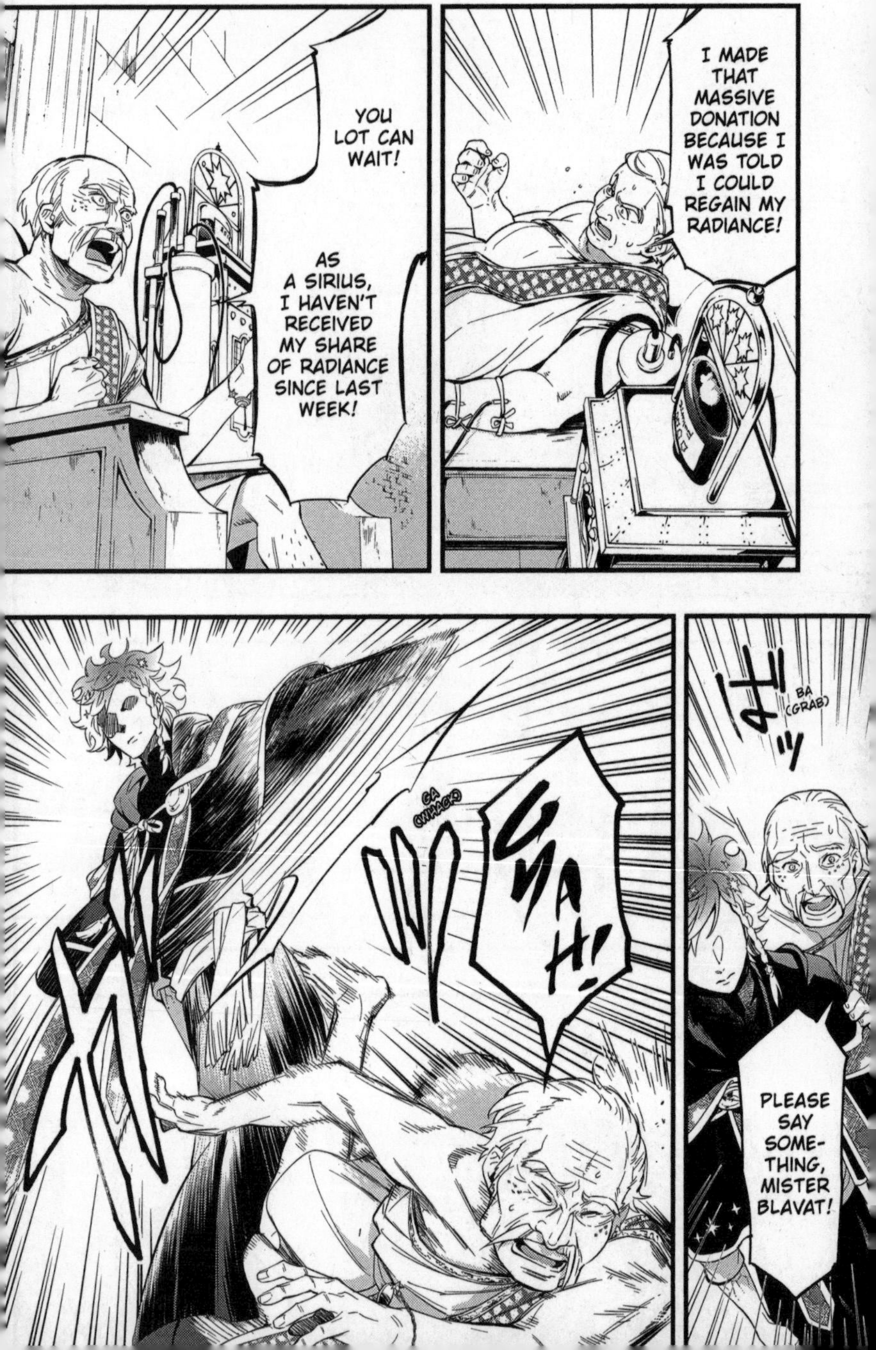
I MADE THAT MASSIVE DONATION BECAUSE I WAS TOLD I COULD REGAIN MY RADIANCE!
YOU LOT CAN WAIT!
AS A SIRIUS, I HAVEN'T RECEIVED MY SHARE OF RADIANCE SINCE LAST WEEK!
BA (GRAB)
PLEASE SAY SOME-THING, MISTER BLAVAT!
GA (WHACK)
UWAH!

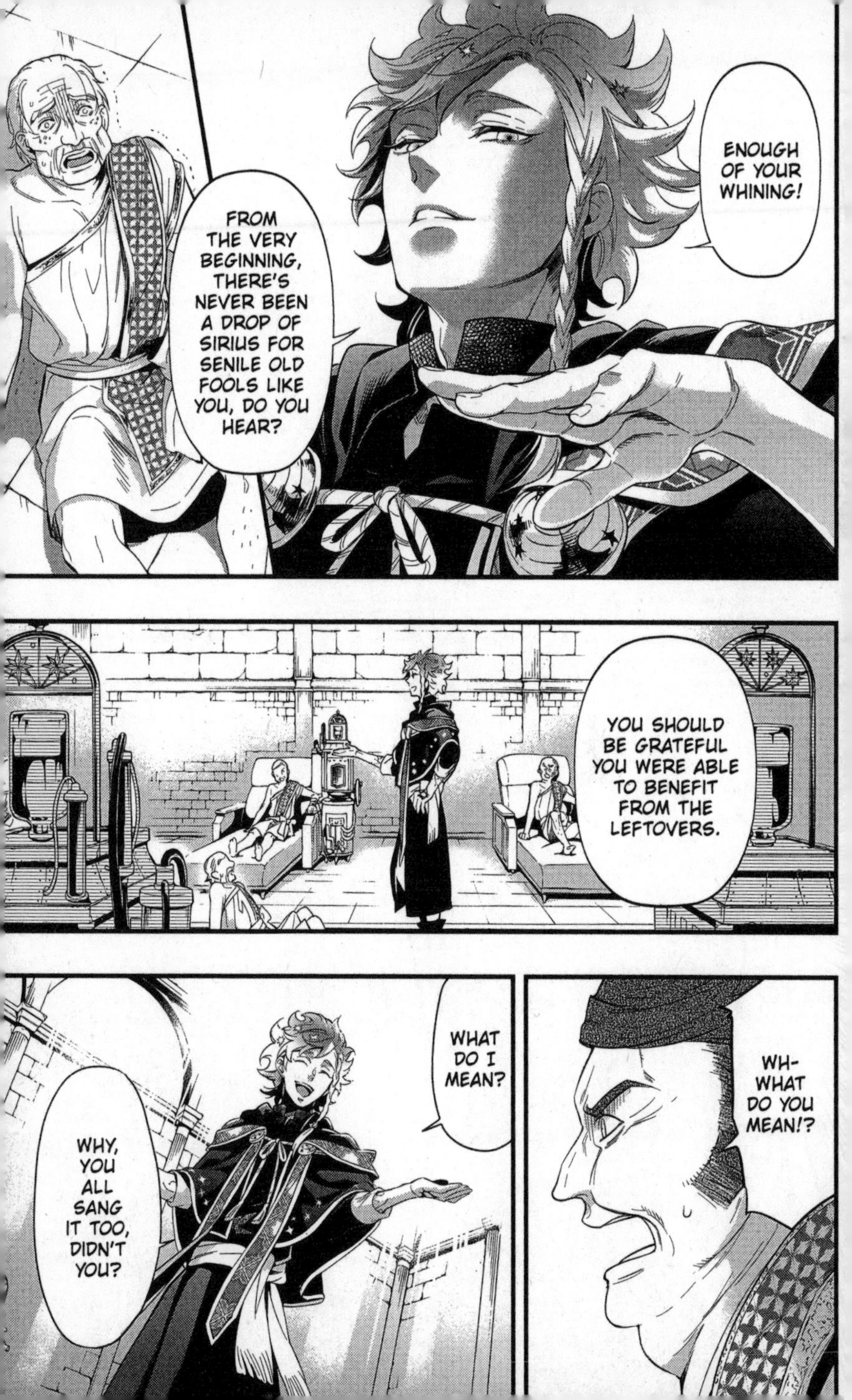
ENOUGH OF YOUR WHINING!
FROM THE VERY BEGINNING, THERE'S NEVER BEEN A DROP OF SIRIUS FOR SENILE OLD FOOLS LIKE YOU, DO YOU HEAR?
YOU SHOULD BE GRATEFUL YOU WERE ABLE TO BENEFIT FROM THE LEFTOVERS.
WH-WHAT DO YOU MEAN!?
WHAT DO I MEAN?
WHY, YOU ALL SANG IT TOO, DIDN'T YOU?

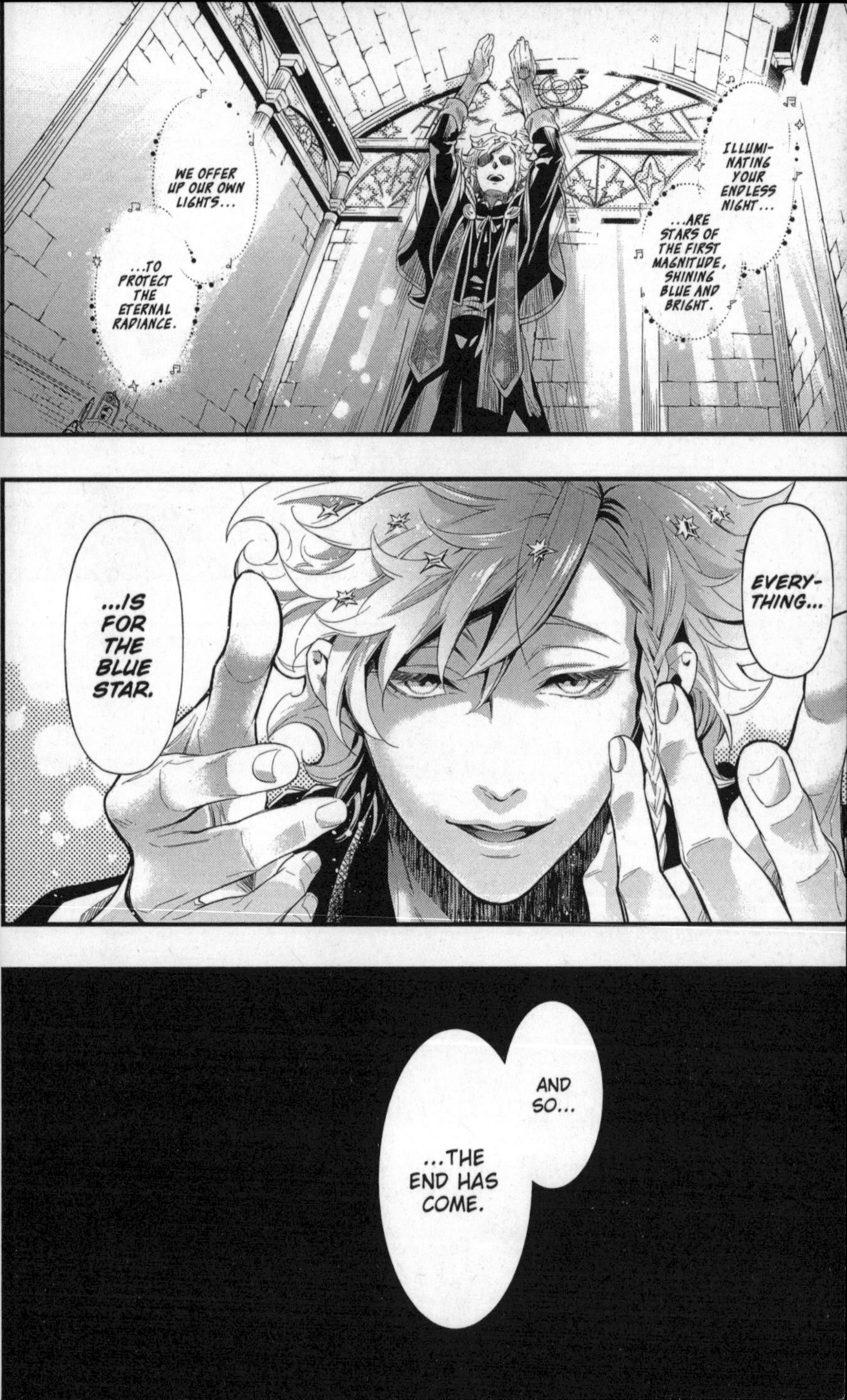
ILLUMINATING YOUR ENDLESS NIGHT...
...ARE STARS OF THE FIRST MAGNITUDE, SHINING BLUE AND BRIGHT.
WE OFFER UP OUR OWN LIGHTS...
...TO PROTECT THE ETERNAL RADIANCE.
EVERYTHING...
...IS FOR THE BLUE STAR.
AND SO...
...THE END HAS COME.

Black Butler

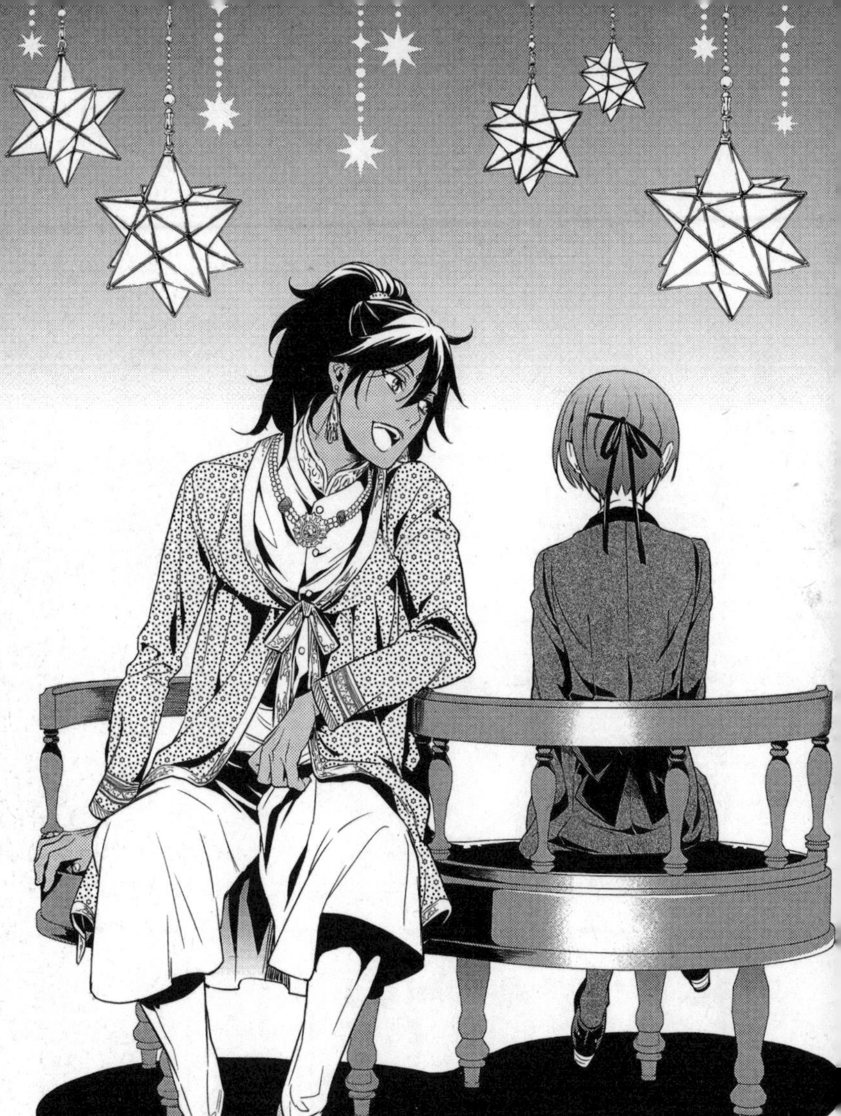

CHAPTER 124

At night : The Butler, Transporting

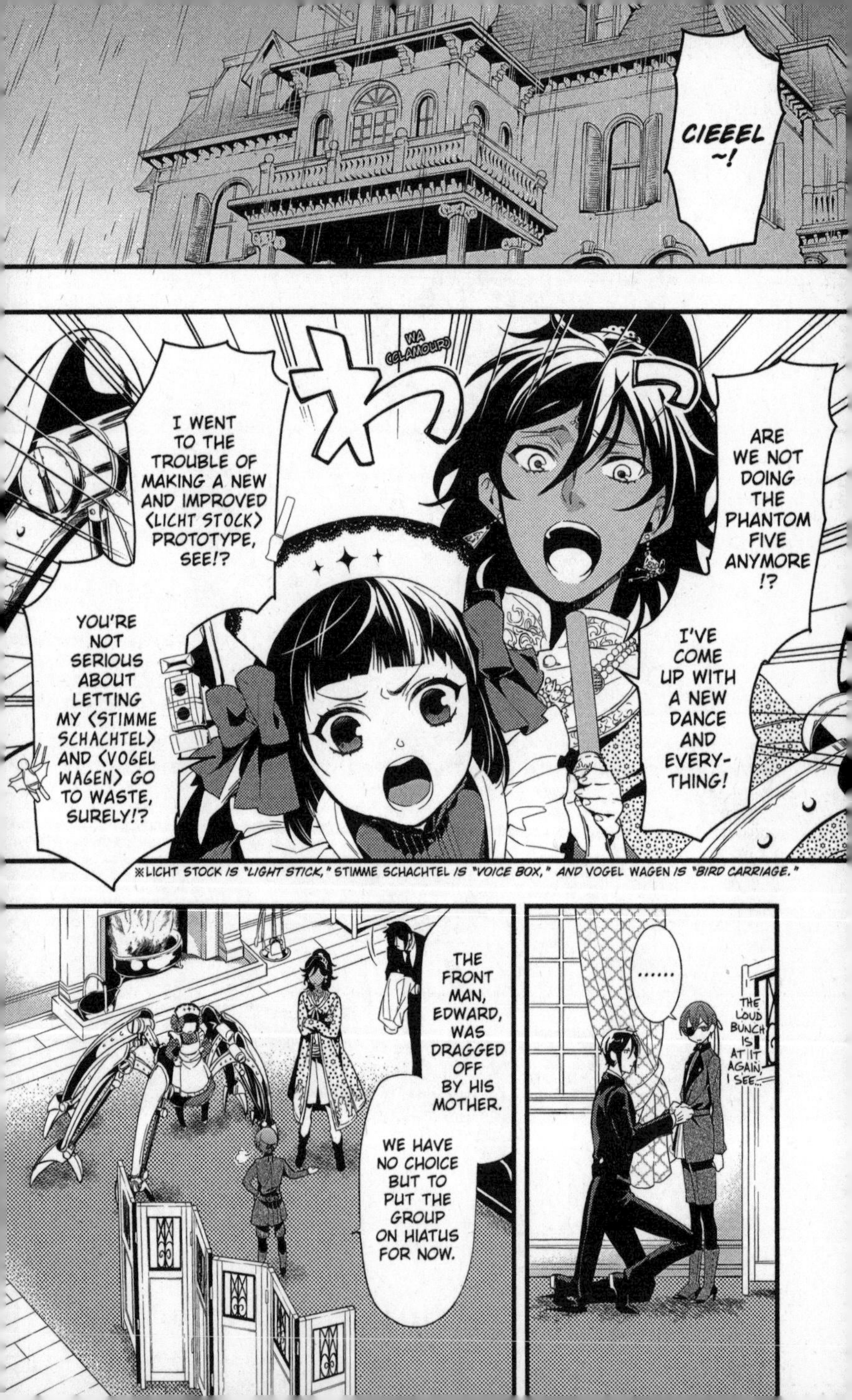
CIEEEL ~!
ARE WE NOT DOING THE PHANTOM FIVE ANYMORE!?
I'VE COME UP WITH A NEW DANCE AND EVERYTHING!
WA (CLAMOUR)
I WENT TO THE TROUBLE OF MAKING A NEW AND IMPROVED 〈LICHT STOCK〉 PROTOTYPE, SEE!?
YOU'RE NOT SERIOUS ABOUT LETTING MY 〈STIMME SCHACHTEL〉 AND 〈VOGEL WAGEN〉 GO TO WASTE, SURELY!?
※LICHT STOCK IS "LIGHT STICK," STIMME SCHACHTEL IS "VOICE BOX," AND VOGEL WAGEN IS "BIRD CARRIAGE."
......
THE LOUD BUNCH IS AT IT AGAIN, I SEE...
THE FRONT MAN, EDWARD, WAS DRAGGED OFF BY HIS MOTHER.
WE HAVE NO CHOICE BUT TO PUT THE GROUP ON HIATUS FOR NOW.

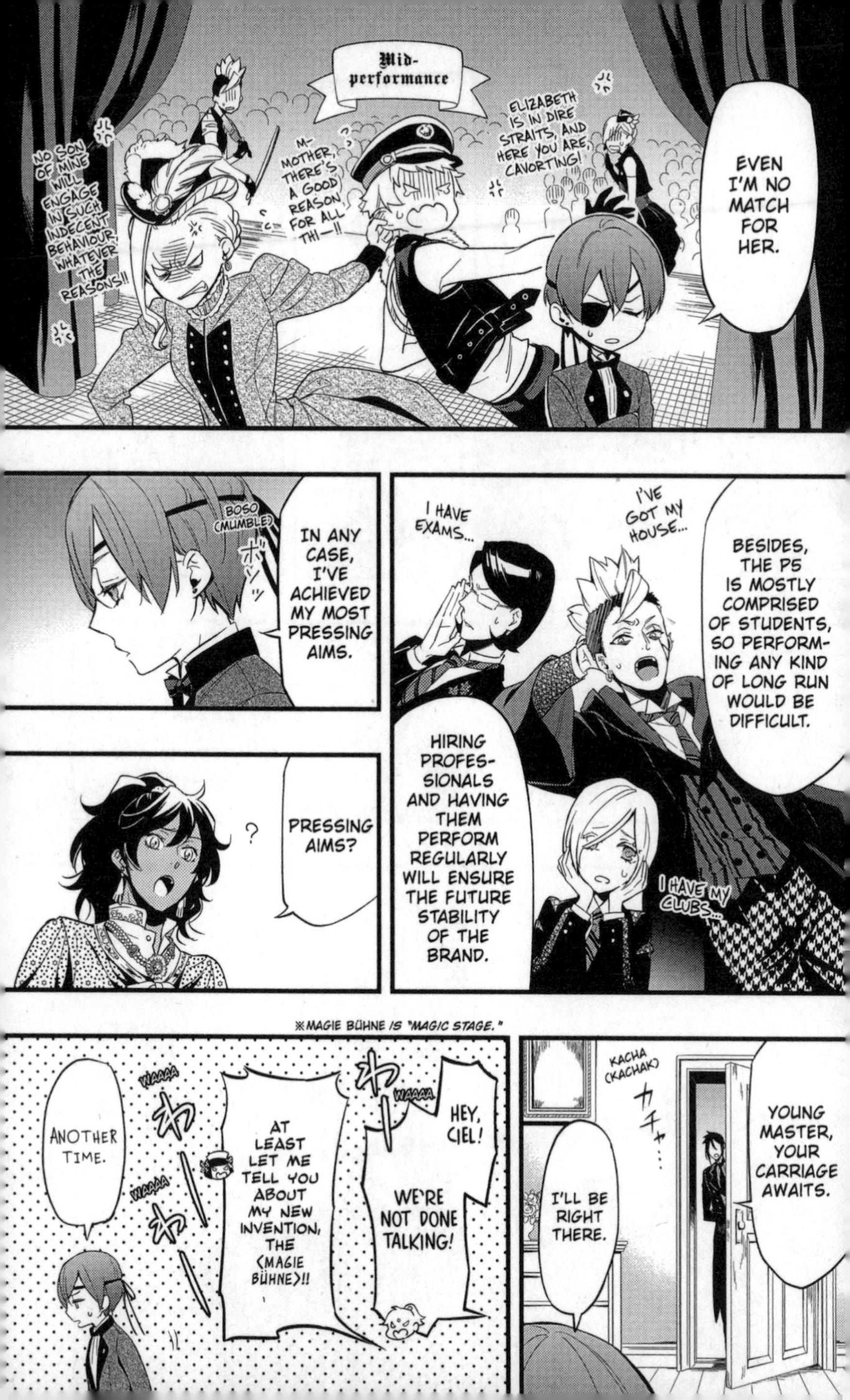
Mid-performance
EVEN I'M NO MATCH FOR HER.
ELIZABETH IS IN DIRE STRAITS, AND HERE YOU ARE, CAVORTING!
M-MOTHER, THERE'S A GOOD REASON FOR ALL THI—!!
NO SON OF MINE WILL ENGAGE IN SUCH INDECENT BEHAVIOUR, WHATEVER THE REASONS!!
BESIDES, THE P5 IS MOSTLY COMPRISED OF STUDENTS, SO PERFORMING ANY KIND OF LONG RUN WOULD BE DIFFICULT.
I'VE GOT MY HOUSE...
I HAVE EXAMS...
HIRING PROFESSIONALS AND HAVING THEM PERFORM REGULARLY WILL ENSURE THE FUTURE STABILITY OF THE BRAND.
I HAVE MY CLUBS...
BOSO (MUMBLE)
ボソッ
IN ANY CASE, I'VE ACHIEVED MY MOST PRESSING AIMS.
PRESSING AIMS?
?
YOUNG MASTER, YOUR CARRIAGE AWAITS.
KACHA (KACHAK)
カチャ...
I'LL BE RIGHT THERE.
HEY, CIEL!
WAAAA
わ
WE'RE NOT DONE TALKING!
AT LEAST LET ME TELL YOU ABOUT MY NEW INVENTION, THE <MAGIE BÜHNE>!!
WAAAA
わ
WAAAA
わ
ANOTHER TIME.

※MAGIE BÜHNE IS "MAGIC STAGE."

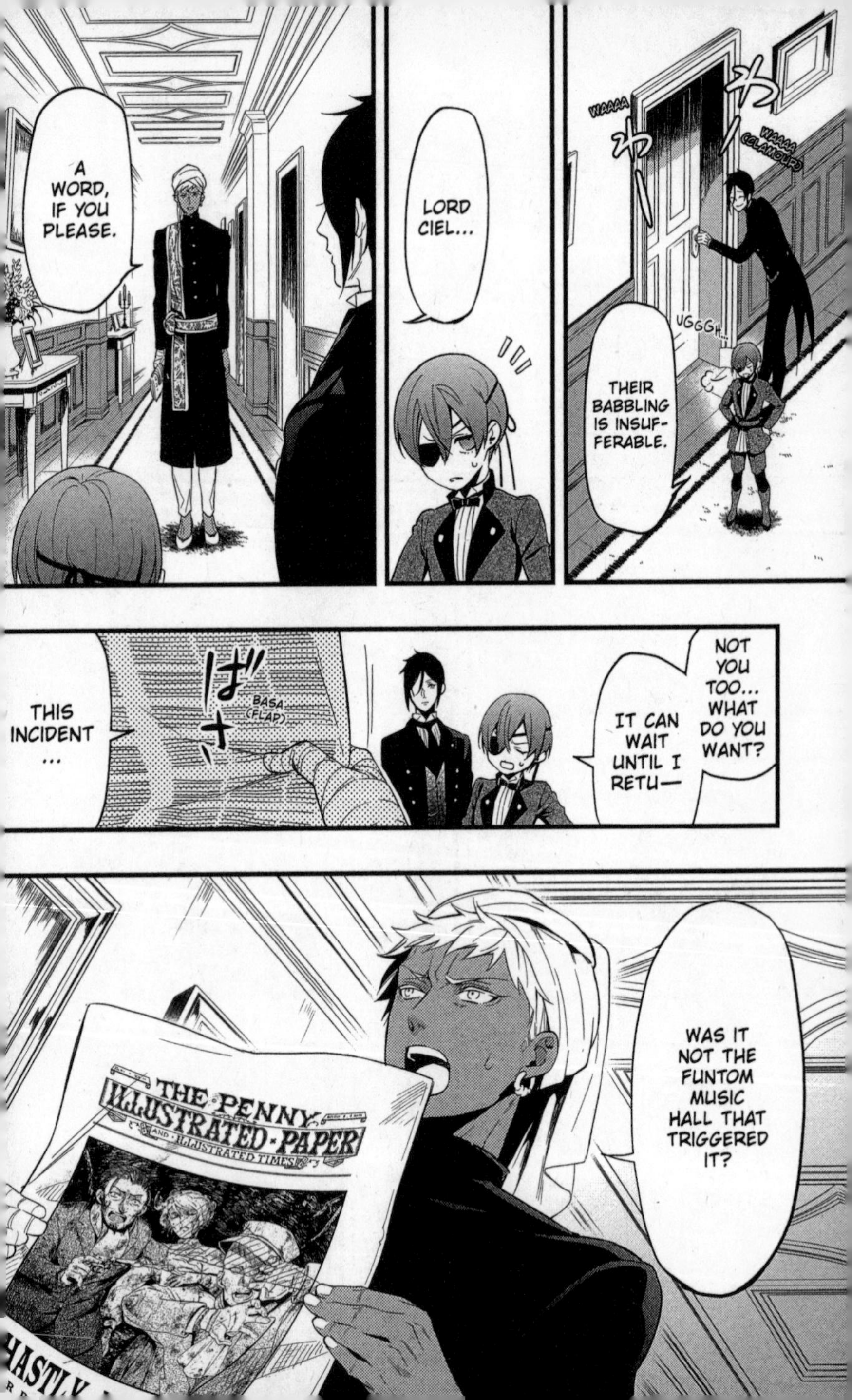
WAAAA
WAAAA (CLAMOUR)
UGGGH...
THEIR BABBLING IS INSUFFERABLE.
LORD CIEL...
A WORD, IF YOU PLEASE.
NOT YOU TOO... WHAT DO YOU WANT?
IT CAN WAIT UNTIL I RETU—
BASA (FLAP)
THIS INCIDENT ...
WAS IT NOT THE FUNTOM MUSIC HALL THAT TRIGGERED IT?
THE PENNY ILLUSTRATED PAPER
AND ILLUSTRATED TIMES

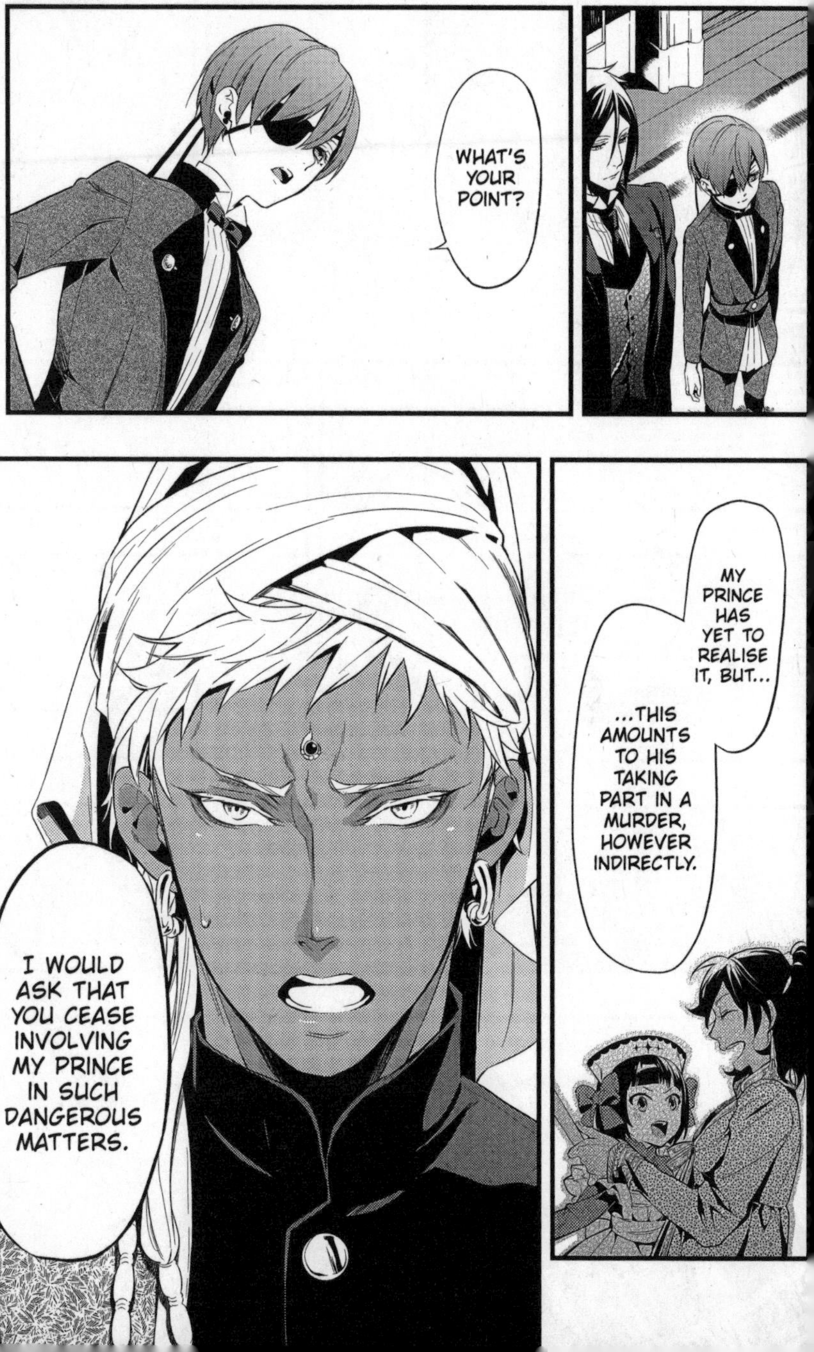
WHAT'S YOUR POINT?
MY PRINCE HAS YET TO REALISE IT, BUT...
...THIS AMOUNTS TO HIS TAKING PART IN A MURDER, HOWEVER INDIRECTLY.
I WOULD ASK THAT YOU CEASE INVOLVING MY PRINCE IN SUCH DANGEROUS MATTERS.

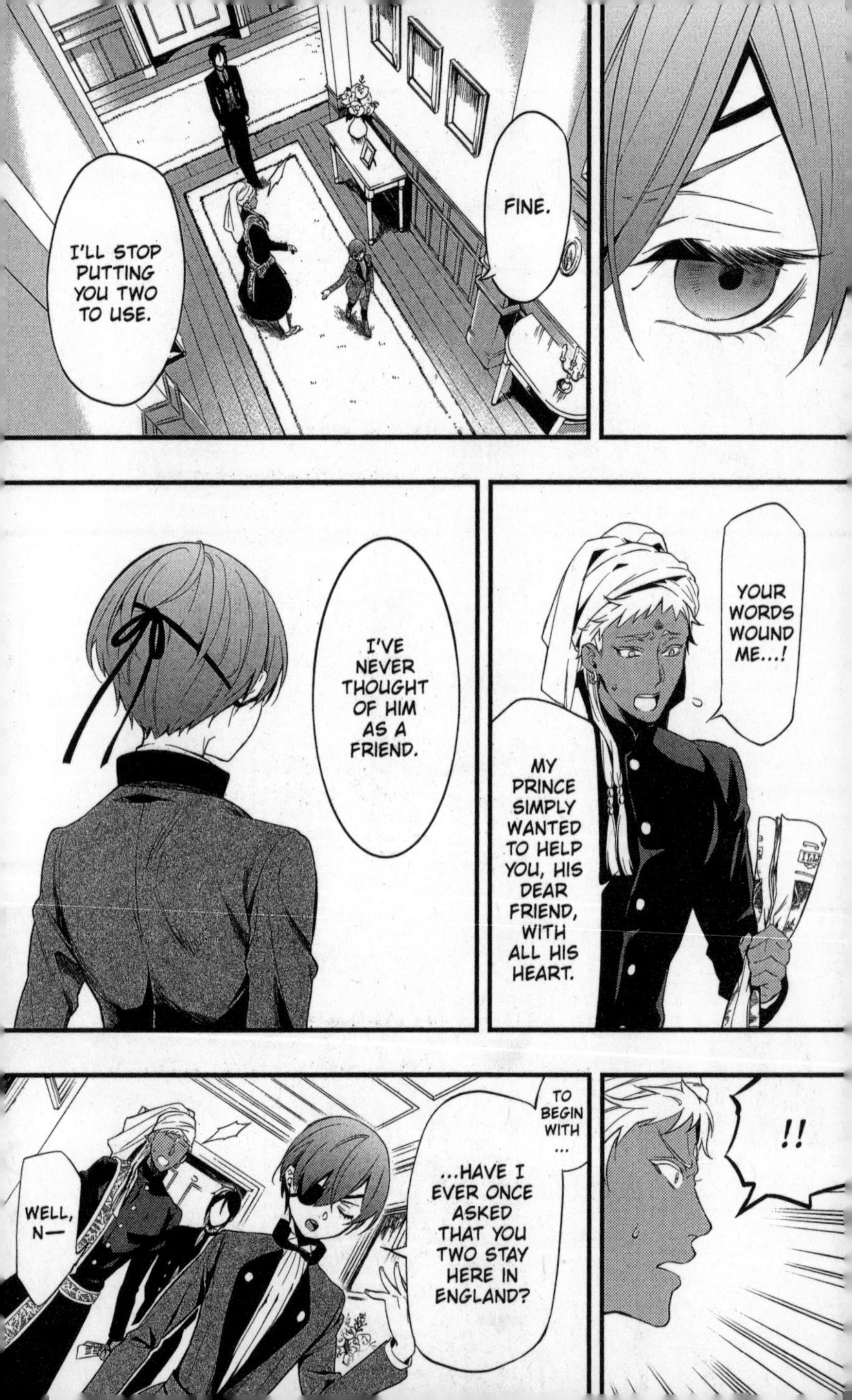
FINE.
I'LL STOP PUTTING YOU TWO TO USE.
YOUR WORDS WOUND ME...!
MY PRINCE SIMPLY WANTED TO HELP YOU, HIS DEAR FRIEND, WITH ALL HIS HEART.
I'VE NEVER THOUGHT OF HIM AS A FRIEND.
!!
TO BEGIN WITH...
...HAVE I EVER ONCE ASKED THAT YOU TWO STAY HERE IN ENGLAND?
WELL, N—

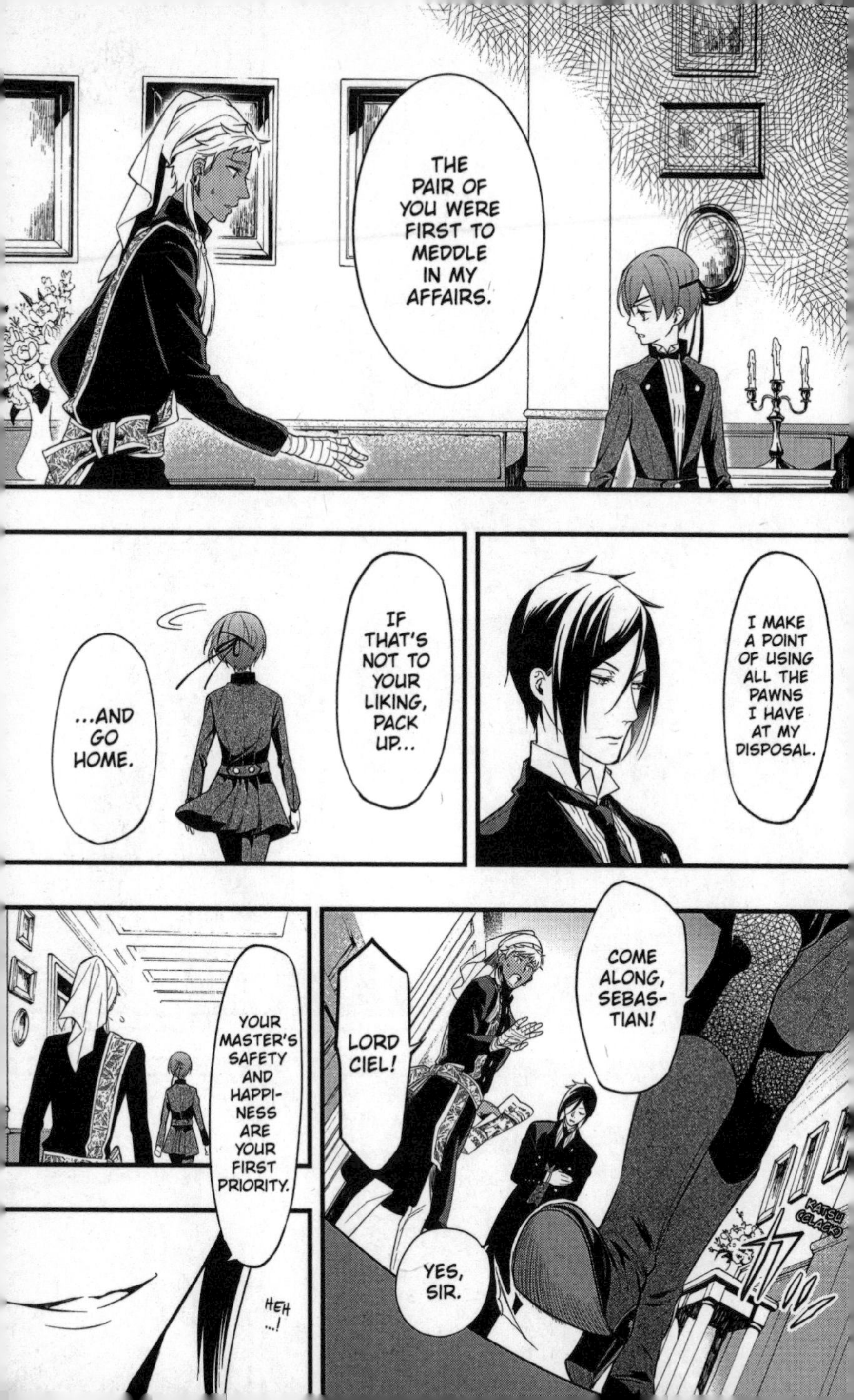
THE PAIR OF YOU WERE FIRST TO MEDDLE IN MY AFFAIRS.
I MAKE A POINT OF USING ALL THE PAWNS I HAVE AT MY DISPOSAL.
IF THAT'S NOT TO YOUR LIKING, PACK UP...
...AND GO HOME.
COME ALONG, SEBAS-TIAN!
LORD CIEL!
KATSU (CLACK)
YES, SIR.
YOUR MASTER'S SAFETY AND HAPPI-NESS ARE YOUR FIRST PRIORITY.
HEH ...!

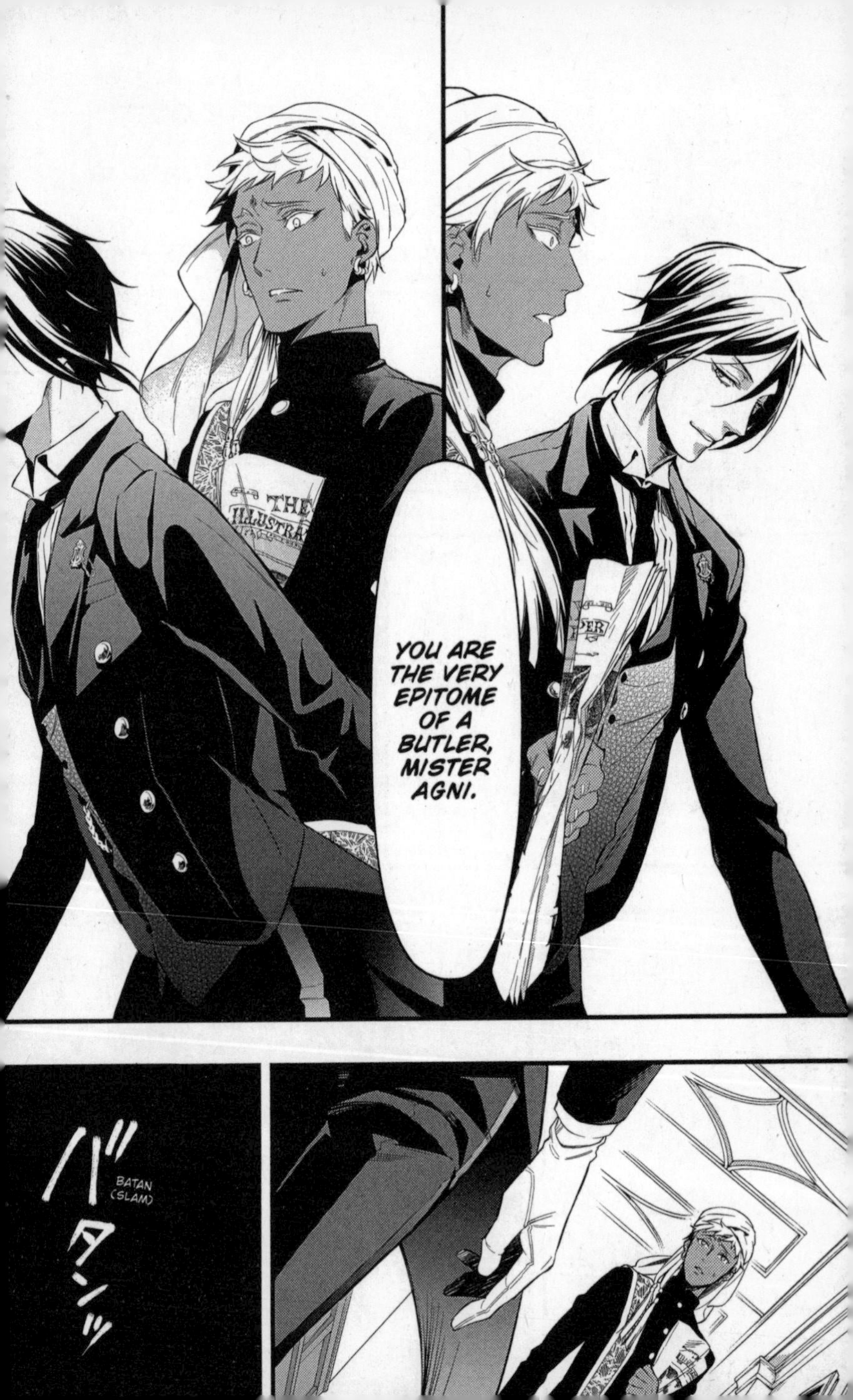
YOU ARE THE VERY EPITOME OF A BUTLER, MISTER AGNI.
バタンッ
BATAN (SLAM)

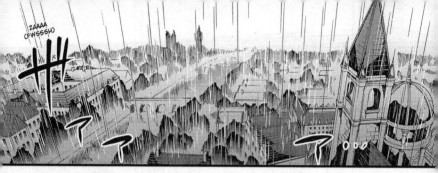

ZAAAA
(FWSSSH)

NO WITNESSES TO BE FOUND IN THE VICINITY OF HYDE PARK.

LET'S HEAD BACK TO THE STATION.

WELL?

PA (PAT)
PA

KARAN
(JINGLE)

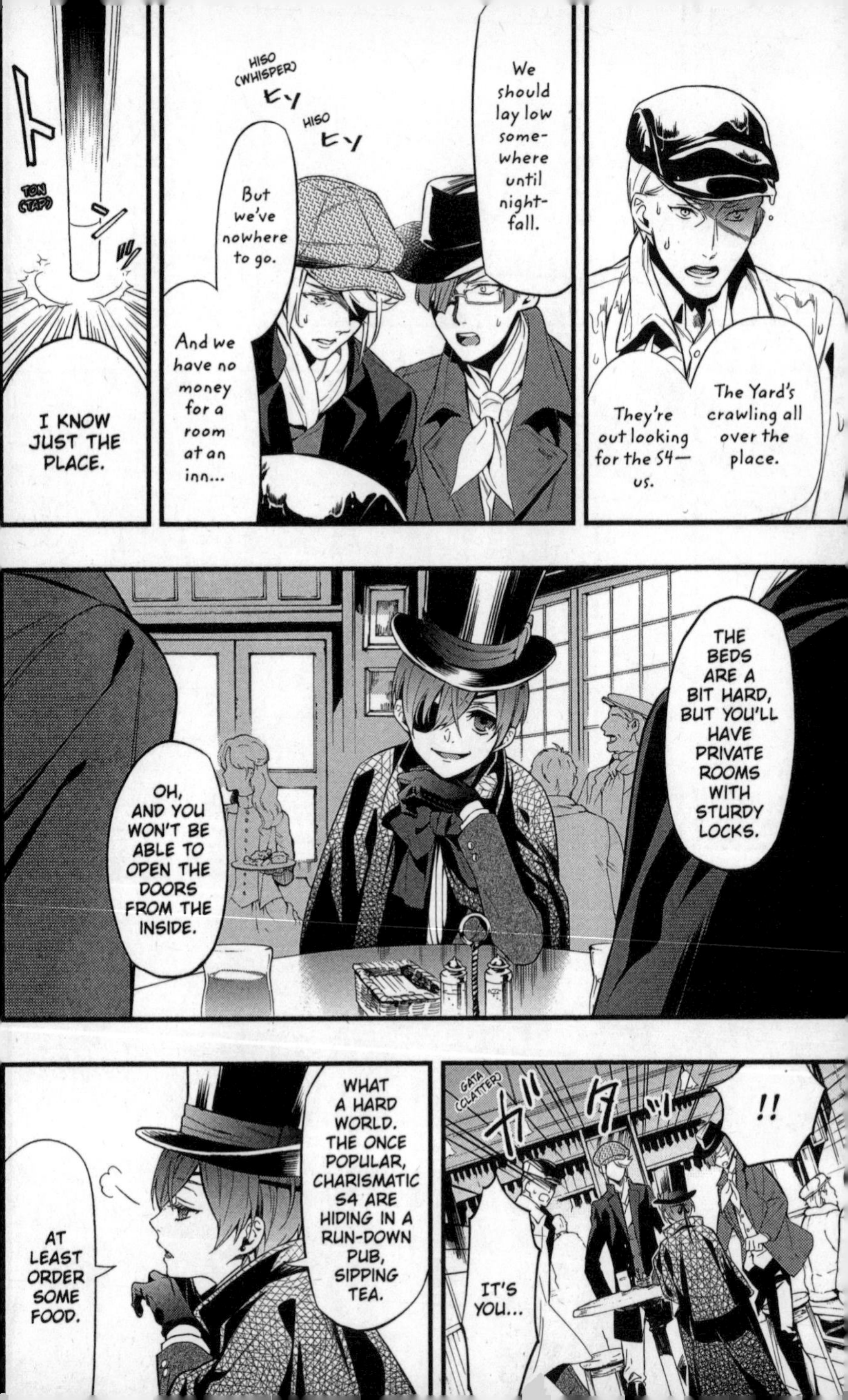
The Yard's crawling all over the place.
They're out looking for the S4— us.
We should lay low somewhere until nightfall.
HISO (WHISPER)
ヒソ
HISO
ヒソ
But we've nowhere to go.
And we have no money for a room at an inn...
TON (TAP)
ト
I KNOW JUST THE PLACE.
THE BEDS ARE A BIT HARD, BUT YOU'LL HAVE PRIVATE ROOMS WITH STURDY LOCKS.
OH, AND YOU WON'T BE ABLE TO OPEN THE DOORS FROM THE INSIDE.
GATA (CLATTER)
ガタッ
!!
IT'S YOU...
WHAT A HARD WORLD. THE ONCE POPULAR, CHARISMATIC S4 ARE HIDING IN A RUN-DOWN PUB, SIPPING TEA.
AT LEAST ORDER SOME FOOD.

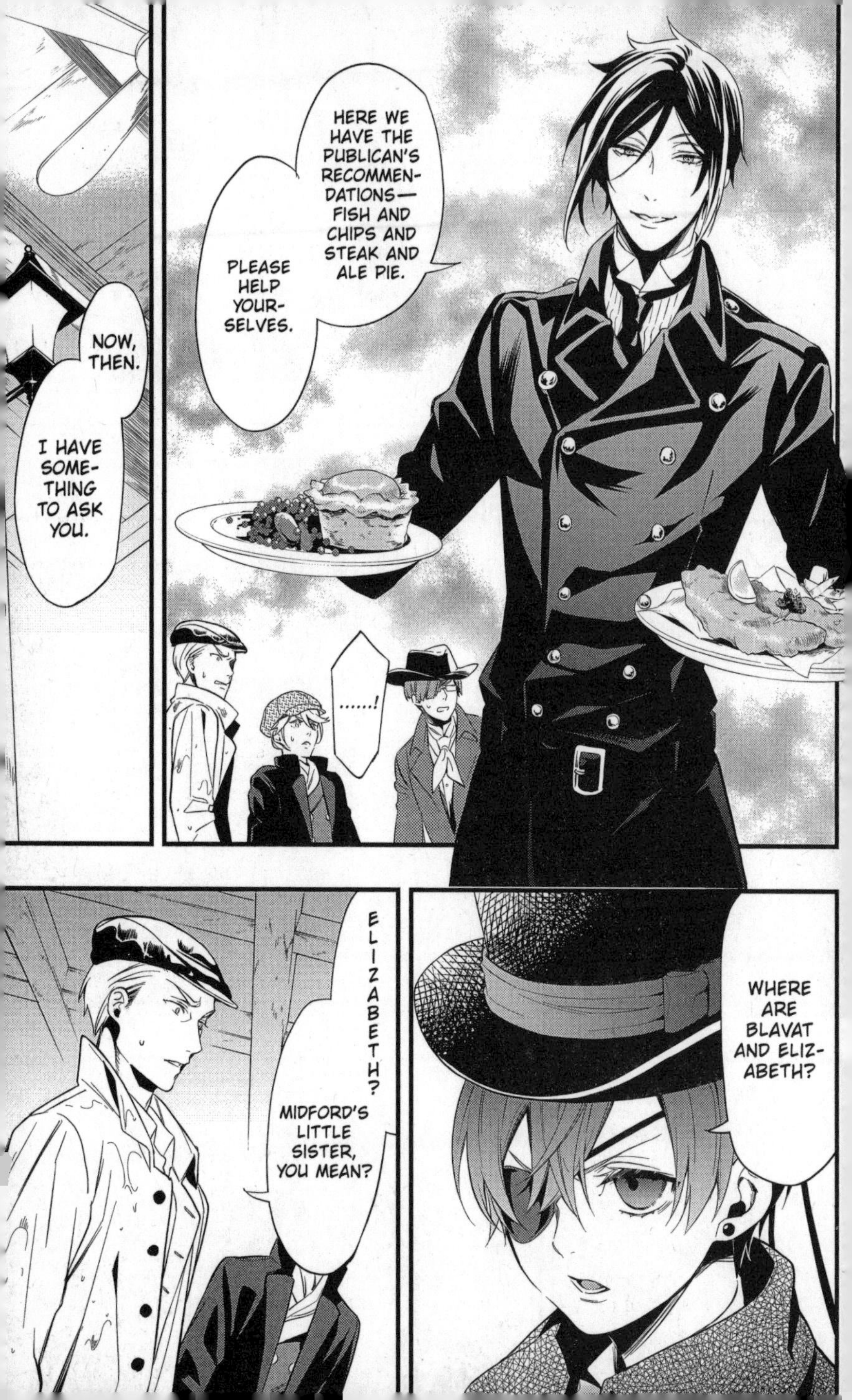
HERE WE HAVE THE PUBLICAN'S RECOMMENDATIONS—FISH AND CHIPS AND STEAK AND ALE PIE.
PLEASE HELP YOURSELVES.
......!
NOW, THEN.
I HAVE SOMETHING TO ASK YOU.
WHERE ARE BLAVAT AND ELIZABETH?
ELIZABETH?
MIDFORD'S LITTLE SISTER, YOU MEAN?

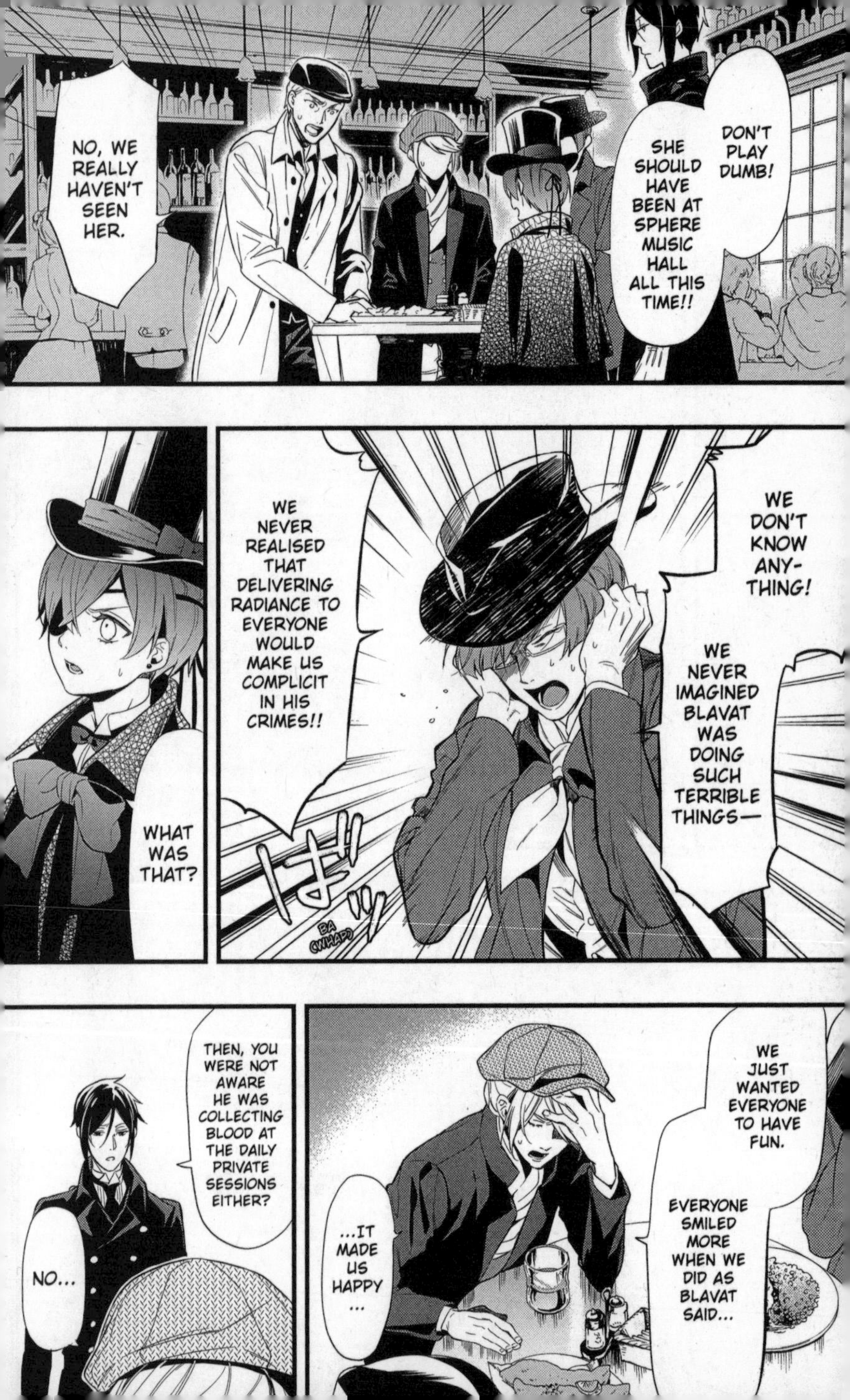
DON'T PLAY DUMB!
SHE SHOULD HAVE BEEN AT SPHERE MUSIC HALL ALL THIS TIME!!
NO, WE REALLY HAVEN'T SEEN HER.
WE DON'T KNOW ANY-THING!
WE NEVER IMAGINED BLAVAT WAS DOING SUCH TERRIBLE THINGS—
WE NEVER REALISED THAT DELIVERING RADIANCE TO EVERYONE WOULD MAKE US COMPLICIT IN HIS CRIMES!!
BA (WHAP)
WHAT WAS THAT?
WE JUST WANTED EVERYONE TO HAVE FUN.
EVERYONE SMILED MORE WHEN WE DID AS BLAVAT SAID...
...IT MADE US HAPPY...
THEN, YOU WERE NOT AWARE HE WAS COLLECTING BLOOD AT THE DAILY PRIVATE SESSIONS EITHER?
NO...

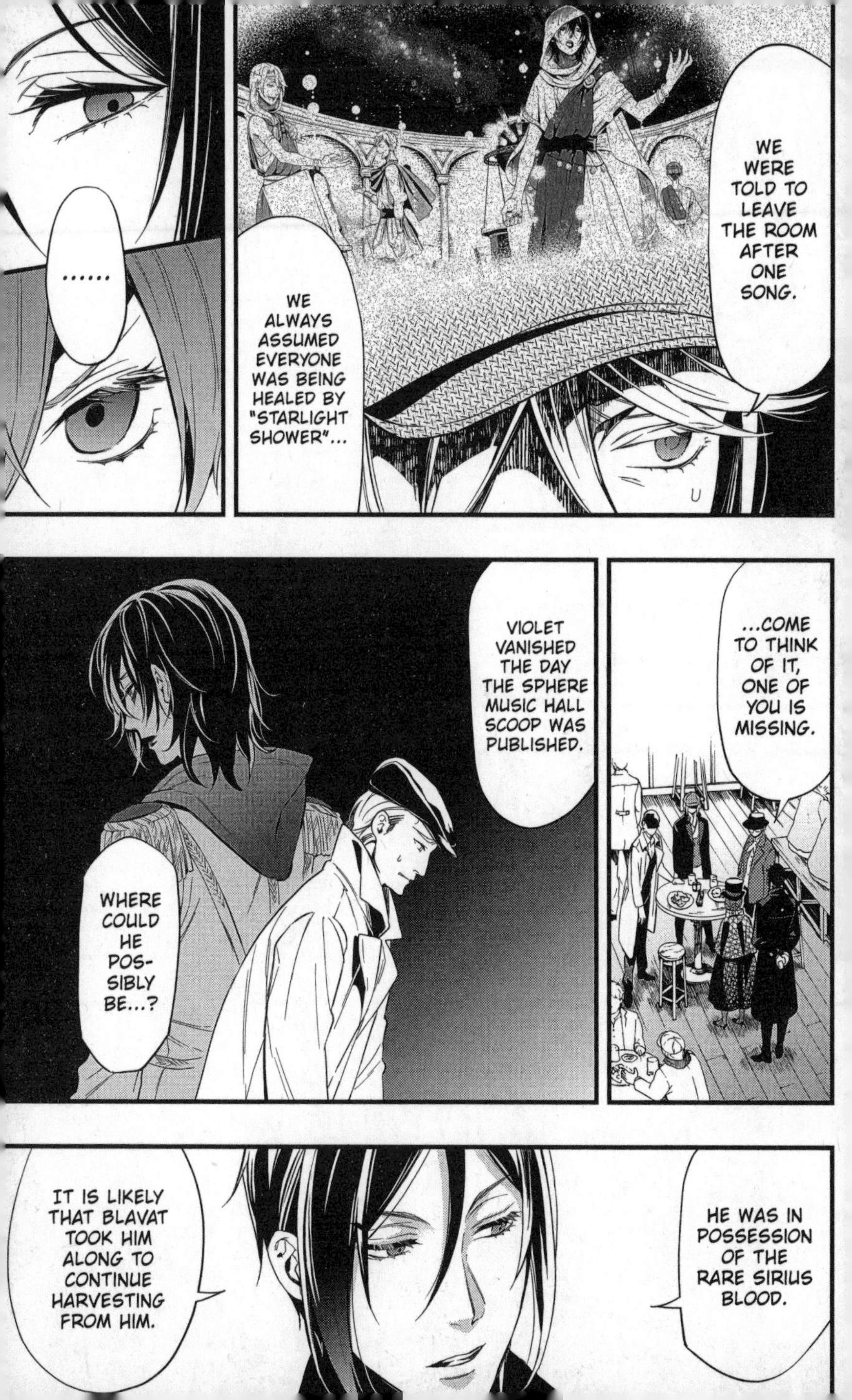
WE WERE TOLD TO LEAVE THE ROOM AFTER ONE SONG.
WE ALWAYS ASSUMED EVERYONE WAS BEING HEALED BY "STARLIGHT SHOWER"...
......
...COME TO THINK OF IT, ONE OF YOU IS MISSING.
VIOLET VANISHED THE DAY THE SPHERE MUSIC HALL SCOOP WAS PUBLISHED.
WHERE COULD HE POS-SIBLY BE...?
HE WAS IN POSSESSION OF THE RARE SIRIUS BLOOD.
IT IS LIKELY THAT BLAVAT TOOK HIM ALONG TO CONTINUE HARVESTING FROM HIM.

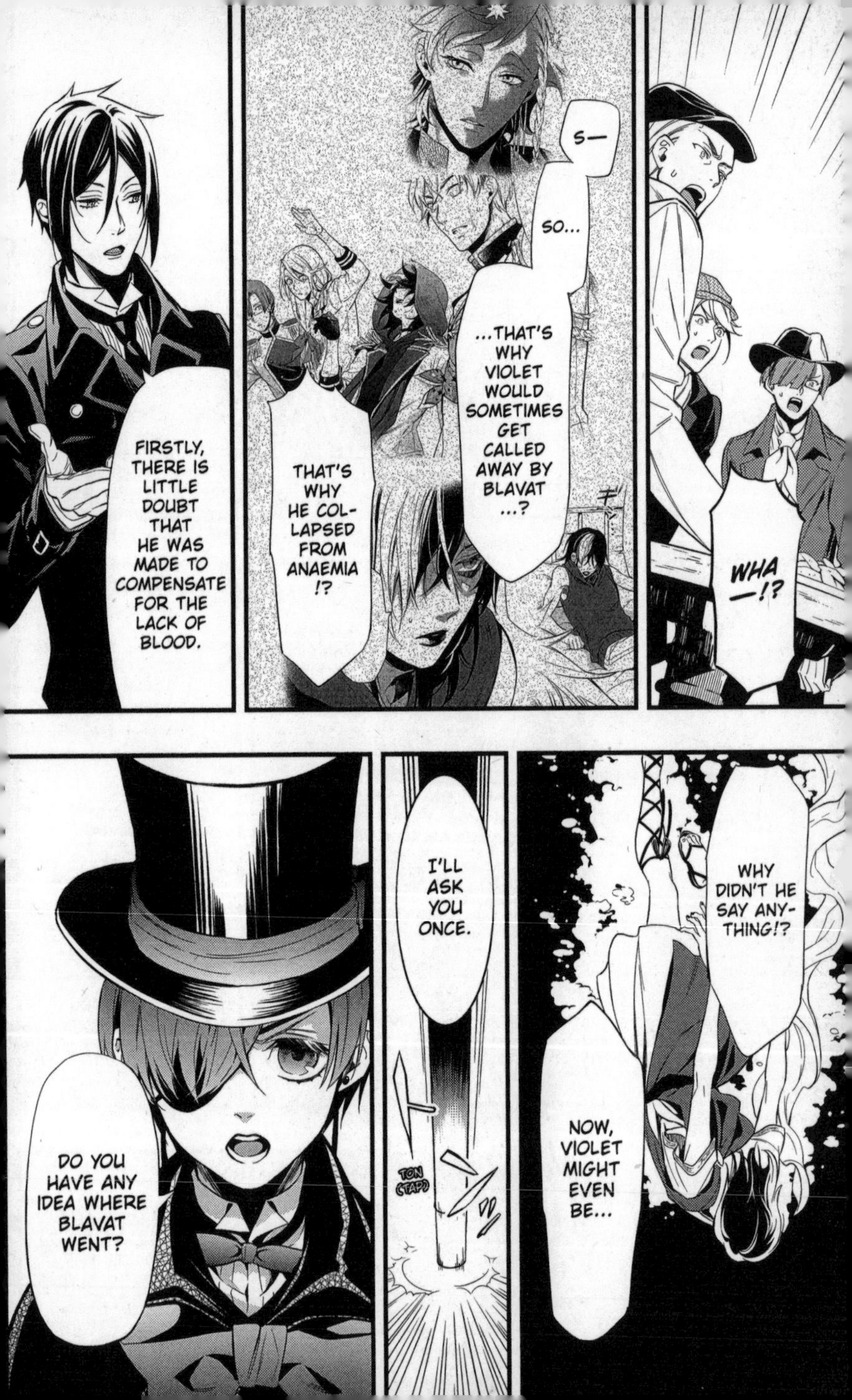
WHA—!?
S—
SO...
...THAT'S WHY VIOLET WOULD SOMETIMES GET CALLED AWAY BY BLAVAT...?
THAT'S WHY HE COLLAPSED FROM ANAEMIA!?
FIRSTLY, THERE IS LITTLE DOUBT THAT HE WAS MADE TO COMPENSATE FOR THE LACK OF BLOOD.
WHY DIDN'T HE SAY ANYTHING!?
NOW, VIOLET MIGHT EVEN BE...
I'LL ASK YOU ONCE.
TON (TAP)
DO YOU HAVE ANY IDEA WHERE BLAVAT WENT?

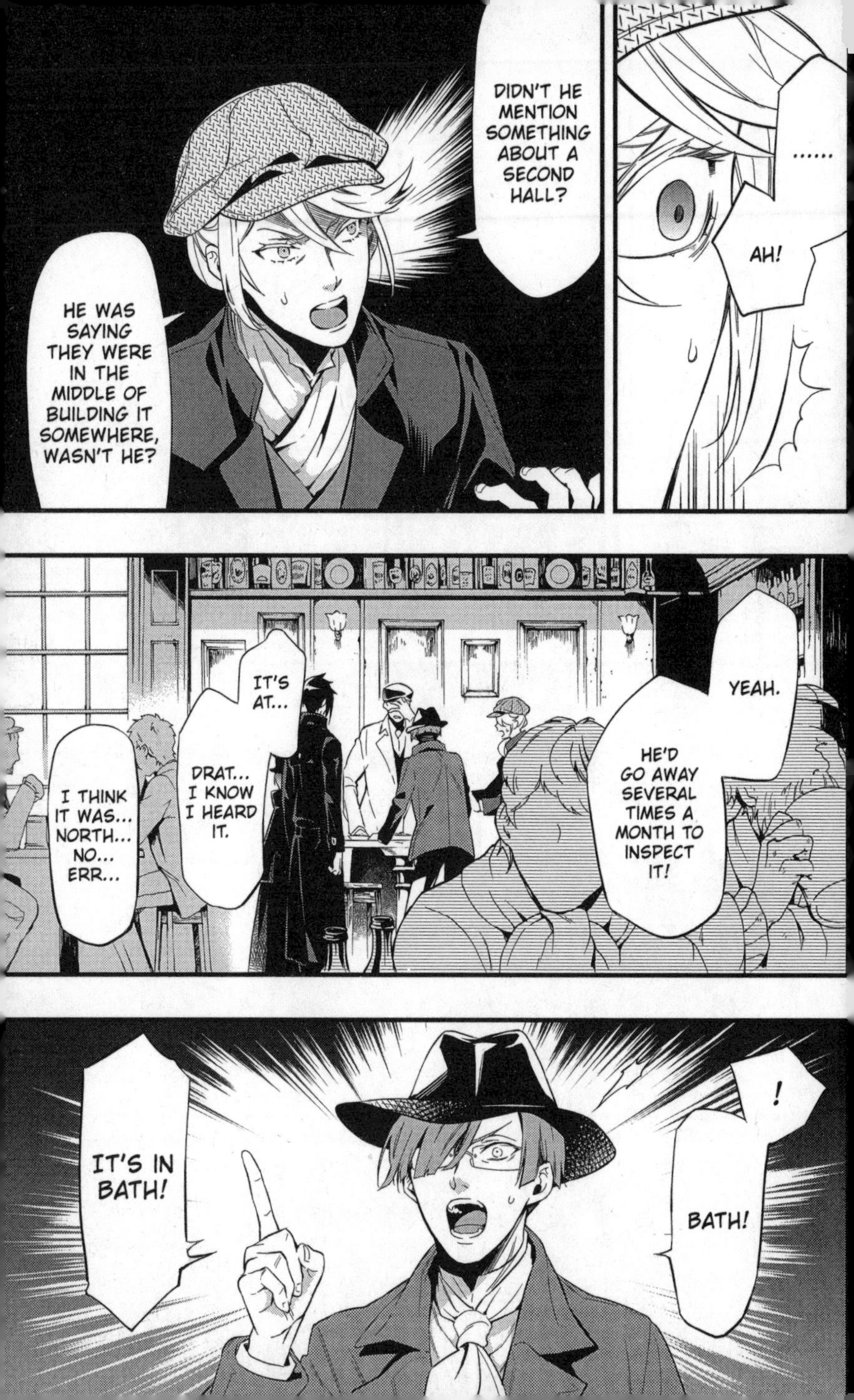
……
AH!
DIDN'T HE MENTION SOMETHING ABOUT A SECOND HALL?
HE WAS SAYING THEY WERE IN THE MIDDLE OF BUILDING IT SOMEWHERE, WASN'T HE?
YEAH.
HE'D GO AWAY SEVERAL TIMES A MONTH TO INSPECT IT!
IT'S AT...
DRAT... I KNOW I HEARD IT.
I THINK IT WAS... NORTH... NO... ERR...
IT'S IN BATH!
!
BATH!

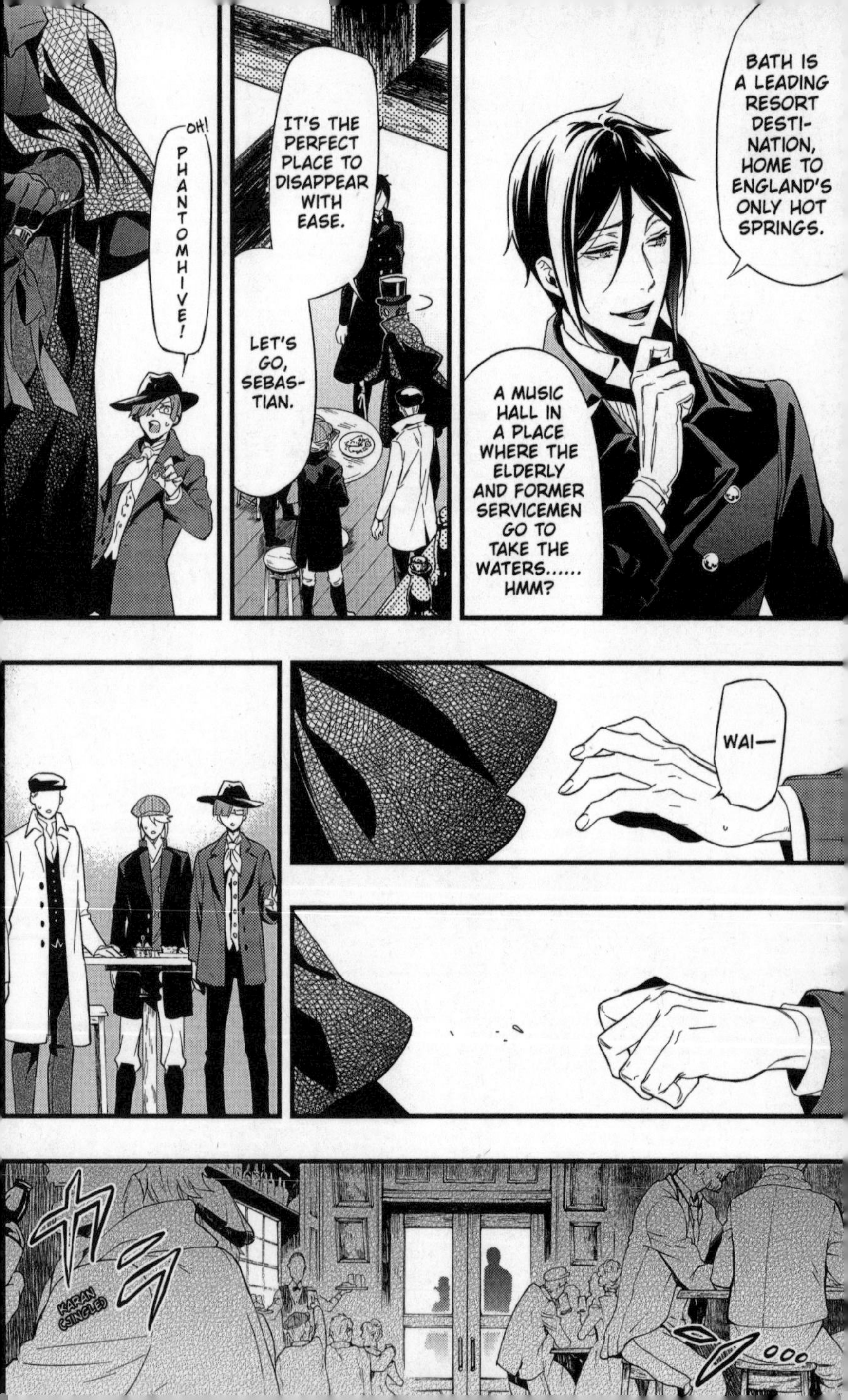
BATH IS A LEADING RESORT DESTINATION, HOME TO ENGLAND'S ONLY HOT SPRINGS.
A MUSIC HALL IN A PLACE WHERE THE ELDERLY AND FORMER SERVICEMEN GO TO TAKE THE WATERS...... HMM?
IT'S THE PERFECT PLACE TO DISAPPEAR WITH EASE.
LET'S GO, SEBASTIAN.
OH! PHANTOMHIVE!
WAI—
KARAN (JINGLE)

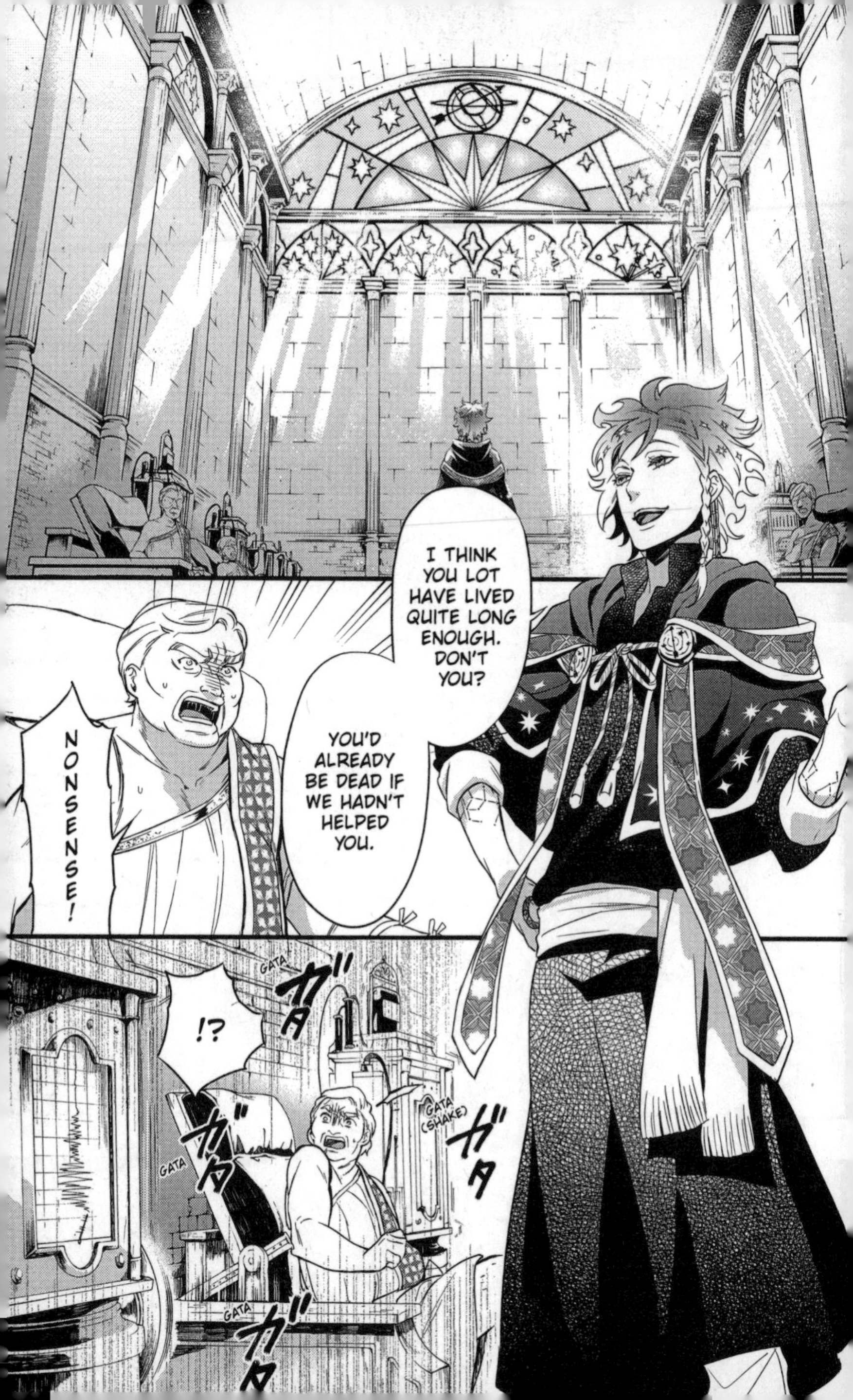
I THINK YOU LOT HAVE LIVED QUITE LONG ENOUGH. DON'T YOU?
YOU'D ALREADY BE DEAD IF WE HADN'T HELPED YOU.
NONSENSE!
GATA (SHAKE)
GATA
!?
GATA
GATA

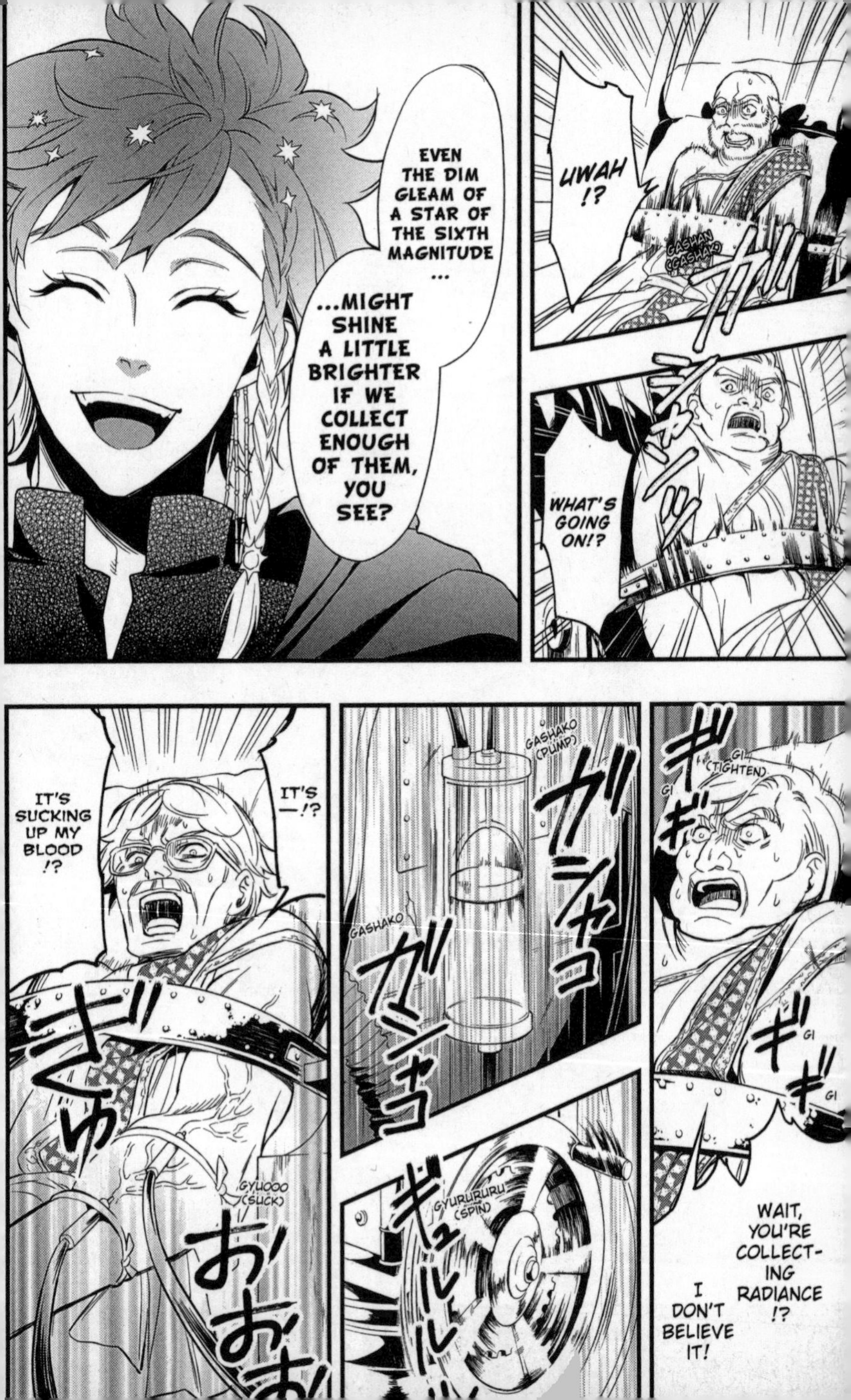
UWAH !?
GASHAN (GASHAKO)
WHAT'S GOING ON!?
EVEN THE DIM GLEAM OF A STAR OF THE SIXTH MAGNITUDE ...
...MIGHT SHINE A LITTLE BRIGHTER IF WE COLLECT ENOUGH OF THEM, YOU SEE?
GI (TIGHTEN)
GI
GI
GI
WAIT, YOU'RE COLLECT-ING RADIANCE !?
I DON'T BELIEVE IT!
GASHAKO (PUMP)
GASHAKO
GYURURURU (SPIN)
IT'S —!?
IT'S SUCKING UP MY BLOOD !?
GYUOOO (SUCK)

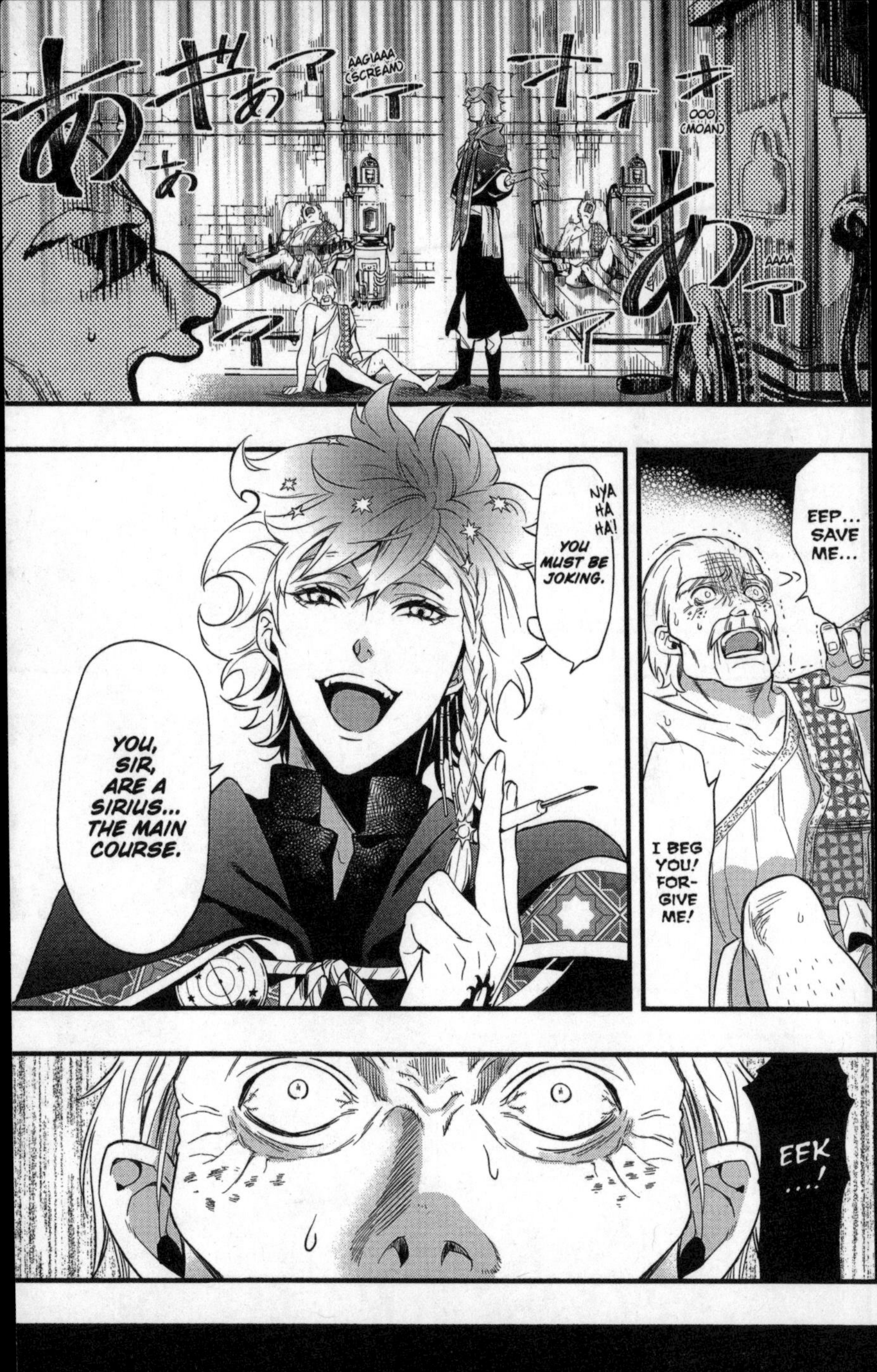
OOO (MOAN)
AAAA
AAGIAAA (SCREAM)
EEP... SAVE ME...
I BEG YOU! FORGIVE ME!
NYA HA HA! YOU MUST BE JOKING.
YOU, SIR, ARE A SIRIUS... THE MAIN COURSE.
EEK...!

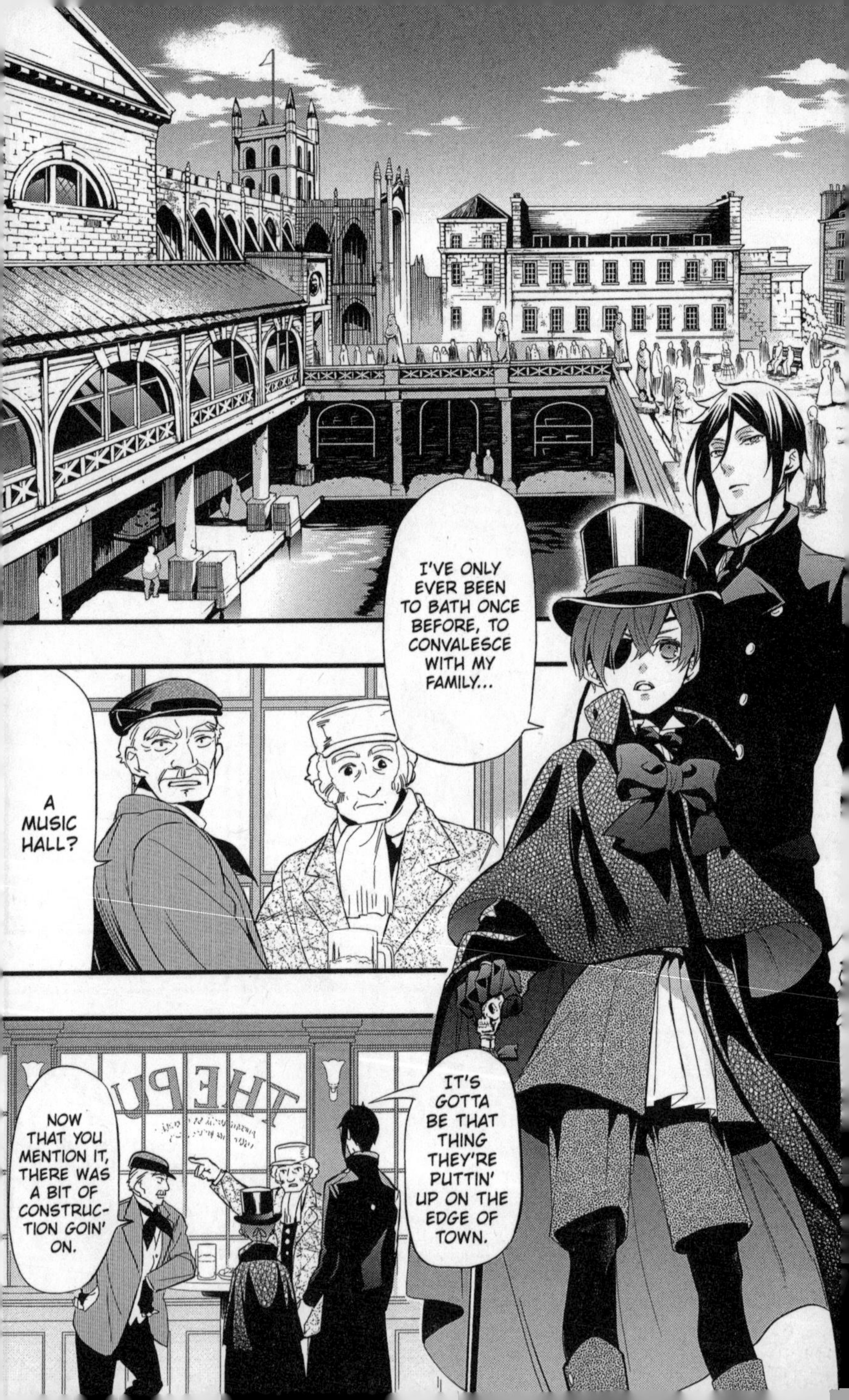
I'VE ONLY EVER BEEN TO BATH ONCE BEFORE, TO CONVALESCE WITH MY FAMILY...
A MUSIC HALL?
IT'S GOTTA BE THAT THING THEY'RE PUTTIN' UP ON THE EDGE OF TOWN.
NOW THAT YOU MENTION IT, THERE WAS A BIT OF CONSTRUCTION GOIN' ON.

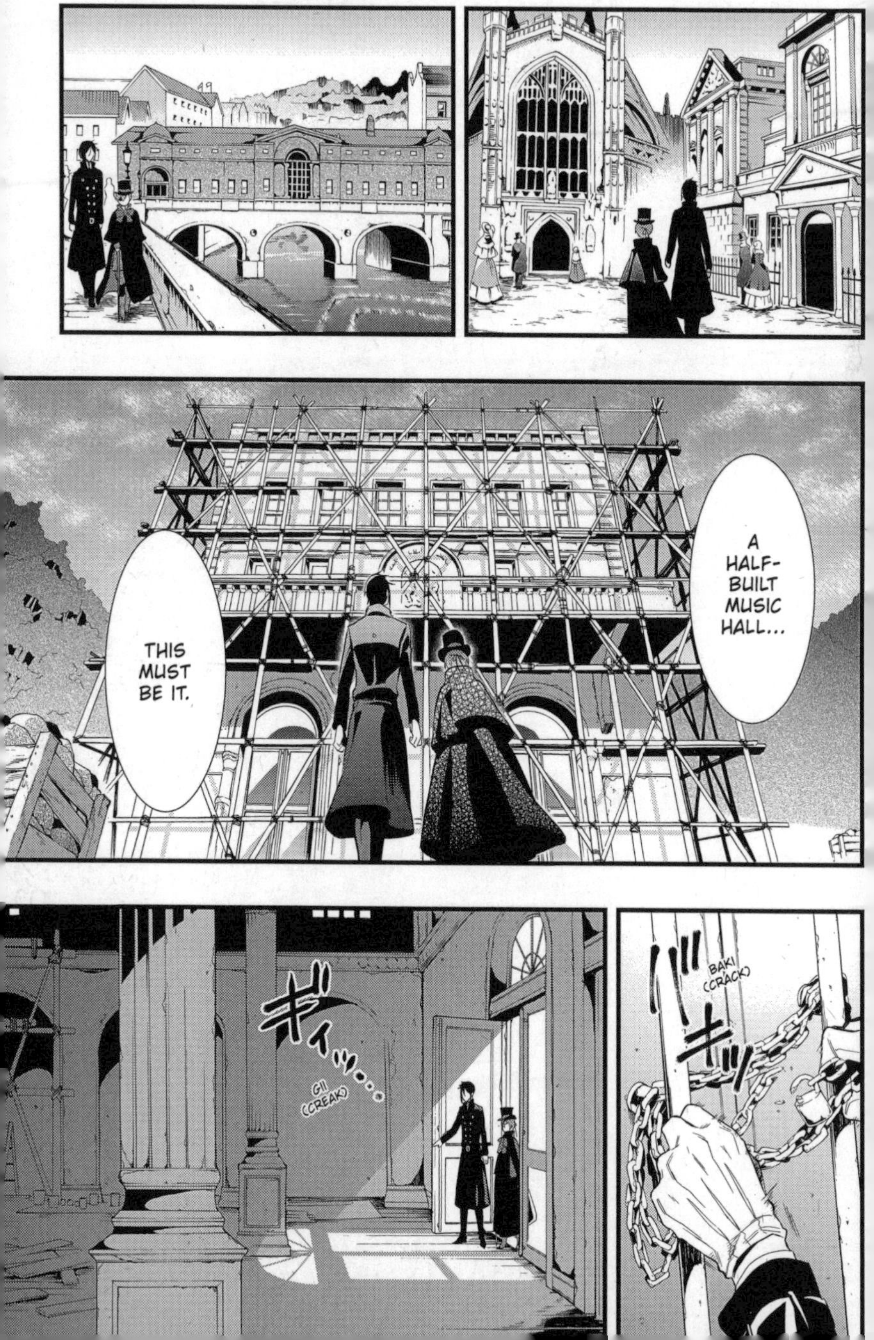
A HALF-BUILT MUSIC HALL...
THIS MUST BE IT.
BAKI (CRACK)
GII (CREAK)

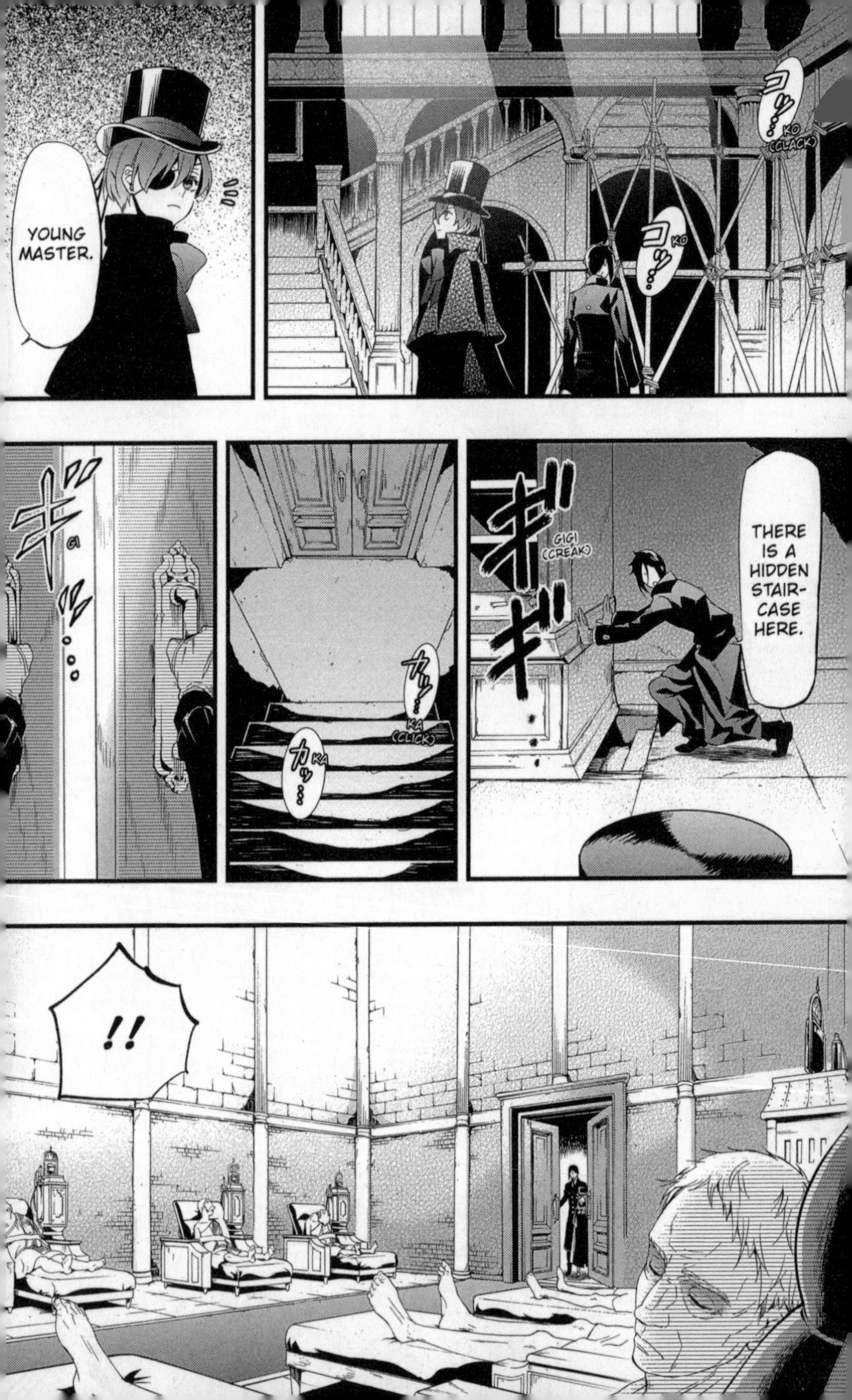

コッ…
KO (CLACK)
コッ…
KO
YOUNG MASTER.
THERE IS A HIDDEN STAIR-CASE HERE.
ギギ
GIGI (CREAK)
カッ…
KA (CLICK)
カッ…
KA
ギ
GI
ギ…
!!

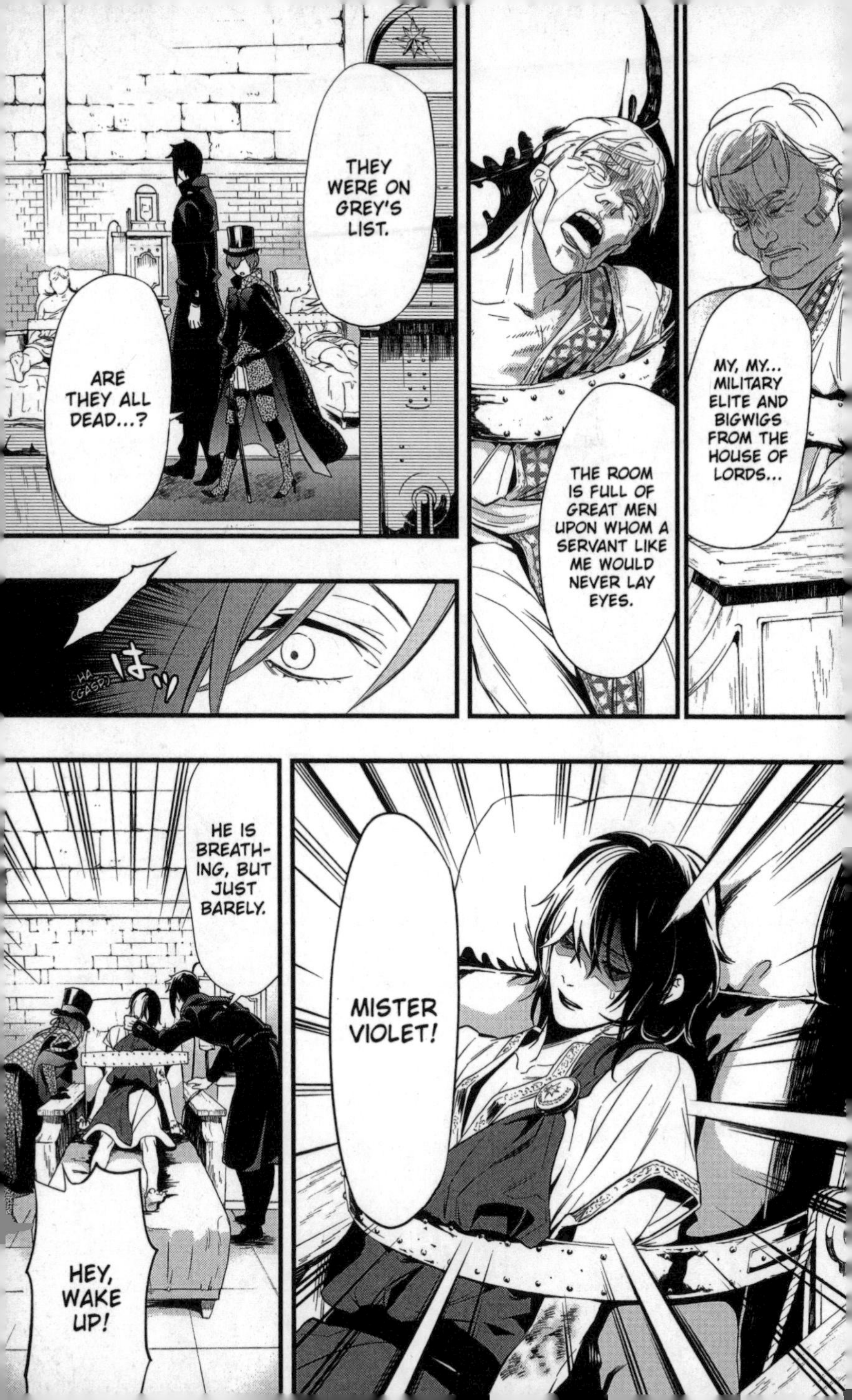
MY, MY... MILITARY ELITE AND BIGWIGS FROM THE HOUSE OF LORDS...
THE ROOM IS FULL OF GREAT MEN UPON WHOM A SERVANT LIKE ME WOULD NEVER LAY EYES.
THEY WERE ON GREY'S LIST.
ARE THEY ALL DEAD...?
はッ HA (GASP)
MISTER VIOLET!
HE IS BREATHING, BUT JUST BARELY.
HEY, WAKE UP!

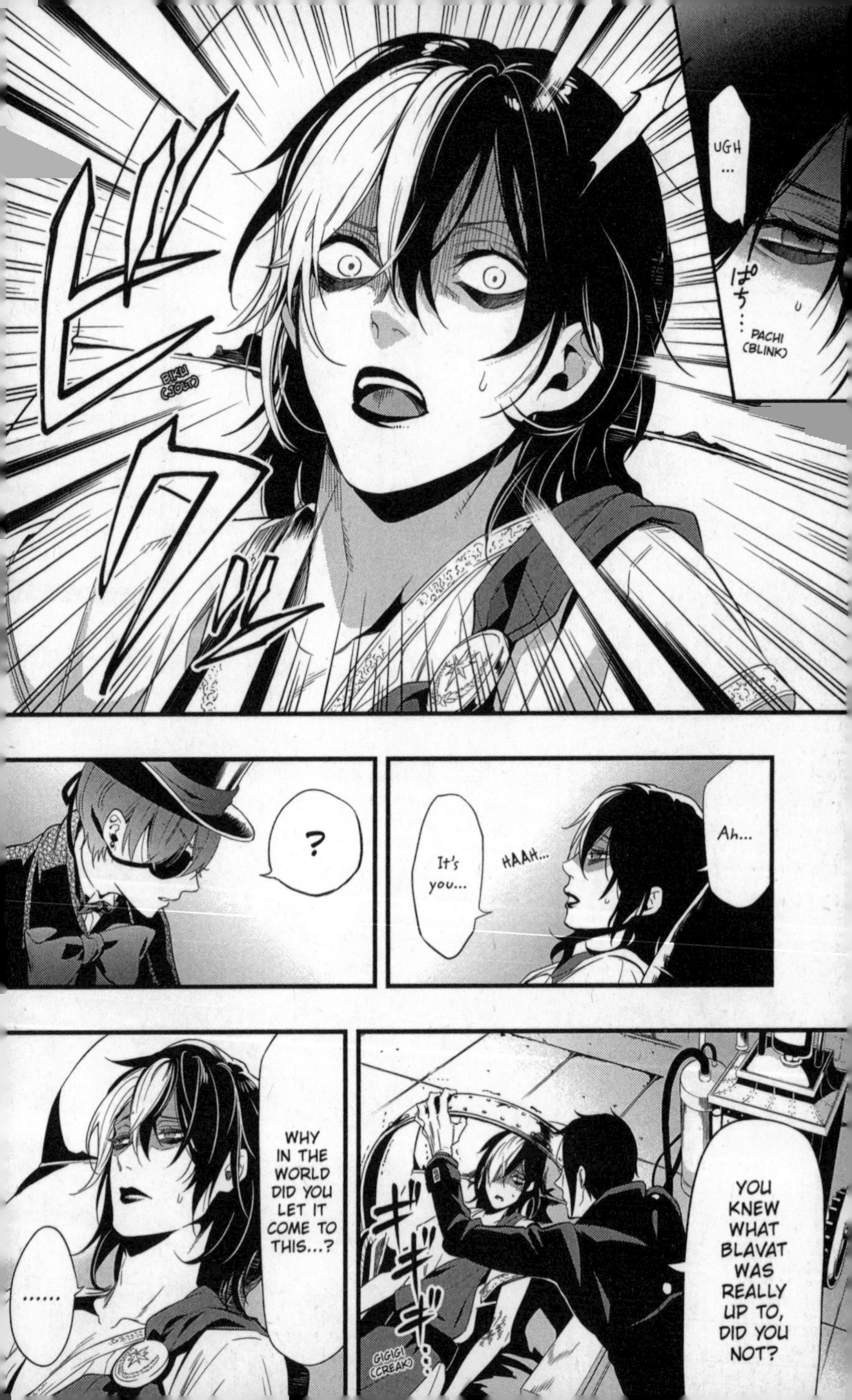
UGH ...
ぱち…
PACHI (BLINK)
BIKU (JOLT)
Ah...
HAAH...
It's you...
?
YOU KNEW WHAT BLAVAT WAS REALLY UP TO, DID YOU NOT?
ギギギ
GIGIGI (CREAK)
WHY IN THE WORLD DID YOU LET IT COME TO THIS...?
......

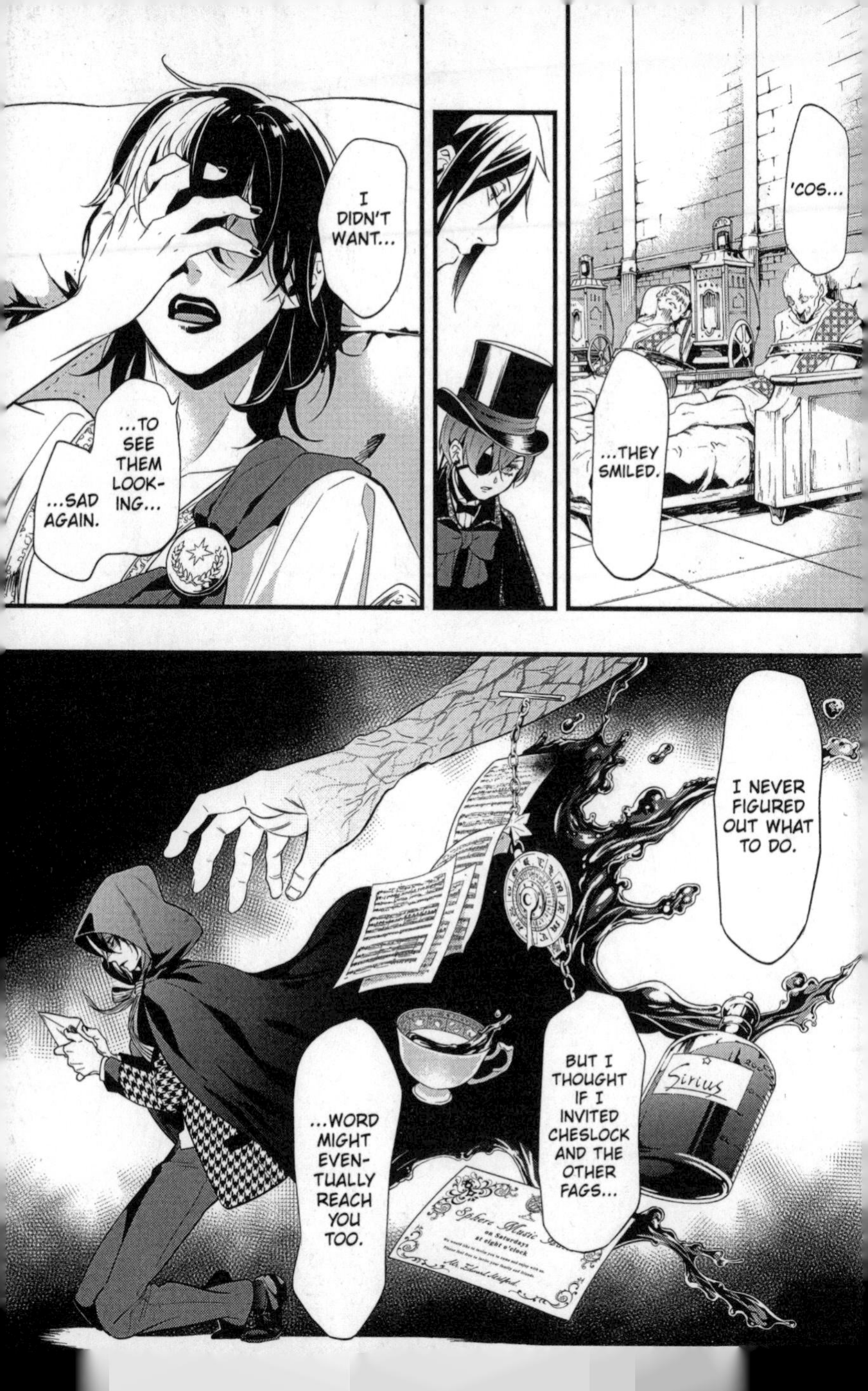
'COS...
...THEY SMILED.
I DIDN'T WANT...
...TO SEE THEM LOOKING...
...SAD AGAIN.
I NEVER FIGURED OUT WHAT TO DO.
Sirius
BUT I THOUGHT IF I INVITED CHESLOCK AND THE OTHER FAGS...
...WORD MIGHT EVENTUALLY REACH YOU TOO.
on Saturdays
at eight o'clock

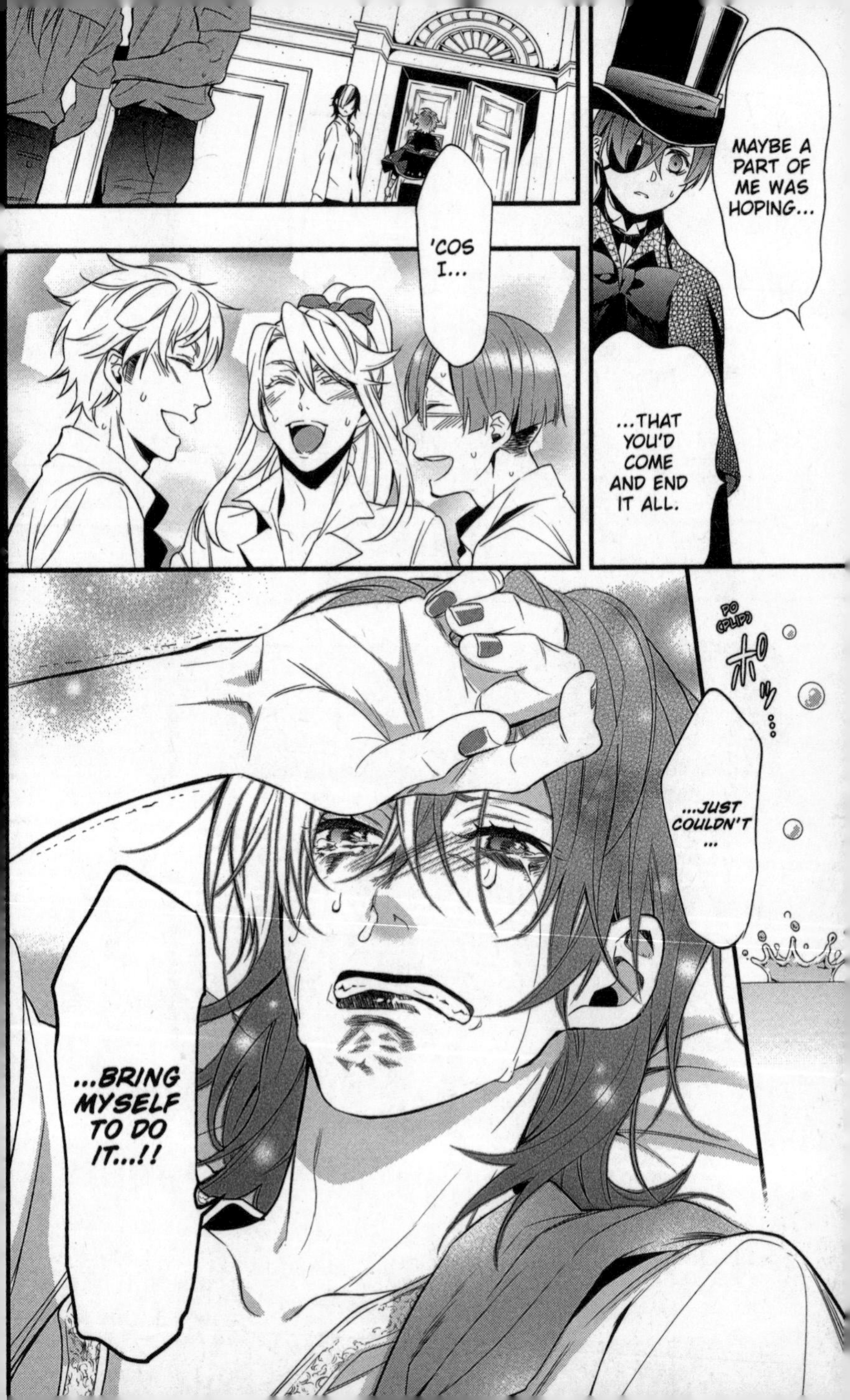
MAYBE A PART OF ME WAS HOPING...
...THAT YOU'D COME AND END IT ALL.
'COS I...
PO (PLIP)
...JUST COULDN'T ...
...BRING MYSELF TO DO IT...!!

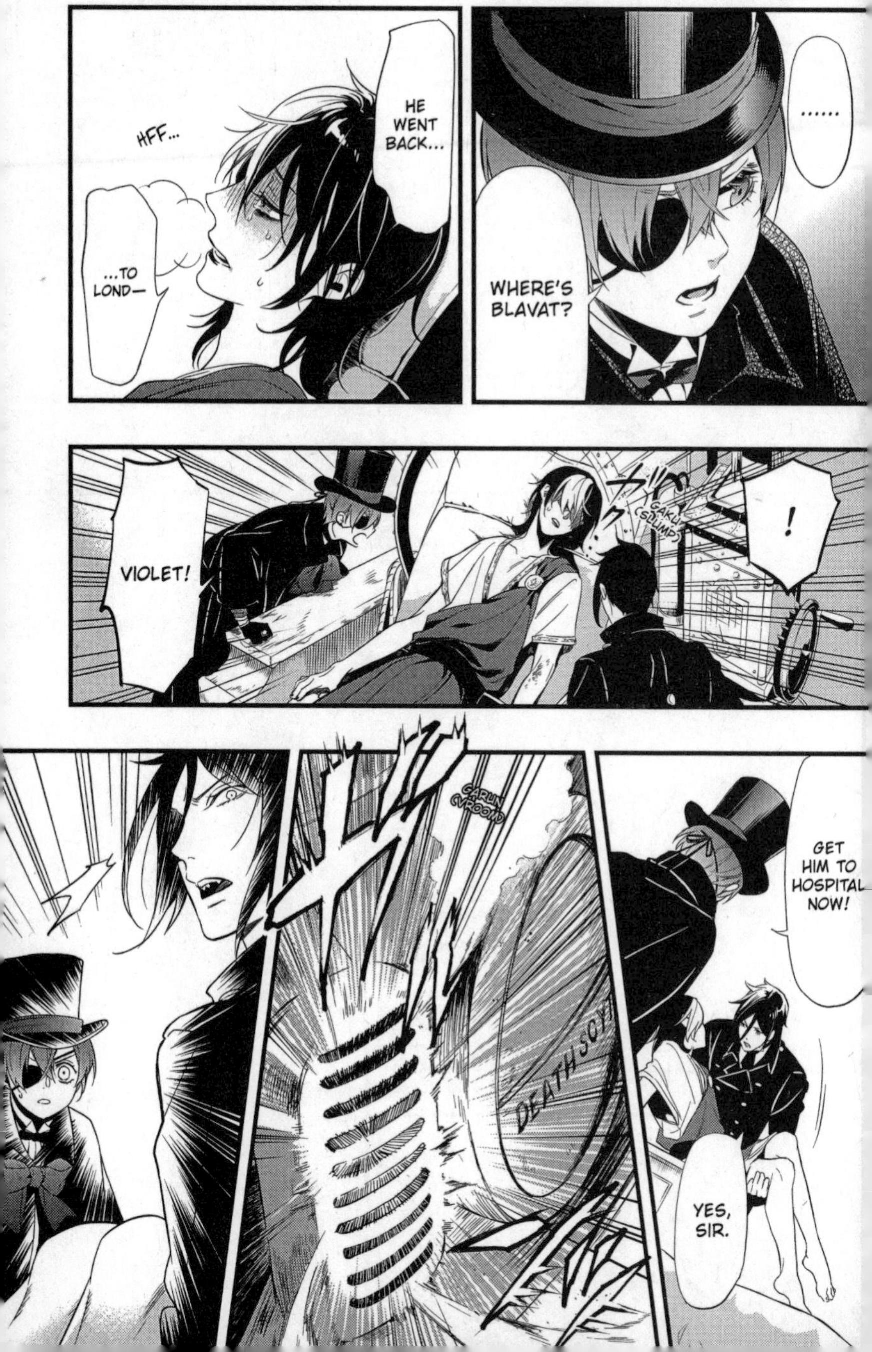
......
WHERE'S BLAVAT?
HE WENT BACK...
HFF...
...TO LOND—
!
GAKU (SLUMP)
VIOLET!
GET HIM TO HOSPITAL NOW!
YES, SIR.
GARUN (VROOM)

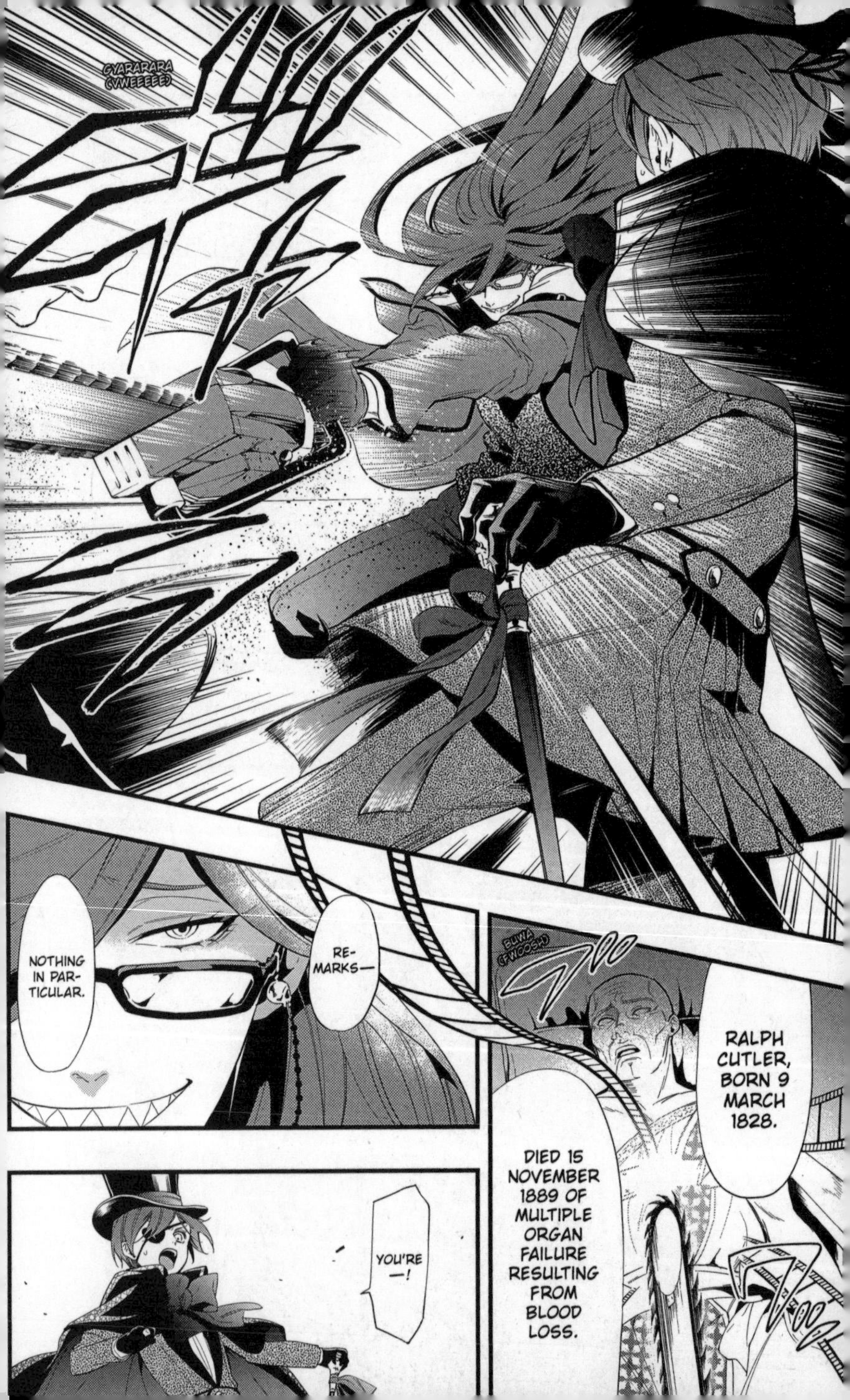
GYARARARA (VWEEEEED)
BUWA (FWOOSH)
RALPH CUTLER, BORN 9 MARCH 1828.
DIED 15 NOVEMBER 1889 OF MULTIPLE ORGAN FAILURE RESULTING FROM BLOOD LOSS.
REMARKS—
NOTHING IN PARTICULAR.
YOU'RE—!

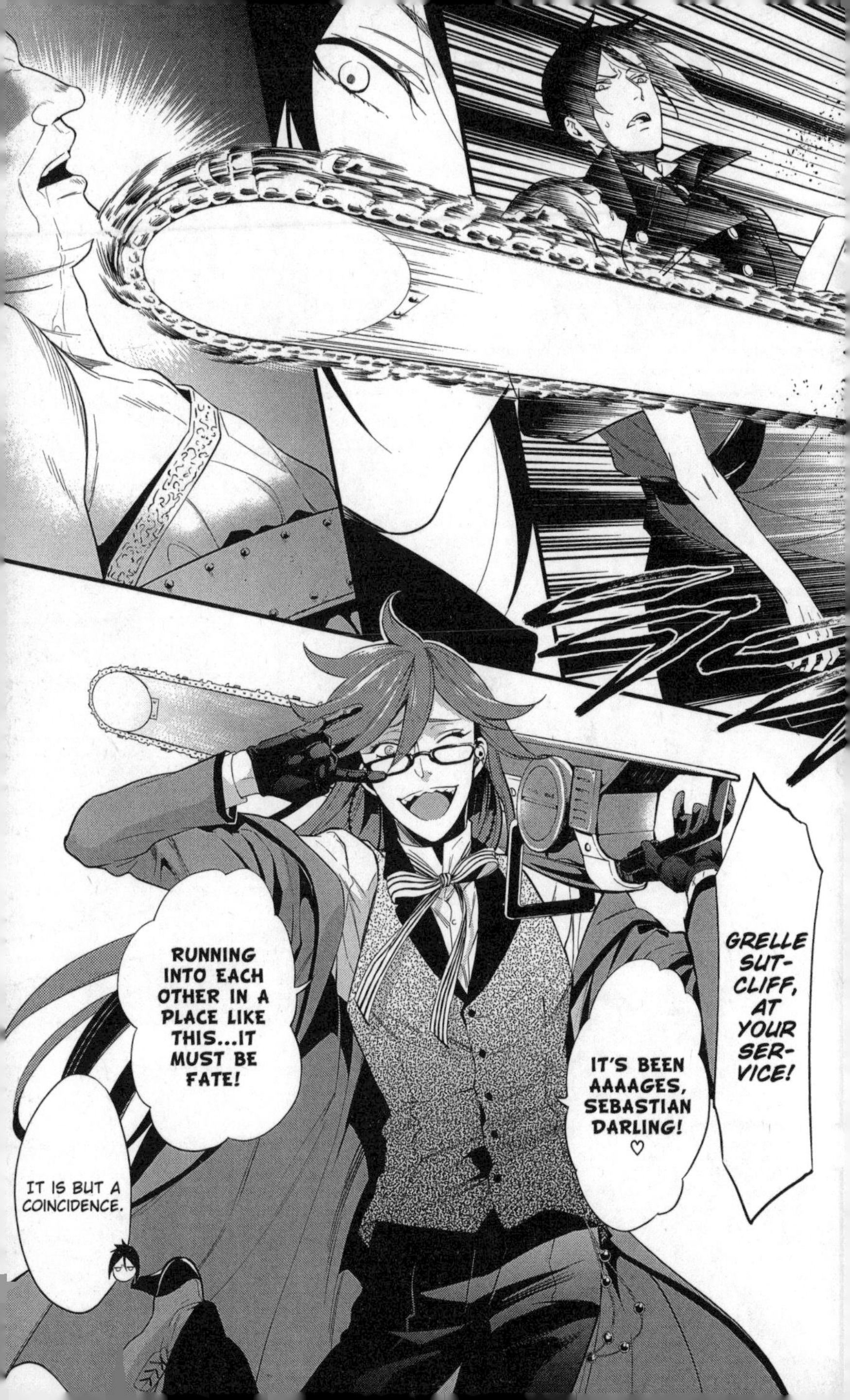
GRELLE SUT-CLIFF, AT YOUR SER-VICE!
IT'S BEEN AAAAGES, SEBASTIAN DARLING! ♡
RUNNING INTO EACH OTHER IN A PLACE LIKE THIS...IT MUST BE FATE!
IT IS BUT A COINCIDENCE.

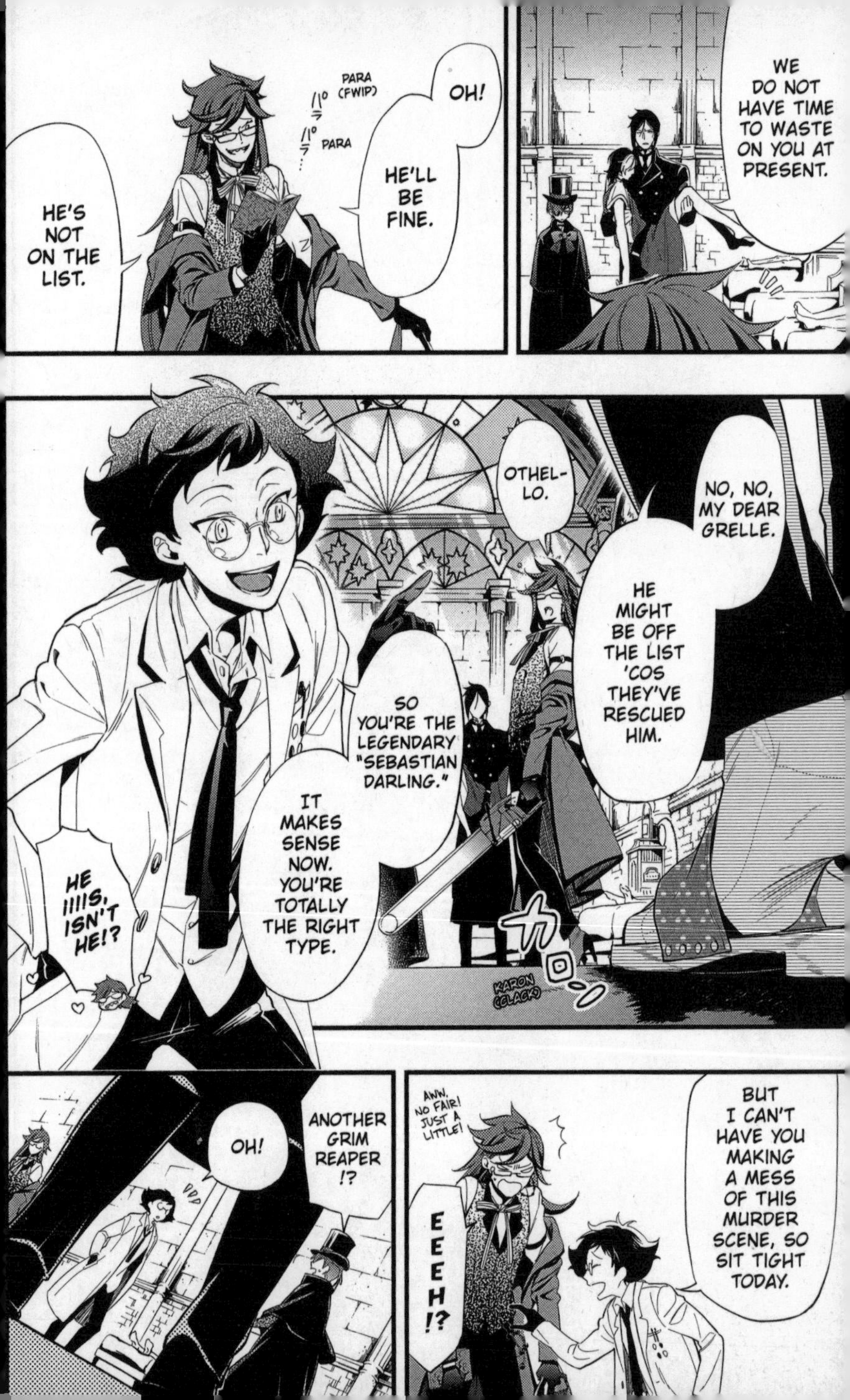
WE DO NOT HAVE TIME TO WASTE ON YOU AT PRESENT.
OH!
PARA (FWIP)
PARA
HE'LL BE FINE.
HE'S NOT ON THE LIST.
NO, NO, MY DEAR GRELLE.
OTHEL-LO.
HE MIGHT BE OFF THE LIST 'COS THEY'VE RESCUED HIM.
SO YOU'RE THE LEGENDARY "SEBASTIAN DARLING."
IT MAKES SENSE NOW. YOU'RE TOTALLY THE RIGHT TYPE.
KARON (CLACK)
HE IIIIS, ISN'T HE!?
BUT I CAN'T HAVE YOU MAKING A MESS OF THIS MURDER SCENE, SO SIT TIGHT TODAY.
AWW, NO FAIR! JUST A LITTLE!
EEEEH!?
ANOTHER GRIM REAPER!?
OH!

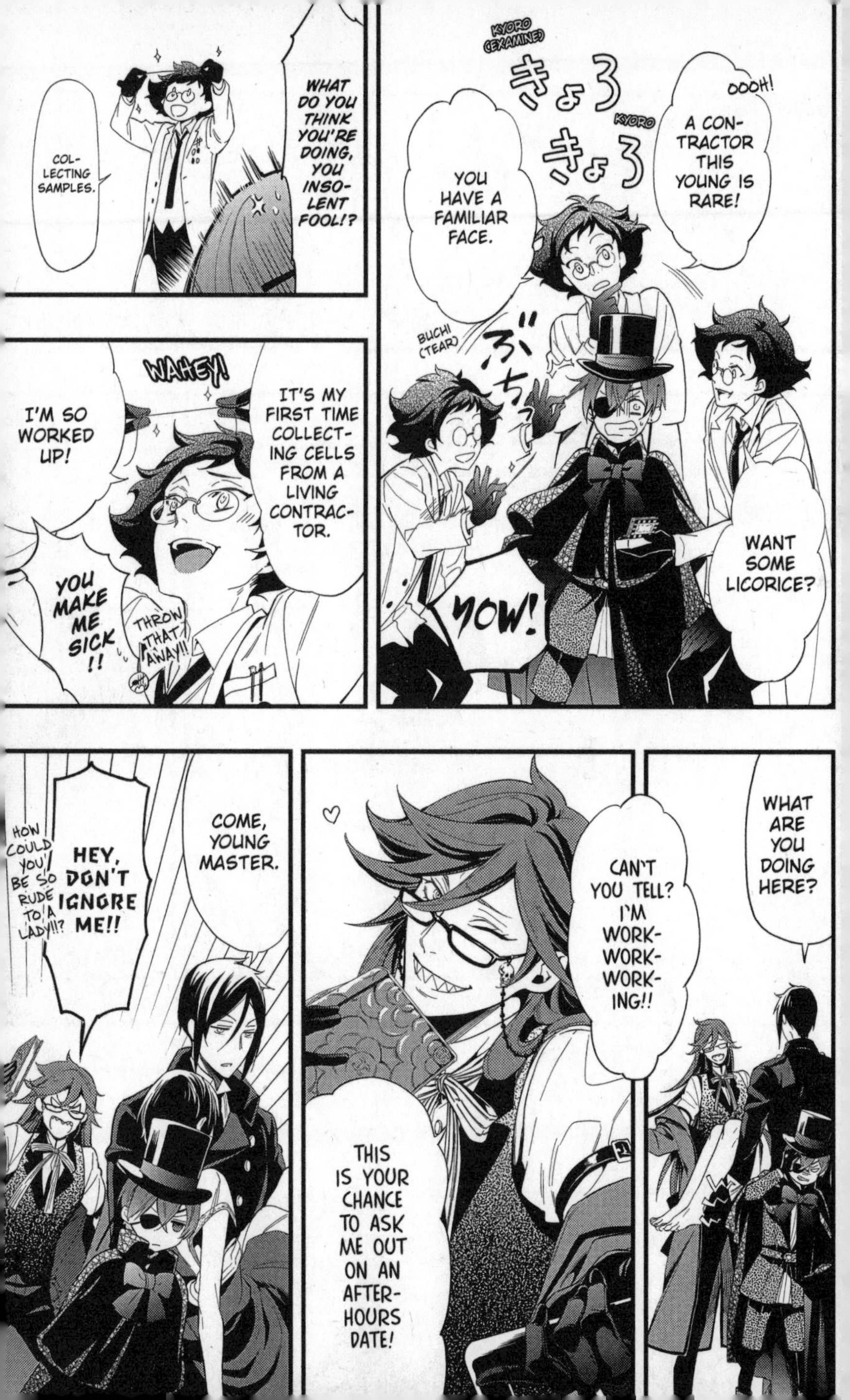
KYORO (EXAMINED)
きょろ
OOOH!
A CONTRACTOR THIS YOUNG IS RARE!
KYORO
きょろ
YOU HAVE A FAMILIAR FACE.
BUCHI (TEAR)
ぶちっ
WANT SOME LICORICE?
YOW!
WHAT DO YOU THINK YOU'RE DOING, YOU INSOLENT FOOL!?
COLLECTING SAMPLES.
IT'S MY FIRST TIME COLLECTING CELLS FROM A LIVING CONTRACTOR.
WAHEY!
I'M SO WORKED UP!
THROW THAT AWAY!!
YOU MAKE ME SICK!!
WHAT ARE YOU DOING HERE?
CAN'T YOU TELL? I'M WORK-WORK-WORKING!!
THIS IS YOUR CHANCE TO ASK ME OUT ON AN AFTER-HOURS DATE!
COME, YOUNG MASTER.
HEY, DON'T IGNORE ME!!
HOW COULD YOU BE SO RUDE TO A LADY!!?

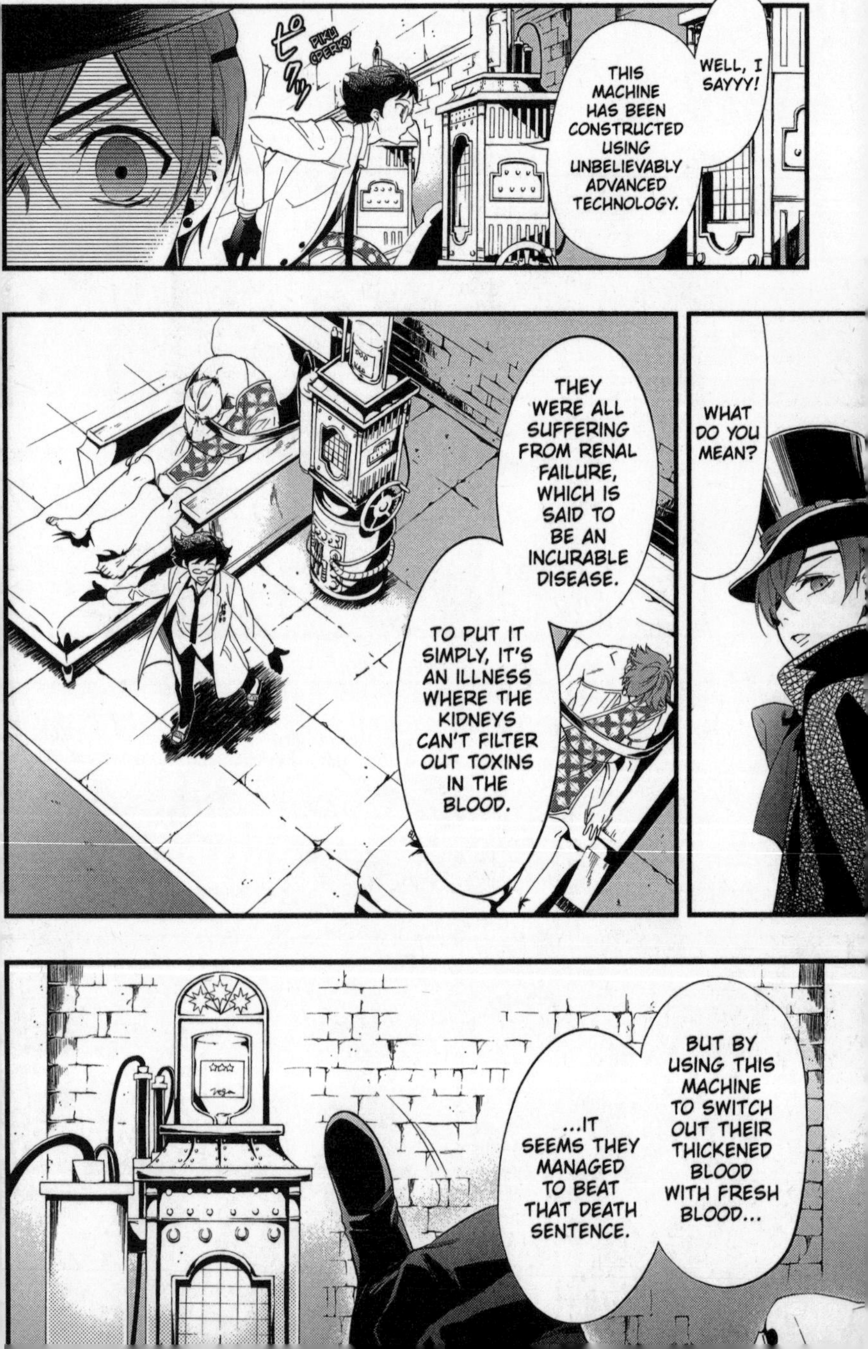
WELL, I SAYYY!
THIS MACHINE HAS BEEN CONSTRUCTED USING UNBELIEVABLY ADVANCED TECHNOLOGY.
PIKU (PERK)
WHAT DO YOU MEAN?
THEY WERE ALL SUFFERING FROM RENAL FAILURE, WHICH IS SAID TO BE AN INCURABLE DISEASE.
TO PUT IT SIMPLY, IT'S AN ILLNESS WHERE THE KIDNEYS CAN'T FILTER OUT TOXINS IN THE BLOOD.
BUT BY USING THIS MACHINE TO SWITCH OUT THEIR THICKENED BLOOD WITH FRESH BLOOD...
...IT SEEMS THEY MANAGED TO BEAT THAT DEATH SENTENCE.

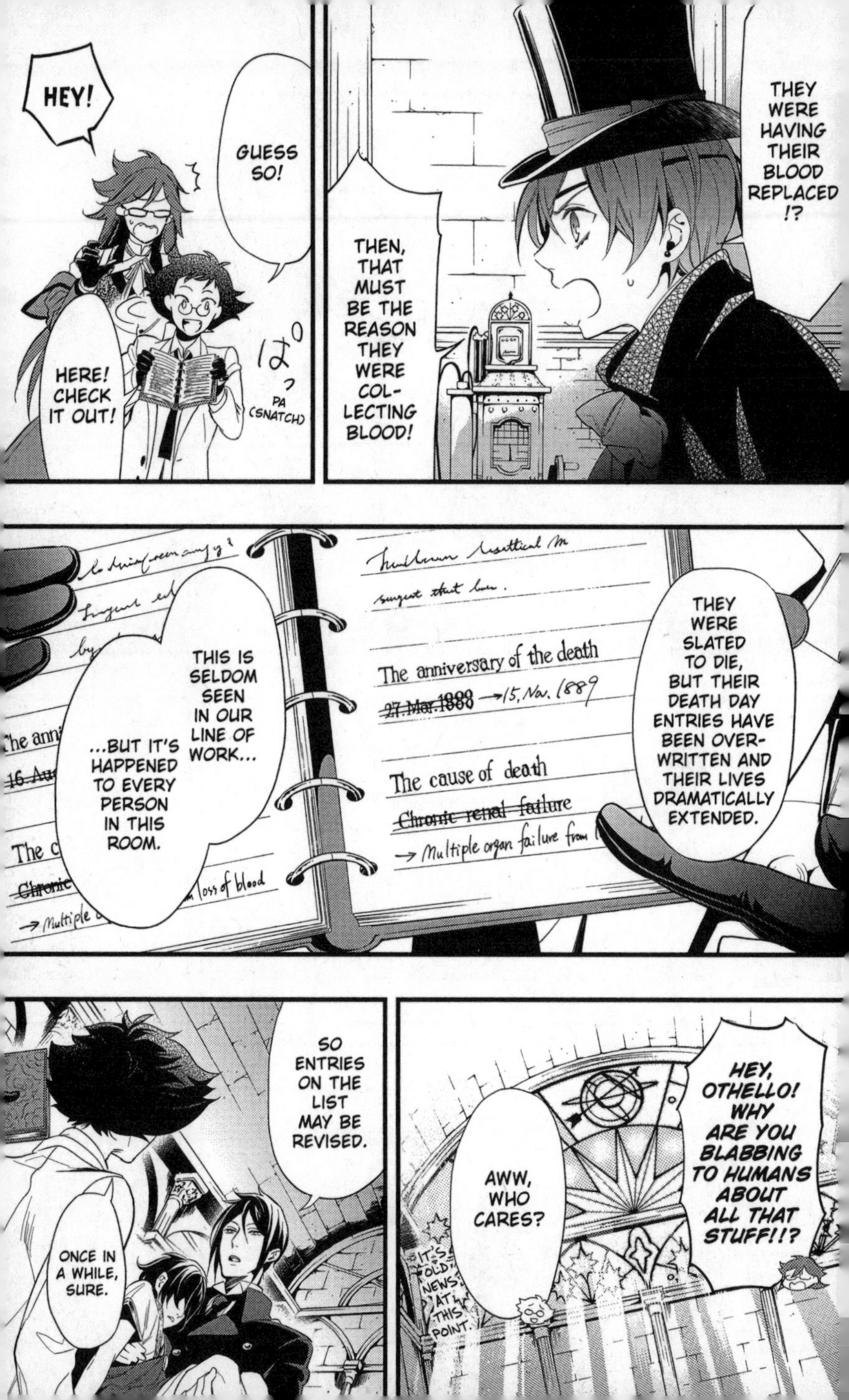
THEY WERE HAVING THEIR BLOOD REPLACED!?
THEN, THAT MUST BE THE REASON THEY WERE COLLECTING BLOOD!
GUESS SO!
HEY!
ぱっ
PA (SNATCH)
HERE! CHECK IT OUT!
The anniversary of the death
~~27.Mar.1888~~ → 15, Nov. 1889
The cause of death
~~Chronic renal failure~~
→ Multiple organ failure from
THEY WERE SLATED TO DIE, BUT THEIR DEATH DAY ENTRIES HAVE BEEN OVER-WRITTEN AND THEIR LIVES DRAMATICALLY EXTENDED.
THIS IS SELDOM SEEN IN OUR LINE OF WORK...
...BUT IT'S HAPPENED TO EVERY PERSON IN THIS ROOM.
loss of blood
→ Multiple
HEY, OTHELLO! WHY ARE YOU BLABBING TO HUMANS ABOUT ALL THAT STUFF!!?
AWW, WHO CARES?
IT'S OLD NEWS AT THIS POINT.
SO ENTRIES ON THE LIST MAY BE REVISED.
ONCE IN A WHILE, SURE.

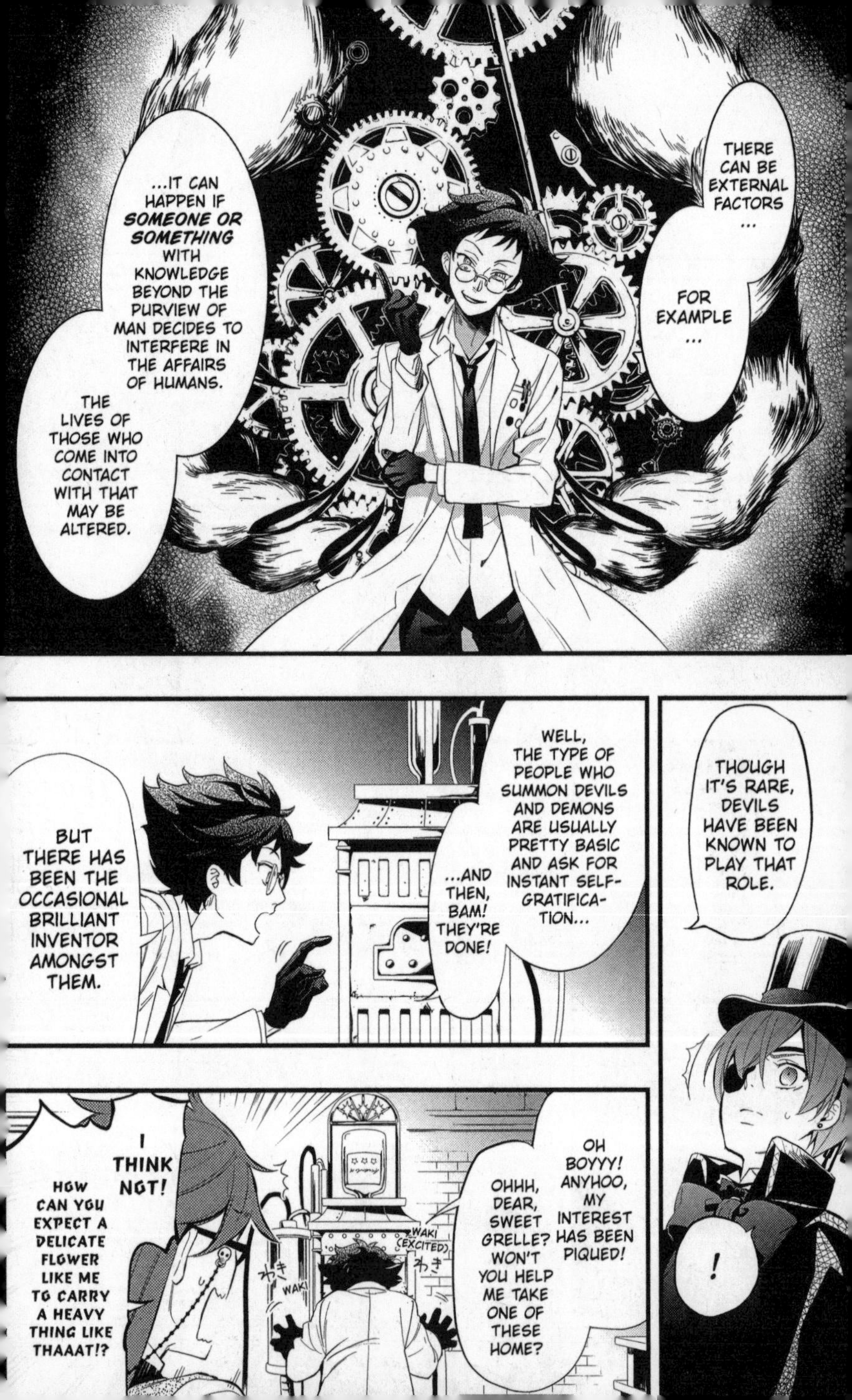
THERE CAN BE EXTERNAL FACTORS...
FOR EXAMPLE...
...IT CAN HAPPEN IF SOMEONE OR SOMETHING WITH KNOWLEDGE BEYOND THE PURVIEW OF MAN DECIDES TO INTERFERE IN THE AFFAIRS OF HUMANS.
THE LIVES OF THOSE WHO COME INTO CONTACT WITH THAT MAY BE ALTERED.
THOUGH IT'S RARE, DEVILS HAVE BEEN KNOWN TO PLAY THAT ROLE.
!
WELL, THE TYPE OF PEOPLE WHO SUMMON DEVILS AND DEMONS ARE USUALLY PRETTY BASIC AND ASK FOR INSTANT SELF-GRATIFICA-TION...
...AND THEN, BAM! THEY'RE DONE!
BUT THERE HAS BEEN THE OCCASIONAL BRILLIANT INVENTOR AMONGST THEM.
OH BOYYY! ANYHOO, MY INTEREST HAS BEEN PIQUED!
OHHH, DEAR, SWEET GRELLE? WON'T YOU HELP ME TAKE ONE OF THESE HOME?
わき WAKI (EXCITED)
わき WAKI
I THINK NOT!
HOW CAN YOU EXPECT A DELICATE FLOWER LIKE ME TO CARRY A HEAVY THING LIKE THAAAT!?

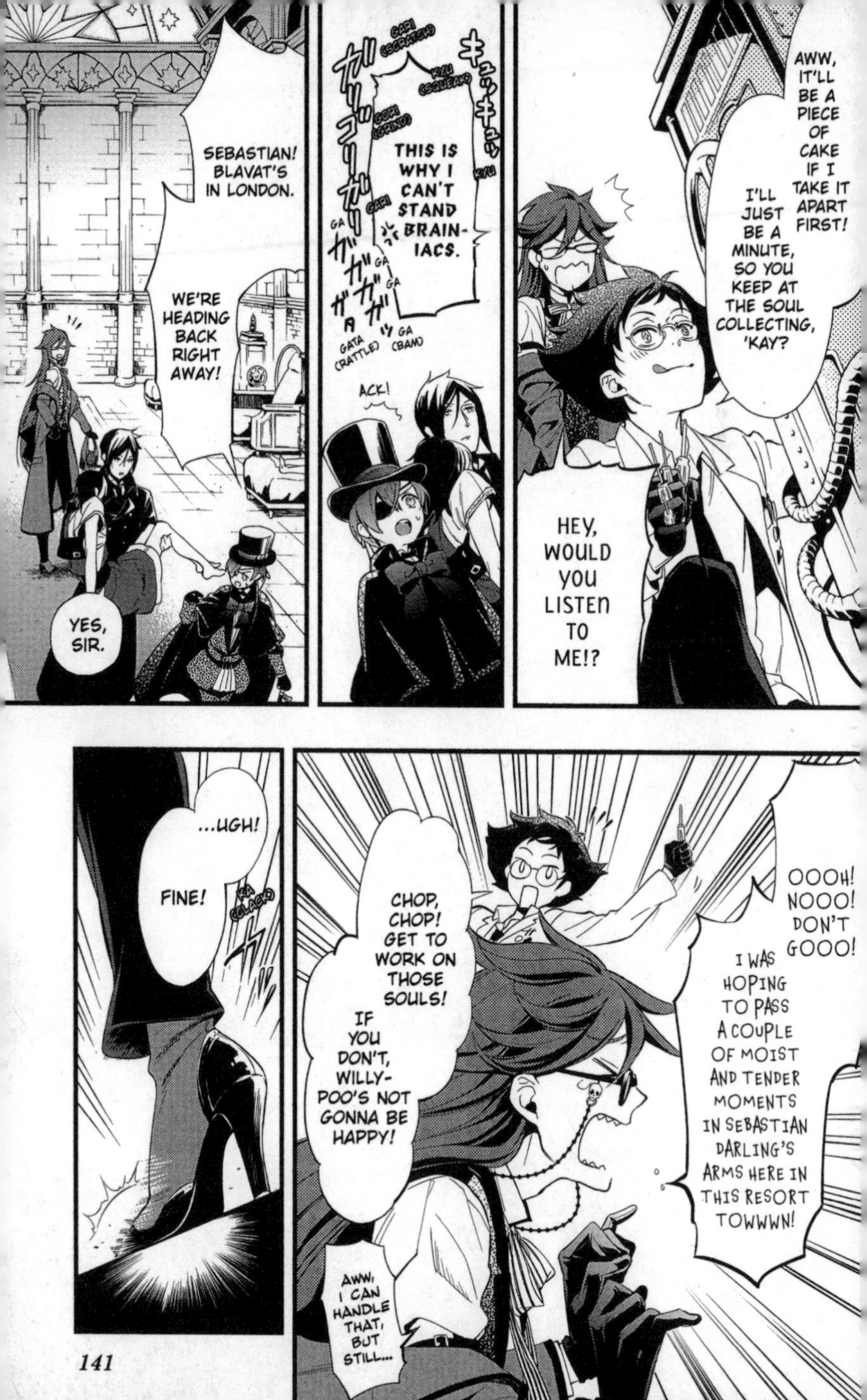
AWW, IT'LL BE A PIECE OF CAKE IF I TAKE IT APART FIRST!
I'LL JUST BE A MINUTE, SO YOU KEEP AT THE SOUL COLLECTING, 'KAY?
HEY, WOULD YOU LISTEN TO ME!?
KYU (SQUEAK)
KYU
GARI (SCRATCH)
GORI (GRIND)
GARI
THIS IS WHY I CAN'T STAND BRAINIACS.
GA
GA
GA
GATA (RATTLE)
GA (BAM)
ACK!
SEBASTIAN! BLAVAT'S IN LONDON.
WE'RE HEADING BACK RIGHT AWAY!
YES, SIR.
OOOH! NOOO! DON'T GOOO!
I WAS HOPING TO PASS A COUPLE OF MOIST AND TENDER MOMENTS IN SEBASTIAN DARLING'S ARMS HERE IN THIS RESORT TOWWWN!
CHOP, CHOP! GET TO WORK ON THOSE SOULS!
IF YOU DON'T, WILLY-POO'S NOT GONNA BE HAPPY!
AWW, I CAN HANDLE THAT, BUT STILL...
...UGH!
FINE!
KA (CLACK)

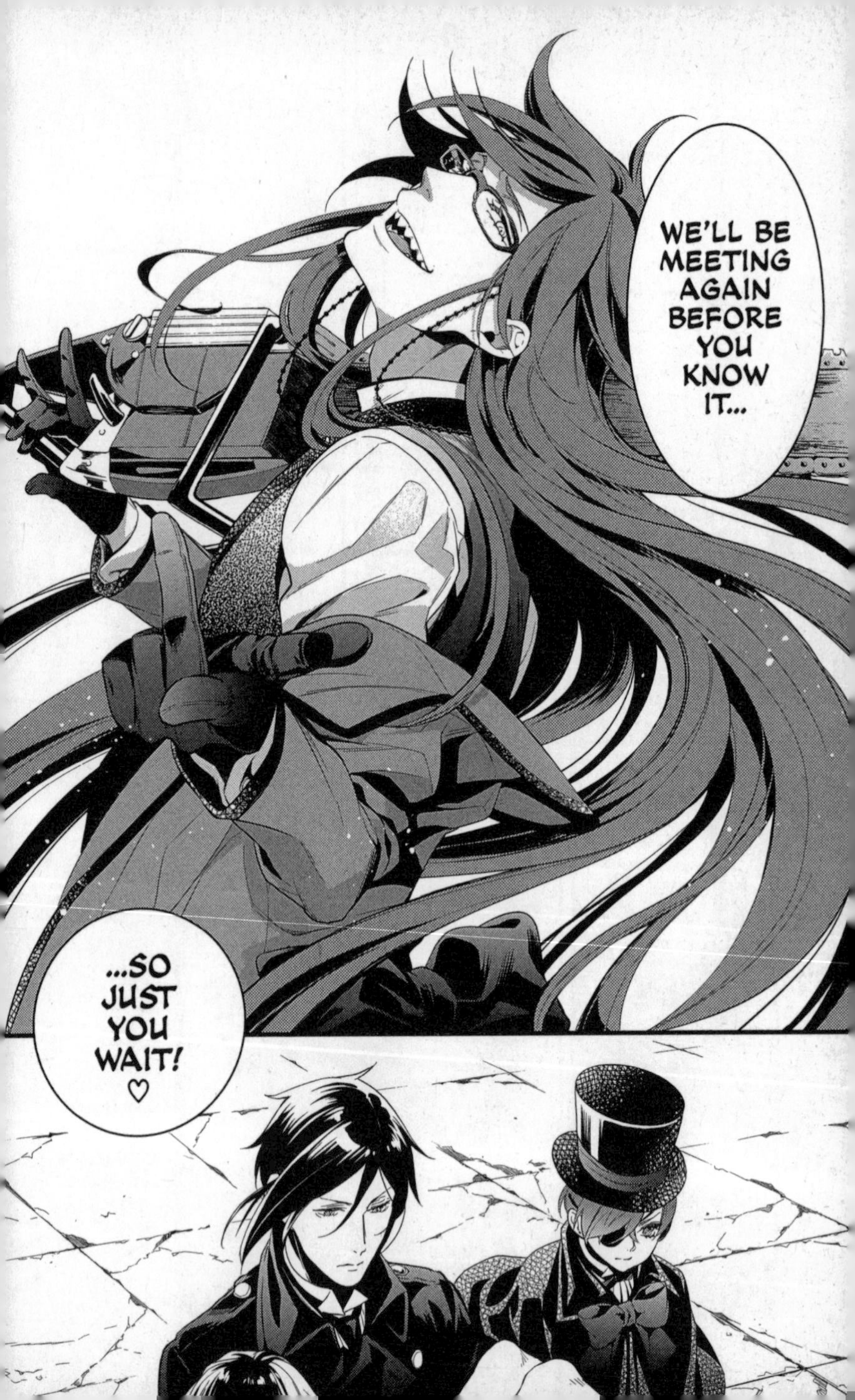
WE'LL BE MEETING AGAIN BEFORE YOU KNOW IT...
...SO JUST YOU WAIT! ♡

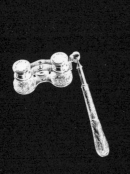

Black Butler

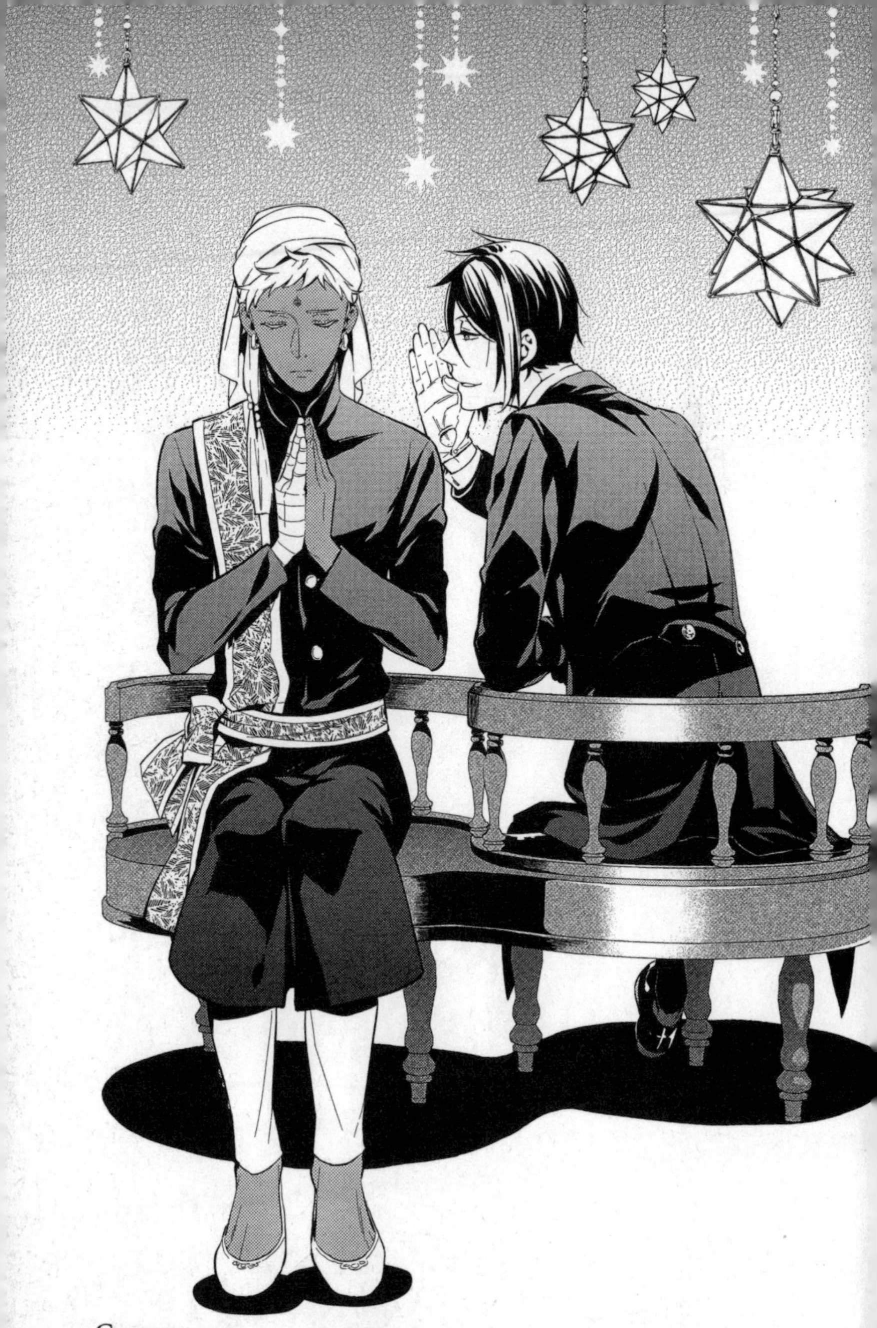

Chapter 125

At midnight : The Butler, Returning Home

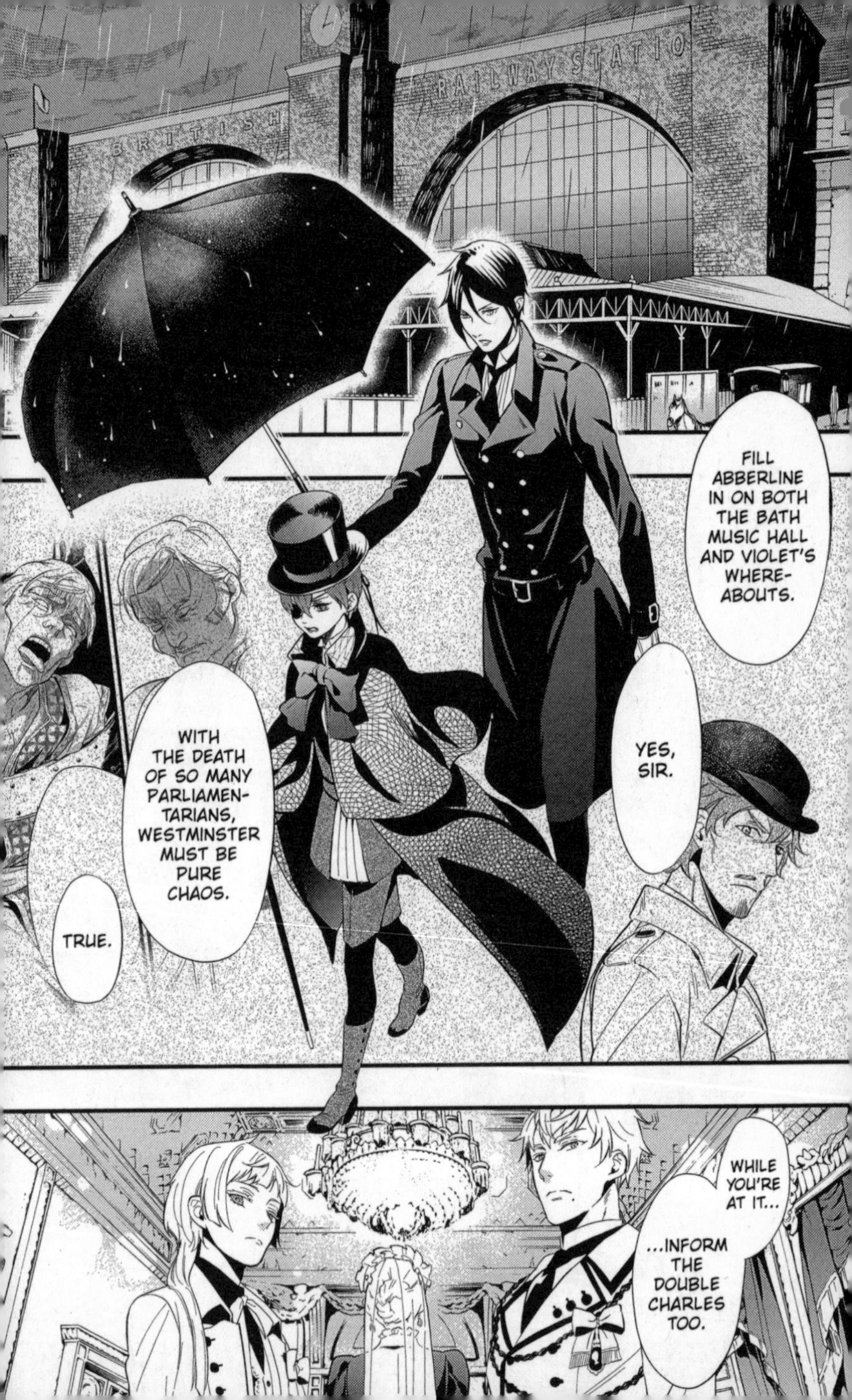
BRITISH RAILWAY STATIO
FILL ABBERLINE IN ON BOTH THE BATH MUSIC HALL AND VIOLET'S WHEREABOUTS.
YES, SIR.
WITH THE DEATH OF SO MANY PARLIAMENTARIANS, WESTMINSTER MUST BE PURE CHAOS.
TRUE.
WHILE YOU'RE AT IT...
...INFORM THE DOUBLE CHARLES TOO.

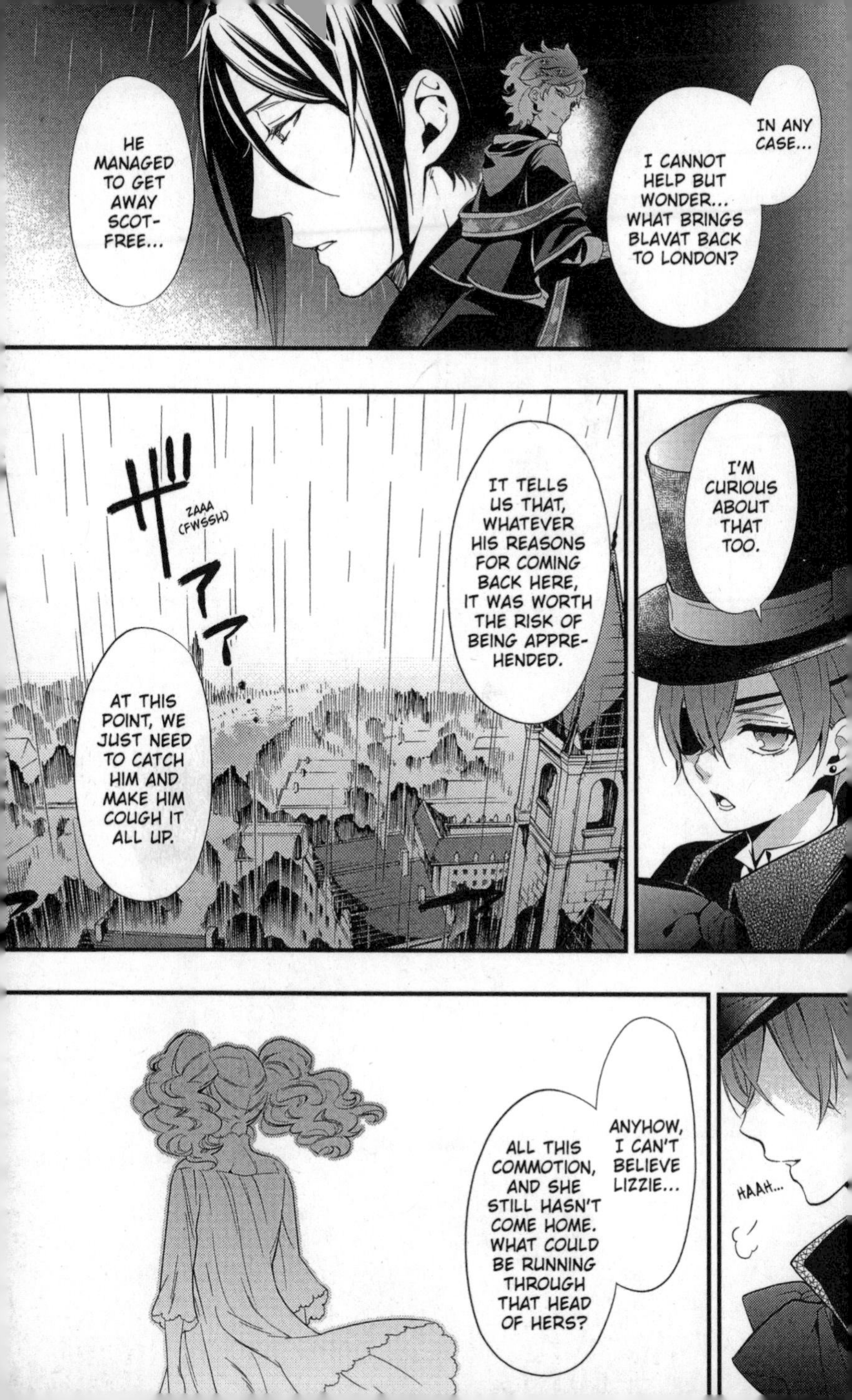

IN ANY CASE... I CANNOT HELP BUT WONDER... WHAT BRINGS BLAVAT BACK TO LONDON?
HE MANAGED TO GET AWAY SCOT-FREE...
I'M CURIOUS ABOUT THAT TOO.
IT TELLS US THAT, WHATEVER HIS REASONS FOR COMING BACK HERE, IT WAS WORTH THE RISK OF BEING APPRE-HENDED.
ザァァ
ZAAA (FWSSH)
AT THIS POINT, WE JUST NEED TO CATCH HIM AND MAKE HIM COUGH IT ALL UP.
HAAH...
ANYHOW, I CAN'T BELIEVE LIZZIE...
ALL THIS COMMOTION, AND SHE STILL HASN'T COME HOME. WHAT COULD BE RUNNING THROUGH THAT HEAD OF HERS?

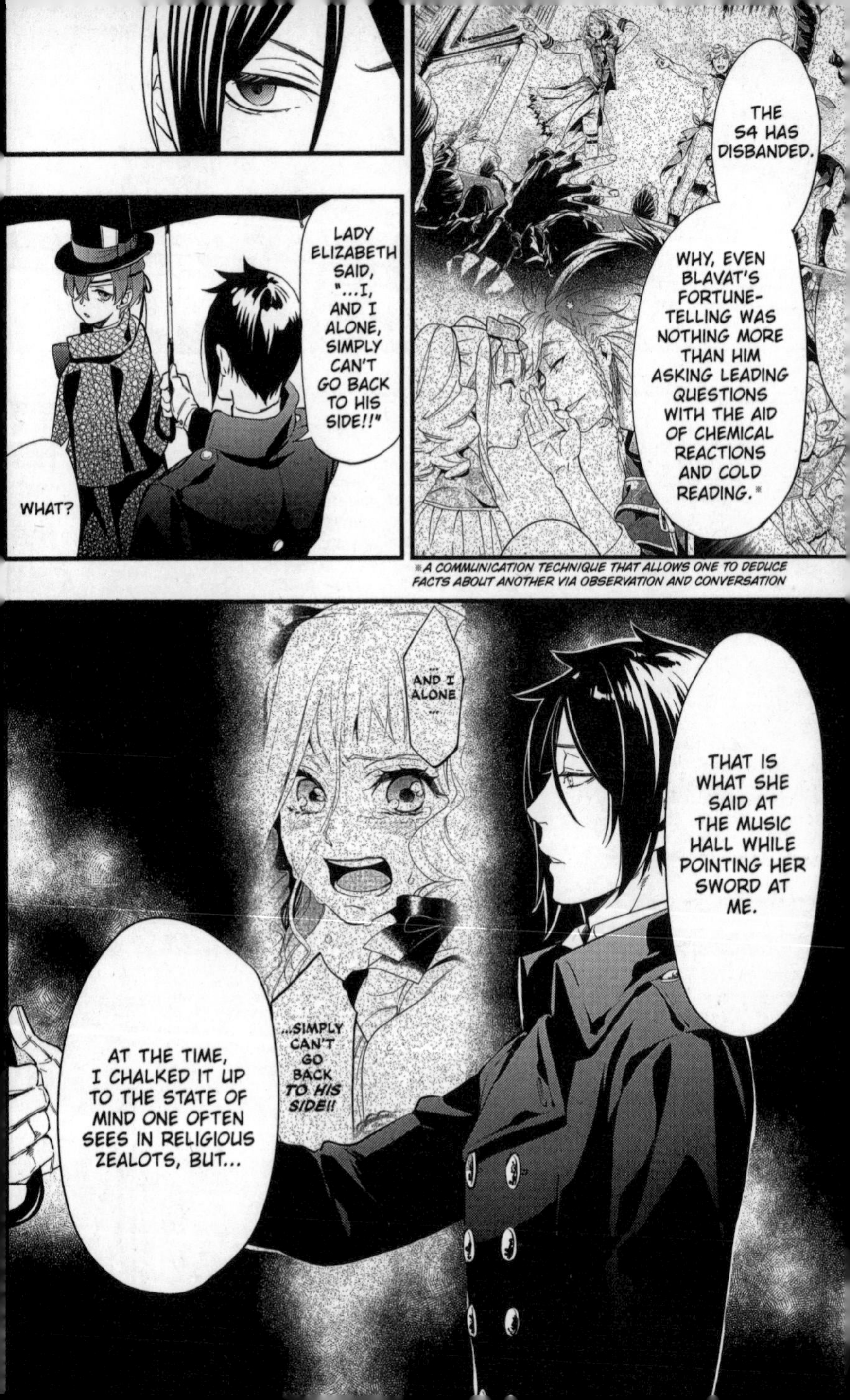
THE S4 HAS DISBANDED.
WHY, EVEN BLAVAT'S FORTUNE-TELLING WAS NOTHING MORE THAN HIM ASKING LEADING QUESTIONS WITH THE AID OF CHEMICAL REACTIONS AND COLD READING.*
LADY ELIZABETH SAID, "...I, AND I ALONE, SIMPLY CAN'T GO BACK TO HIS SIDE!!"
WHAT?
*A COMMUNICATION TECHNIQUE THAT ALLOWS ONE TO DEDUCE FACTS ABOUT ANOTHER VIA OBSERVATION AND CONVERSATION
THAT IS WHAT SHE SAID AT THE MUSIC HALL WHILE POINTING HER SWORD AT ME.
...AND I ALONE...
...SIMPLY CAN'T GO BACK TO HIS SIDE!!
AT THE TIME, I CHALKED IT UP TO THE STATE OF MIND ONE OFTEN SEES IN RELIGIOUS ZEALOTS, BUT...

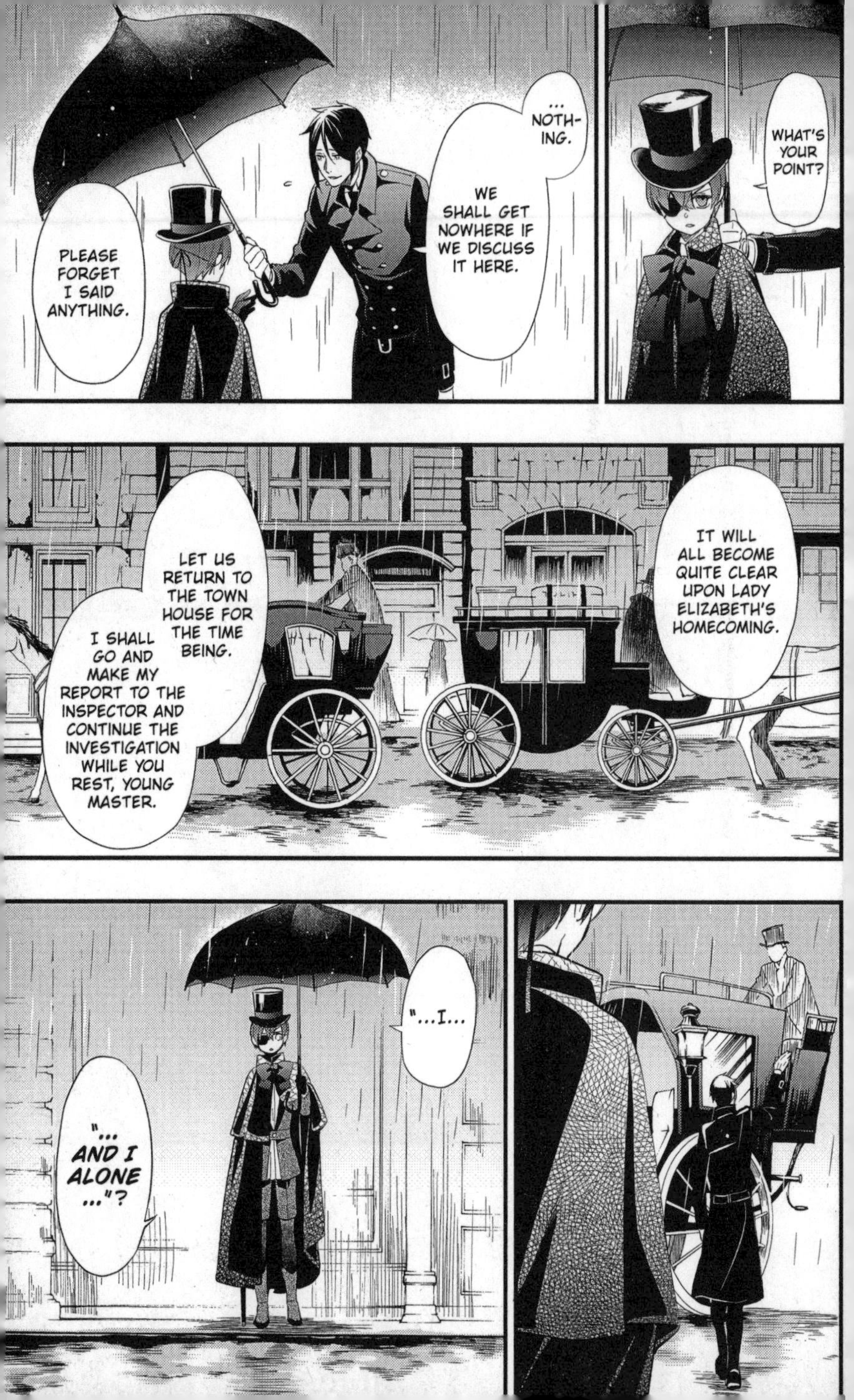
WHAT'S YOUR POINT?
...NOTH-ING.
WE SHALL GET NOWHERE IF WE DISCUSS IT HERE.
PLEASE FORGET I SAID ANYTHING.
IT WILL ALL BECOME QUITE CLEAR UPON LADY ELIZABETH'S HOMECOMING.
LET US RETURN TO THE TOWN HOUSE FOR THE TIME BEING.
I SHALL GO AND MAKE MY REPORT TO THE INSPECTOR AND CONTINUE THE INVESTIGATION WHILE YOU REST, YOUNG MASTER.
"...I...
"... AND I ALONE ..."?

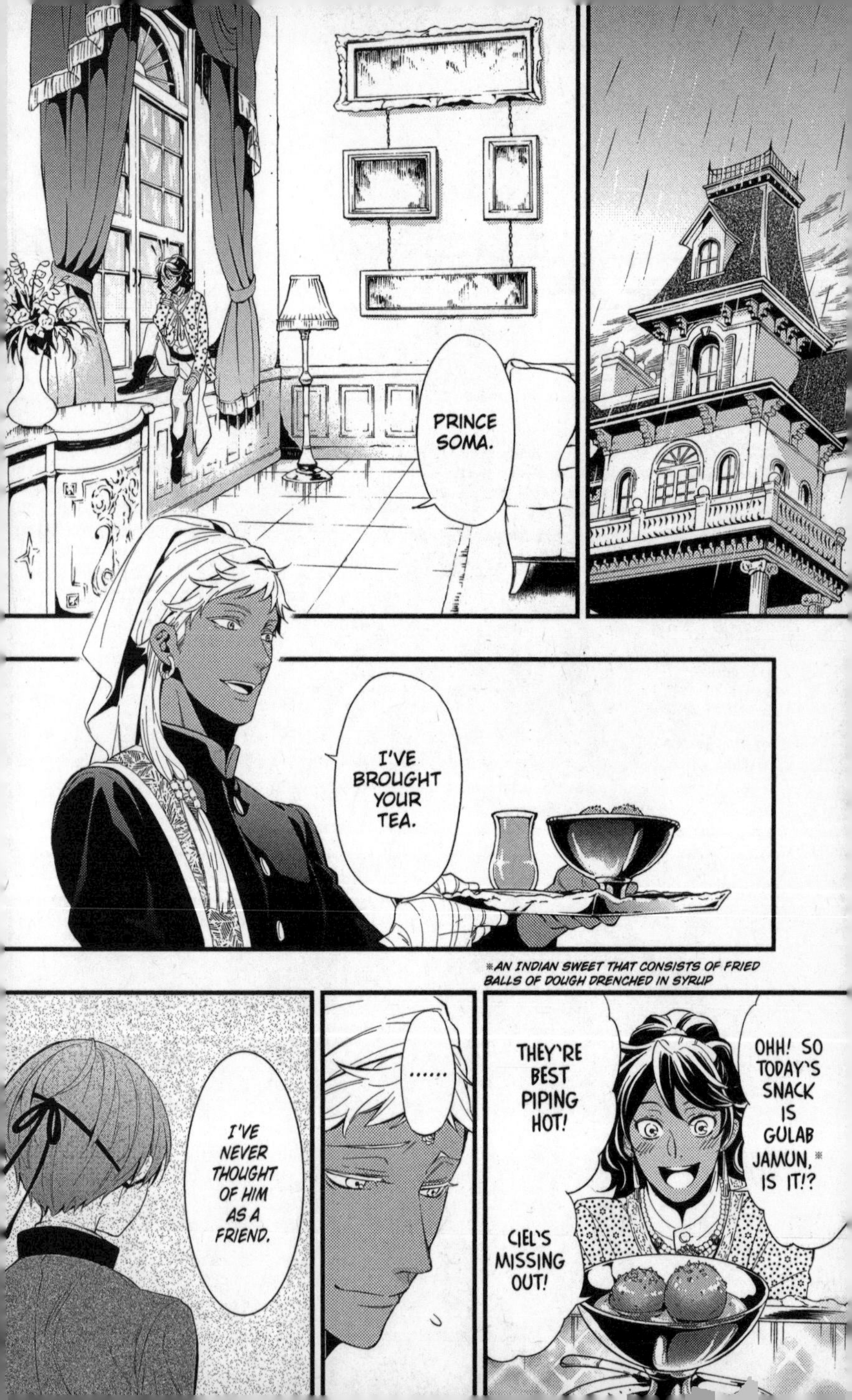
PRINCE SOMA.
I'VE BROUGHT YOUR TEA.
※AN INDIAN SWEET THAT CONSISTS OF FRIED BALLS OF DOUGH DRENCHED IN SYRUP
OHH! SO TODAY'S SNACK IS GULAB JAMUN,※ IS IT!?
THEY'RE BEST PIPING HOT!
CIEL'S MISSING OUT!
......
I'VE NEVER THOUGHT OF HIM AS A FRIEND.

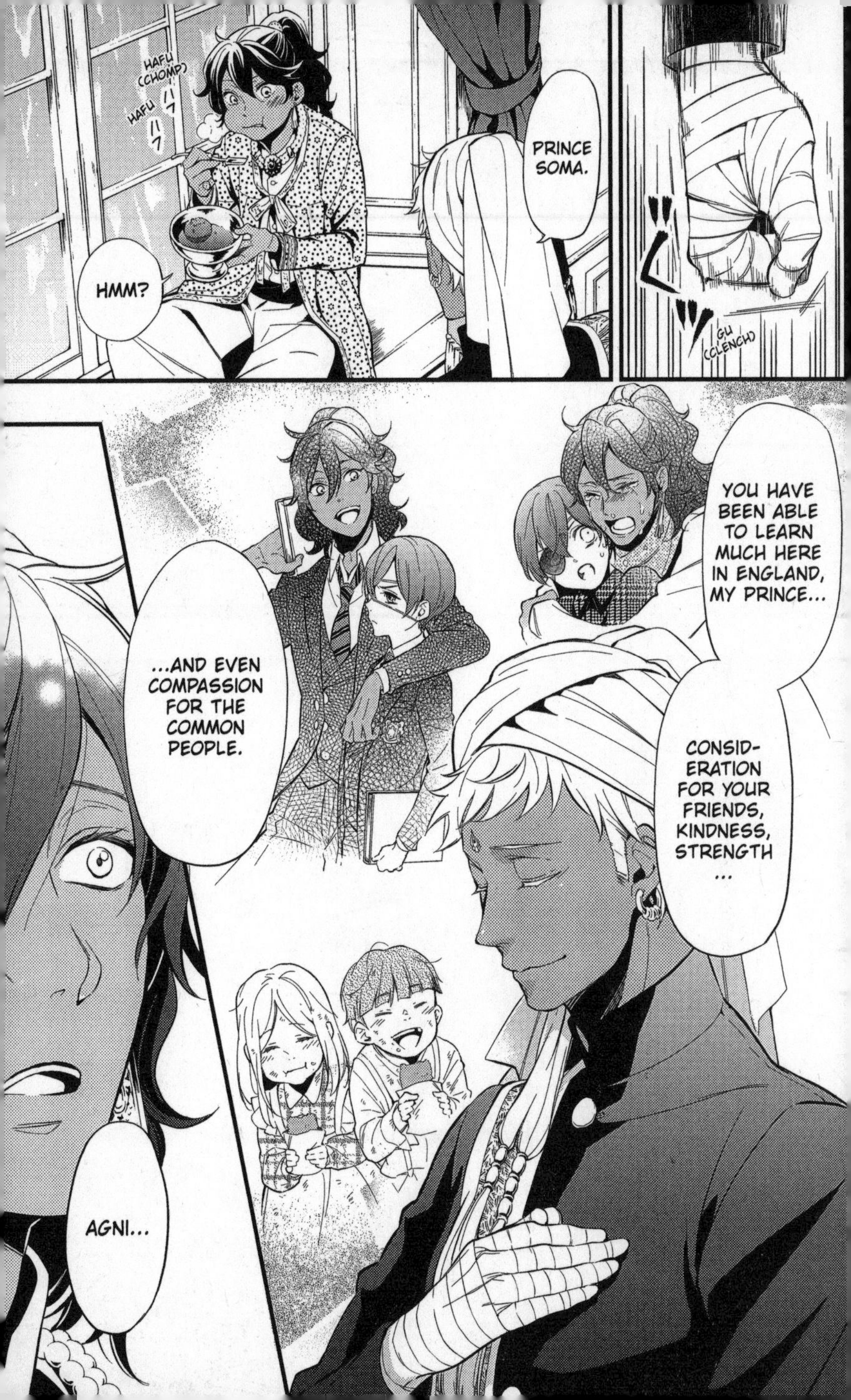
GU (CLENCH)
PRINCE SOMA.
HAFU (CHOMP) HAFU
ハフ ハフ
HMM?
YOU HAVE BEEN ABLE TO LEARN MUCH HERE IN ENGLAND, MY PRINCE...
CONSID-ERATION FOR YOUR FRIENDS, KINDNESS, STRENGTH...
...AND EVEN COMPASSION FOR THE COMMON PEOPLE.
AGNI...

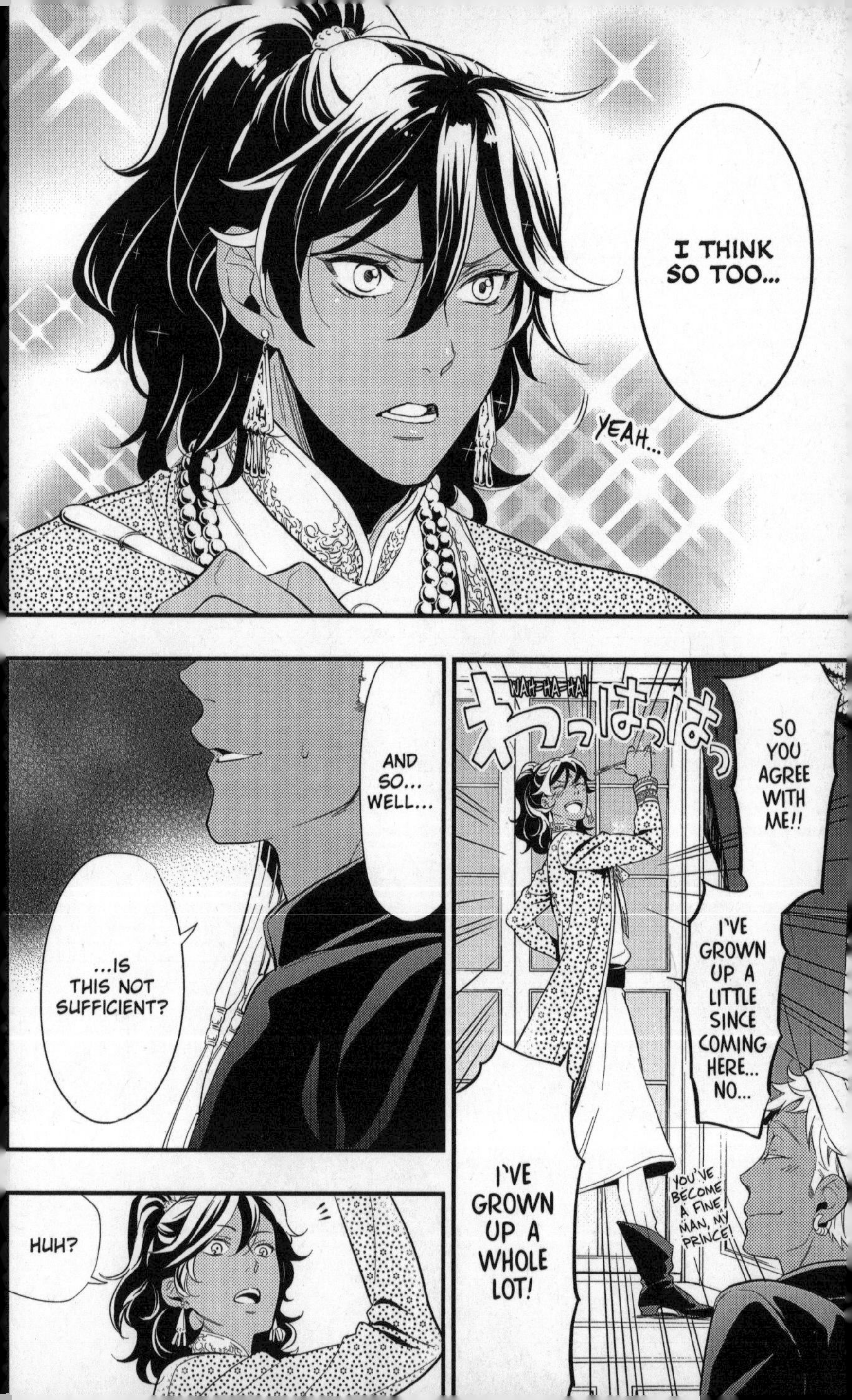
I THINK SO TOO...
YEAH...
WAH-HA-HA!
わっはっはっ
SO YOU AGREE WITH ME!!
I'VE GROWN UP A LITTLE SINCE COMING HERE... NO...
YOU'VE BECOME A FINE MAN, MY PRINCE!
I'VE GROWN UP A WHOLE LOT!
AND SO... WELL...
...IS THIS NOT SUFFICIENT?
HUH?

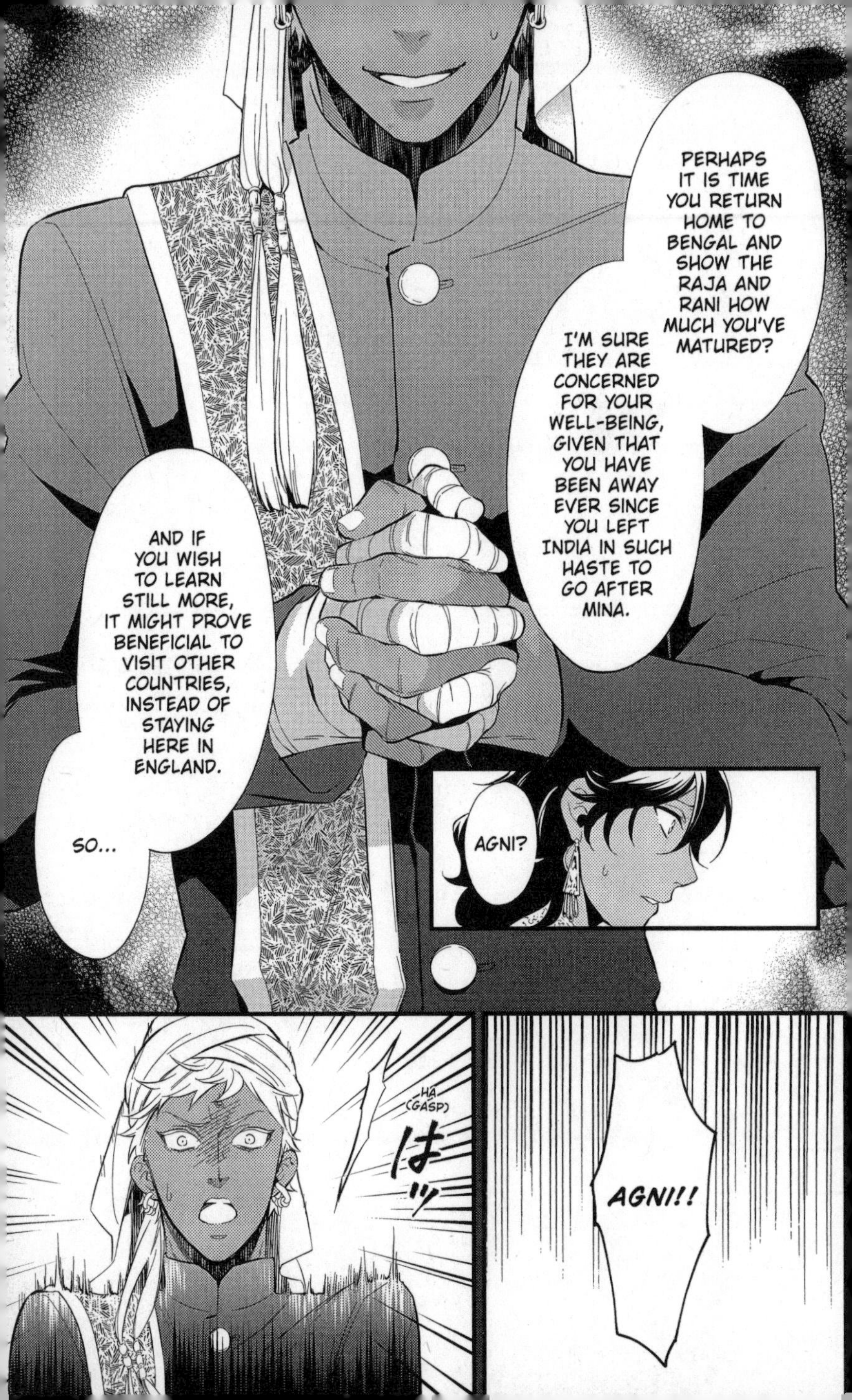
PERHAPS IT IS TIME YOU RETURN HOME TO BENGAL AND SHOW THE RAJA AND RANI HOW MUCH YOU'VE MATURED?
I'M SURE THEY ARE CONCERNED FOR YOUR WELL-BEING, GIVEN THAT YOU HAVE BEEN AWAY EVER SINCE YOU LEFT INDIA IN SUCH HASTE TO GO AFTER MINA.
AND IF YOU WISH TO LEARN STILL MORE, IT MIGHT PROVE BENEFICIAL TO VISIT OTHER COUNTRIES, INSTEAD OF STAYING HERE IN ENGLAND.
SO...
AGNI?
AGNI!!
HA (GASP)
はッ

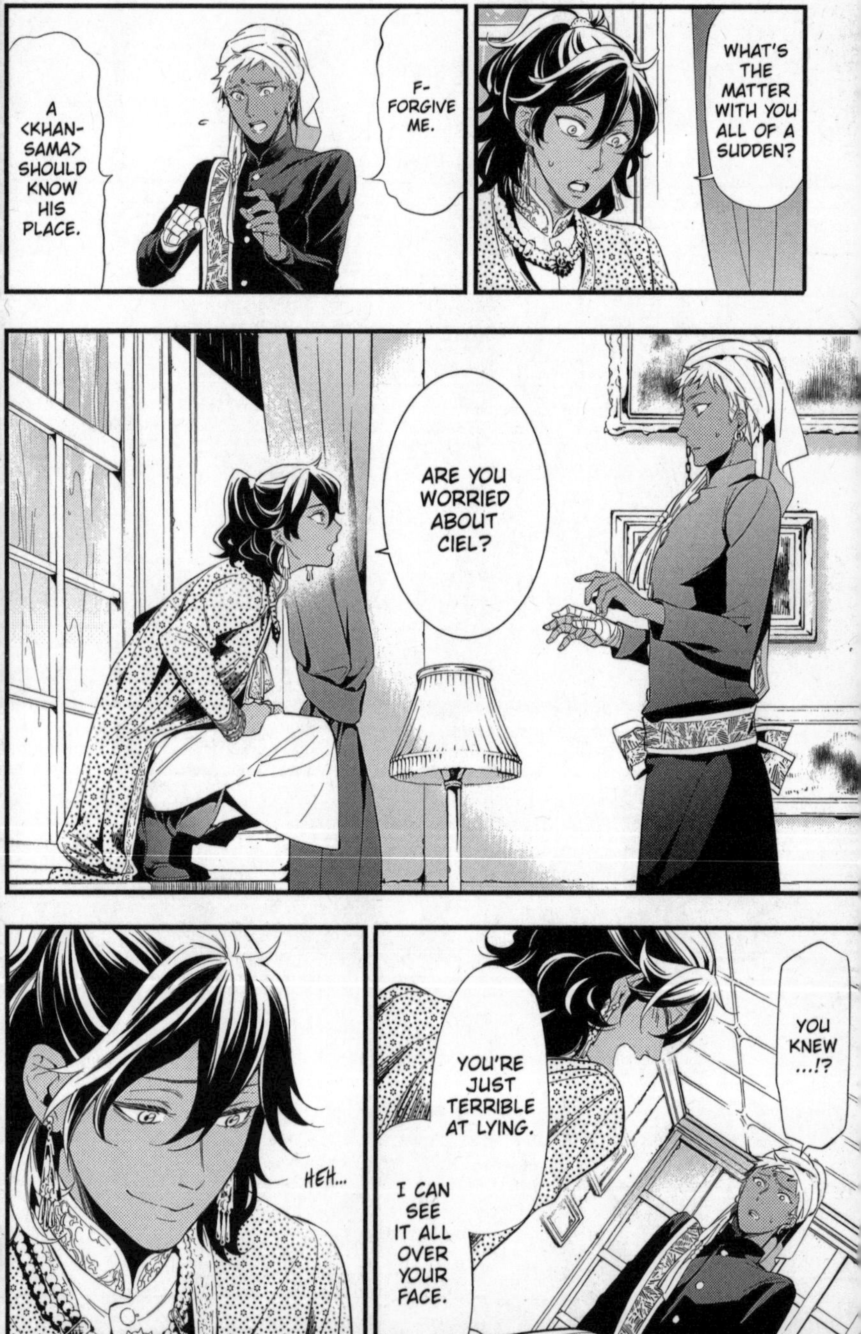
WHAT'S THE MATTER WITH YOU ALL OF A SUDDEN?
F-FORGIVE ME.
A <KHAN-SAMA> SHOULD KNOW HIS PLACE.
ARE YOU WORRIED ABOUT CIEL?
YOU KNEW ...!?
YOU'RE JUST TERRIBLE AT LYING.
I CAN SEE IT ALL OVER YOUR FACE.
HEH...

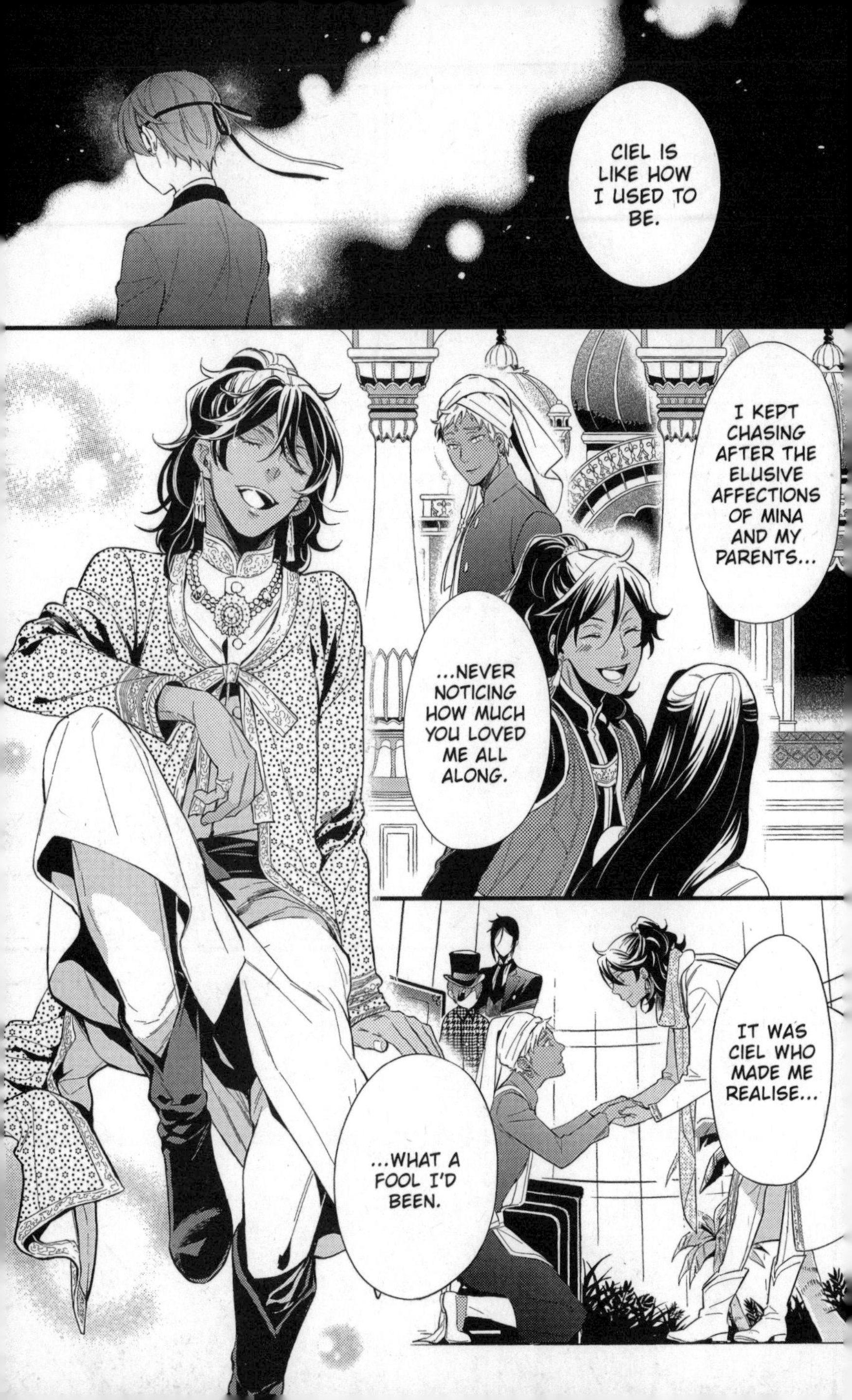
CIEL IS LIKE HOW I USED TO BE.
I KEPT CHASING AFTER THE ELUSIVE AFFECTIONS OF MINA AND MY PARENTS...
...NEVER NOTICING HOW MUCH YOU LOVED ME ALL ALONG.
IT WAS CIEL WHO MADE ME REALISE...
...WHAT A FOOL I'D BEEN.

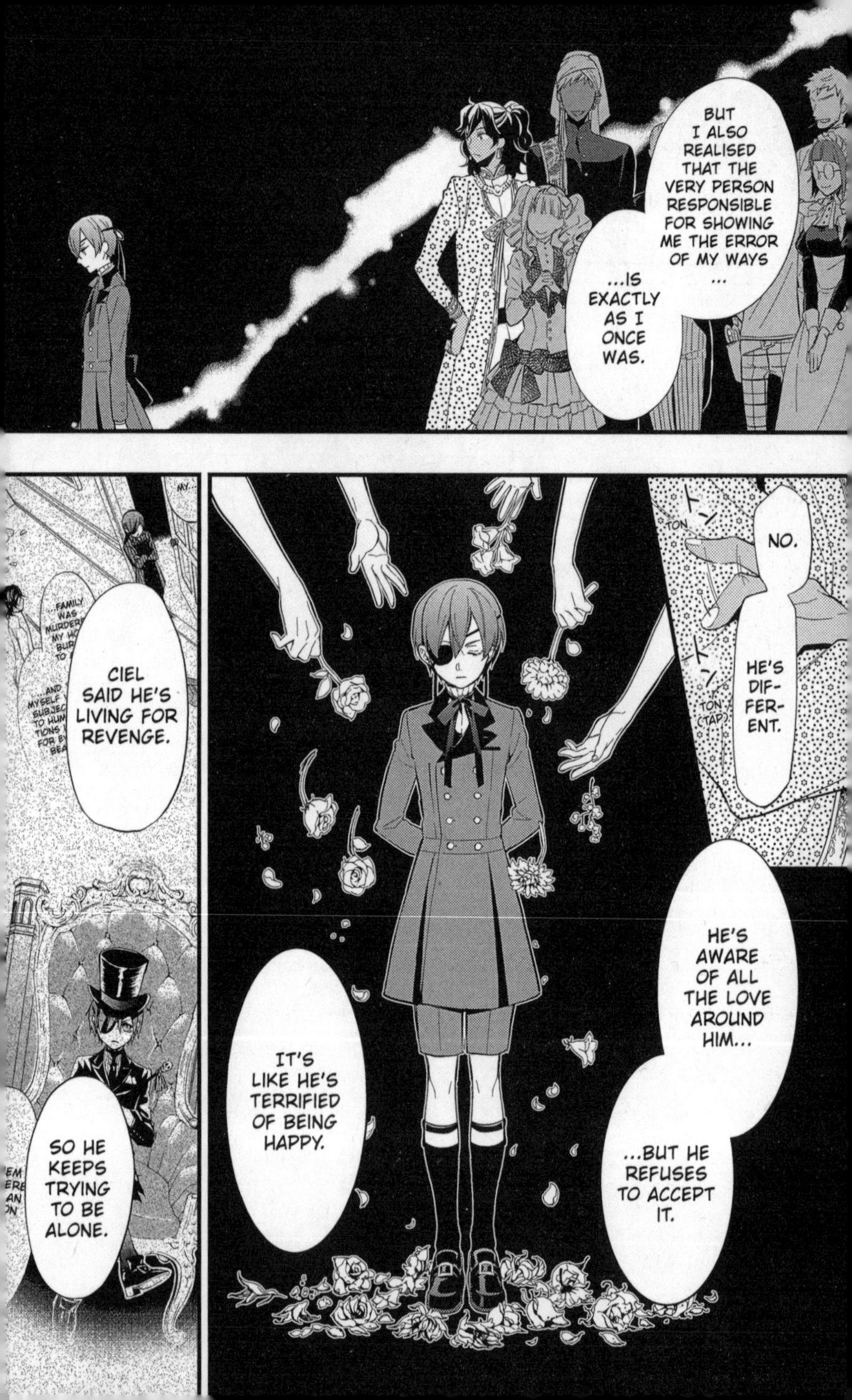
BUT I ALSO REALISED THAT THE VERY PERSON RESPONSIBLE FOR SHOWING ME THE ERROR OF MY WAYS ...
...IS EXACTLY AS I ONCE WAS.
TON
NO.
TON (TAP)
HE'S DIF-FER-ENT.
HE'S AWARE OF ALL THE LOVE AROUND HIM...
...BUT HE REFUSES TO ACCEPT IT.
IT'S LIKE HE'S TERRIFIED OF BEING HAPPY.
MY...
CIEL SAID HE'S LIVING FOR REVENGE.
SO HE KEEPS TRYING TO BE ALONE.

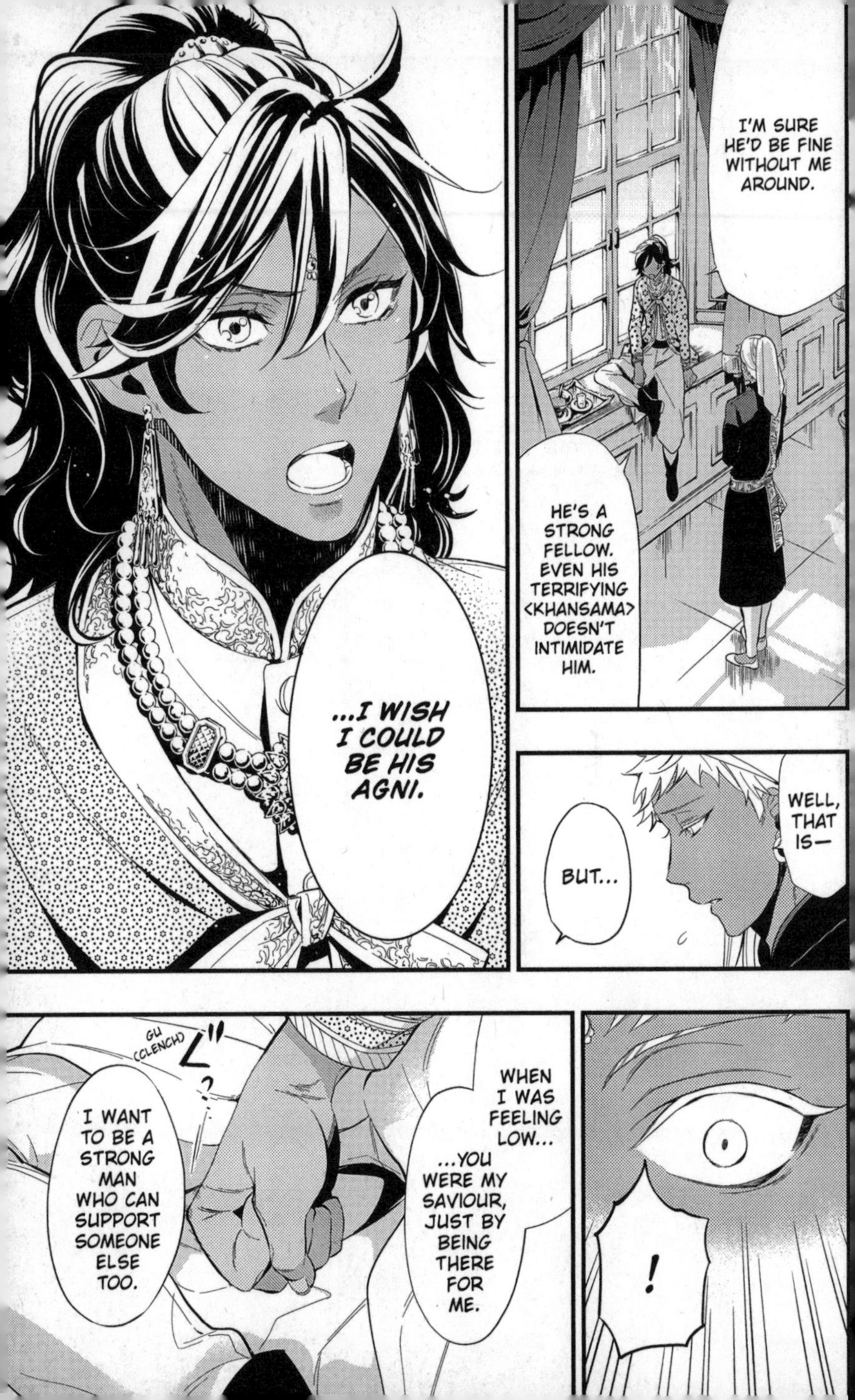
I'M SURE HE'D BE FINE WITHOUT ME AROUND.
HE'S A STRONG FELLOW. EVEN HIS TERRIFYING <KHANSAMA> DOESN'T INTIMIDATE HIM.
WELL, THAT IS—
BUT...
...I WISH I COULD BE HIS AGNI.
!
WHEN I WAS FEELING LOW...
...YOU WERE MY SAVIOUR, JUST BY BEING THERE FOR ME.
GU (CLENCH)
I WANT TO BE A STRONG MAN WHO CAN SUPPORT SOMEONE ELSE TOO.

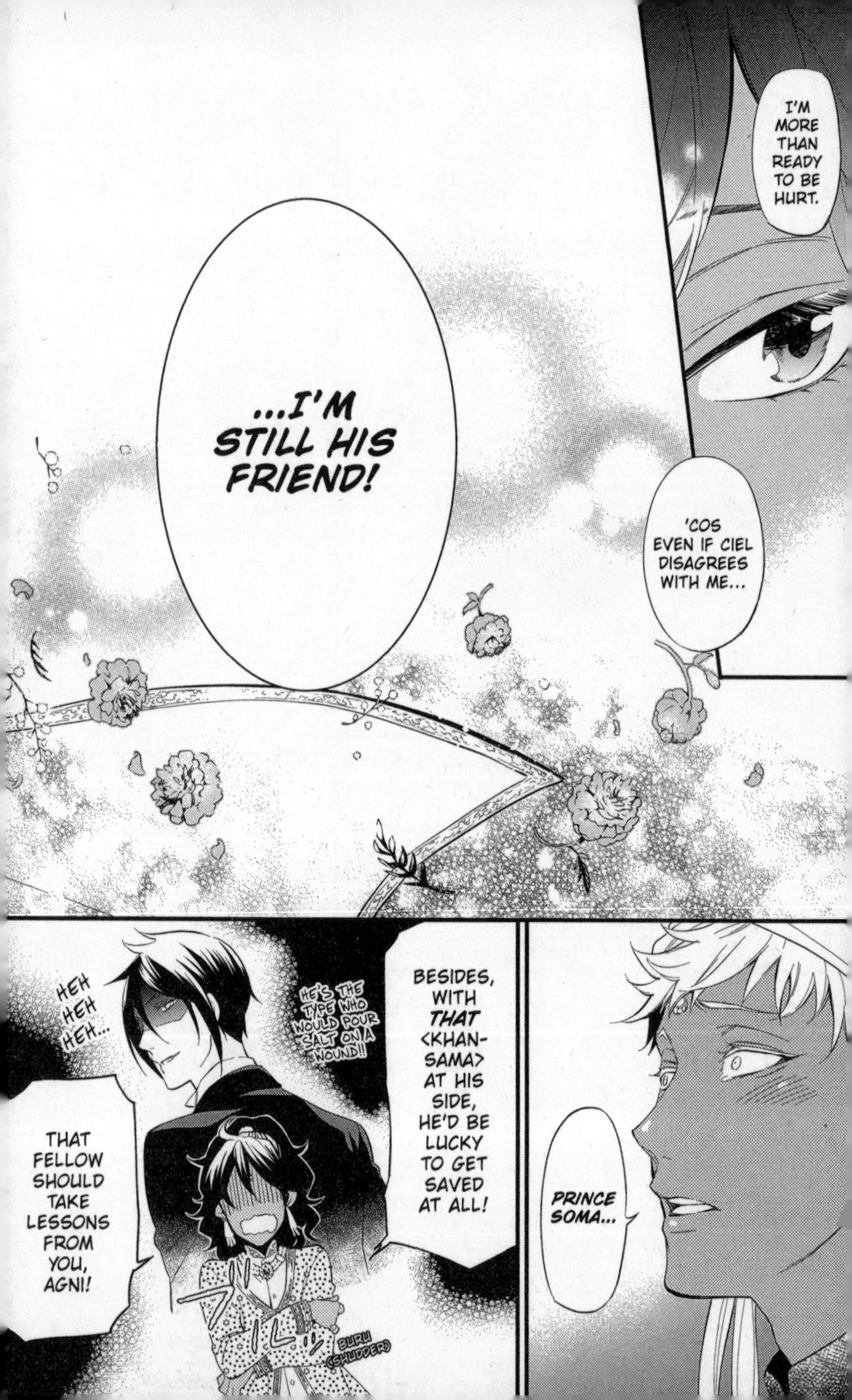
I'M MORE THAN READY TO BE HURT.
'COS EVEN IF CIEL DISAGREES WITH ME...
...I'M STILL HIS FRIEND!
PRINCE SOMA...
BESIDES, WITH *THAT* <KHAN-SAMA> AT HIS SIDE, HE'D BE LUCKY TO GET SAVED AT ALL!
HE'S THE TYPE WHO WOULD POUR SALT ON A WOUND!!
HEH HEH HEH...
THAT FELLOW SHOULD TAKE LESSONS FROM YOU, AGNI!
BURU (SHUDDER)

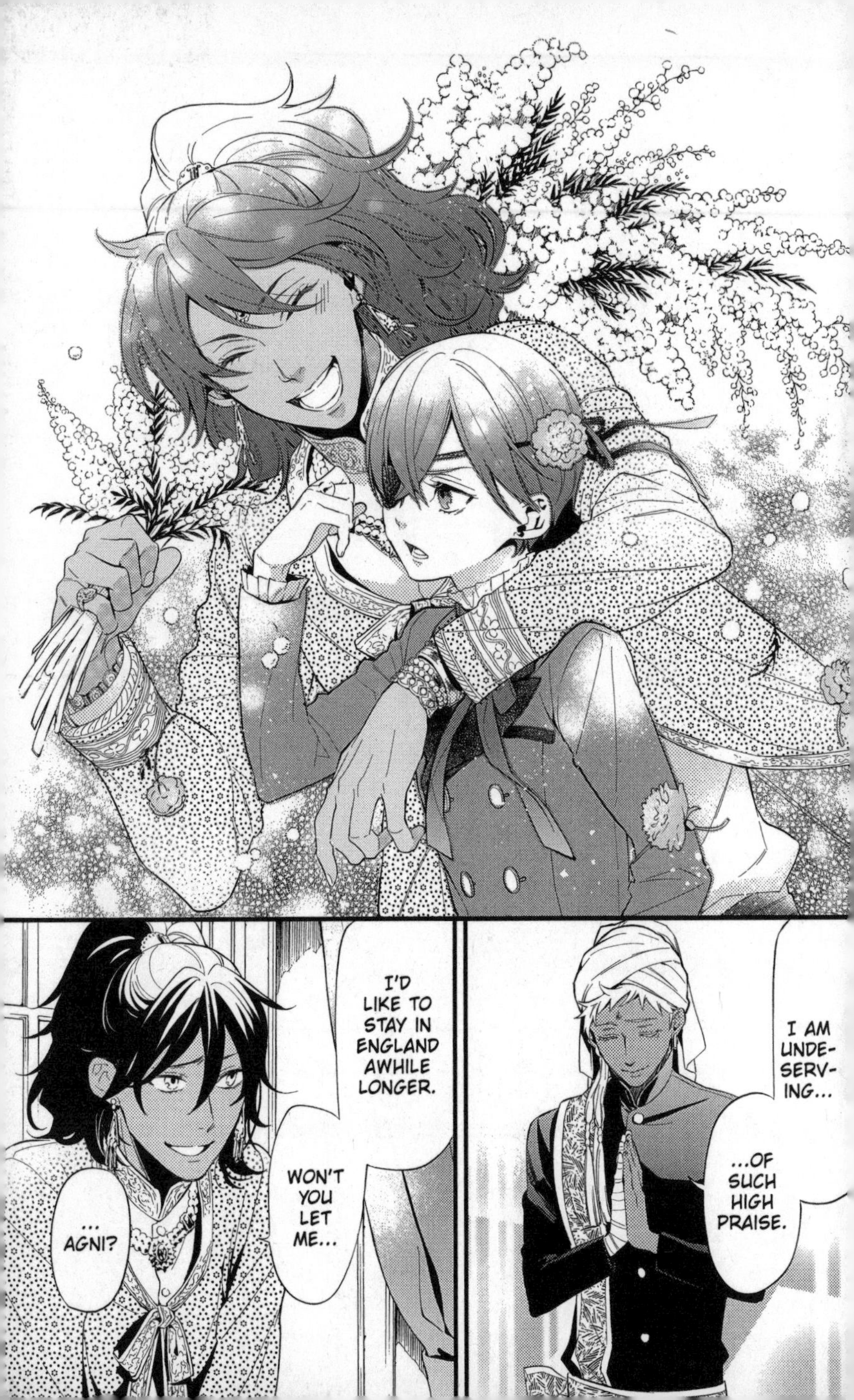
I AM UNDE-SERV-ING...
...OF SUCH HIGH PRAISE.
I'D LIKE TO STAY IN ENGLAND AWHILE LONGER.
WON'T YOU LET ME...
...AGNI?

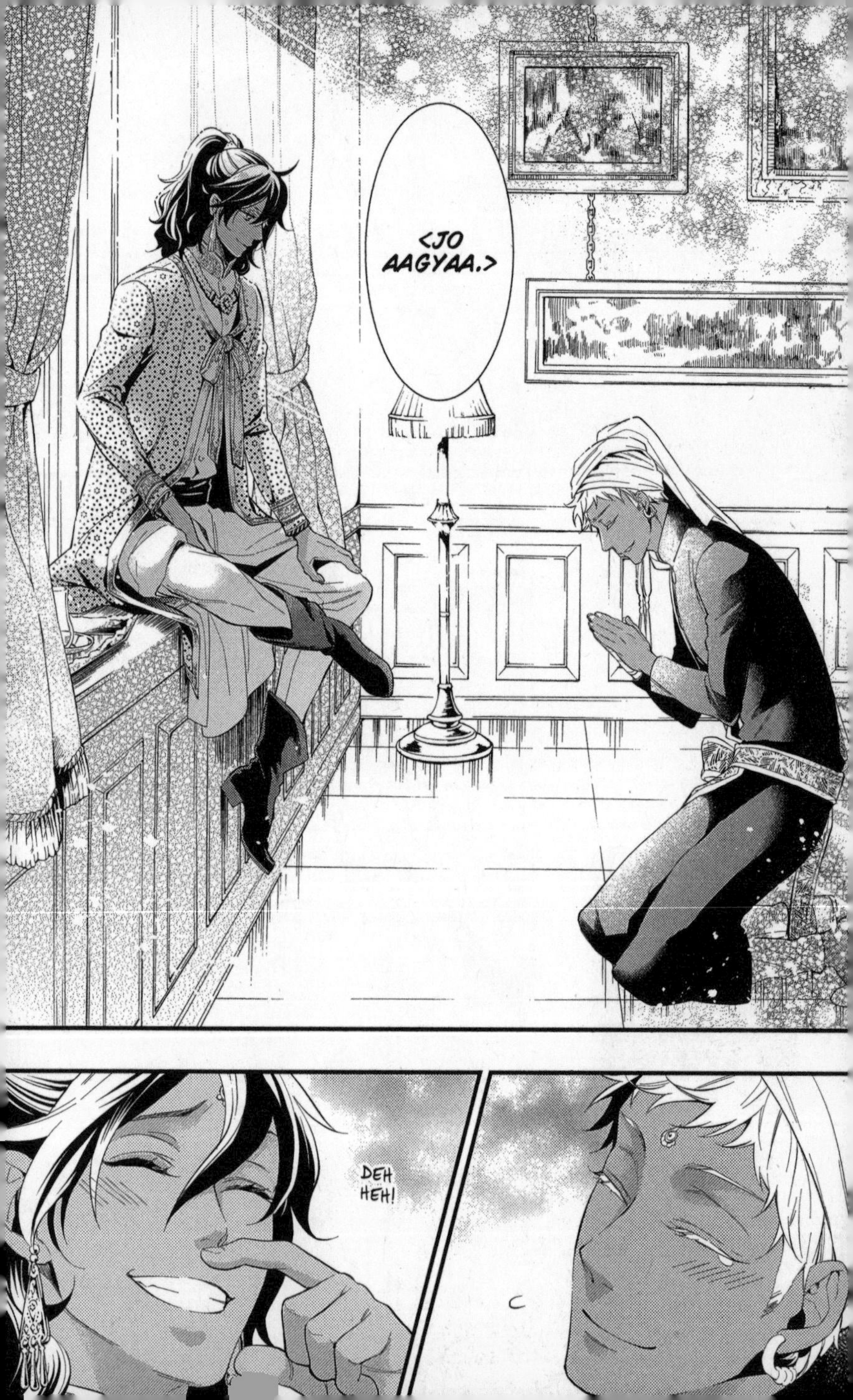
<JO AAGYAA.>
DEH HEH!

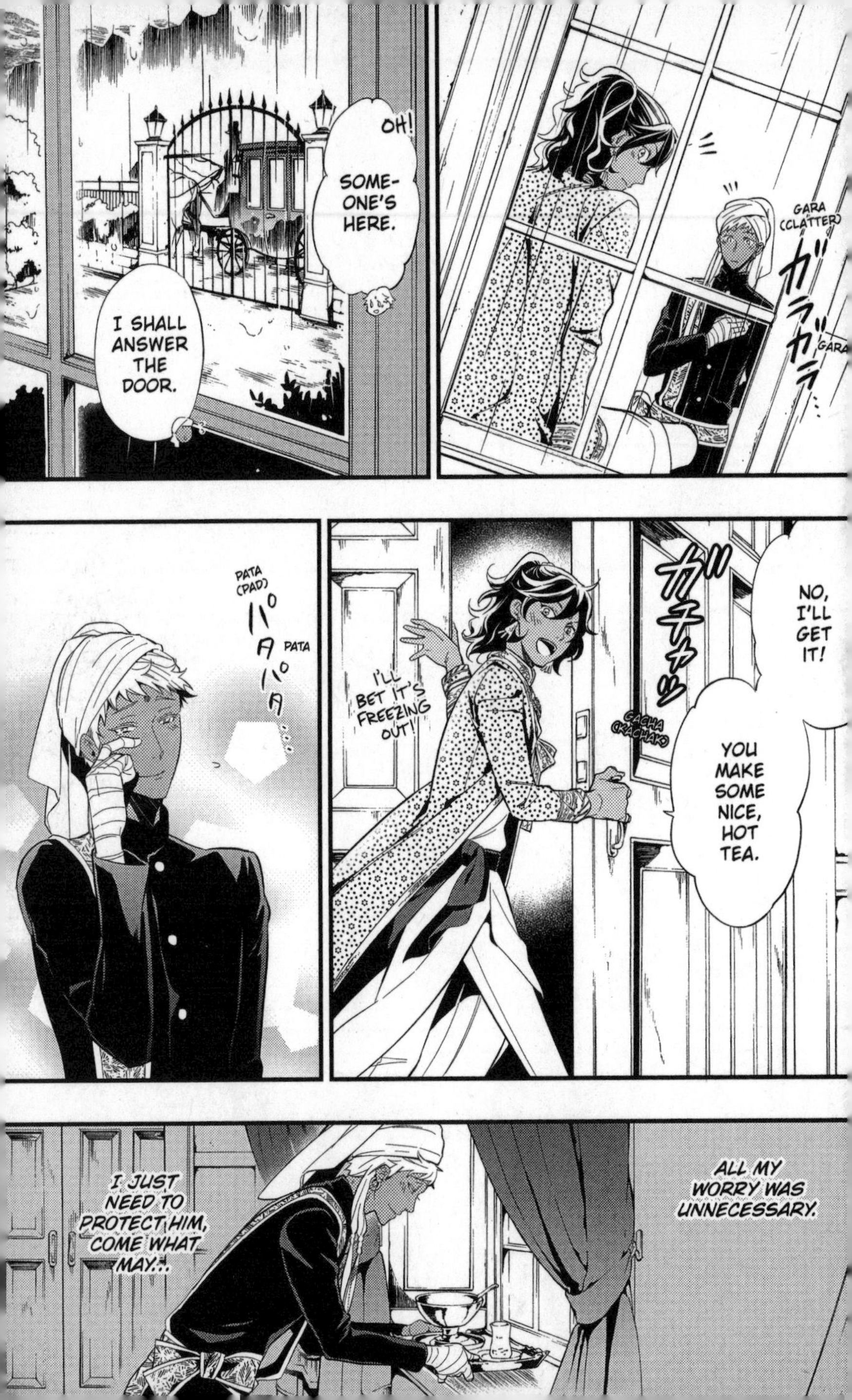
GARA (CLATTER)
GARA
OH!
SOME-ONE'S HERE.
I SHALL ANSWER THE DOOR.
NO, I'LL GET IT!
YOU MAKE SOME NICE, HOT TEA.
GACHA (KACHAK)
I'LL BET IT'S FREEZING OUT!
PATA (PAD)
PATA
ALL MY WORRY WAS UNNECESSARY.
I JUST NEED TO PROTECT HIM, COME WHAT MAY...

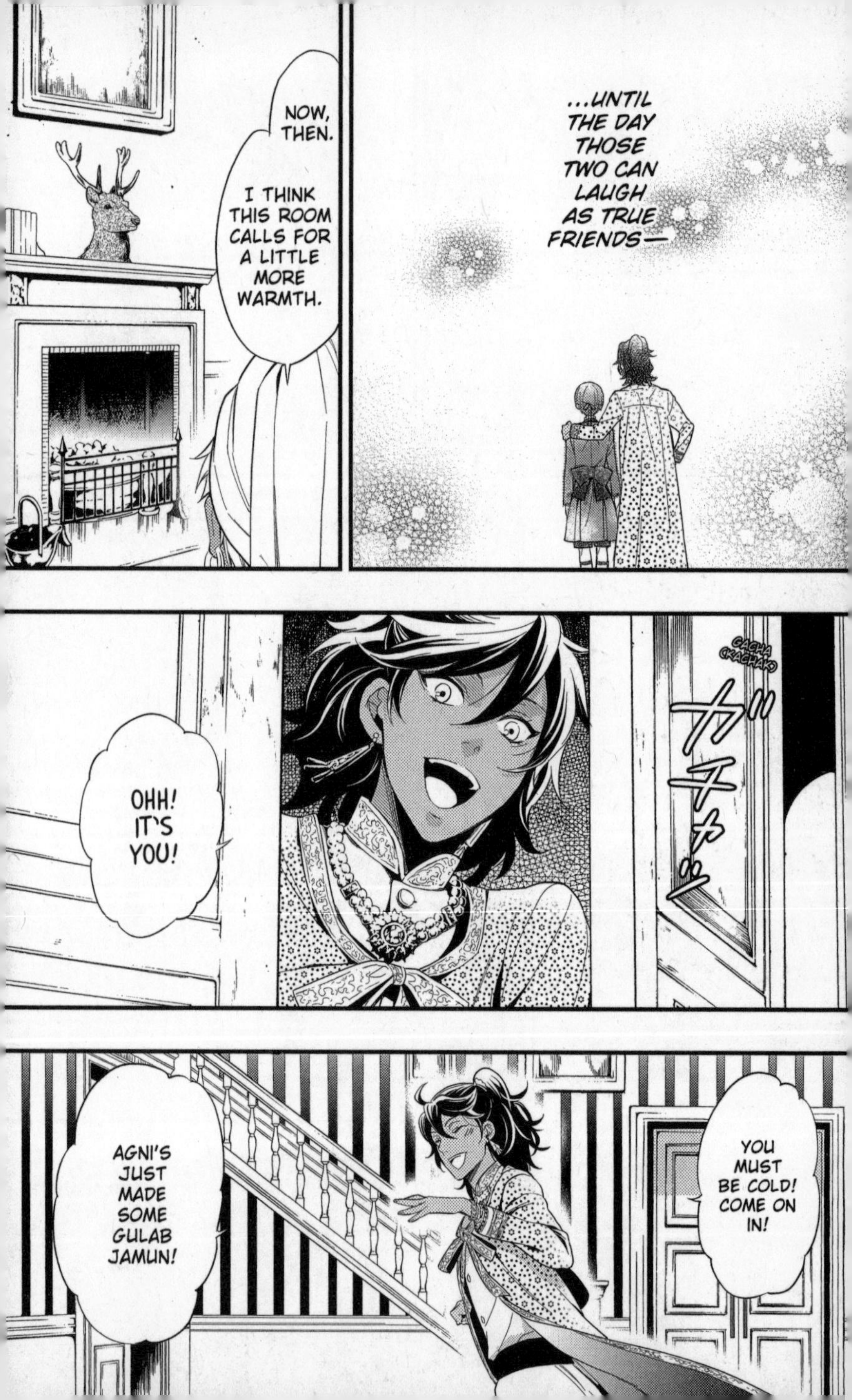
...UNTIL THE DAY THOSE TWO CAN LAUGH AS TRUE FRIENDS—
NOW, THEN.
I THINK THIS ROOM CALLS FOR A LITTLE MORE WARMTH.
GACHA (KACHA)
ガチャッ
OHH! IT'S YOU!
YOU MUST BE COLD! COME ON IN!
AGNI'S JUST MADE SOME GULAB JAMUN!

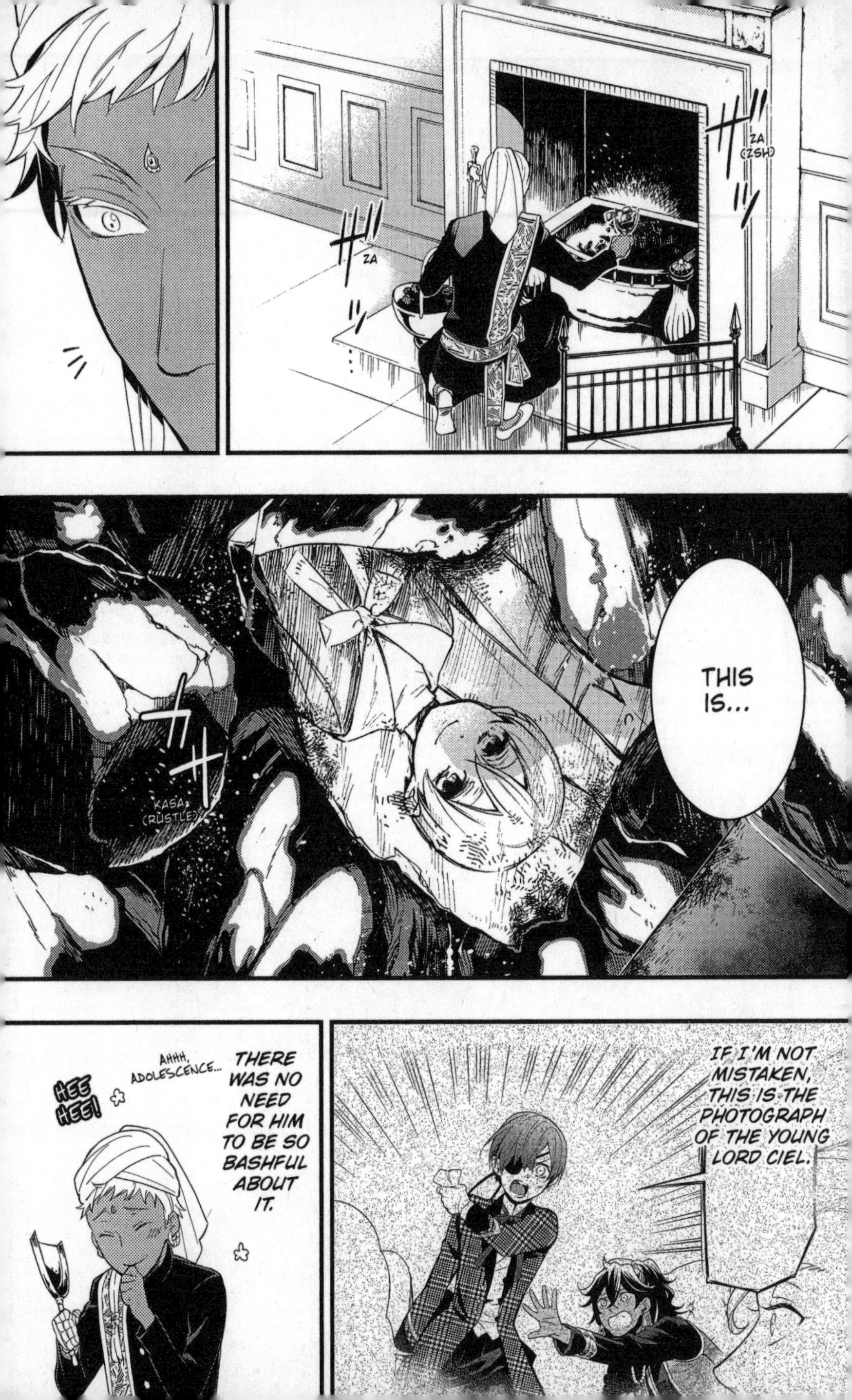
ZA (ZSH)
ZA
THIS IS...
KASA (RUSTLE)
IF I'M NOT MISTAKEN, THIS IS THE PHOTOGRAPH OF THE YOUNG LORD CIEL.
THERE WAS NO NEED FOR HIM TO BE SO BASHFUL ABOUT IT.
AHHH, ADOLESCENCE...
HEE HEE!

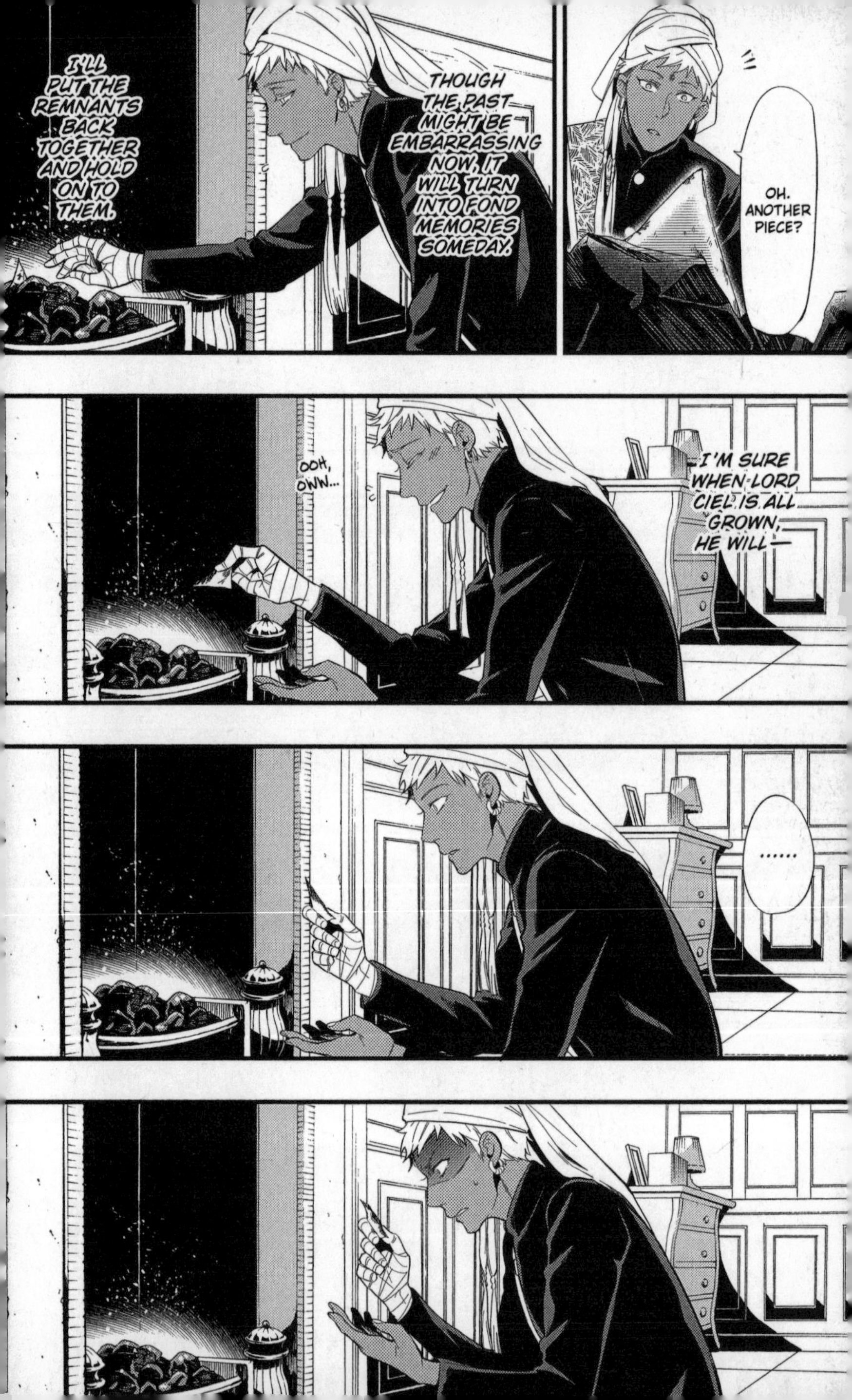
OH. ANOTHER PIECE?
THOUGH THE PAST MIGHT BE EMBARRASSING NOW, IT WILL TURN INTO FOND MEMORIES SOMEDAY.
I'LL PUT THE REMNANTS BACK TOGETHER AND HOLD ON TO THEM.
I'M SURE WHEN LORD CIEL IS ALL GROWN, HE WILL—
OOH, OWW...
......

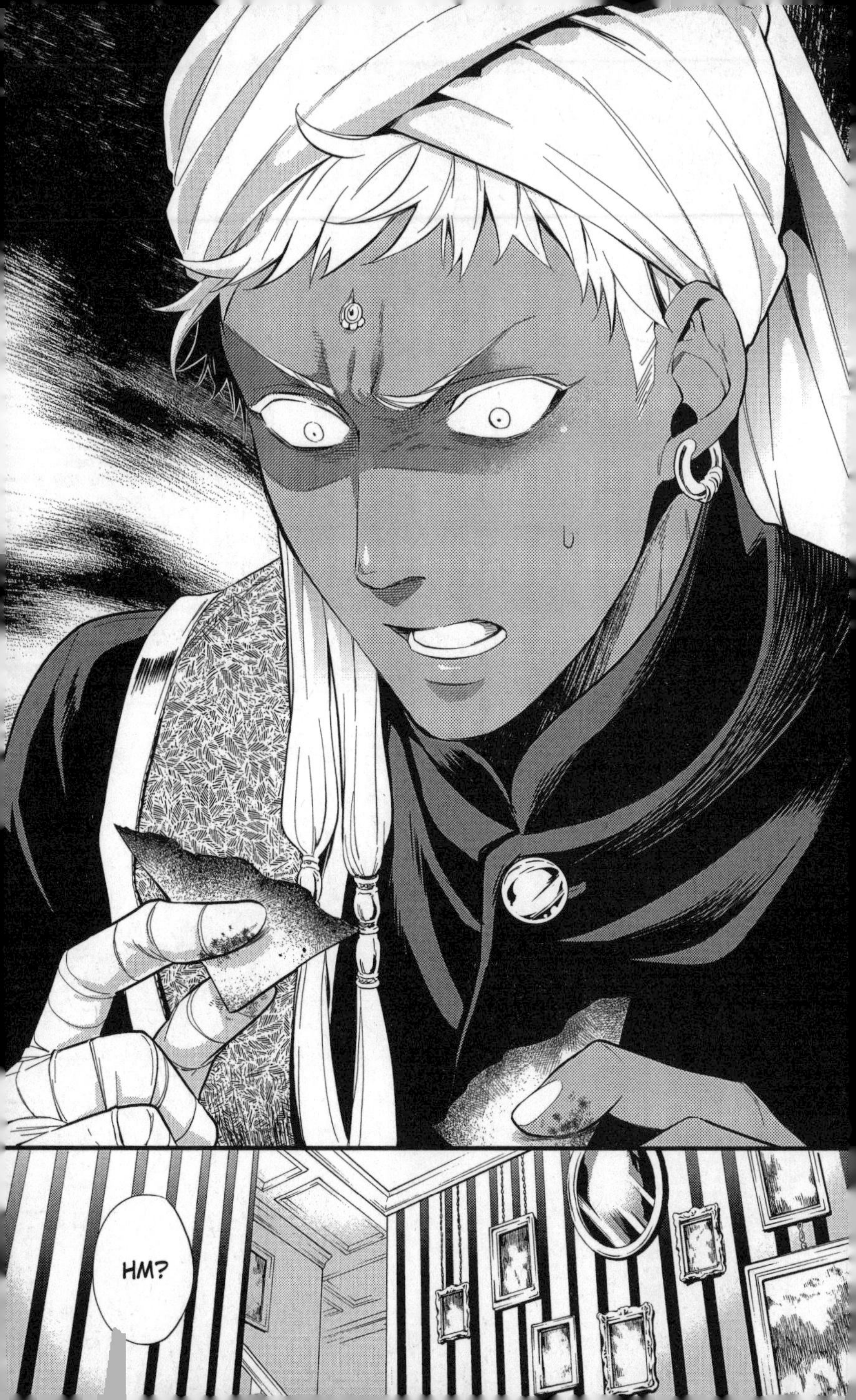
HM?

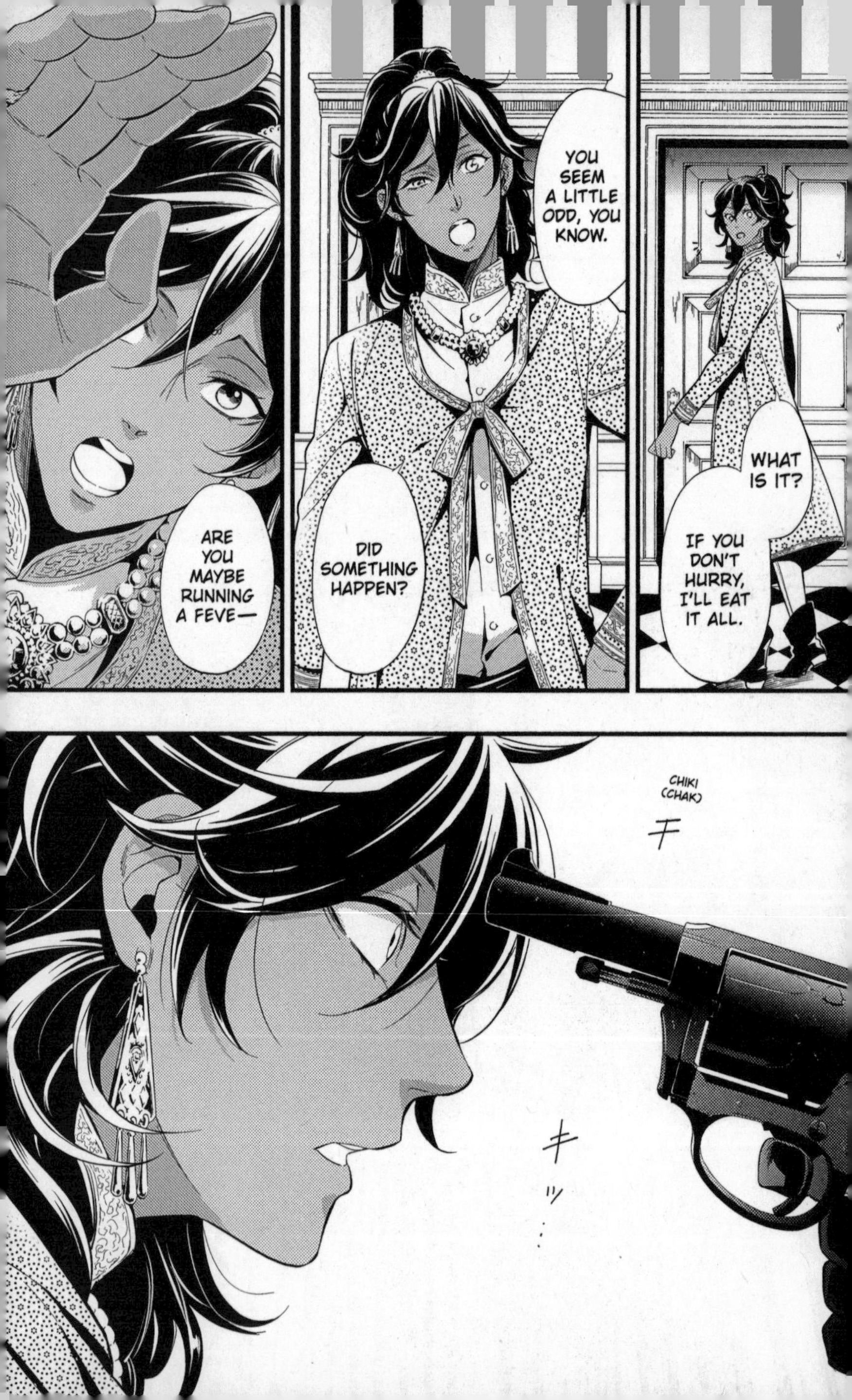
WHAT IS IT?
IF YOU DON'T HURRY, I'LL EAT IT ALL.
YOU SEEM A LITTLE ODD, YOU KNOW.
DID SOMETHING HAPPEN?
ARE YOU MAYBE RUNNING A FEVE—
CHIKI (CHAK)
チキッ

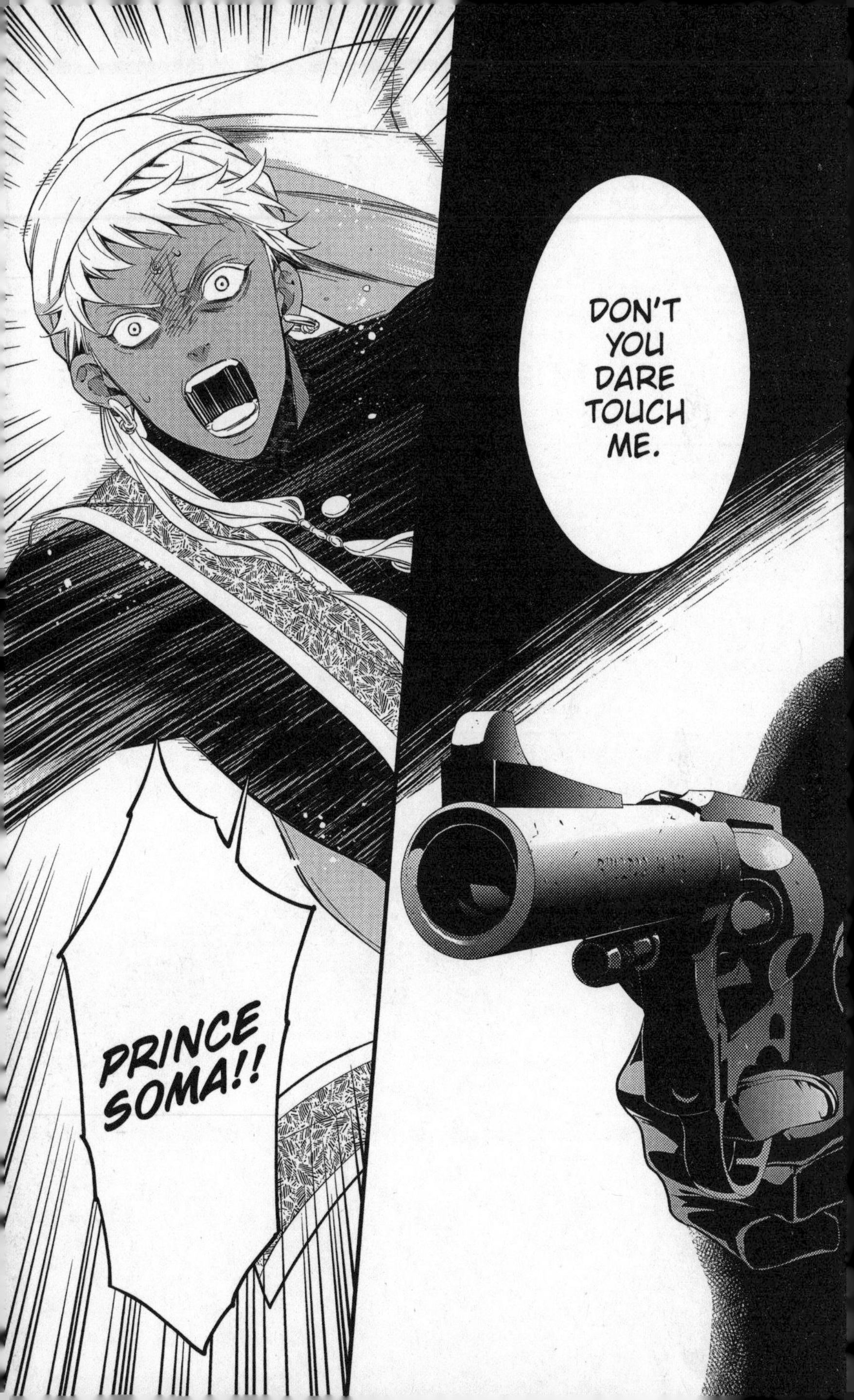
DON'T YOU DARE TOUCH ME.
PRINCE SOMA!!

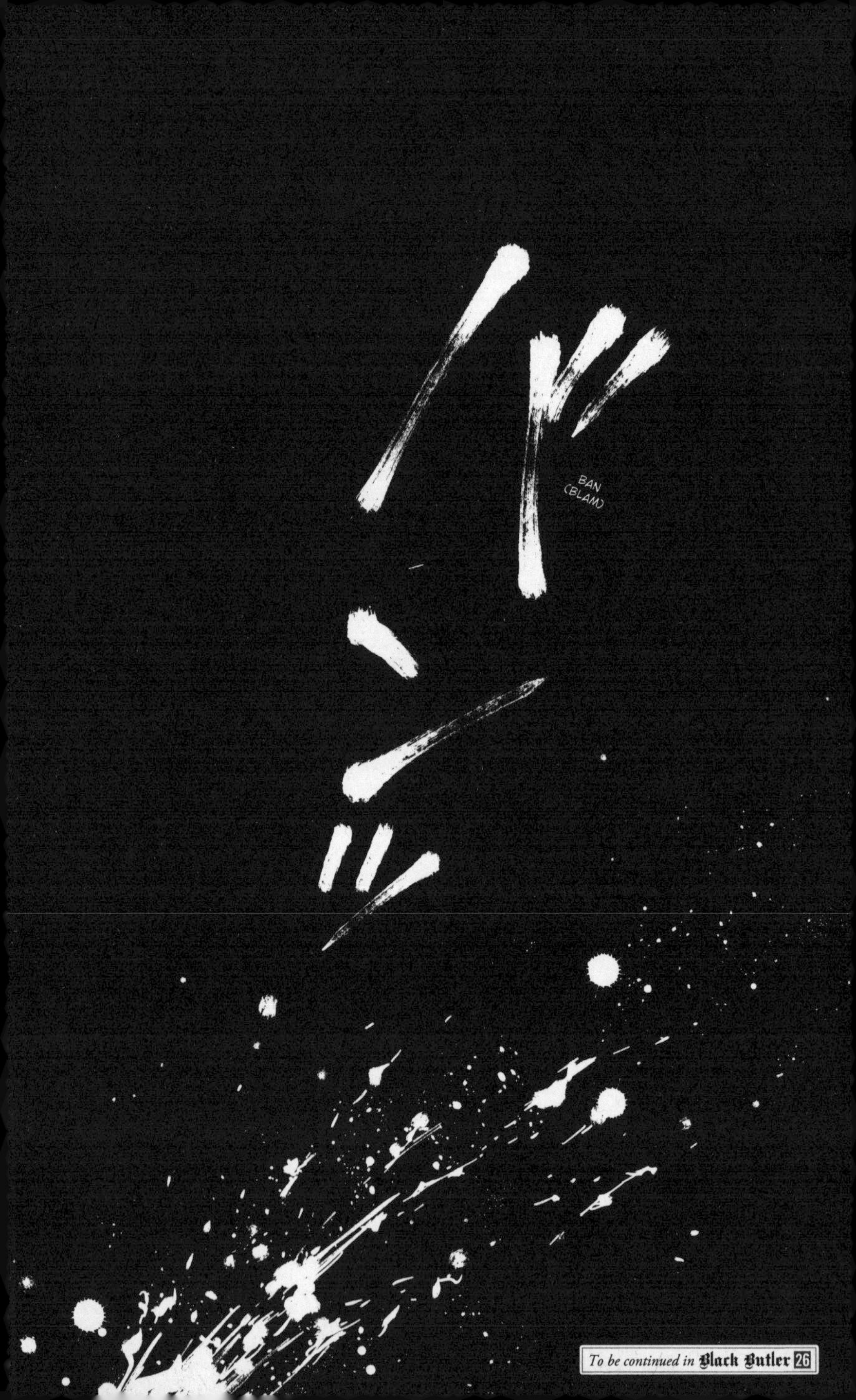
BAN
(BLAM)

To be continued in **Black Butler** 26

⇒Black Butler⇐

黒執事

✦

Downstairs

Wakana Haduki
7
Tsuki Sorano
Chiaki Nagaoka
Sanihiko
Seira

*

Takeshi Kuma

*

Yana Toboso

Adviser

Rico Murakami

Special thanks to You!

NEXT VOLUME

Black Butler

26

COMING SOON!

Translation Notes

Nezumi Kozou
Othello is dressed as Nezumi Kozou, a famous thief of Edo-period Japan, who only stole from the mansions of feudal lords. The legends describe him as a kind of Robin Hood.

Kan'ei tsuuhou
Theses coins with square holes were widely circulated during the Edo period.

Koban
The oval-shaped coins are *koban*, gold coins of the Edo period. A *koban* was worth one *ryou*, a currency unit of the time.

Senryoubako
Othello is carrying a *senryoubako*, a wooden box used to store large quantities of *koban*. "*Sen*" means "one thousand," so a *senryoubako* could hold one thousand *ryou* worth of *koban*.

Inside back cover
Bugyou
Tanaka-san is dressed as a *bugyou*, or magistrate, who maintained order in the city of Edo. There were two *bugyou* offices in the city, the north office and the south office.

Hitsuke touzoku aratame kata
Snake is dressed as a *hitsuke touzoku aratame kata*, officers who were tasked with policing arsonists, thieves, and gamblers.

Sasumata
Snake holds a *sasumata*, a weapon with a "U"-shaped tip that was used to capture criminals by holding and pushing them against a wall or the ground. With a length of around seven to ten feet, the *sasumata* worked well against Edo-period felons wielding knives and swords. *Sasumata* are still used by Japanese police today.

Okappiki
Finny is dressed as an *okappiki*, the lowest rank of the Edo-period police. Commoners hired by *bugyou* offices and *hitsuke touzoku aratame kata*, they functioned as informants and patrolmen for their employers.

Jitte
Finny has a *jitte*, a weapon used by okappiki as a symbol of their jobs and a weapon in arresting

offenders. *Jitte* were made either of metal or wood and each had a hook near the handle, which was used to capture sword blades when necessary.

Goyou **lantern**
Finny is holding a lantern that reads "*goyou*," or "You're under arrest." When taking a suspect into custody, the *okappiki* would utilise these tools.

Policewoman's uniform
Mey-Rin is wearing a modern Japanese policewoman's uniform.

Page 61
Meissen
Meissen is a German porcelain manufacturer based in Meissen, a town near Dresden. It was established in 1710 and developed the first European hard-paste porcelain, which is normal material for Chinese porcelain.

Page 79
"Watch the birdie!"
This phrase originated in the late nineteenth century, when portrait photographers would use a mechanical bird to catch the attention of their subjects for the perfect shot. The original "birdie" from around 1879 is said to have been a live bird.

Page 80
The Penny Illustrated Paper and Illustrated Times
The *Penny Illustrated Paper* was an illustrated weekly newspaper aimed at the working classes. It was published from 1861 to 1913.

Page 115
Hyde Park
Hyde Park is a large park in London and one of London's eight Royal Parks. The Great Exhibition of 1851 was held in the park, and the Crystal Palace was built there.

Page 117
Steak and ale pie
Standard British pub fare. Beef and vegetables are stewed with ale, then baked in pastry.

Page 121
Bath
160 kilometers west of London, Bath is a spa resort in the English countryside that is known for its Roman-era baths.

Yana Toboso

AUTHOR'S NOTE

I recently started using Twitter. People from all over the world talk to me there, and I'm moved that **Black Butler** is being read in so many countries. By the way, people outside Japan apparently call my self-portrait "the Devil," but it's nothing that pretentious. It's just a germ. And so, here's Volume 25!

The Phantomhive family
has a butler who's almost
too good to be true...
or maybe he's just too
good to be human.
And now you can find
him in two places at once!

Read the latest chapter of

on the same day as Japan!

Available now worldwide at your favourite e-tailer!

www.yenpress.com

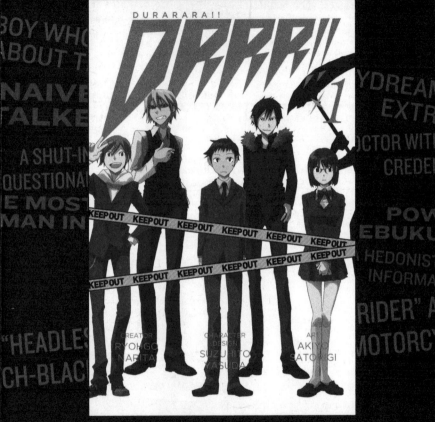

BLACK BUTLER ㉕

YANA TOBOSO

Translation: Tomo Kimura
Lettering: Bianca Pistillo

KUROSHITSUJI Vol. 25 © 2017 Yana Toboso / SQUARE ENIX CO., LTD. First published in Japan in 2017 by SQUARE ENIX CO., LTD. English translation rights arranged with SQUARE ENIX CO., LTD. and Yen Press, LLC through Tuttle-Mori Agency, Inc.

English translation © 2018 by SQUARE ENIX CO., LTD.

Yen Press
1290 Avenue of the Americas
New York, NY 10104

Visit us!
† yenpress.com
† facebook.com/yenpress
† twitter.com/yenpress
† yenpress.tumblr.com
† instagram.com/yenpress

First Yen Press Edition: January 2018
The chapters in this volume were originally published as ebooks by Yen Press.

Yen Press is an imprint of Yen Press, LLC.
The Yen Press name and logo are trademarks of Yen Press, LLC.

The publisher is not responsible for websites (or their content) that are not owned by the publisher.

Library of Congress Control Number: 2010525567

ISBNs: 978-0-316-48011-6 (paperback)
       978-1-9753-2697-5 (ebook)

10 9 8 7 6 5 4 3 2 1

BVG

Printed in the United States of America